# FEMINIST ISSUES
## RACE, CLASS, AND SEXUALITY

Edited by
## NANCY MANDELL
York University

Prentice Hall Canada Inc.
Scarborough, Ontario

**Canadian Cataloguing in Publication Data**

Mandell, Nancy
    Feminist issues

Includes bibliographical references.
ISBN 0-13-076365-9

1. Feminism. 2. Women–Social conditions.
I. Title.

HQ1206.M35 1995 305.4 C94-931366-1

Prentice-Hall, Inc., Englewood Cliffs, New Jersey
Prentice-Hall International (UK) Limited, London
Prentice-Hall of Australia, Pty. Limited, Sydney
Prentice-Hall Hispanoamericana, S.A., Mexico City
Prentice-Hall of India Private Limited, New Delhi
Prentice-Hall of Japan, Inc., Tokyo
Simon & Schuster Asia Private Limited, Singapore
Editora Prentice-Hall do Brasil, Ltda., Rio de Janeiro

ISBN 0-13-076365-9

Acquisitions Editor: Marjorie Munroe
Production Editor: Kelly Dickson
Production Coordinator: Sharon Houston
Page Layout: Jaytype Inc.


1 2 3 4 5 RRD 99 98 97 96 95

Printed and bound in the USA.

Every reasonable effort has been made to obtain permissions for all articles and data
used in this edition. If errors or omissions have occurred, they will be corrected in future
editions provided written notification has been received by the publisher.

*For Lionel, Jeremy, Dan, and Adam*

# TABLE OF CONTENTS

# Preface

This collection of chapters addresses a variety of feminist questions that have received little attention in Canadian texts. All of the pieces, were written specifically for this volume with the intention of providing an overview and summary of the most up-to-date material in each field. Authors explore the range and diversity of contemporary feminist perspectives applied to critiques of gender, race, class, sexuality, disability, and poverty. The lives of previously forgotten and silenced women are brought to the forefront as their experiences of work, family, violence, sexuality, law, aging, health, and education are examined. The result is an innovative, challenging, and comprehensive survey of Canadian feminist issues today.

Undergraduate students should find this book particularly accessible as authors have been asked to present their arguments in as clear and compelling a fashion as possible. Our purpose is to answer a number of central questions: How (in what ways) is a particular topic a feminist issue? What have feminists researching health care or education, for instance, discovered as systemic and persistent biases against women? How have feminists addressed inequities revealed through feminist analyses? What sorts of personal and institutional responses have been taken to redress the mislabelling and misdirection of women, such as gender tracking in high schools? And finally, what are the immediate and long-term consequences of feminist intervention and analysis? Has the discovery of the "double day" of wage and domestic labour, for which women are responsible, in fact lessened or redistributed their load? Students, as members of groups usually ignored and as members of institutional settings in which they are often silenced, may find, for the first time, their lives, their experiences, their feelings, and their histories explored. Students may find such revelation unsettling, contentious, validating, and liberating. It is unlikely they will emerge untouched.

Putting this book together has been truly enjoyable. An excellent group of contributors have broadened previous feminist critiques by incorporating debates around race, class, sexuality, disability, poverty, and violence into everyday explanations of women's omission and oppression. I am immensely enriched by and delighted with the excellent work of Canadian feminist academics and activists who continually contest mainstream definitions and struggle to expand the boundaries of our collective enterprise.

# Introduction

In the last twenty-five years, a forceful but largely peaceful revolution has altered the lives of Canadian women and men. Traditional relationships between the sexes, dating and courtship rules, family structures, workplace scenarios, and leisure patterns have given way to more varied, diverse, and nonconventional forms. Fuelling these structural and institutional rearrangements are a host of cultural and personal demands for variety and flexibility. Women who now anticipate a lifelong combination of wage and domestic labour need and want more participatory, interchangeable, and pliable arrangements in order to cope with their responsibilities. Men, who no longer self-identify solely through their jobs, share more fully in raising their children with same or opposite sex partners. The institutions in which we work, receive health care, and become schooled have begun, slowly, to shift their foci in response to individual and social claims for greater flexibility and individuality.

These and other trends have led to the virtual demise of traditional ideas of femininity and masculinity. Gender ideologies created in everyday and institutional practices no longer condemn women and men to restrictive patterns of behaviour. Women are no longer assumed to be more passive, unassertive, caring, kind, and helpful than men. Conversely, men no longer conform to 1950s stereotypes as cool, unemotional, domineering, and career-driven. Relationships between and among women and men have also modified. The century-long trek toward the liberation of individuals from the oppressive features of patriarchy has fostered the emergence of the "postmodern" relationship. Individuality, diversity, and plurality prevail.

Societal and personal innovation have altered the landscape of Canadian universities in profound and irrevocable ways. Student bodies are finally becoming more variegated, international, and incomparable. A healthy tension of diversity charges the atmosphere. Academic programs are moving toward models of inter- and multidisciplinarity as traditional intellectual boundaries are expanded. Women students and faculty have been leaders in fashioning new courses out of shifting interests.

Gender challenges have been collected under the rubric of "Women's Studies," a label that pulls together into one curriculum any courses that place the study of women and women's own experiences at the centre of their investigation. Women's Studies endorses the fundamentally simple, yet radical, belief in an approach to knowledge that places women at the centre of an intellectual analysis and critique of androcentric/phallocentric systems of knowledge, ones in which men's experiences and priorities have traditionally been seen as central and representative of all (Robinson 1993). Such a recentering of knowledge has wide-reaching implications for our teaching and research within the disciplines and the academy in general.

The changing nature of women's lives resonates in academic pursuits. Women's Studies was initially seen as supplying missing information, both historical and contemporary, about women's activities. Did women ever have a renaissance? What were women doing in pre-agricultural communities? Women's invisibility has resulted in part from our own silence about ourselves. Women have tended to be excluded from public discourse, have rarely been taught to read or write, and their work, when it has been published, has not been seen as interesting or worthy. This lack of interest in women can be traced to a general devaluation of women: women's work is ignored because it is produced by women.

Women's Studies also corrects misconceptions about men and women. Some serious misconceptions about women's bodies, mental capacities, activities, and achievements are widely believed. Myths about "man-the-hunter" ignored women's foraging. Conceptualization of women as irrational and hysterical ignored women's powerlessness and victimization by abusers. In some cases, these misconceptions are the result of too narrow a focus of study. In other cases, they come from entrenched ideological beliefs and practices.

In the past, both women and men have studied women from a predominately male perspective largely because, until recently, all theories about humans, our nature and behaviour, have been "man-made" (Spender 1981). Observations and their resulting interpretations within each discipline reflect male perspectives of reality, meaning these narratives are simply not as "true" for women as for men. Explanations do not correspond with women's understandings and thus may be poor guides for predicting women's attitudes and behaviour. Women's Studies attempts to rectify this appalling lack of knowledge through historical recovery and contemporary investigation.

Emanating from the women's movement, the establishment, within the academy, of Women's Studies journals, courses, and programs in the early 1970s in Canada represented a profoundly political act. Feminist academics, by questioning conventional knowledge claims to "objectivity," "truth," and the separation of experience from theory, transformed teaching, learning, and research. Feminist critiques of objectivity, inquiries into feminist methods of research, and the linking of feminist research with the political goals of the women's movement challenged basic methods and presuppositions in established disciplines. Women's Studies also produced new bodies of knowledge that both corrected and complemented the established disciplines while slowly constituting itself as a new academic discipline of its own.

Central to the creation of woman-centred knowledge and its dissemination through feminist pedagogies remains the fusion of experience and politics. Conventional ideas that research and teaching have been about, and not for, women is counteracted by Women's Studies insistence that women's experiences as workers, as lesbian mothers, as political activists, and so on, not be left outside the classroom, separate from the serious job of theorizing. Therefore, feminist learning connects with the everyday world of women's daily lives as well as with their sexuality and emotional life.

The feminist classroom offers the possibility of dialogue between women with different conceptions and relationships. It offers a safe space within which to explore the idea of the contradiction between women's lived experience and perceived feminist ideas. A widely diverse group, with differing motives, take Women's Studies courses. Varied student expectations lead to challenge and conflict within the classroom as students feel the right to demand, discharge, and disclose in ways unthinkable in traditional disciplines. At the same time as it politicizes its students, Women's Studies faces the dilemma of being co-opted and deradicalized as it enters the university mainstream. In terms of its activist connections, feminist teachers are sometimes viewed as corrupted by a male hierarchy that demands obedience to a patriarchal orthodoxy, or as careerists unconnected to the women's movement, or as token feminists (Robinson 1993).

Such criticisms fail to acknowledge how political an act teaching Women's Studies remains in most Canadian institutions. Women's Studies is far from mainstreamed or institutionalized in most universities. Indeed, most programs seem precariously perched, dependent on the goodwill of administrators and a pool of part-time instructors. Such criticisms also deny the energy and effort feminist instructors expend in maintaining feminist programs, taking for granted their hard work. Moreover, faculty, staff, and students still find it difficult to survive as feminists, as out lesbians, as Native, Black, poor, or disabled women in the institution. Indeed, feminism's recent focus on "forgotten women" has attempted to lessen these burdens by accepting a diversity of feminist approaches, classrooms, and pedagogies, all aimed at the empowering of students to create social and political change. In fact, empowering energy, capacity, and potential has become the 1990s feminist goal (Shrewsbury 1987). This collection aims to encourage student's empowerment through knowledge and thus to further the feminist project.

## PART ONE: THEORIZING WOMEN: HISTORY, POLITICS, AND PLACEMENT

The first chapter, *"Feminist Theories"* by *Patricia Elliot and Nancy Mandell*, provides a thoroughly accessible and comprehensive review of feminist theories.

Feminists are born and move into particular arrangements that shape all aspects of their lives. These arrangements confer obligation and responsibility, and share access to economic resources, power, and privilege. As Elliot and Mandell point out, feminist theories emerge from the various explanations of women's oppression. Feminist theories are thus visions guided by experiences and experiences corrected by visions.

Masculine models, such as patriarchy, are constituted and validated through social arrangements of power. By producing knowledge we affirm what counts as reality, as truth and progress, and what counts as experience, identity, desire, and the "good." New models of society, feminist ones, arise with new structurings of power. New knowledge, constructed along with social power, is reflexive and demonstrates that which has been forgotten, denied, or invalidated. Misogynist influences on theory and history expose a bias toward a single, immutable, static, and fixed set of "truths." However, feminists studying both the natural and social sciences have shown the ways in which masculine self-images and desires permeate intellectual work previously situated as "objective" and "universal." Feminist scholars like Nancy Hartsock, Jane Flax, and Carol Gilligan reveal that an author's standpoint or theoretical perspective results from her social location and that knowledge claims are forms of discourse and as such are meaningful only as social interchanges. Feminists, as producers of knowledge, all produce theories or interpretations of events and, in the process, deconstruct traditional scripts.

Elliot and Mandell review traditional feminist theories, including liberal feminism, Marxism, socialist and radical feminism, before moving into an engaging discussion of antiracist feminism, psychoanalysis, and poststructuralism. All of this sounds daunting to the new Women's Studies student, but Elliot and Mandell present a simple, precise, and demystified account of what are complicated bodies of thought—an encouraging incentive to read on.

They conclude with an historical summary of the interface between feminism, as a political movement, and its academic counterpart, Women's Studies programs. Women's Studies examines relations of power between women and men that are social processes through which ideas about masculinity and femininity, sexual identities, and sexual preferences are continually constructed. This analysis necessarily involves us in a massive critique of society's institutions, ideologies, and day-to-day relations. As Elliot and Mandell point out, the tools for this endeavour are the questions raised by feminist theories that critique the current distribution of power and privilege.

In the next chapter, *"Silenced and Forgotten Women: Race, Poverty, and Disability,"* Barbara Cassidy, Robina Lord, and Nancy Mandell provide an overview of the ways in which the second wave of feminism has largely ignored the history and contemporary experiences of many groups of women. Feminism, the political movement that aims to liberate all women, is revealed as historically and geographically specific. Its analysis of the origins of women's oppression and the solutions it proposes tend to be relevant only to middle-class White women. White solipsism (Spelman 1988)—thinking, imagining, and speaking as if whiteness described the world—has dominated feminist writing, thinking, and activism.

By focusing on five groups of women—First Nations, African-Canadians, immigrant, disabled, and poor—the authors attempt to partially redress this imbalance. They highlight central historical events that have shaped these women's understandings of, and engagement in, Canadian social life.

They point out the role of First Nations women in ensuring the survival of voyageurs and merchants in the North by acting as interpreters and guides and making items such as snowshoes. They also describe the destruction of matrilineal and matrilocal systems of kinship and marriage and the loss of status that Native women suffered as White men and women colonized natives. First Nations women enjoyed equal status with men, laboured alongside men growing crops and trapping animals, and held important community positions. Attempts to civilize natives and to decimate native culture, while partially successful, have been strenuously resisted by continual struggle against white society.

The history of African-Canadians can be seen within the context of legalized slavery. While Canadians tend to remain smug about their relatively non-violent and non-exploitative past, a more careful and cynical reading reveals a legacy of abuse and degradation. Missing also from this story are the many successes of Black women as they founded companies, joined police forces, held political office, and raised families, all the while battling prejudice and discrimination.

The history and contemporary experiences of immigrant women reveal their simultaneous experience both as victims of class and ethnic discrimination and as heroines in a new land. Racist immigration policies made it virtually impossible for many women to join their husbands in Canada. The result was split-family households with husbands and wives separated for many years. When women did finally begin to arrive, immigration afforded many of them new opportunities and experiences they might not have encountered otherwise. Rather than being portrayed as victims of oppression, many immigrant women prefer to envision themselves as hard workers whose years of domestic and wage labour enabled their families to achieve their goals of security, educational advancement, and financial stability.

The lives of women with disabilities remain relatively unknown in feminist writing. Their struggles for political recognition as activist groups, their international organizations, and their influence on current political and social agendas are largely unrecognized. This historic invisibility reflects their obliteration in feminist and sociological work. Little is written about disabled women's day-to-day experiences, their struggles with teachers in the education system, their difficulties in overcoming the innumerable institutional barriers to their engagement in ordinary social life. Norms of femininity and myths of beauty are described as negatively constructing women whose bodies and minds are seen as deviant. The omission of women with disabilities reminds us that feminist theorizing and activism needs to reevaluate its goals.

Poor women also receive insufficient attention in feminist work. Poverty rates for the growing number of female-headed, single-parent families attest to the contemporary social fact that women without access to male wages often live in poverty. Also, increasing numbers of women remain "unattached," often by choice, for increasing periods of time as adolescents, as young mothers, and as elderly women. Feminist writing needs to reflect upon the challenges and conflicts that poor women face. Economic discrimination, coupled with systemic racism, heterosexism, and disability prejudice leave far too many women embattled and beleaguered. While help exists in the form of government assistance, often it is too little. Food banks, clothing drives, and demands for safe and affordable housing suggest that basic needs of this growing population of women are not being met.

In "What Makes Lesbianism Thinkable?: Theorizing Lesbianism from Adrienne Rich to Queer Theory," Kathleen Martindale provides a comprehensive overview of the ways in which the concepts of "lesbianism" and "sexuality" have been elaborated by historians and used by lesbians and feminists. Contextualizing lesbian theory means studying the history of lesbianism as a sexual practice, an identity, and a politics of same-sex female desire that parallels, but is not identical to, the history of feminism. Martindale tells us that lesbian theorists do not agree as to whether lesbians or lesbianism existed before the end of the nineteenth century. Lesbianism existed in that lesbians have always been present, but not as self-conscious groups such as those which emerged in large Euro-American cities at the end of the nineteenth century. Heterosexuality was a term invented in 1901, thirty years after sexologists invented homosexuality as a social category.

Beginning in the 1970s, theorists differed as to definitions of lesbianism. Definitions raise the question of what lesbianism means for feminism. Should lesbianism be construed broadly as a form of womanly bonding rather than a sexual practice, or narrowly as a self-conscious sexual identity? Adrienne Rich's critical 1980 article attempted to decrease homophobia in the women's movement and build bridges between all feminists by defining lesbianism as "woman identified woman," a broad definition characterized by desires, experiences, and self-perceptions rather than social categories. Lesbianism, it was argued, is shaped by ideological and political preferences as much as by explicit sexual practices.

The year 1982 marked the beginning of the sex wars between those lesbians who were cultural feminists and those who were sex radicals. These differences reflected conflicting perspectives of basic meanings of femaleness and lesbianism with which women have long struggled. Sex radicals argued that feminism is of limited usefulness for lesbians and other sexual minorities. What became obvious was that feminism had produced lots of theories and texts on gender oppression, but no adequate theory of female sexuality.

Postmodernism provides a way out of the divisions among lesbian theorists. Rejecting a minoritizing view of homosexuality, one that sees lesbian and gay issues as being of interest only to a minority, Martindale favours a universalizing view, one that sees the production of the category of the homosexual minority as interesting to everyone as it constructs and normalizes the heterosexual majority which would not make sense without it. "Queer Theory," a postmodern outgrowth fashioned in 1991, attempted to force a paradigm shift in our ways of thinking about links between gender and sexuality. Postmodern feminist lesbianism seeks to break out of the gay/straight theoretical impasse by formulating a new way of relating lesbianism to feminism that refuses to centre or naturalize either discourse. Such tensions between lesbians and feminists, Martindale reminds us, can be politically and theoretically productive.

## PART 2: WOMEN'S EXPERIENCES: ENGENDERING DIVERSITY

In a compelling fashion, *Sharon Abu-Laban and Susan McDaniel in "Aging Women and Standards of Beauty"* demonstrate that women cannot escape the cultural message that their worth is judged by their appearance. Attractiveness is a central dimension of the schema for femininity and sexual desirability, and girls are motivated to strive towards beauty (Unger and Crawford 1992). Women learn early in their lives that beautiful women are more likely to gain material and economic rewards, that "beauty power" is female.

Standards of beauty for women have actually become more restricted just as women's public and legal independence has risen. Few women can measure up to the ridiculously thin body image that is rarely applied to men. Nor are most of the world's women White, class-advantaged, tall, lanky, and heterosexual. What is the effect of such culturally and socially restrictive definitions on aging women? If very young women worry constantly about their weight, their attractiveness, and their desirability to men, how do older women feel?

Abu-Laban and McDaniel cite all the ways in which women attempt to starve, vomit, purge, and carve themselves into beautiful sex objects. Deprivatory dieting begins early in women's lives and often leads to anorexia and bulimia. Trips to the plastic surgeon, excursions only financially secure women can afford, become commonplace.

Aging is an experience that differs greatly for men and women. For women, aging means they are seen to be getting older faster than men, that women are more likely to be seen as less empowered, and that women receive a disproportionate share of caring for others. Learning to care, to be self-sacrificing and self-deprecating is often the same thing as learning to be a good woman. Predictably, women experience stress, illness, depression, and anxiety that result from women's caring for others and not themselves being cared for. Less well documented, though, are the experiences of aging lesbians, visible minority women, and women with disabilities. Abu-Laban and McDaniel note that considerable research needs to be done to fill in these missing gaps.

In *"The Psychology of Women," Nikki Gerrard and Nayyar Javed* present a rich and detailed account of the many ways in which psychology, as a discipline, objectifies and positions women as "other." Biologically, socially, culturally, and politically, women are viewed as "less than," "different than," and "inferior to" men. Connected with this theorization and treatment of women as deficient lies the actual material and psychological oppression of women. Interconnected and multiple oppressions, exemplified through objectification and the writing of women out of language, leave women psychologically vulnerable. Women grow into adulthood convinced of their inadequacy as people.

How did it come about that half the population exhibits feelings of inferiority? Perhaps no other discipline has put so much time and energy into demonstrating the ways women differ from men. Psychology has generated a series of theories and practices that negatively construct women. Male standards for health, mental health, leadership, culture, competence, judgment, relationship, and personal freedom constitute our recorded and received social reality. Gerrard and Javed lead us through a devastating review of psychology's damaging placement of women. Beginning with its methodological borrowing from physics, psychology dichotomizes women's experiences, contrasting them constantly and artificially with those of men. Sex difference research, for example, tries to draw distinct gender differences, but in fact posits far fewer than might be imagined. Freud's ideas of psychosexual development come under close scrutiny as does Kohlberg's moral maturation sequence and Piaget's cognitive development scheme. All three theorists, long revered in psychology, are exposed as sexist.

Gerrard and Javed also point out that virtually all psychological theory, traditional or feminist, assumes heterosexuality as its norm. Rather than questioning the hegemony of heterosexuality, psychologists marginalize homosexuality. Lesbians are mislabelled and misdiagnosed, overmedicated and shocked, in the mistaken belief that their depression, anxiety, or other manifestations of alienation represent individual pathology. Gerrard and Javed expand the boundaries of psychological analyses by noting the social origins of women's illnesses and separation from self that emanate from social isolation.

On an optimistic note, the authors end with a summary of "new directions in the psychology of women." From the uncovering of new research areas to the revisioning of traditional theories, feminist psychologists have renamed, reframed, and redefined most of psychological theory and practice. Gerrard and Javed have traced, in precise detail, this restructuring as well as providing an excellent "road map" for future feminist psychologists.

In *"The Feminist Challenge: Knowing and Ending the Violence,"* Ann Duffy points out that one of the greatest accomplishments of modern feminism has been the naming and exposure of violence against women. In a chilling portrayal, she documents the extent to which large numbers of Canadian girls and women are exposed to and experience violence in their lives. In both public and private spheres, women face harassment, sexual assault, date rape, woman assault, and intimate femicide. These experiences of violence unite all women across political and cultural grounds: violence against women represents male demonstrations of power, control, and domination. Fear of violence restricts women's behaviour, making them unwilling to assert their needs, unsure of their public use of space.

Sexual violence, even that directed against little girls, is not related to sexual needs. Victims are usually chosen because they are available and powerless, easy targets for male coercion and abuse. The greater women's social and individual powerlessness, the more likely they are to find themselves victimized. Native women face eight times the risk of family violence as non-Native women. Every day the newspapers report incidents of assault directed against women with disabilities, older women, and visible minority women.

The feminist response to violence against women has shaped the political agenda. Government funding for transition houses for battered women helps maintain many of the more than 200 shelters across the country. The "battered woman's syndrome" has been used, successfully, as a legal defence for women who have killed their abusive partners. Federal incidence surveys, a royal commission, and numerous government projects have highlighted woman assault as a national problem. Many feminists decry the use of public funds for more data gathering on what they see as a well-acknowledged problem. Indeed, many feel the money should be used to implement prevention projects. Concerted research has produced a mass of data confirming the enormity of its destructive influence. Duffy reminds us that violence against women remains a horrendous social problem around which all women must unite in order to eliminate it.

What is the position of men in feminism? *Norman Morra and Michael Smith, in "Men in Feminism: Reinterpreting Masculinity and Femininity"* provide numerous answers to this question from the positioning that men are equally as subordinated as women to suggesting that, as oppressors, men cannot occupy any space at all. Those who see men as historically, culturally, and politically duped prefer to rename "Women's Studies" as "Gender Studies," thus emphasizing the social production of gender. Opponents view such categorization as obscuring and depoliticizing the relations of power between women and men.

Those who support the principle of "woman-only" courses and discourage profeminist men from teaching in Women's Studies do so from a position of political suspicion. Feminists wonder if sympathetic men privately and publicly act on their academic beliefs, if sympathetic men monopolize classroom interaction, if sympathetic men endorse feminist studies as a politically correct career decision. Of course, all of these criticisms could equally be applied to "sympathetic women."

Morra and Smith realized, when they set out to write their chapter, that they were entering a politically contested arena. Feminists feel passionately about their goals and vigorously defend their right to define and interpret subject matter. They also recognize, however, that men can make important contributions to feminist scholarship and practice. It is men who must end violence against women.

In a wide-ranging look at feminist research, especially in the area of sexual violence, and at the historic construction of gender identities, Morra and Smith draw out the similarities in men's and women's experiences of isolation, indifference, brutality. Under capitalism, men were just as likely as women to hold low-paying and unrewarding jobs and to suffer abuse at the hands of other men. Power over other men has long been the preserve of only a few men even though all men enjoy more privileges than women. Feminism has prompted men to rethink masculinity and to envision themselves as non-violent, equal partners with women. While it is often easier to state what the new masculinities do not constitute, Morra and Smith make a heartfelt plea for feminists to "leave open the lines of communication vital to the creation of more compatible masculinities."

## PART THREE: RESTRUCTURING INSTITUTIONS: CHALLENGES AND CONFLICTS

Does the legal system act to advance the interests of women or is it an instrument of oppression? In a compelling and detailed fashion, *Mary Jane Mossman, in "The Paradox of Feminist Engagement with Law,"* probes the inherent contradictions in the workings of the Canadian legal system. The system, paradoxically, both acts to facilitate change and constrains women's achievement of both formal and substantive equality in law.

Beginning historically with the early twentieth century, Mossman outlines women's struggles to achieve legal recognition for their fundamental claims to participate in public life. Women's legal claims, during the early years of this century, can be characterized as efforts to establish the civil or political status of women. These claims were based on the idea of women's equality, defined as having access to the same status as men in terms of citizenship. Women's legal claims defined women's equality entirely in terms of men's existing rights and responsibilities and asserted women's right to participate in public life.

Until 1897, Canadian women could not vote and were not eligible to be legislators, judges, or jurors. Achieving the vote occurred in 1916 in some provinces, although Aboriginal women and men could not, up until 1960, vote unless they gave up their Indian status. The famous "Persons" case of 1929 declared women were persons as well as men and thus were eligible to hold appointments to the Senate.

The years between 1960 and 1980 witnessed numerous changes in the practice and substance of law. Beginning in the early 1970s, women entered the legal profession in unprecedented numbers. The Royal Commission on the Status of Women in 1970 articulated needed legislative changes in the areas of family law, tax, child-care allowances, social assistance, immigration and criminal law. The commission thus asserted the role of law as a significant component in achieving changes in the interests of women. In addition, numerous cases questioned women's traditional status. Family property claims were raised by the famous *Murdoch* v *Murdoch* case. By 1980, every common-law province except Quebec had enacted legislation amending the arrangements for sharing property between a husband and wife at the time of separation or divorce. Men and women were treated as economic equals. This recognition of the "formal" equality between men and women ignored the fact that the "substance" of their economic situations is often quite different. Other cases, including changes in the Indian Act, Morgentaler's challenges to abortion laws, equal pay cases, and the deportation of Jamaican workers, represented a preoccupation with property, equality, and equal pay legislation.

Since the 1980s, women's interests, as represented by legal claims, have widened. Most legal battles have taken place over readings of the Canadian Charter of Rights and Freedoms, which was enacted in 1982 even though its equality clause did not take effect until 1985. Charter cases around work, family, and sexuality reveal the contradictory way in which the law both advances and constrains women's search for fair and equitable treatment. While women's equality claims have advanced, so too have men's. In some cases, interpretations of the Charter have actually hampered women's claims; in others, the claims of some women may undermine those of others.

In *"Women's Work and Family Lives,"* Marion Lynn and Milana Todoroff call for a revision in our thinking about the ways women organize their lives in families and in paid employment. Previous biases in family literature have resulted in a sexist, conservative, monolithic, and microstructural analysis of family forms and structures. Lynn and Todoroff demonstrate that a postmodernist reading of "family" critiques universalistic and essentialist analyses and stresses the social location of the speaker.

The postmodern family represents a variety of family patterns, forms, and structures combined together. Family history, as a unified story, is fractured. History, when viewed from various contexts, reveals a rich variety of patterns, including split households and egalitarian arrangements.

The interface of work and family is revealed in statistical patterns. Labour force participation rates for women have steadily grown over the century although employment is not evenly distributed. Fewer Aboriginal women, four in ten, are employed while seven out of ten women of colour work (Khosla 1993). Women with disabilities are even less likely to be in the labour force. They do not have equitable access to training and educational programs, and this restricts their access to the labour force. Unemployment rates are higher for women who cannot depend on a partner for support. A gendered wage gap still prevails for women in all occupational sectors. The majority of women remain clustered in just five occupations: clerical, teaching, nursing or other health-related occupations, and sales or service. Sexual harassment and institutional racism keep women marginalized, vulnerable, and literally shut out of certain graduate schools and workplaces. Even though women comprise 45 percent of the labour force, only 30 percent of women are unionized.

Lynn and Todoroff outline four current family forms: dual-earner, single-parent families, common-law marriages, and lesbian families. In a careful and precise manner, the authors touch on what they consider to be central issues for each of these family types. In dual-earner families, affordable day care, the division of household labour, and time spent on child care are contentious issues. Single-parent families, one of the fastest-growing types in Canada, face problems of poverty as women's wages and gendered labour force patterns mean their take-home pay is less than men's. Lesbian families face homophobic reactions to their living arrangements by neighbours, school officials, and children's friends. They fear losing custody of their children. The chapter ends with a quick look at extended families and kinship systems. Kinship has increasingly been "feminized" as women, acting on an ethic of care, uplift and strengthen entire communities (Collins 1990).

Feminist analysis of schooling has raised questions about the ways in which traditional beliefs about women and men have been used as inappropriate and inequitable sorting and streaming mechanisms. In a sweeping and comprehensive overview, *Cecilia Reynolds, in "The Education System,"* assesses the cumulative effect of the structure and practices of schooling on the life chances of females. Her conclusions are daunting. Rather than consistently acting as instruments of promotion, too often schools reproduce sexist practices commonly found in the larger society.

Rather than diminishing gender differences, schools construct experiences for males and females that facilitate differential outcomes. Clearly, as Reynolds suggests, some kind of "gender tracking" (Mandell and Crysdale 1993) appears to be at work in which extensive gender segregation of domestic labour, schooling, and workplaces means that women and men live, work, and study in different areas. High school streaming leads young men and women into different types of job experiences and/or postsecondary education.

Even though women have had formal access to schooling for over 100 years, their participation varies from that of men. While women have achieved horizontal equity, that is, formal equality of educational opportunity, vertical gender inequity, concentration with categories, still persists in high schools and postsecondary institutions (Mandell and Crysdale 1993). Women are disproportionately found in the humanities and social sciences, in business and health care courses.

From their inception, schools have always favoured boys over girls. Deficit models constructed young girls as lacking in the talents, skills, and abilities needed to progress. Reynolds demonstrates the ways in which the "hidden curriculum" advances the interests of males over females. Young boys receive more "air time," more praise, and more reprimands from teachers. Teachers devote more time and energy to engaging males in classroom discussions by demonstrating more interest in their answers. In numerous ways, the process of schooling suggests males are more worthy of attention, more likely to succeed.

The linkages between schooling and labour markets remain relatively underexamined in Canada. Reynolds points out the similarities between the "chilly climate" females experience in school with the "culture of coercion" they often find at work. She suggests that a number of social policy proposals need to be implemented to transform colleges and universities into "women-friendly" environments. While feminists do not always agree on the importance of the educational system as an instrument for change for women, their exclusion from organized forms of knowledge remains a political battle.

In *"Women and Health: Challenges and Changes," Pat Armstrong* demonstrates the ways in which women's health is defined by and shaped in social, psychological, and economic environments. While race, class, disability, and age distinguish women's health experiences, women do share certain health concerns. Women's bodies remain contested terrain. The biological context is neither fixed nor separate from the social context in which women live and work. The health of women's bodies and women's minds is shaped by history, culture, economics, and the environment. Native women, for example, experience twice the rate of miscarriage as the general Canadian population.

Armstrong points out that the health care that women receive is influenced by the structures within which health care is delivered. In short, she argues that both the institution of medicine and the effects of medical practice are bad for women. Focusing almost exclusively on doctors as purveyors of perilous practice, Armstrong suggests that both male and female doctors practice medicine in such a way that their own backgrounds of class, ethnicity, and gender engender practices that are largely negative for women. Drug prescriptions for tranquilizers are much more likely to be written for women than men; contraceptive practices frequently harm women in their focus on readjusting female, rather than male, bodies; breast implants were not carefully scrutinized for negative consequences. The professionalization of midwives represents women's desire to choose the kinds of births they want and the kinds of people with whom they want to share the experience.

Women's health, at home and in the workplace, is often fraught with problems. Women's greater responsibility for domestic labour means they are more time-stressed than men and visit doctors more often. Motherhood brings immense joy to many women but can also be experienced as a time of increased stress, depression, isolation, and sleep deprivation. Women with labour force jobs enjoy better mental and physical health than women who work exclusively at home. But, even paid labour jobs can be hazardous to women's health. Telephone operators and airline booking agents work at high speed and under close supervision. Clerical workers face repetitive back strain and other technologically-induced illnesses. Women, it seems, face health risks in their dual capacity as domestic and wage labourers.

Finally, we end with a tribute to women's historic contributions, through their paid and unpaid labour, to Canada's social and economic development. Who was the famous Mohawk woman born in 1736 who became a diplomat, crop farmer, and expert in the medicinal qualities of herbs? Who was Canada's first woman explorer? Who was our first Black newspaperwoman? Who was the first North American woman to hold police duties? Who was the first woman to legally practice medicine in Canada? Who was the first woman barrister in the Commonwealth? Who was the first woman principal of a public school? And who was the British Columbian suffragist and trade unionist who ensured that equal pay was written into the constitution of the Vancouver Trades and Labour Council in 1915?

*William Whitla's "A Chronology of Women in Canada"* represents a unique attempt to write women back into history. It highlights women's struggle to overcome gender-based stereotypes and discrimination, emphasizes women's employment patterns of being alternatively drawn into and pushed out of the labour force, and reminds us of the enormous amount of historical recovery still waiting to be done for African-Canadians, First Nations, immigrant, and visible minority women. Government documents yielded almost no information for Whitla, confirming his theory that our historical record has largely been "whitewashed." Whitla's fascinating reconstruction resembles a detective story in which all manner of extremely time-consuming and original research had to be conducted in order to present a comprehensive view of Canadian history. Whitla offers this chronology as merely a first attempt to capture women's past and hopes students will be motivated to fill in the missing details.

## CONCLUDING REMARKS

Each of the chapters in *"Feminist Issues: Diversity, Challenge, and Change"* questions prevailing myths and stereotypes about women's past and current lives. Traditional gender role notions are seen as ideological, as fostering beliefs that no longer match the social reality of women's experiences. While it may be unsettling to have long-held ideas challenged, the process of rethinking women's lives can also be profoundly liberating, not only for women but also for all those with whom they eat, sleep, work, and play. It no longer makes sense to talk about certain behaviours or beliefs as solely the domain of either men or women. The dynamic quality of social life, responding as it does to material, historical, and cultural forces, conflicts with static conceptions of gender roles. Negotiating future contestations over prescribed social patterns remains our challenge. It is hoped that these chapters will provide some guidance for that journey.

## BIBLIOGRAPHY

Collins, Patricia Hill. *Black Feminist Thought: Knowledge, Consciousness, and the Politics of Empowerment*. Boston, Mass.: Unwin Hyman, 1990

Khosla, Punam. *Review of the Situation of Women in Canada*. National Action Committee on the Status of Women, Ottawa, 1993.

Mandell, Nancy and Crysdale, Stewart. "Gender Tracks: Male-Female Perceptions of Home-School-Work Transitions." In *Transitions: Schooling and Employment in Canada*, edited by Paul Anizef and Paul Axelrod, 21-24. Thompson Educational Publishers, 1993.

Robinson, Victoria. "Introducing Women's Studies." In *Thinking Feminist: Key Concepts in Women's Studies*, edited by Diane Richardson and Victoria Robinson, 1-26. The Guilford Press: New York, 1993.

Shrewsbury, Carolyn. "What is Feminist Pedagogy?" *Women's Studies Quarterly: Feminist Pedagogy*, XV (3 and 4), Fall/Winter 1987, 6-14.

Spelman, Elizabeth. *Inessential Woman: Problems of Exclusion in Feminist Thought*. Beacon Press: Boston, 1988.

Spender, Dale, ed. *Men's Studies Modified*. Pergamon, Oxford, 1981.

Unger, Rhoda and Crawford, Mary. *Women and Gender: A Feminist Psychology*. Toronto. McGraw-Hill, 1992.

# Acknowledgements

A number of people have read numerous versions of each chapter and suggested significant contributions and improvements. Others have tirelessly typed. The contributors and I express our heartfelt thanks to Ann Gibbens, Johanna Stuckey, Shelagh Wilkinson, Marion Lynn, Eimear O'Neill, Ann Duffy, Dorothy Chunn, Susan Ehrlich, Sandra Pyke, Paula Caplan, Marion Pirie, Kathryn McPherson, and Lorna Erwin. The editorial guidance provided by Michael Bickerstaff, Ed O'Connor, and Kelly Dickson is much appreciated. And to the "boys," Lionel, Jeremy, Ben and Adam: "Thanks for your support." One day this may all make sense to you.

**PART 1**

# THEORIZING WOMEN: HISTORY, POLITICS, AND PLACEMENT

# CHAPTER 1

# FEMINIST THEORIES

*Patricia Elliot and Nancy Mandell*

The Clarion: *Rebecca West*
*"I myself have never been able to find out precisely what feminism is: I only know that people call me a feminist whenever I express sentiments that differentiate me from a doormat...."*

## INTRODUCTION

Why, some students bemoan, do feminist academics always begin their courses with a month of readings on feminist theory? What has theory got to do with how I live my life or the manner in which I resolve my everyday problems? Why do I need to review the writings of Canadian feminists?

While you may not enjoy theory more as a result of reading this chapter, we hope it will provide you with an understanding of the ways in which theoretical assumptions guide our decision-making process. Theories are nothing more than blueprints we use, often subconsciously, in leading our lives. What type of consumer goods we purchase, who we live with, and the ways in which we try to raise our children are examples of major and minor life choices based on our theoretical assumptions about how we should lead our lives. Too frequently, it is not possible to realize our dreams, but the obstacles do not necessarily force us to relinquish our beliefs, only to clarify their content.

Feminist theories vary in nature, content, and consequence just as do any other set of theories found in academic disciplines. This cursory introduction outlines some of the most important trends in contemporary feminist theory and focuses on the ways in which theories are used to understand and explain concrete issues and problems in women's lives. By understanding hidden assumptions and by identifying particular positions, the reader will acquire the tools with which to situate theoretical debates and to clarify his or her own position within these debates. Only then can one discuss different theoretical perspectives on current issues raised in the following chapters, such as date rape, employment equity, and spousal benefits for gay and lesbian couples.

## DEFINITIONS OF FEMINISM

"Feminist" as a word gained widespread usage in the western world in the 1890s. It emerged at this time as a way to identify individuals who supported not merely an increased public role for women but also women's right to define themselves as autonomous beings. However, throughout the past century, as women's private and public roles have expanded and altered, the definition of a feminist has also broadened to include political, cultural, economic, sexual, racial, and ethical dimensions. Today, were instructors to require students to define feminism or feminist, we doubt consensus would be found.

To the American writer Adrienne Rich (1979), feminism is not a frivolous label but is an ethics, a methodology, a more complex way of thinking about and acting upon the conditions of our lives. To the British social scientist Chris Weedon (1987), feminism is a politics directed at changing existing power relations between women and men in society. To the American literary critic bell hooks (1984), feminism constitutes a social, economic, and political commitment to eradicating race, class, and sexual domination and to reorganizing society so that individual self-development takes precedence over imperialism, economic expansion, and material desires. To Canadian activist and academic Linda Carty (1993), white feminism needs to recognize that gender is not the only or always the primary consideration in the struggle for women's liberation.

Despite definitional differences, feminist theorists generally share four concerns (Jaggar and Rothenberg, 1984). First, feminist theorists seek to understand the gendered nature of virtually all social and institutional relations. These arrangements determine who does what and for whom, what we are, and what we might become. Second, gender relations are constructed as problematic and as related to other inequities and contradictions in social life. Family, education and welfare, worlds of work and politics, culture and leisure are socially structured through relations of gender, power, class, race, and sexuality. Third, gender relations are not viewed as either natural or immutable but as historical and sociocultural productions, subject to reconstitution. In particular, feminist analyses deconstruct errors and myths about women's abilities, add to knowledge about women's empirical realities, and construct theory by and about women. Fourth, feminist theorists tend to be explicitly political in their advocacy of social change. Feminists challenge what they call traditional race-class-sexuality-power arrangements which favour men over women, whites over non-whites, adults over children, able-bodiedness over non-able-bodiedness, residents over non-residents, and the employed over the non-employed. Although comprehensive feminist theories remain unfinished, struggles to embrace inclusivity continue.

One way to understand the various dimensions of feminist theories is to locate them within broader philosophical and political perspectives. In the rest of this chapter, we outline some of the basic tenets of liberal feminism, socialist feminism, radical feminism, anti-racist feminism, psychoanalytic feminism, and postmodernist feminism. Subsequent chapters in the book explore and build on particular theories in more detail.

## LIBERAL FEMINISM

The philosophical tradition of liberalism grew out of the major social, political, and economic transformations of the late 1600s to the late 1700s. In this period, called the "Age of Enlightenment" or the "Age of Reason," social dislocation inevitably led to the emergence of theories contesting traditional authority held by the church, the aristocracy, and the propertied classes. Previously held feudal beliefs were eschewed in favour of citizens' rights, individual rationality, and equal opportunity. In particular, the new, burgeoning middle class questioned long-standing traditions including the divine right of kings and aristocrats to rule, the seemingly incontestable authority of the church, and the lack of political participation for non-propertied classes. Changes brought about by the American and French revolutions, by industrialization and urbanization, and by the consolidation and expansion of a world system of capitalism led to urban crowding, development of slums, pollution and waste, poverty and crime, and new tensions in family life (Anderson, 1993). Fierce arguments erupted about the ability and rights of ordinary men to participate in public life, to vote and hold political office, and to hold property in their own names. The emergence of scientific laws, in biology, in geography, and in Newtonian and Galilean physics emphasized reason over tradition. Liberal philosophers and politicians extended these natural laws to human society and concluded that every individual has certain inherent natural rights, such as those to life, liberty, and the pursuit of happiness, upon which governments may not intrude.

These ideas represent the legacy of the Enlightenment: the ascendancy of reason over tradition, the outreach of humanitarianism to dispossessed groups, and the general improvement in the condition of humanity. At heart, liberalism constitutes a philosophy based on the principle of individual liberty, in which every person should be allowed to exercise freedom of choice, unfettered by either public opinion or law. In principle, every person was to be given equal opportunities and civil rights (Anderson, 1993). In reality, progress and justice were only intended to be extended to men.

Early liberal feminists attempted to correct misconceptions about women. In her *Vindication of the Rights of Woman*, first published in London in 1792, Mary Wollstonecraft (1759–1797) vigorously defended women's rights. Fifty years later, Harriet Taylor Mill (1807–1858), along with her collaborator John Stuart Mill (1806–1873), published a series of essays advocating the emancipation of women. "The Subjection of Women," first published in 1851, indicts traditional arrangements of work and family as tyrannizing women and denying them freedom of choice. Both Wollstonecraft and the Mills point out that women are human beings capable of rational thought and deserving of the same natural rights granted to men. Since women have been constructed primarily as sexual beings, they have been educated to acquire qualities such as chastity, gentleness, and obedience. Their so-called "natural" weaknesses, their irrationality and their wandering minds actually result from their lack of education and freedom of choice, their dependence on men and faulty socialization.

Foretelling generations of feminists, these authors identify goals still central to the liberal feminist agenda: ending women's legal, economic and social dependence upon men; obtaining the freedom and opportunity to engage in education and training; promoting open competition and a laissez-faire, non-interventionist operation of the economic market; accelerating the process of modernity in which social organizations support the principle of meritocracy; and enacting laws and public policies guaranteeing equality of choice and equality of opportunity, both of which are thought to lead to improvements in women's status.

### Contemporary Liberal Feminism

Throughout this century, liberal feminists continue to assume that the inequality of women stems from the denial to them of equal rights and from their learned reluctance to exercise such rights. They identify socialization and education in shaping individuals as central in constructing gender differences in attitudes, expectations, and behaviours. By reshaping individual beliefs and values, new socialization processes will be created in institutional and non-formal settings. More liberated and egalitarian gender relations will presumably derive from this altered process of social learning.

Contemporary liberal feminists also seek female equality with men by extending to women those rights and privileges being offered to men. They advocate social and legal reform through policies designed to create equal opportunities for women, such as achieving citizens' rights, introducing companionate marriages, and ensuring educational opportunities. Social policy is viewed as an important force in establishing access to economic opportunities and civil rights.

Often we fail to acknowledge just how radical were the demands of Canadian feminists one hundred years ago. As Bill Whitla outlines in the

Epilogue to this book, liberal feminists engaged in a wide range of diverse activities aimed at improving women's status. Mary Ann Shadd established schools for black children in the 1850s in Windsor. Physicians Emily Stowe and Augusta Stowe-Gullen established in 1883 the Canadian Women's Suffrage Association and emphasized getting women into education. Pauline Johnson focused in the 1890s on self-enfranchisement for First Nations women. Lady Aberdeen, in 1893, founded the National Council of Women of Canada. Emilie Carrier LeBlanc wrote newspaper articles on suffrage and education for women. As a journalist, Ella Cara Hind promoted women's rights. In 1907, Marie Gerin-Lojoie, Caroline Beique, and Josephine Marchand-Dandurand established the Fédération Nationale Saint-Jean-Baptiste, a francophone and Catholic organization for women concerned with education, social service, and the relations of women's lives to the economy in wages, working conditions, trade unions, and other associations.

Liberal feminist activities culminated in the 1918 federal enfranchisement of women over 21 who received the vote and in the famous 1929 "Persons Case." Nellie McClung, Emily Murphy, Louise McKinney, Irene Parlby, and Henrietta Muir Edwards petitioned the Supreme Court of Canada and eventually the Judicial Committee of the British Privy Council to declare that women were persons and so eligible for appointment to the Canadian Senate. First wave feminists eliminated barriers and enabled women to gain entrance into education, politics, social service, and the professions.

Second wave feminists, whose agenda of concerns officially arose from the 1970 Royal Commission on the Status of Women, continued the liberal feminist tradition of trying to fit women into existing social structures. Goals included ensuring married women access to wage labour, parental sharing of child care, protection of maternity, and special treatment of particularly disadvantaged groups of women. It was not until the 1984 Abella Report (Abella, 1984) that liberal feminists introduced the idea of employment equity into government discourse and recognized the rights of marginalized groups of women as requiring special advancement in order to redress systemic discrimination. Throughout the second wave, as Mary Jane Mossman tells us in Chapter 8, preferred forms of action include legal reforms, educational advances, and public policy accommodations.

### Critiques of Liberal Feminism

Working within existing institutions, liberal feminists stress the principle of equal opportunity and social reform and focus on achieving social change by constructing legislation and regulating employment practices. Since liberal feminists believe in the power of reason and knowledge to facilitate social reform, their practical solutions to inequality include programs that prohibit discrimination and resocialize children and adults. Nineteenth and twentieth century women's rights movements include extending the natural rights doctrine of the Enlightenment to women, gaining the right to vote, changing married women's status by protecting married women's property, improving women's legal position in child custody cases, liberalizing divorce laws, providing married women with economic autonomy, and ensuring women access to higher education, wage labour, and the professions.

Liberal reforms have resulted in increased opportunities for women and increased public consciousness of women's rights, marking liberal feminism as the most mainstream and popular feminist perspective. Yet, critics suggest these reforms have not been shared equally by all women because changes have not addressed issues of socially structured inequality. They focus on how to achieve collective equality without jeopardizing individual freedom. But, they fail to recognize that inequities of class, race, ethnicity, and disability are institutionalized and difficult to dislodge through individual action.

Liberal feminist theories also presume a distinction between the private world of the home and the public lives of individuals without analyzing the ways in which the private and the public spill over into one another. For instance, assuming a rigid private/public dichotomy continues dualistic thinking about gender roles. Men are more likely to be associated with the rational, instrumental, mechanistic, scientific, secular, and public domain while women are associated with the irrational, sacred, emotional, and private world. Moreover, assuming that legal changes such as married women's property acts and no-fault divorce legislation will equalize women's status in marriage fails to recognize that women's continued responsibility for domestic duties interrupts their opportunities to participate in paid labour. Twentieth century liberal feminist thinking left women economically independent but still fulfilling traditional roles of wife and mother. It was up to socialist feminists to point out the discrepancies, conflicts, and contradictions in the liberal feminist agenda.

## Socialist Feminism

### Roots of Socialist Feminism

Like the liberal tradition, socialism has its roots in the political, intellectual, and socio-economic changes taking place in the middle and late nineteenth century in Western Europe and North America. This climate of social reform set the stage for the British suffrage movement and the Canadian feminist movement of the late nineteenth and early twentieth centuries. The spread of industrial capitalism, rapid industrialization, urban poverty, family upheavals, and role transitions spawned both a liberal and a socialist response.

While the liberal perspective emphasizes learned gender roles and the denial of opportunities as the primary causes of women's oppression, socialist feminists see women's relationship to the economy as the origin of women's oppression. Gender is conceptualized as a social, political, ideological, and economic category that takes a particular shape under capitalism. While liberal feminism takes women's equality with men as its major political goal, socialist feminists set as their goal transforming basic structural arrangements of society so that categories of class, gender, sexuality, and race no longer act as barriers to equal sharing of resources.

Socialist feminists critique liberal theories as maintaining class and race hierarchies at the same time as categories are widened to include women. In fact, most socialists consider the liberal concept of isolated individuals with abstract rights and choices a harmful myth that perpetuates inequalities. Socialist feminists view individuals as social beings embedded in a network of concrete social and economic relationships. Capitalist relations actually force people to compete with and exploit one another in order to survive economically. By failing to analyze the ways in which dominant institutions are organized through gender, race, and class oppression, liberal feminists improve the lot of privileged women but leave untouched the social organization of everyday life.

The socialist stress on capitalism reminds feminists to pay attention to the ways in which economic circumstances condition choices and opportunities. Eliminating exploitative structures alleviates the social consequences that such arrangements encourage such as the feminization of poverty, inequity in wages, and unpaid work. With social class as the main category of analysis, socialist feminists focus on the social and economic organization of work in capitalist systems, on the relations between paid and unpaid labour, and the interconnection between production and reproduction, the private and the public.

### Marxist Feminists

The same year, 1848, that liberal philosopher John Stuart Mill published *On Liberty*, Karl Marx (1818–1883) and his collaborator, Friedrich Engels (1820–1895), published *The Communist Manifesto* in Paris. Marxist feminists take as their starting point Engels' 1884 text "The Origin of the Family, Private Property, and the State." Following Marx and Engels, Marxist feminists see women's oppression as originating with the introduction of private property. Private ownership of the means of production by relatively few persons, mostly male, instituted a class system that forms the root cause of most inequality and misery in the world. Ultimately, women are oppressed, not by sexism, but by capitalism. Gender inequality will only disappear when capitalism is replaced with socialism. Once women's economic dependence on men dissolves, the material basis for women's subordination will also fade.

Marxist feminists see women as relating differently to the means of production in capitalist systems. First, capitalism has an inherent division of labour by sex.

Women who work in the home tend to be responsible for the production of goods and services that have no exchange value. Hence, women's housework and child-care work is not considered "real work" since they do not produce money. Men who work in the public sector are directly engaged in commodity production, of products created for exchange on the market. Second, the association of women with the private home relegates their public labour to a secondary status. The cultural prescription that women belong in the home situates women as a "reserve army of labour." Women will be paid less, be first fired or laid off, and returned to the home when the economy no longer needs their paid labour (Benston, 1969).

The family under capitalism becomes a microcosm of society's larger class relations. Wives resemble the proletariat, monogamous marriage develops as part of the formation of private property, and the division of private and public labour becomes gendered. All wives, regardless of their paid labour commitments, are responsible for household management, child care, the emotional nurturing of dependants, and the general well-being of the family. The work of housewives, their domestic slavery, represents both a private service to the male head of the household and an unpaid economic service to society as a whole. Only the abolition of capitalism and private property frees women from gender oppression.

## Contemporary Socialist Feminists

Classical Marxist feminists see the oppression of women as stemming primarily from capitalism in which women are defined as the property of men and the accumulation of profit necessitates the exploitation of women's labour. Recent socialist feminists criticize traditional Marxist feminists as putting too much emphasis on the economic origins of gender inequality, noting that female subordination also occurs in precapitalist and socialist systems. In fact, socialist feminists accuse Marxist feminists of being "sex blind," of only adding women into their existing critique of capitalism (Hartmann, 1981).

Moreover, they suggest Marxist feminists have stagnated the debate about women by focusing endlessly on the connection between the economy and gender relations. One way to advance theory about women's oppression lies in enlarging traditional Marxism by expanding our understanding of the mode of production. This includes not only providing for our basic material needs of food, clothing and shelter, but also incorporating all the ways in which individuals organize to produce and distribute the means of satisfying their needs for reproduction, for sexuality, nurturance, and babies.

Another way socialist feminists have advanced theoretical boundaries is by analyzing the ways class and gender relations intersect. Economic class relations are important in determining women's status but gender relations may be equally significant. Eradicating social class inequality alone will not necessarily eliminate sexism. Patriarchy, a system in which men dominate both women and younger or less privileged men, existed prior to capitalism and continues to exist in both capitalist and non-capitalist political-economic systems.

Socialist feminists today tend to focus their analyses on five central concerns. The first involves examining the role of the household in propping up the entire capitalist system by reproducing gender, race, sexual, and class relations. In 1969, Margaret Benston, in "The Political Economy of Women's Liberation," exposed domestic labour as a crucial form of women's work, unpaid, undervalued, and rendered invisible within the home. Numerous Canadian and international studies emanated from Benston's work, all aimed at recognizing and legitimating women's ongoing domestic responsibilities. Meg Luxton's (1980) qualitative study of Flin Flon women carefully analyzes women's domestic labour, revealing both its tedious and enriching qualities. Pat and Hugh Armstrong's (1978) material analysis of the occupational segregation of women in gendered labour markets initiated more detailed analyses of paid work. Ann Duffy, Nancy Mandell, and Noreen Pupo's 1989 study of the interface of paid and unpaid labour in the lives of women reveals the lack of choices women face in "choosing" part-time or full-time labour. Domestic labour studies have been enormously influential in gaining public recognition for unpaid labour and for the ways in which this added responsibility constrains women's paid work, limits their leisure time, and increases their likelihood of facing poverty.

A second area of concentration discusses the relation of women as wage earners to modes of production. Far from being liberated by their entrance into paid labour, as Engels predicted, women are confined to a double day of paid and unpaid labour. Moreover, cultural definitions of femininity are closely linked to definitions of good mothering, making it difficult for women to escape feelings of obligation, guilt, and anxiety when their time and attention is diverted from caring for dependants. The role of women as wage earners has also sparked concern with female job segregation. Noting that women earn a 64-cent dollar and cluster in five traditionally low-paid occupational areas, studies show how definitions of women as primarily wives and mothers contributes a secondary status to their roles as paid labourers (Briskin, 1993). Investigations into the origin of wage differentials and occupational segregation have led to critiques of the "family wage" ideology in which men are seen to be breadwinners who need to be paid a wage sufficient to support their dependent wives and children (see Chapter 9).

A third focus dissects the relation of women and social class. Questions arise as to which social class women belong to. Women have contradictory class status as wives carrying the status of their male partners and as workers imbued with their own class positions. Another question probes class differences among women. All women's experiences are not similar. Working-class women face daily hardships and worries about economic survival that middle-class professional women avoid. To what extent does socialist feminism assume a monolithic, middle-class bias in its analysis of women's lives? What common experiences unite all women across class lines? Do public policy and legal gains made for some classes of women actually harm others?

The role of the family in the ideological socialization of women, men, and children represents the fourth area of concentration. More than any other group of theorists, socialist feminists have dissected the strategies families employ in inculcating traditional values and behaviours. The stereotypical behaviour expected of women and men is functional to the capitalist system (Hartmann, 1981). Men are socialized into competitiveness, aggressiveness, rationality, and independence, traits assumed necessary for achieving success in a capitalist economy. In contrast, women are socialized into relational, contextual, integrative, and life-affirming relationships presumably suited to their main chores of childrearing and kin-keeping.

Finally, concepts of praxis, consciousness raising, and ideology are central to socialist feminist studies. Consciousness raising and praxis, practical action, form the basis of feminist methodology. According to Nancy Hartsock (1983), the practice of consciousness raising in small groups, with its stress on examining and understanding experience and on connecting personal experience to the structures that define our lives is the clearest example of the method basic to feminism. Socialist feminists stress the development of alternative arrangements that provide models for change and, in the process, alter women's consciousness. Rape crisis centres, woman assault shelters, small businesses, and collective daycares are examples of new structures that stimulate alternative thoughts and behaviour.

The analysis of ideology guides socialist feminist work. Ideology is used in multiple ways including the Marxian sense of false consciousness rooted in ruling-class interests as well as the generic sense of ideology as a process by which meaning is produced, challenged, reproduced, and transformed. Feminist engagement with public policy, law, intimate encounters, educational authorities, and other social relations represents the contested terrain on which ideology is constructed. Families, for example, ideologically and concretely reproduce social class through the socialization of their children. Cultural capital is passed on to children through daily practices of interaction in schooling, friendships, and leisure activities. Childrearing, a lifetime activity, changes women's consciousness as they experience the contradictions of entrapment and exhilaration. While the family may be experienced as a "haven" for some, a location in which to experience personal freedom and consumption, too often for women family life becomes burdensome (Lasch, 1977).

### Critiques of Socialist Feminism

Socialist feminist theory begins with the point that class and gender relations intersect in shaping women's lives. Recently, concerns with sexuality, race, ethnicity, and disability have been added into the interaction of class and gender. For the most part, early socialists argue that social and biological reproduction are conditioned by a society's economic mode of production. Yet, many socialist feminists suggest that class relations may not be the most critical relations defining women's place in society. Rather, class analysis must be considered with analyses of patriarchy. Patriarchy refers to an analytically and historically distinct system of male domination that affects and is affected by class systems. Women and men do not share common interests because the interpenetration of capitalism and patriarchy modify and support one another to produce historically specific forms of female oppression.

More recently, socialist feminists have addressed patriarchy and capitalism as concretely intertwined and mutually supportive systems of oppression. Women's subordination within capitalism results from their economic exploitation as wage labourers and their patriarchal oppression as mothers, domestic labourers, and consumers. This patriarchal oppression has both a material and an ideological basis. Ideologically, the sexes are assumed to be different in temperament and aptitude. Practically, these presumed differences are institutionally inscribed in the sexual division of labour and the heterosexual, nuclear family.

Radical feminist and other feminist critiques suggest that the socialist ideology of separate spheres for men and women does not apply to diverse family forms. Immigrant families, split-family households, working-class families, First Nations and Inuit families, gay and lesbian families, single-parent households, and numerous other arrangements do not adhere to strict gender role divisions in expectations and tasks. Also, the ideology of women's role places concrete limitations on women's aspirations and actions, such as their capacity to organize and implement change.

Critics of socialist feminism suggest it is problematic to argue that women's domestic responsibilities explain the origin and reproduction of gender segregation in the labour market. Social constructions of skill contain beliefs about valued work. Male control of the workplace relates to power relations within the family. A more complex answer is required to explain historical patterns of occupational segregation than the limits placed on women's time and energy.

In spite of considerable ideological and structural change in conceptions of gender, sexual divisions persist. This had led some feminists to suggest that answers lie in psychoanalytic theory which permits the location of subjectivity and sexual difference in the unconscious and in language, rather than in nature or material conditions.

## Radical Feminism

Most radical feminists agree that women's oppression is the first, the most widespread, and the deepest form of human oppression. To claim that women's oppression is the most fundamental form of oppression includes the following meanings: that historically women were the first oppressed group; that women's oppression is widespread and international; that women's oppression is the hardest form of oppression to eradicate; that enormous suffering results for women; and that women's oppression provides a conceptual model for understanding all other forms of oppression (Jaggar and Rothenberg, 1984).

What oppresses women is not what oppresses men but is rather a special form of life called patriarchy through which men appropriate all superior social roles and keep women in subordinate and exploited positions. Radical feminists define patriarchy as a "sexual system of power in which the male possesses superior power and economic privilege." (Eisenstein, 1979:17) They view patriarchy as an autonomous social, historical, and political force (Anderson, 1993:330). In particular, male control of female sexuality and male domination in social institutions lead to women's devaluation and continued subordination. Feminism becomes the study of the socio-political formation of patriarchy itself and constitutes its own social theory rather than being a sub-set of a broader philosophical theory such as Marxism or psychoanalysis.

### Feminist Separation

Only the elimination of patriarchy and the destruction of male control will liberate women. But given its historical, culturally pervasive, and invasive nature, how does one get rid of patriarchy? Clearly this is not an easy task. Radical feminists suggest we begin by eliminating gender, specifically sexual status, role, temperament, and social constructions as they have been constructed under patriarchy (Tong, 1989:96). As patriarchy is organized through men's relationships with other men, unity among women is the only effective means for liberating women. Separation by women calls for isolation from men and from institutions, relationships, roles, and activities that are male-defined, male-operated, benefit males and maintain male privilege.

Lesbian feminism and cultural feminism are two types of feminist separations advocating the creation of a woman-identified world through the attachments women have to each other. The emergence of lesbian separatism positions lesbianism as more than a purely personal decision, as an outward sign of an internal rejection of patriarchal sexuality (Rich, 1980). Lesbianism becomes a paradigm for female-controlled female sexuality, the kind of sexuality that meets women's own needs and fulfills their own desires (see Chapter 3).

Another popular strategy for resisting patriarchy has been to redefine social relations by creating women-centered cultures that emphasize the positive capacities of women by focusing on the creative dimensions of their experiences. Cultural separation involves the development of women's culture and women's relationships with other women. Radical feminists, more than any other feminist theoretical tradition, have made considerable contributions to women's culture. We now celebrate a long and previously unimaginable list of women's accomplishments because radical feminists dared to imagine and create alternative structures. Feminist art, spirituality, food, ecology, reproduction, mothering, gender, and sexuality have all been nurtured in women-only spaces. Women's co-operatives, clinics, clubs, shelters that emphasize decision by consensus, tapping of spiritual resources, and giving of mutual aid shatter male power and privilege.

### Women's Bodies: Reproduction, Mothering, Sexuality, and Violation

Biological inequality between the sexes and hence reproduction, or making babies, was assumed by early radical feminists to be the cause of women's oppression (Firestone, 1970). There were calls to eliminate the family as a biological and an economic unit in which individuals possess neither private property nor private children. Freeing women from the tyranny of reproduction was thought to be emancipatory. Technology was viewed as liberating women. Recent critiques suggest the opposite. Technologies such as artificial insemination, in vitro fertilization, sex preselection, embryo transplantation, fetal monitoring, and eventual cloning make the womb the province not of women, but of scientists and doctors who wish to control it (Petchesky, 1980).

Describing women as out of control of their own destinies led radical feminists to question mothering under patriarchy (Rich, 1976). The current institution of mothering is one in which men have convinced women that unless they become mothers, they are not really women. "Good mothering" constitutes women's only significant job. "Good mothers" are not supposed to have any personal friends or plans unrelated to those of their family, are on call 24 hours a day and love every minute of it, and are blamed for whatever goes wrong in their children's lives. Moreover, husbands demand that women help them raise their sons to be "real" men who grow up to oppress women. In short, under patriarchy, women don't experience childbearing and childrearing on their own terms.

Socialist feminists see women's oppression as stemming from their work in the family and the economy. Many radical feminists see sexual relations, men's dominance over women, and male control of female sexuality as the central cause of women's oppression. For radical feminists, sexual relations are political acts, emblematic of male/female power relationships (McKinnon, 1982). Socially constructed gender and reproductive roles restrict women's identity and behaviour and make it exceedingly difficult for women to identify and develop their own sexual desires and needs. As long as women's sexuality is interpreted in terms of men's sexuality, women will never be men's full political, economic, or social equals and heterosexual relations will not be egalitarian (Tong, 1989).

Heterosexist ideology exaggerates biological differences between men and women, making certain that men always have the dominant or masculine roles and that women always have the subordinate or feminine ones (Tong, 1989:96). Heterosexism institutionalizes male hegemony by legitimating and normalizing sexual practices built on aggressive male behaviour and passive, submissive female behaviour. Through socialization in the family, the church, the academy and so on, men secure consent of the very women they oppress. Each institution justifies and reinforces women's subordination to men with the result that most women internalize a sense of inferiority to men. Men use coercion to accomplish what conditioning fails to achieve (Millett, 1970:8).

Men construct female sexuality to serve their needs and desires. Restrictive contraception, sterilization, abortion laws, and violence directed against women through pornography, sexual harassment, rape, incest, violence directed against lesbians, and assault are examples of ways men control female sexuality. All over the world, patriarchy is established, supported, and maintained through these sexually violent and misogynist practices (Dworkin, 1974).

The elimination of violence against women is a main goal of radical feminist politics and practice. Liberal feminists assume that, given the introduction of fair legal and political practices, heterosexual relations will be voluntary, egalitarian, and just. Most socialist feminists assume that given non-exploitative economic institutions, heterosexual relations will cease to be alienating or oppressive. Radical feminists believe women will always be subordinate to men unless sexuality is reconceived and reconstructed in the image and likeness of women. Only then will the power and spirit of the female body be able to emerge and allow the development of women's reproductive and sexual powers in new ways.

## The State as an Instrument of Patriarchy

While liberals see the state as disembodied reason, socialists see the state primarily as a reflection of material interests (McKinnon, 1989). Liberal political analyses of the state treat women as an interest group with rights like any other lobby group. For socialists, the state is a tool of dominance and a force that legitimates ideology. Women are one of many subordinated groups. Both groups demand the state intervene to equalize rights and opportunities. Sexual abuse, divorce law, and equal pay are examples of specific areas in which women have entrusted the state to protect their rights.

For radical feminists, the state is an instrument ensuring male control of women's sexuality. Although it assumes objectivity through the enactment of presumably neutral laws, in practice women are raped by the state just as they are raped by men (Tong, 1989). As long as the state is male, meaning that its meaning systems, its mode of operations, and its underlying assumptions are based in masculine power, women will be unable to overcome their subordination through state actions.

### *Critiques of Radical Feminism*

Radical feminists have brought immensely valuable insights to feminist theorizing. Identifying the ways in which male practices construct women as passive and submissive allows women to make their personal experiences political and to figure out strategies of resistance. Celebrating women as actors, not victims, empowers women to act on their own behalf to reverse or eliminate negative acts. Even if there is no such thing as a supremely nurturant, wise, and essential female nature, it is empowering to think that it is good to be a woman (Grant, 1993).

Recently, poststructuralist developments have emerged in response to theoretical dissatisfactions with radical feminism. Specifically, critics charge radical feminists with essentialism, romanticism, ethnocentrism, and ahistoricism. Most feminist theorists now find radical feminist explanations of patriarchy, women, and experience as essentialist and analytically unhelpful. For instance, women's natures and bodies are defined as biologically fixed, unchanging, and determined. Men and women are seen as possessing an "a priori" essence that is as predetermined as our genetic makeup (Tong, 1989). Individuality and historical variability are ignored, as are racial, cultural, sexual, and class differences.

Radical feminists fall into the trap of essentialism, the conviction that men are men and women are women and that there is no way to change either's nature. Such a trap represents an analytic dead end as well as a political danger (Tong, 1989). Agreeing, for example, that women are by nature compassionate and nurturing and that men are aggressive and competitive suggests that radical feminists accept and promulgate the very stereotypes they are trying to avoid. How does one alter or change that from which one cannot escape? Women are trapped inside their bodies and biology becomes their destiny. Politically, such rigidity fuels a deep conservatism (Elshtain, 1981).

Essentialist and romanticist charges have rendered the category "woman" one of the most contested within contemporary feminism. The notion of a universal female experience is seen as necessary in order to ground feminism (Grant, 1993). Yet the terms "woman," "universal," and "experience" mean different things to different groups of women. If, as the poststructuralists argue, experience is multiple, fractured, and diverse, whose experience counts as "real"? To whom do we listen? How do we assert "truths" about women? Generalizing from one point of view erases, ignores, or invalidates the experiences of others. But if no experience can be privileged, then the fear is that we will be led down a spiral to a completely relativistic, pluralistic, ever-expanding additive model of theories of knowledge (Grant, 1993). In later sections we will see that searching for answers to these questions has led feminists to poststructuralism.

## Anti-Racist Feminism

Critics of radical feminism wonder to whom and to what radical feminists refer when they talk about women, experience, and personal politics. Standpoint theory represents a different strategy than socialist or universalist approaches in that it attempts to talk about women, women's experiences, and politics in concrete and historicized ways. Standpoint feminism abandons the idea that there is a unified female identity or a single female perspective and moves to the idea that there are many female standpoints (Grant, 1993:91).

Women of colour were among the first to conceptualize the multiplicity of female experience and to criticize liberal, socialist, and radical feminists for ignoring race as a category of oppression and analysis (Brand, 1993; Das Gupta, 1995). Previous feminist theorizing suffers from white solipsism, thinking, imagining, and speaking as if whiteness describes the world (Spelman, 1989). White, middle-class, heterosexual women's experiences are taken as the norm while the specificity of black, native, and other ethnic and cultural experiences are ignored.

Feminism purports to liberate all women yet it takes the experience of white women as the universal social norm. By assuming that gender is the primary form of subordination, oppressions of class, sexuality, and race become extensions of patriarchal domination. Such assumptions divide minority women and men and provide little explanation of the powerlessness that minority men and women experience together. For instance, radical feminists' insistence that eliminating sexism is the key to eliminating racism has a hollow ring to women of colour as they experience racism from feminist women as well as from men (Grant, 1993).

Feminist theories remain incomplete without an analysis of the intersections of race, sexuality and gender. So severe are these limitations that Chapter 2 and Chapter 3 in this book give voice to previously silenced women: First Nations, African Canadian, immigrant, disabled, poor, and lesbian women. We have been deliberately brief here in order to direct the reader to these more detailed explanations.

## Psychoanalytic Feminism

Feminists have not been quick to embrace either psychoanalytic theory or therapy since both have been used historically to assert female inferiority and to enforce passivity. Some feminists, like Simone de Beauvoir (1970), Betty Friedan (1963), Kate Millett (1970), and, more recently, Gloria Steinem (1994) condemn Freudian psychoanalysis as a tool of women's oppression. Other feminists, however, claim psychoanalysis is useful for feminism, that the insight it provides into the unconscious aspects of the human psyche can help women to better understand both the personal and the political dimensions of our lives. These feminists, referred to as "psychoanalytic feminists," are interested in exploring the hidden dynamics at work in personal, interpersonal and social relations, the unconscious dynamics that shape the way we think, feel, and act in the world. Of particular interest to psychoanalytic feminists is the analysis of the social construction of gender which psychoanalysis provides. This analysis can be utilized in understanding and transforming women's position as subordinate. It is clear, then, that unlike those feminists who condemn psychoanalysis, those who find it helpful do not interpret Freud as prescribing women's subordination. Rather, they read Freud as describing a process that takes place within a patriarchal culture, a process women need to alter in order to end our oppression.

Since the publication of Juliet Mitchell's book *Psychoanalysis and Feminism* in 1974, the field of psychoanalysis and feminism has expanded, producing many fascinating books, articles, and debates (see Brennan, 1989; Feldstein and Roof, 1989). The publication in 1992 of a critical dictionary entitled *Feminism and Psychoanalysis* (edited by Elizabeth Wright) demonstrates the continued and international interest in this field. Although the relationship between feminism and psychoanalysis is fraught with all the tensions, disputes, negotiations, and reconciliations that accompany any passionate relationship, it appears to grow stronger over time (Gallop, 1982). Those who develop the relationship between psychoanalysis and feminism constitute a rather diverse group who bring different questions, readings, experiences, and insights to bear on this field. Whereas some feminists working in this area are practising psychoanalysts, others are academics working in diverse disciplines such as film, literary theory, cultural studies, sociology, and political theory. In what follows, psychoanalytic feminism will be distinguished from other feminisms, and an overview of some of the major psychoanalytic feminist theories will be sketched.

At least two of the three central concerns of all feminist analyses as stated earlier in this chapter are addressed by psychoanalytic feminism. These concern the deconstruction of myths about women's nature and the construction of theory by and about women. Psychoanalytic feminists may share the politics of radical, Marxist or socialist feminists, but the kinds of questions they ask concern another scene, a scene other feminists do not always know how to acknowledge. Psychoanalytic feminism involves a particular kind of inquiry into the nature and functioning of women's oppression, an inquiry that engages us in a rethinking of what it means to be a gendered subject. The aim is to develop a critique of gendered subjectivity which produces a hierarchy of masculine over feminine subjects, a hierarchy in which women are made subordinate. Psychoanalytic feminist critiques of gender extend beyond the conscious level of experience to the unconscious level where gender-specific desires and meanings are constituted or formed. The method involves tracing representations of gender back to crucial moments of psychosexual development where dilemmas of desire and identity arise and get resolved in different ways depending on individual, cultural, and symbolic factors. For some psychoanalytic feminists these moments centre on the dual mother-child relationship (the pre-oedipal relationship), whereas for others these moments centre on the triangular relationship of mother-child-father (the oedipal relationship). Theorizations of how we actually become gendered subjects vary depending on how one reads psychoanalysis and depending on what school of psychoanalysis one finds most convincing (Elliot, 1991).

The most influential feminist psychoanalytic theory in the United States is that of Dorothy Dinnerstein (1976) and Nancy Chodorow (1978). Both draw on a school of psychoanalysis called "Object-relations theory," developed by Melanie Klein (1957), D.W. Winnicott (1965), and others. Object-relations theorists criticize Freud's preoccupation with the role of the father and oedipal conflict, focusing instead on the child's early relationship to the mother and on pre-oedipal identification. For both Dinnerstein and Chodorow, gender is understood as an effect of the sexual division of labour and, in particular, of the fact that women (at least in our society) are the primary childrearers. Although Dinnerstein and Chodorow understand the process of reproducing masculinity and femininity in somewhat different ways, both of them argue that this process is the result of exclusive female mothering. Exclusive female parenting is seen to be the cause of gender inequality, creating, at least in males (and, for Dinnerstein, in females as well) a repression of connection with the mother. Chodorow (1978:214) claims that "the very fact of being mothered by a woman generates in men conflicts over masculinity, a psychology of male dominance, and a need to be superior to women." For Dinnerstein, female mothering also generates conflicts in women, especially an ambivalence towards other women which accounts for a certain amount of collusion with male dominance. For both of these theorists, fear of an imagined all-powerful mother causes at least males to reject her, and reproduces the motivation for the continued oppression of women, a motivation that will remain until both men and women share parenting.

Many feminists find the focus on the mother's role in childrearing developed by Dinnerstein and Chodorow a welcome development. Critics argue, however, that this theory leaves many troublesome aspects of gender untouched. If, for example, poor gender relations are produced by exclusive female parenting alone, then there is no need to examine gender itself as a construct; it becomes the simple reflection of social roles.

For French psychoanalyst Jacques Lacan and those feminists who read Freud through Lacan (1977) — both British feminists Juliet Mitchell and Jacqueline Rose, and French feminists Luce Irigaray and Julia Kristeva — the concept of gender is rendered much more complex. In fact, it is traded in for the concept "sexual difference" because the concept of gender is seen to represent a false image of the subject as stable, unified, whole, and fixed. Sexual difference refers to the process by which one assumes (or is subjected to) the position of "woman" or "man." In a patriarchal society, the meaning attributed to the difference between the sexes is determined by at least two factors: 1) the symbolic importance of the father (whose presence makes the fantasy of mother-child unity an impossibility); and 2) the imagined anatomical privilege of men and the imagined anatomical "lack" or disadvantage of women (both privilege and lack are cultural constructs).

Feminists who developed this understanding of psychoanalysis through reading Lacan have responded by either rejecting or accepting his interpretation of Freud. Mitchell and Rose have been the most vocal champions of Lacan, considering the political implications of his theory for feminism (Mitchell and Rose, 1982). Mitchell (1984) has utilized Lacan to show how gender identity is achieved and how women come to see themselves as lacking or incomplete. Rose (1986), on the other hand, utilizes Lacan to show how gender identity is precarious, unstable, and uncertain. Both Mitchell and Rose insist that the images of women as lacking or incomplete, and of men as self-possessed and autonomous, are socially constructed (as opposed to biologically given) and can be reconstructed differently.

French feminist Julia Kristeva also accepts Lacan's descriptions of sexual difference, developing the implications of these for women (see Moi, 1986). She asks what it means for women to be the "other sex" in relation to men and in relation to a patriarchal social order. Perhaps her most important essay for feminism, "Women's Time," places the western women's movement in historical perspective and describes three different political concerns or stages in the movement. Interestingly enough, these are organized around the question of sexual difference. The first political concern is to demand equality through demanding the same rights as men and through denying specific differences between the sexes. The second political concern, in opposition to the first, demands recognition for women's differences and specificity with respect to men. In this historical moment, femininity is revalued, and masculinity devalued, as the source of women's oppression. Kristeva argues that this moment is important in that differences are acknowledged, but that the hierarchical oppositions characteristic of a patriarchal construction of gender are merely reversed here, not eliminated or undermined. The third political concern (endorsed by Kristeva) involves the recognition that our patriarchal society is based on the repression and sacrifice of femininity. The crucial question for Kristeva becomes not how can women reverse the situation and sacrifice masculinity, but how can we preserve difference without sacrificing either gender? Kristeva's solution is complex, but it involves developing a new ethics or politics whereby neither femininity nor masculinity is sacrificed, but where the ideal of a fixed or stable identity for either sex is given up as a fantasy.

Kristeva's recommendation that women reject both the identity assigned to us and any other fixed identity has not been well received by feminists who want to create a new identity for women (Elliot, 1991; Oliver, 1993). But if, as Kristeva claims, "the paths of desire ensnarl the paths of knowledge," then we cannot expect agreement on issues of key importance to feminist politics and identity (Kristeva, in Moi: 307).

In contrast to Kristeva, French feminist theorist Luce Irigaray is less interested in dismantling sexual difference than in reconstructing and re-theorizing the feminine. Irigaray (1985a, 1985b) criticizes both Freud's and Lacan's understanding of sexual difference as the product of male fantasy. Irigaray explores the question, what does it mean to be "woman," to be "the other"? turning her attention to the specifics of female pleasure and desire. In her book *Speculum of the Other Woman*, she argues that the psychoanalytic tradition, like all male thought, can only theorize woman as lack, as castrated male. She claims man has set himself up as the standard or yardstick against which woman is measured in a negative light. One of Irigaray's criticisms of Lacan is that he speaks about feminine sexuality without knowing anything about it. For example, she criticizes his claim that one can understand feminine pleasure by looking at Bernini's famous statue of St. Teresa in Rome. Irigaray's humorous response attacks several notions at once, including the location of woman's pleasure in a statue. She replies: "In Rome? So far away? To look? At a statue? Of a saint? Sculpted by a man? What pleasure are we talking about? Whose pleasure? For where the pleasure of the Teresa in question is concerned, her own writings are perhaps more telling." (1985b:91)

Irigaray's own theories of femininity return us to the mother-daughter relation. Female sexuality is described here not as lack or "castrated," but as plural, fluid, excessive, without boundaries, an idealized conception. Lacan's emphasis on the symbolic importance of the father is replaced by an imaginative rewriting of the female body and feminine pleasure. Irigaray believes this rewriting constitutes a radical potential for subverting the patriarchal organization of sexual difference, with its boundaries, divisions, and suppression of women's desire. Predictably, Irigaray's privileging of the female body has been interpreted as a kind of essentialism that makes claims about the nature of femininity (Plaza, 1978; Elliot, 1991). Some critics argue that her celebration of women's bodily difference risks being appropriated by a patriarchal culture to oppress women. Sympathizers argue that we need to take this risk, that theorizing the feminine as something other than lack is crucial to establishing equivalence between the sexes (Cornell, 1993). At the very least, Irigaray has raised important questions about the representation of sexual difference that continue to be debated today.

To conclude this discussion, it should be clear that psychoanalytic feminists do confront myths about women and do contribute in various ways to the construction of theory by and about women. In addition to these tasks, psychoanalytic feminism provides insight into the ways in which fantasies of "woman" and "man" are constructed, how we participate in these fantasies, and how we resist them.

Most important, perhaps, and despite the differences in these theories, all of them draw our attention to processes of oppression that operate on an unconscious level. These processes must be made conscious if they are to be transformed.

## Postmodernist Feminism

Major debates in contemporary feminist theory centre on whether, or to what extent, feminists ought to ally ourselves with postmodern theory, culture, and politics. Part of the difficulty in writing any kind of summary of these debates is that there are different interpretations of what the term "postmodern" means. Some commentators define it very narrowly, others define it broadly, and some avoid defining it at all! Andreas Huyssen (1990), who provides a detailed history of the term, claims that postmodernism describes contemporary postindustrial culture, so that we are in it whether we like it or not. He further claims that postmodern culture comes after modernism and has been made possible in part because of the impact feminism has had on culture in general and on the ways we think about gender in particular. Other characteristics of postmodern culture, according to Huyssen, are its challenge to imperialism, its ecological sensibility, and its critique of modernism's ethnocentric domination of "others" (270). As a theoretical approach, postmodernism is often confused with "poststructuralism," which shares some of its critical goals and methods (Butler and Scott, 1992: xv), but which is said to be distinct in other ways (Huyssen: 258-267). Whether they understood postmodernism as a culture, a philosophy or as a critical method, most commentators agree that it involves a critical response to beliefs, values, and ideals that came to dominate the modernist period or culture. In what follows, some central aspects of the postmodern response to modernism will be briefly sketched out, with the understanding that the diversity and complexity of both feminist and nonfeminist views cannot be captured here. Given that the critical response called postmodernism has been read by some feminists as a breath of fresh air and by others as a disastrous mistake, feminist objections to postmodernism will be discussed. The last word will go to those feminists sympathetic to postmodernism, especially those who work with the "poststructuralist" theories of Jacques Lacan (psychoanalysis), Michel Foucault (discourse theory), and Jacques Derrida (deconstruction) to further feminist goals. Poststructuralist theories, although distinct from each other, have been associated with a postmodern perspective (broadly defined) because they are all critical of various aspects of modernism. As a result of this critical association, both postmodern and poststructural feminisms will be considered here.

From the perspective of postmodern criticism, the ideals and beliefs that dominated modernity bear the mark of a specific period in the history of the western world and can no longer be sustained today. According to Jane Flax, these modernist ideals and beliefs include the idea that individuals comprise stable, coherent, and rational subjects; that reason, with its scientific laws, provides an objective, reliable, and universal basis for knowledge; that the rational use of scientific knowledge will lead to freedom and progress for everyone; and that such knowledge is neutral and socially beneficial (Flax: 41). These ideas concerning the centrality and importance of "rational man" belong to a supposedly democratic theory known as "humanism." One theme of postmodern criticism is that these humanist ideals and beliefs are not only unattainable but have themselves produced certain forms of oppression. Thus, some postmodern critics claim that a crisis in modern ideals and beliefs has already occurred (Huyssen). Others believe we are in the midst of the crisis and that various forms of criticism, including some feminist theory, are producing an alternative set of beliefs. For example, Mary Poovey argues that "feminism must assist...historical transformation [to postmodernity and]...must stop trying to resuscitate the humanist subject." (1992:50-51) Putting aside the question of whether the dominant beliefs of modernity are still with us, postmodernists share an alternative set of beliefs. These include a conception of the individual as unstable, contradictory, and socially constructed; a conception of what forms of authority or knowledge are legitimate, namely multiple, anti-hierarchical, and participatory forms; a conception of history as non-linear, not necessarily progressive, and as always read through the limited perspective of the present, as well as through particular social contexts; and a conception of community as an achievement based on valuing differences without opposition (Lather: 160).

Since the mid 1980s, increasing numbers of feminists have been exploring the implications of postmodernism for feminism, discussing the common ground between them and even describing their own theories as postmodern or poststructural. In her anthology *Feminism/Postmodernism*, editor Linda Nicholson claims there are "many points of overlap between a postmodern stance and positions long held by feminists," thus making the two "natural allies." (1990:5) She points out that feminism has produced its own critique of scientific rationality, objectivity, and the autonomous self as masculinist constructions. Furthermore, critiques of white, western feminists' tendency to generalize from a limited perspective have been made by women of colour and women from developing countries. These criticisms, added to those of lesbian, disabled, and working-class women, have produced a rethinking of key concepts in feminism that has led to more historically and culturally specific work. For example, gender is understood as a socially constructed, politically charged category, one which is intertwined with other socially constructed categories such as race, class, and sexual orientation. According to Nancy Fraser and Linda Nicholson, if feminism pursues this trend towards a more historical, non-universalizing, non-essentialist theory, one that addresses differences among women, then feminism will become "more consistently postmodern." (1990:34) However, such a trend also means that feminism must give up universal claims about gender, about patriarchy, and about women or "woman." For many feminists, this means giving up too much. Feminists who adopt Sandra Harding's theory based on the standpoint of women, or who adopt Carol Gilligan's view that women share specific ways of thinking, acting or speaking, find their theory does not fit especially well with a postmodern critique. Many feminists hostile to postmodernism imply it is a patriarchal plot to silence women at a time when women are better prepared to speak out than before: "Why is it [Nancy Hartsock asks], just at the moment in western history when previously silenced populations have begun to speak for themselves and on behalf of their subjectivities, that the concept of the subject and the possibility of discovering/creating a liberating 'truth' become suspect?" (cited in Di Stefano, 1990:75).

In her critique of postmodernism, Christine Di Stefano summarizes four major feminist arguments against postmodernism as follows: First, that postmodernism expresses the claims and needs of a constituency (white, privileged men of the industrialized West)"...."Secondly, that the objects of postmodernism's various critical and deconstructive efforts have been the creations of a similarly specific and partial constituency. Third, that mainstream postmodernist theory has been remarkably blind and insensitive to questions of gender. Finally, that the postmodernist project, if seriously adopted by feminists, would make any semblance of a feminist politics impossible (75-76). Readers familiar with feminist thought will recognize in this debate the return of what Ann Snitow has identified as an unavoidable "central feminist divide" on the question of just how gendered we are. In fact, Snitow refers to this debate between what she calls "cultural feminists and poststructuralists" as yet another example of how the issue of gender identity gets played out (1990:16). Nor does this debate disappear when one turns to the question of which theory "best serves the contemporary needs of women in Western society," as Di Stefano and others have hoped it would (Di Stefano: 66). For postmodern feminists, the question of which theory best suits women's needs is "undecidable" because it is a question that falsely assumes needs can be clearly defined for all women. As more feminists adopt and develop postmodern insights and methods, the suspicions Hartsock casts on what may have been in 1987 a predominantly male pursuit become much less convincing. Postmodern feminists respond to their feminist critics by claiming that modernist conceptions of gender, reason, truth, and so on have been as oppressive to women as they have been helpful to men (and more oppressive to some women than others); that insensitivity to gender issues on the part of some male postmodern theorists does not invalidate the entire postmodern project; that many feminists do find postmodern theory insightful in theorizing oppression; that contemporary feminist political practice, far from being made impossible, is "already implicitly postmodern." (Fraser and Nicholson: 35)

Debates among feminists continue, sometimes becoming decidedly nasty. A recent example is the exchange between Laura Lee Downs and Joan W. Scott, whose mutual criticisms are instructively entitled "If 'Woman' is Just an Empty Category, Then Why Am I Afraid to Walk Alone at Night? Identity Politics Meets the Postmodern Subject" and "The Tip of the Volcano." However rich and provocative these heated exchanges may be, Snitow is probably correct to suggest that there is no bridging the feminist divide on the question of gender, and that we might as well learn to embrace the tension between the two positions.

Feminists who employ postmodernism as a critical resource continue to raise what some of us find important and challenging questions. For example, in *Feminist Practice and Poststructuralist Theory*, Chris Weedon develops her version of "feminist poststructuralism," based on what she takes to be the most productive theory for feminism. In her view, feminists "need a theory of the relationship between subjectivity and meaning, meaning and social value, the range of possible normal subject positions open to women, and the power and powerlessness invested in them." (1987:19) In *Gender and Knowledge: Elements of a Postmodern Feminism*, Susan J. Hekman recommends Foucault's theory as one feminists "should employ in both theory and practice," (1990:188) advice that has been widely followed, to judge by the popularity of other feminist explorations of Foucault (Butler, 1990). In the Introduction to their anthology *Feminists Theorize the Political*, Judith Butler and Joan Scott raise 15 questions about the intersection between feminism and postmodernism, questions that illustrate their own view of poststructuralism as not "*a position*, but rather a critical interrogation of the exclusionary operations by which 'positions' are established." (1992: xiv) For Butler, the term postmodernism appears to be an "artificially constructed whole" that says more about people's desire to position themselves either with or against a clearly defined theory than about the clarity of the theory itself (1992:5). Nevertheless, both Butler and Chantal Mouffe, a contributor to the anthology, argue that feminist politics improve, becoming more radical and more democratic, when informed by poststructuralist theory. How is this possible?

Feminists hostile to postmodern theory claim that no feminist politics is possible once one has called into question the nature of gender identity and subjectivity. For Butler and Mouffe, however, it is the continual questioning of these concepts, the ability to inquire into the processes by which they are formed, that produces a radically democratic feminist politics. Butler, who wants feminism to become more self-critical of its own theory, asks, "Through what exclusions has the feminist subject been constructed, and how do those excluded domains return to haunt the 'integrity' and 'unity' of the feminist 'we'?" (1992: 14) Similarly, Mouffe claims that if feminists are to "struggle against the forms of subordination which exist in many social relations...an approach that permits us to understand how the subject is constructed through different discourses and subject positions is certainly more adequate than one that reduces our identity to one single position — be it class, race, or gender." (1992:382) According to Butler, all the categories feminism uses in its political struggles, including the category "women," must be open to questioning and redefinition.

Newcomers to this field may suspect that this postmodern insistence on continuous questioning constitutes a purely academic exercise. In some cases, this may be true. But for most postmodern theorists, the point is to make us more sensitive to what we can and cannot know, and to the nature of our claims, especially when it comes to generalizing about others. Feminists are drawn to the postmodern project not as something foreign, but as a field of criticism they can use to advance feminist projects, and to realize what they take to be feminism's radically democratic promise.*

## CONCLUSION

We assess the adequacy of theories by their ability to address fundamental issues in feminist thought. What are the origins of women's universal oppression? In what way are social relations gendered, problematized, and interwoven with other systems in inequity? What errors and myths exist about women's natural abilities and accomplishments? What political actions can be taken to ameliorate these injustices?

We have seen feminist theories provide explanations for a wide range of particular issues including relating the ideology of sexism to the social institutions in which it is produced, describing the process and content of gender socialization, explaining the relationship of "nature" to "nurture," interpreting women's status in work and the family, analyzing the social control of female reproduction, health, and sexuality, and interpreting intersections of race, sexuality, disability, and class with gender.

We have also seen that feminist theories remain partial, imperfect, and unfinished. Feminist theory has been enriched and expanded through the clash of different perspectives. Rather than rejecting some theories for others, the feminist movement needs to draw on the strengths of all theories. For succeeding generations of women and men, this remains the challenge.

*We thank Joan Mason-Grant, Alison Weir, and Marion Lynn for providing detailed comments and suggestions.

## BIBLIOGRAPHY

Abella, R. S. 1984. *Equity in Employment: A Royal Commission Report.* Ottawa: Ministry of Supply and Services.

Anderson, Margaret. 1993. Third Edition. *Thinking About Women: Sociological Perspectives on Sex and Gender.* New York: Macmillan.

Armstrong, Pat and Hugh Armstrong. 1978. *The Double Ghetto: Canadian Women and Their Segregated Work*. Toronto: McClelland and Stewart.

Benston, Margaret. 1969. "The Political Economy of Women's Liberation," *Monthly Review*, 21:13-27.

de Beauvoir, Simone, 1970. *The Second Sex*. H.M. Parshley, trans. New York: Bantam.

Brand, Dionne. 1993. "A Working Paper on Black Women in Toronto: Gender, Race and Class." In *Returning the Gaze: Essays on Racism, Feminism and Politics*, edited by Himani Bannerji, 220-241, Toronto: Sister Vision Press.

Briskin, Linda. 1993. "Women, Unions and Leadership." In *Work in Canada*, edited by Graham S. Lowe and Harvey J. Krahn, 284-291, Toronto: Nelson.

Butler, Judith. 1990. *Gender Trouble. Feminism and the Subversion of Identity*. New York and London: Routledge.

———— 1992. "Contingent Foundations: Feminism and the Question of Postmodernism." In *Feminists Theorize the Political*. Judith Butler and Joan W. Scott, eds.

Butler, Judith and Joan W. Scott, eds. 1992. *Feminists Theorize the Political*. New York and London: Routledge.

Brennan, Teresa, ed. 1989. *Between Feminism and Psychoanalysis*. New York and London: Routledge.

Carty, Linda, ed. 1993. *And Still we Rise: Feminist Political Mobilizing in Contemporary Canada*. Toronto: Women's Press.

Chodorow, Nancy. 1978. *The Reproduction of Mothering*. Berkeley: University of California Press.

Cornell, Drucilla. 1993. *Transformations: Recollective Imagination and Sexual Difference*. New York and London: Routledge.

Das Gupta, Tania. 1995. "Families of Native Peoples, Immigrants, and People of Colour." In *Canadian Families: Diversity, Conflict and Change*, edited by Nancy Mandell and Ann Duffy, 141-174, Toronto: Harcourt Brace.

Derrida, Jacques. 1982. *Positions*. Alan Bass, trans. Chicago: University of Chicago Press.

Dinnerstein, Dorothy. 1976. *The Mermaid and the Minotaur: Sexual Arrangements and Human Malaise*. New York: Harper and Row.

Di Stefano, Christine. 1990. "Dilemmas of Difference: Feminism, Modernity, and Postmodernism." In *Feminism/Postmodernism*. Linda J. Nicholson, ed.

Downs, Laura Lee. 1993. "If 'Woman' is Just an Empty Category, Then Why Am I Afraid to Walk Alone at Night? Identity Politics Meets the Postmodern Subject." In *Comparative Studies in Society and History*. 35: 414-437.

Duffy, Ann, Nancy Mandell and Norene Pupo. 1989. *Few Choices: Women, Work and Family*. Toronto: Garamond.

Dworkin, Andrea. 1974. *Woman Hating*. New York: E. P. Dutton.

Elliot, Patricia, 1991. *From Mastery to Analysis: Theories of Gender in Psychoanalytic Feminism*. Ithaca: Cornell University Press.

Eisenstein, Zillah, ed. 1979. *Socialist Feminism and the Case for Capitalist Patriarchy*. New York: Monthly Review Press.

Elshtain, Jean Bethke. 1981. *Public Man, Private Woman*. Princeton: Princeton University Press.

Feldstein, Richard and Judith Roof, eds. 1989. *Feminism and Psychoanalysi*s. Ithaca: Cornell University Press.

Firestone, Shulamith. 1970. *The Dialectic of Sex: The Case for Feminist Revolution*. New York: William Morrow.

Flax, Jane. 1990. "Postmodernism and Gender Relations in Feminist Theory." In *Feminism/Postmodernism*. Linda J. Nicholson, ed.

Foucault, Michael. 1980. *The History of Sexuality: vol. 1 An Introduction*. New York: Vintage Books.

Fraser, Nancy and Linda J. Nicholson. 1990. "Social Criticism without Philosophy: An Encounter between Feminism and Postmodernism." In *Feminism/Postmodernism*. Linda J. Nicholson, ed.

Freud, Sigmund, 1977. *On Sexuality*. The Pelican Freud Library, vol. 7. James Strachey, trans. Angela Richards, ed. Harmondsworth: Penguin Books.

Friedan, Betty. 1963. *The Feminine Mystique*. Harmondsworth: Penguin Books.

Gallop, Jane. 1982. *The Daughter's Seduction: Feminism and Psychoanalysis*. Ithaca: Cornell University Press.

Gilligan, Carol. 1982. *In a Different Voice*. Cambridge: Harvard University Press.

Grant, Judith. 1993. *Fundamental Feminism: Contesting the Core Concepts of Feminist Theory*. New York and London: Routledge.

Harding, Sandra. 1986. *The Science Question in Feminism*. Ithaca: Cornell University Press.

Hartmann, Heidi. 1981. "The Unhappy Marriage of Marxism and Feminism: Towards a More Progressive Union." In *Women and Revolution*, edited by Lydia Sargent, 1-41. Boston: South End Press.

Hartsock, Nancy. 1983. *Money, Sex, and Power*. New York: Longman.

Hekman, Susan J. 1990. *Gender and Knowledge: Elements of a Postmodern Feminism*. Boston: Northeastern University Press.

hooks, bell. 1984. *Feminist Theory: From Margin to Center*. Boston: South End Press.

Huyssen, Andreas. 1990. "Mapping the Postmodern." In *Feminism/Postmodernism*. Linda J. Nicholson, ed.

Irigaray, Luce. 1985a. *Speculum of the Other Woman*. Gillian C. Gill, trans. Ithaca: Cornell University Press.

———— 1985b. *This Sex Which is Not One*. Catherine Porter, trans. Ithaca: Cornell University Press.

Jaggar, Alison and Paula Rothenberg. 1984. *Feminist Frameworks: Alternative Theoretical Accounts of the Relations Between Women and Men*. 2nd ed. New York: McGraw-Hill.

Klein, Melanie. 1957. *Envy and Gratitude*. London: Tavistock.

Kristeva, Julia. 1986. "Women's Time." In *The Kristeva Reader*. Toril Moi, ed. New York: Columbia University Press.

Lacan, Jacques. 1977. *Ecrits: A Selection*. Alan Sheridan, trans. New York: W. W. Norton.

Lasch, Christopher. 1977. *Haven in a Heartless World: The Family Beseiged*. New York: Basic Books.

Lather, Patti. 1991. *Getting Smart. Feminist Research and Pedagogy With/in the Postmodern*. New York and London: Routledge.

Luxton, Meg. 1980. *More Than a Labour of Love: Three Generations of Women's Work in the Home*. Toronto: Women's Educational Press.

McKinnon, Catherine. 1989. *Toward a Feminist Theory of the State*. Cambridge: Harvard University Press.

McKinnon, Catherine. "Feminism, Marxism, Method, and the State: An Agenda for Theory," *Signs* 7 (Spring 1982): 515-44.

Millett, Kate. 1970. *Sexual Politics*. New York: Avon Books.

Mitchell, Juliet. 1974. *Psychoanalysis and Feminism*. New York: Vintage.

———— 1984. *Woman: The Longest Revolution*. New York: Pantheon.

Mitchell, Juliet and Jacqueline Rose, eds. 1982. *Feminine Sexuality: Jacques Lacan and the école freudienne*. New York: Pantheon Books.

Moi, Toril, ed. 1986. *The Kristeva Reader*. New York: Columbia University Press.

Mouffe, Chantal, 1992. "Feminism, Citizenship, and Radical Democratic Politics." In *Feminists Theorize the Political*. Judith Butler and Joan W. Scott, eds.

Nicholson, Linda J., ed. 1990. *Feminism/Postmodernism*. New York and London: Routledge.

Oliver, Kelly. 1993. *Reading Kristeva. Unraveling the Double-bind*. Bloomington and Indianapolis: Indiana University Press.

Petchesky, Rosalind. "Reproductive Freedom: Beyond a Woman's Right to Choose," *Signs* 5 (Summer 1980):661-85.

Plaza, Monique. 1978. "Phallomorphic Power and the Psychology of Women." In *Ideology and Consciousness* 4:5-36.

Poovey, Mary. 1992. "Feminism and Postmodernism — Another View," *boundary 2* 19: 34-52.

Rich, Adrienne. 1976. *Of Woman Born: Motherhood as Experience and Institution*. New York: W.W. Norton.

Rich, Adrienne. 1979. *On Lies, Secrets, and Silence: Selected Prose*. 1966-1978. New York: W.W. Norton.

Rich, Adrienne. "Compulsory Heterosexuality and Lesbian Existence," *Signs* 5 (Summer 1980):531-60.

Rose, Jacqueline. 1986. *Sexuality in the Field of Vision*. London: Verso.

Scott, Joan W. 1993. "The Tip of the Volcano," *Comparative Studies in Society and History*, 35: 438-443.

Snitow, Ann. 1990. "A Gender Diary." In *Conflicts in Feminism*. Marianne Hirsch and Evelyn Fox Keller, eds. New York and London: Routledge.

Spelman, Elizabeth. 1988. *Inessential Woman: Problems of Exclusion in Feminist Thought*. Boston: Beacon Press.

Steinem, Gloria. 1994. *Moving Beyond Words*. New York: Simon and Schuster.

Tong, Rosemarie. 1989. *Feminist Thought: A Comprehensive Introduction*. Boulder: Westview Press.

Weedon, Chris. 1987. *Feminist Practice and Poststructuralist Theory*. London: Basil Blackwell.

Winnicott, D.W. 1965. *The Maturational Processes and the Facilitating Environment*. New York: International Universities Press.

Wright, Elizabeth, ed. 1992. *Feminism and Psychoanalysis: A Critical Dictionary*. Oxford: Basil Blackwell.

# CHAPTER 2

# SILENCED AND FORGOTTEN WOMEN: RACE, POVERTY, AND DISABILITY

*Barbara Cassidy, Robina Lord, and Nancy Mandell*

## FEMINIST CRITIQUES OF RACE, CLASS, AND DISABILITY

The second wave of the women's movement has finally begun to address criticisms that White, middle-class feminists have denied, dismissed, and denigrated the experiences of differently raced, abled, and classed women. Some charge the mainstream women's movement with being so narrow in orientation that, among others, poor women, women of colour, and women with disabilities find their concerns, their issues, and their agendas being ignored. Feminism, they say, has taken on the mantle of being universal while its shape has been specific (Bhavnani 1993).

Feminism, the political movement that aims to liberate all women, is actually historically and geographically specific. Its analysis of the origins of women's oppression and the solutions it proposes tend to speak only to middle-class White women. Its description of White, middle-class women's experiences is taken as the norm and other women's experiences have been treated as "different." White solipsism, as Spelman (1989) calls it, includes thinking, imagining, and speaking as if whiteness described the world. Racism, for example, engenders white solipsism by allowing White women the power to make it seem as if their own experience is wholly representative of all women's experience. Black women, Native women, disabled women, in fact, most other women, are left out without anyone noticing they are absent (Thornhill 1991).

Feminist erasure and denial of the significance of race, class, and disability has generated a narrow discussion of oppression. Differently abled, raced, and classed women decry feminists as bourgeoise, avant-garde types who maintain, in inverted form, the dominant values. Capitalism, it seems, is ready to incorporate as many feminists as necessary to generate co-optation. Thus, feminist theory has tended to emerge from privileged women whose perspectives and experiences rarely include knowledge and awareness of the lives of marginalized women and men.

In order for feminists to take difference into account, they need to understand the ways women's experiences position them within certain social locations. We are here trying to further this project by discussing five particular constructions with which we are most familiar: Black women, Native women, immigrant women, women with disabilities, and poor women. Among us, we have raised seven Native-Jewish-White children; lived alone, with their fathers, and with other men; struggled to pay the bills and remain permanently off the welfare roll; raised disabled siblings; and handled the anxieties and problems immigrant families confront. The only commonality we share as co-authors is our privileged position as educated women. While not inclusive, these discussions articulate social patterns and processes by which differently located women are marginalized within feminism. The challenge, of course, consists of re-theorizing difference so that feminist theorizing—teaching and practice—escapes its narrowly constructed boundaries.

## FIRST NATIONS WOMEN

Before white contact, most native societies were matrilineal, matrilocal, and matrifocal. They were also egalitarian, enlightened and peaceful. Many of the "old ways" have almost disappeared and indeed now many Native men believe that patriarchy is embedded in native history (Weaver 1993:221). However, the teachings of First Nations ancestors sustain many Native women.

In native agrarian societies such as the Iroquois, women controlled the distribution of food. If Native men wished to wage war but lacked the support of the women, women would withhold food and effectively negate any chance of war. After white contact, Jesuit missionaries refused to deal directly with women who were traditionally regarded as controlling agriculture (Wagner 1990:221). One of the first examples of white corruption of

First Nations' culture that led Native men into patriarchal and capitalist arrangements came when missionaries forced Native men to take over women's work. Prior to white contact, although work was divided by gender and age, all work was treated with equal respect and the work of women was not devalued or demeaned.

Similarly, women had the power to elect chiefs and to remove them from their jobs if they did not perform as women expected. The mainstream notion of the power of chiefs clashes with native ideas. For Aboriginals, power is not having control over somebody or something: power is something found in nature—in thunderstorms, waterfalls, animals—and within humans.

Some authors suggest that when British and French settlers first ventured onto Canadian soil, their initial contacts with Aboriginal people were reasonably co-operative, mutually beneficial, even symbiotic. They traded with each other, assisted one another in the expanding fur trade and intermarried with Native women in an indigenous rite known as "customary marriages." Fur trading was, after all, largely a White male pursuit (Elliott and Fleras 1992).

A more cynical reading suggests that what began with the establishment of English and French settlements in the late 1400s and 1500s was a process of colonization of Aboriginal people, of bringing territory and people under new and more stringent forms of control. For First Nations people, white contact was indeed the beginning of the end of aboriginal culture.

For most of the 1700s, Indians were treated with the cautious respect accorded allies in war and partners in trade. Native women's skills in hunting, gathering, skinning and preserving furs, their skills in trade and diplomacy, and their knowledge of several native languages made their services invaluable to the fur traders. Numerous interracial unions were sanctioned in recognition of Native women's "usefulness." Journals from those early days record the degree to which European traders relied on the Native wives' skills to survive the harsh Canadian winters (Jamieson 1986).

As long as the fur trade flourished, Native women and men possessed skills necessary for the Europeans. By 1812, agriculture had replaced fur trade as the main economic activity. Ironically, agriculture was the economic basis for many First Nations groups, such as the Huron. Interracial marriages were outlawed by 1806 as White women, heretofore virtually unknown and unseen in the fur trade, slowly settled in agricultural posts across the country. By the 1820s, Native women's status had declined so precipitously that 20 percent of contracted servants in the trading posts were Métis. By the 1850s, 50 percent of Métis were engaged in seasonal labour in transportation and general labouring around the posts (Jamieson 1986).

By the early 1800s, government policy deliberately set out to achieve assimilation, to absorb Natives into the mainstream by shedding native languages, customs, religious beliefs and traditional structures (Ponting 1993). Traditional aboriginal customs and traditions were totally disregarded as individual and state policies were pursued that destroyed aboriginal political, economic, kinship, and, in most cases, religious systems. Institutional racism was ideologically bolstered by official state policy decreeing Natives as inferior savages and heathens in need of "Christianizing" and "civilizing." A series of acts, culminating with the Indian Act of 1878, was instituted to force assimilation. The creation of a reserve system, the establishment of a series of boarding schools, and the institution of punitive legal guardianship of Natives were some of the more notorious state attempts to force integration through the destruction of "primitive" native culture (Frideres 1993).

Europeans declared Indian ways of governing their communities too primitive and too uncivilized to even compare with the British civil code. As "uneducated savages," Natives were deemed unable to care for practically any aspect of their lives. The Indian Act created a paternalistic system of dependency and tight control by placing all Natives under the jurisdiction of the department of Indian Affairs and Northern Development. Natives were stripped of their political sovereignty, residentially segregated on often economically unproductive reserves, and subject to state control directly through Indian agents and indirectly through their elected band councils.

The Indian Act resulted in a foreclosure of social and economic opportunities for Natives while simultaneously ensuring the annihilation of their language and culture. Physically, Natives were pushed into smaller and smaller areas. An 1890s amendment to the Indian Act appropriated native land by legislating that "surplus or idle" Indian land could be available for use by non-Indians (Elliott and Fleras 1992).

Cultural racism consists of a type of social imperialism in which the dominant group seeks to impose its values, morality, norms, and standards upon the minority. Ponting (1993) suggests the most unmitigated form of cultural racism in Canadian history was the effort by government and missionaries to "civilize" the Aboriginal people through their church-run boarding schools. Native children were physically removed from their parents' homes and sent to residential schools where they were strapped for speaking their own language, physically and sexually abused by staff members, and subjected to daily ridicule of their culture and values.

How has this legacy of colonial imperialism affected the lives of First Nations women? In the words of Mavis Goeres (1992:217):

> So we've had a long hard struggle. I think what kept us going was our heritage and our sticking together. Maybe we didn't have all the same ideas but we all had the one main goal in mind—equality for the women. We're just as good as the men. I think what kept us going is our determination to seek what is rightfully ours. And that is our heritage....being Indian is our heritage.

According to the Epijig Ag Unjuana Project (1992) "Women and Their Children," a research project on Native single mothers carried out by Anduhyaun and sponsored by the Advisory Council on the Status of Women, the main problems faced by the women interviewed were:

(1) Accommodation: 32 percent of women reported that finding appropriate housing was a major concern

(2) Health: 40 percent of women reported that depression was their main health issue

(3) Education: 20 percent of women reported that they needed more education themselves

(4) Social Life: 42 percent of women responded that loneliness was their most pressing issue

(5) Employment: 36 percent of women stated they needed job training

(6) Law: 24 percent of women reported their need for legal advice

(7) City Orientation: 27 percent of women stated they were not familiar with the city

(8) Economics: 46 percent of women stated that food and clothing costs were their most immediate problems.

While volumes could be written on any of these issues, this section will deal primarily with issues of family, health, and law.

First Nations families are not inherently patriarchal nor are women as devalued as they are in Western society (Monture 1993:96). A long tradition of female independence was maintained by the community. In traditional Navajo culture, if a man was caught physically, sexually, or verbally abusing his wife or children, the community immediately intervened. The man was removed for spiritual and practical guidance from the elders. The wife and children received similar guidance. If the abuse continued, the man was exiled from the group, the ultimate punishment in an interdependent society. If the abuser came from a "good family," he was allowed the option of suicide to "clear the family name" (Native Women's Resource Center 1993; Cassidy 1994).

Unfortunately, these methods are not available in contemporary times and too often First Nations women must contend with a society deeply imbued with sexism, racism, and classism. In addition, these women must deal with abuse from First Nations men. In urban areas, women lack support from extended families and groups.

Violence in First Nations families reflects internalized patriarchy by Native men. History and anthropology texts portray First Nations women as weak, passive, quiet, unresisting, and subservient. In most pre-Colonial native cultures, quite the opposite existed. In historical Ojibway culture, if a man spoke abusively to a woman, the women in the group tied him to an undomesticated, wild horse and turned the horse loose. In historical Lakota culture, if a man abused a woman, the men of the group were obligated to intervene and correct the abuser by "beating him up" (Brooks 1993).

Today, such organizations as Native Child and Family Services of Toronto (NCFST) are trying to recapture the essence of the "old ways" and speak of "supreme values." Supreme values refer to such traits as kindness, strength, bravery, humility, honesty, sharing, trust, and respect and are at the core of what NCFST is trying to recapture and perpetuate.

White colonization eroded women's community strength. First Nations women ceased to be seen as human beings. Adopting white culture included adopting woman abuse as a regular practice. Native children were systematically beaten in residential school systems for speaking their own language, for practicing their spirituality or for perceived infractions of the rules. These children learned that abuse was a way of life, a practice alien to traditional First Nations lifestyles. While not all victims of residential schools went on to abuse women, a significant number replicated the violence. Rather than dealing with systemic causes of violence against women, mainstream society has attributed abuse to the First Nations issues of substance abuse and propensity for savagery.

Despite high rates of violence against women, Native men continue to recognize the importance of Native women. Women are still perceived as "the backbone of the nation, the backbone of our families. They hold us together. They pass on the culture, the teachings. They make sure the family works...women have worked hard to keep that going" (Transition, December 1991:4).

For First Nations women, the ideal of an extended, community-supported family form remains strong. In pre-contact times, children were seen as a sacred gift from the Creator, born inherently good and deserving of physical, emotional, and spiritual space in which to develop. The day-to-day duties of caring for children were done by the community, not just the immediate family as in the European paradigm. Children were raised not just by their biological parents but by the group as a whole. Today, it is not uncommon for a single Native woman with biological children of her own to adopt other Native children rather than let them be turned over to Children's Aid and risk placement in non-native foster homes.

According to the Epijig Study (1992), the majority of Native women who are single parents are between the ages of 25 and 29 (31 percent as compared to 13 percent for non-Native women) and can range in age from 15 to 19 (11 percent as compared to 0 percent for non-Natives) and to 45 and over (5 percent as compared to 0 percent for non-Natives). This indicates a strong trans-generational commitment to children (Young 1990:21).

As families are scattered in urban areas, community support becomes essential but at the same time problematic for these women. As child-care practices have become fractured by white contact, continued support from native cultural centres, residences, and family services remains crucial. Despite this, the future of First Nations families currently appears promising as evidenced by the following: "Mothers help one another. We take care of each other's children. You'll never find an orphan among us" (Cantryn 1993:247).

The demolition of native culture by whites has had several repercussions on native parenting skills. Years of residential schools and forced adoption have left a generation of Aboriginal women who have no mothers, grandmothers, or great-grandmothers. No intergenerational link between women exists, a link that historically was of major importance in maintaining family continuity. Parenting skills are no longer passed along from one generation to the next in ways supportive of native culture. The result is the further annihilation of First Nations culture.

Native definitions of health are intricately linked to native definitions of family and community life, all of which differ dramatically from those in mainstream society. Middle-class feminists are fighting for abortion rights, while Native women are struggling for the right to give birth to and raise healthy children. Mainstream culture tends to measure and research health as "death, disease, disability, discomfort and dissatisfaction" (Young et al. 1992:2). Native definitions emphasize health as a holistic state based on the balance or imbalance of the mind, body, heart (emotions), and spirit. Health is represented by a circle with these four equal parts. If any one of these parts is damaged or destroyed, the whole is affected. Within the circle are other circles including ones for self, family, community, nation, and at the outermost ring, the Creator. Traditional native healing methods, which are spiritual, non-intrusive, holistic, and collective, are used when an individual's four parts are imbalanced. Healing centres are being used, for example, to stop abusive Native men and substance abuse.

The wearing away of native culture has had a profoundly negative effect on virtually all aspects of Native women's health (Monture 1989:3). The circle of health has been broken and harmony between mind, body, heart, and spirit is shattered. Many First Nations women believe that the only way to regain health and to reclaim some measure of sanity and balance is to return to traditional ways.

Canadian law regarding native rights, especially those of women, remains problematic. Patricia Monture (1989:147) discusses racism as involving the institutional power to define laws as well as an individual state of "not-knowing." Despite current policies designed to rectify past wrongs, laws and their enactment continue to oppress Native women.

Mary Two-Axe Early was a Mohawk woman who married a White man and subsequently lost her Indian status (Indian is the legal term for a First Nations person). She and her children continued to visit the reserve from which she came and lived in a house willed to her by her parents in accordance with Mohawk traditions (Krosenbrink-Gelissen 1993:337). Other on-reserve Natives agreed with this practice. In 1967, she was informed by the band council that, because of provisions specified in the Indian Act, she could not continue this practice and was not entitled to property on the reserve. In 1968, she presented to the Royal Commission on the Status of Women her case, which highlighted the sex discrimination in the Indian Act. Furthermore, Native women were also reported by the commission as suffering from "factionalism, favouritism and male chauvinism" on reserves (Fifth Standing Committee 1988). Subsequent amendments to the Indian Act in 1985, An Act to Amend the Indian Act or Bill C-31, protected the Indian status of Native women who married non-Indians. This bill eliminated the most blatant sexism contained in the Indian Act but did not eliminate discrimination based on sex and in fact rendered this discrimination more covert than it had been previously. Accordingly, it is much more difficult to fight.

One example concerns the ability of reinstated persons to transmit status to their offspring (Penner 1986:15). If a child has only one reinstated parent, namely an Aboriginal woman who married a non-Indian, s/he becomes a registered Indian and is eligible for status and conditional band membership (Penner 1986:17). If a child has both parents with Indian status (this might include an Indian man married to a non-Indian woman), s/he can be registered and is eligible for status and band membership. This means that if a First Nations brother and sister married non-Natives, the offspring of the sister would be eligible for conditional band membership whereas the brother's offspring would be given unconditional Indian status. It is evident that discrimination based on sex is far from absent in the new Act.

There are numerous issues Native women face as part of their daily living that cannot be addressed here. First Nations women, ranging from those who comprise the Native Women's Association of Canada to the "woman in the street," are struggling to reclaim their culture. Like many other women, Aboriginal women must deal with discrimination based on gender, class, and race. The struggle to remain separate and strong is a difficult one and one that cannot be adequately explained in such a short space. However, the following story is an illustration of the struggles of First Nations women as related by Maggie Hodgson (1993).

> There is a story about a shark who was swimming through the ocean he had discovered and he meets dinner, the mackerel. Just before he was going to swallow the mackerel, the shark said, "Let's assimilate!" Now who's perception do we look at? Do we look at it from the shark's or the mackerel's perception? Of course the shark thinks he is doing the mackerel a favor because he will provide him with a nice warm stomach to swim around in and certainly things will be better for him there. From the mackerel's perception he will think if it is at all possible I do not want to end up as part of that shark, I am a mackerel and free.

## AFRICAN-CANADIAN WOMEN

Historically, Canada's treatment of indigenous peoples and visible minorities has been racist. Institutionalized racism existed, and still exists, in Canada in the form of direct and deliberate discrimination against racial minorities through the conscious application of exclusionary laws and programs (Elliott and Fleras 1992). In short, racism was legally sanctioned. Africans were brought to Canada and remained enslaved for over 200 years. Until the 1954 passage of the "Fair Accommodation Practices Act," restaurants, recreational clubs, hotels, and movie theatres were racially segregated. Windsor, Ontario had outright bans on the entrance of Blacks and Jews. In 1975 Windsor was the last municipality to desegregate its public facilities (Ponting 1994).

Slavery was a constituent feature of pioneer life in colonial Canada. Slavery was institutionalized in 1685, and, from the late 1600s until the 1800s, African-Canadian slaves were held in Quebec, Nova Scotia, New Brunswick, and Ontario. The difficulty and expense involved in obtaining African slaves meant they belonged to the wealthy merchant class and to religious patriarchs, and were generally reserved for domestic service. First Nations peoples, a more abundant, cheap, and dispensable labour pool, were commonly enslaved and used for agricultural and manual labour.

Colonization of Canada was bolstered by racist ideologies and practices. Slaves were without rights, could not vote, could not associate with White people as equals, could not think of interracial marriage, were not welcome in white churches, and were segregated in black schools (Thomson 1979). Social Darwinism, which labelled Blacks as "fun loving, imitative, and naturally obsequious," was quoted by White supremacists as theoretical justification for owning and abusing slaves. White settlers considered themselves the dominant race, as "men of the north; a superior race of people, more manly, and more real, than the weak narrow-bones superstition of an effeminate South" (Berger 1966). Blacks were thought to be at the bottom of the race hierarchy since they originated from hot lands. They were compared with apes. Since both were considered to be "tropical animals," neither flourished in cold countries (Berger 1966). White colonialists used this racist ideology as justification for their enslavement of Black peoples.

Canadian slavery is often contrasted with its American counterpart. The former is described as benevolent and humane, whereas the latter is constructed as disgustingly abusive. It is claimed that the very nature of Roman Catholicism and its doctrine created a tolerant benevolence and more humane laws in New France than in other countries (Williams 1989). Many historians fail to comment on the brutalities endured by slaves. The "Code Noir," a set of practices to regulate the behaviour of Black slaves, was adopted from France as the customary law in New France. It was harsh and punitive:

Si le Noir s'évade, on lui coupe les oreilles et on le marque au fer rouge d'une fleur de lys a l'épaule; s'il recidive, on lui coupe les jarrets. S'il ose recommencer une troisième fois, c'est la mort.

*(Williams 1989:10)*

(Translated: If the Negro escapes, his ears will be cut off and he will be branded on his shoulder with a fire-red fleur de lys; if he tries again, he will have his legs cut off at the knees. If he dares a third attempt, he will die.)

In 1793, upon learning that she was about to be sold, Marie Joseph Angelique, a New France slave, set fire to her master's home. The fire spread and destroyed a part of the city of Montreal. Angelique was recaptured and sentenced to hang for arson (Shadd 1987; Hill 1981). In further retaliation, she was savagely tortured and then executed:

On the day of her execution, Angelique was first tortured until she confessed her crime. Then she was driven through the streets in the scavenger's wagon...A burning torch had been placed in her hand. At the main door of the parish church in Place d'Arnes she was made to kneel...and her hand was cut off. Then, once again, she was placed in the scavenger's wagon and taken to the place of execution and hanged. After her body was burnt at the stake, her ashes were then scattered in the wind. (Williams 1989:9)

Contrary to popular belief, the first underground railroad did not run from the United States to Canada. Rather, it was established in Canada to help liberate escaped slaves from the provinces under British rule to the slave-free northern states of the United States (Winks 1969). The institution of slavery ended in Canada in the early 1820s. During the 1820s and 1830s, significant numbers of free Blacks and escaped slaves left the United States for Toronto. Canada was envisioned as a land of safety and wealth; therefore, Blacks fled north.

By 1837, there were at least fifty Black families settled in Toronto. Despite racist sentiment, for many of them their dreams of liberty, wealth, and security had been realized: they had become successful in business enterprises, had purchased homes, had built churches, and had organized themselves into "benevolent and fraternal organizations." The majority of Blacks in Toronto were home owners and some possessed valuable property (Hill 1963). After 1850, many American Blacks fled to Southern Ontario. Estimates suggest that approximately 30,000 Blacks settled in Toronto and Southern Ontario.

Work outside the home has been a crucial site of Black women's oppression, from the institution of slavery in the Americas to current exploitative work structures (Brand 1993). Structural and cultural racism have historically denied Black women access to certain job categories. As a result, the types of jobs Black women are doing has not changed significantly since slavery. Up until the 1930s, Black women worked as indentured labour. Domestic work represents the contemporary version of this form of bondage (Brand 1993). For example, in 1941,

80 percent of Black adult females in Montreal were employed as domestic servants (Walker 1980). Likely the same situation existed for Black women in other Canadian cities. Until World War Two, Black women were denied access to factory jobs (Pierson 1986). Similarly, racism meant that nursing, teaching, and other professions open to White women remained closed to Black women. As Dionne Brand's oral histories reveal, Black women recall that the only work available was as cleaners or domestics:

> You couldn't get any position (in Toronto in 1920), regardless who you were and how educated you were, other than housework, because even if the employer would employ you, those that you had to work with would not work with you (Brand 1992:37).

A 1981 study noted that Black women are concentrated in such job ghettos as nursing assistants (as aides and orderlies), personal service occupations, nursing, and electronic data processing equipment operation (Reitz et al. 1981). Black women's recent concentration in nursing follows a pattern similar to one found in Britain in which nursing is seen as an escape from domestic work. Becoming a nurse can be seen as a trajectory from maid/servant/domestic help to helping, caring subordinates (Brand 1993).

The labour force participation rate for racial minority women is slightly higher than for women as a group. Racial minority women are underrepresented in middle- and upper-level management positions, overrepresented in the manual field, and, like women as a group, are heavily concentrated in the clerical field (Ontario Women's Directorate 1993c). Today, Black women in Toronto are to be found mainly in service jobs as domestics, nurses, nurses' aides; in factory work; in food and service work; and as telephone operators, hotel workers, and clerks (Brand 1993).

Black women, along with immigrant women and other women of colour, rank as the lowest-paid waged workers. Black women's concentration within low-paid segregated occupations accounts for their low wages. In 1979, Black and Italian women were the lowest paid in the Metro Toronto labour force (Reitz et al. 1981). Even when women and men have similar education levels, men's earnings far exceed women's. In the clerical field, where 14 percent of racial minority women and 7 percent of men in the general population have university degrees, racial minority women earn approximately 32 percent less (Ontario Women's Directorate 1993c). Visible minority populations are over represented in service occupations and in machining and product-fabrication (Agocs and Boyd 1993). In addition to low wages, job security is lowest among Portuguese and Black women (Reitz et al. 1981).

Within the workplace, Black women have always resisted exploitation. In factories, Black women point out when the clock has been deliberately set back, do not stand at the machine to wait for their break to use the facilities, and are known to be intractable; therefore, they are unpopular with factory owners (Brand 1993).

Growing up, Black women are taught the centrality of both work and education. They value education and recognize its significance for obtaining secure and stable employment. As one young Black woman related to Canadian sociologist Carl James during an interview on her aspirations:

> Education definitely gets your foot in the door. You need some kind of qualification and credibility.... Other types of skills are important.... Like being able to talk.... In Canadian society, talking goes a long way. (James 1993:10)

Systemic racism depresses Black men's education and wages, thus making it impractical for Black women to depend on Black men's incomes (Brand 1993). Learning self-sufficiency, valuing education, and preparing for a lifetime of hard work are thus lessons passed on from one generation of women to the next. As Dionne Brand (1993:231) relates:

> Every black woman has a mother or grandmother who has told her that she had to do it, probably alone, and that she had to continue to find ways of surviving, that she must be cognizant that no man would rescue her. This vision is reflected in the proportion of women-headed households in the black community (thirty-five percent) and in our participation in waged work.

Even though education is highly valued and promoted, culturally racist schooling practices poison the process. Many young Black women and men can be found in lower-stream high schools leading to terminal high school diplomas or community college courses (Brand 1993). Rarely is the educational experience enjoyable. One woman describes her experiences of elementary school:

> School was the most awful experience. It was a horrible experience because, first of all, I was the only black child in the entire school that year. Secondly, I was being confronted by a group of bigger kids, who usually surrounded me in a circle shouting "nigger, nigger" over and over until I was crying. It was very terrifying for me and I felt very trapped. The children made fun of my skin colour and my lips by calling me "chocolate face" and "liver lips." They also associated me with the jungle by calling me "jungle bunny." One girl at school hated me so much that she told me if she had a gun, she would shoot me. (ASEIN 1993: 101–102)

Studies reveal that young Blacks perceive being Black or "visible minority" as particularly significant in terms of society's expectations of them and consequently of their life chances and opportunities (Fuller 1983; James 1993). James (1993) suggests that although racism does not dampen their aspirations, it does alter strategies they employ to obtain and maintain their jobs. While not underplaying its effects, racism is seen as a "hurdle," not a "barrier." The longer one searches for and engages in work, the more one becomes aware of the systemic nature of racism. As one young man related to Carl James (1993:10) during his interviews:

> (Earlier on in my employment) I wasn't aware of the extent to which it (racism) existed...the degree to which it is entrenched in large systems. I wasn't aware of how difficult it is to change somebody's mind with regards to their perceptions

of other people, in terms of race, colour, sex...(now) I am very aware of how deep a part of this society it is.

These perceptions match social reality. As many as 15 percent of the population exhibit blatantly racist attitudes while another 20 to 25 percent have some racist tendencies. Institutions restrict the life chances of non-White individuals through a variety of seemingly neutral rules, regulations, and procedures. A mid-1980s study conducted by Henry and Ginzberg (1985) reveals substantial discrimination in employment offers, job advancement, job retention, and level of earnings.

Black women's wages have always been essential to the total family income. Some Black women may have to support two or three children on their income alone. The contemporary extended family in the black community is a woman-built system resting on three social building blocks: the imperative of waged work; the stress of child bearing and rearing; and an understanding of children as grace. The extended family is basically matrilineal, including sisters, grand-mothers, nieces, aunts, and older children, both male and female. Its scope may extend to women in the family of the child's father and to friends and neighbours. The rearing of children is its central feature (Brand 1993).

Political organizing has always been a necessary part of the lives of Canadian Black women because, without it, they could not survive (Bristow 1993). Blacks were rejected by white churches and white society (Walker 1980). The Ku Klux Klan opened chapters in British Columbia, Saskatchewan, and Ontario in the 1920s (Hamilton 1993). Racism was pervasive.

Early black organizing took place through churches, missionary societies, mothers' clubs, benevolent societies, and more overt political organizations. Black women have a strong tradition of organizing against gender, race, and class oppression. In 1882, Black women established the Women's Home Missionary Society with Elizabeth Shadd Shreve as the first president. The Ladies' Union Aid Society was formed in 1878 by a group of women in Chatham. In 1902, in Montreal, the Colored Women's club was started and the Phillis Wheatley Club was later established. Most Black women's organizations were local ones until the Canadian Negro Women's Club was started in 1951 in Toronto. It sponsored the Congress of Black Women, with chapters all over Canada. In 1920, African-Nova Scotian women organized the first-ever convention of "coloured" women in Canada to address a range of community, educational and spiritual concerns (Hamilton 1993). More recently, black community groups and organizations have developed including the black Heritage Programme, the black Workers' Group, African Liberation Support Committees, the Rastafarian Cultural Workshop, the Immigrant Women's Job Placement Centre, the Organization of Parents of Black Children, the African Sisterhood Organization, Black Working Women, the Committee Against the Deportation of Immigrant Women, and the Coalition of Visible Minority Women. Many groups are under the leadership of women who draw strength from each other as they develop distinctive female culture (Bristow 1993).

Contemporary racism exists in various forms throughout all Canadian institutions. In recent years, the criminal justice system has been criticized for its discriminatory treatment of racial minorities. Fourteen Black men and one Black woman, most of whom were unarmed, have been shot by police in the provinces of Ontario and Quebec, six of them in 1991 (Simms 1993:345). Audrey Smith, a 39-year-old female tourist from Jamaica, was the subject, in Toronto, of a public inquiry into an alleged strip-search in the early hours of August 10, 1993 after police accused her of having drugs (*The Toronto Star* 1994).

What is contemporary life like for the majority of Black women in Canada whose lives have always been oppressed by racism as well as sexism? In the words of Dolores Gabriel (1993:153), a teacher in Halifax:

> Life for ME, a black woman in Nova Scotia, has been a life filled with hardships, struggles, pain rejection, and most importantly ANGER. So much to be angry at, and always the knowledge that there was so little that I could do about it. The fact that this society has placed ME, a black woman, at the bottom of the ladder has not only served to limit my political, social, and economic power but also tried, and I repeat, tried, to take away all the good that is inside of ME.

## IMMIGRANT WOMEN

Immigrant women are not a clearly identifiable group with similar backgrounds, aspirations, values, or needs. Rather, immigrant women in Canada are a heterogeneous, diverse, and complex group, differing with respect to class, age, and country of origin. In fact, their only commonality lies in their difference, making any comprehensive analysis of the issues they face the subject of an entire text, not a few pages.

In 1986, 3.9 million immigrants were living in Canada, representing about 16 percent of the population. Canada's immigrant population is split evenly between those who arrived before and after 1967, but there have been major changes in the distribution of immigrants from different parts of the world (Badets 1990). Between 1945 and 1970 when 4.4 million individuals landed in Canada, the majority were from Europe. Since 1967, the sources of immigration have shifted away from Europe. Between 1981 and 1986, of all persons entering Canada, 29 percent were from Europe, 43 percent from Asia, 10 percent from South and Central America, 7 percent from the United States, 6 percent from the Caribbean, and 5 percent from Africa and Oceania (Elliott and Fleras 1992). Nearly two-thirds of Canada's immigration total is now comprised of visible minorities. If present immigration trends continue, visible minorities are expected to reach 9.6 percent of Canada's population by 2001. Immigrants are more likely to live in large cities, particulary Toronto, Montreal and Vancouver. In 1986, 36 percent of people living in Toronto and 30 percent of Vancouver residents, were immigrants.

Historically, immigrant women have had to fight to enter Canada. Canadian immigration policies have been steeped in the notion of white superiority. Immigration laws were built on the assumption that the closer a prospective immigrant's resemblance to the White, Anglo-Saxon Protestant in appearance and manner, the better chance s/he had of adjusting to Canadian life and contributing to the development of the country. Although our immigration laws and practices have been amended several times in the recent past to be more racially tolerant, it was not until 1976 that an immigration act came into force that did not discriminate on the basis of race, national or ethnic origin, colour, religion, or sex (Simms 1993).

A particulary inflammatory and infamous quote displays past attitudes of many White Canadians:

> We welcome as brother all white men still,
> But the shifty yellow race
> Whose work is vain, who oppress the weak,
> Must find another place. (Ward 1978:xii)

Early Canadian immigration legislation is replete with racist practices. These policies have been described by many as racially selective, segregationist, and assimilationist (Elliott and Fleras 1992; Ponting 1994; Simms 1993). Immigration policies were selective in that they gave preferential entrance to Canada based on an individual's or group's race by way of their country of origin. Citizens of the "preferred" countries were Anglo-Saxon.

Initially, those from Northwest Europe and eventually those from Eastern Europe were invited into Canada while Jewish and Mediterranean peoples were discouraged from applying to emigrate and required special permits to be considered. Peoples from Asia, South America, the West Indies, and Africa were not even acknowledged as potential immigrants. Policy makers adopted what some have called a "taps on/taps off" approach (Elliott and Fleras 1992). The "on" periods, which corresponded with intense nation-building, allowed visible minorities an opportunity to emigrate. Chinese and Indians, for example, were able to enter Canada to perform the gruelling work of building the Canadian Pacific Railway, a task Canadian residents apparently found too menial and physically demanding. Upon completion of the railroad, the taps were turned off and an outright ban was effected (Ponting 1994).

Chinese workers who first arrived in Canada from China and San Francisco in the 1860s and 1870s were men. Women were specifically excluded on the grounds that Chinese men were merely temporary workers. Cultural racism, as exemplified by this quotation worked to establish ways to keep Asians out of Canada.

> No yellow slave shall eat our children's bread
> Let no Chinese leper cross our threshold. (Ward 1978:41)

In order to ensure that only men emigrated, a federal head tax of $100 was levied on any Chinese immigrant who entered the country. This tax was increased to $500 in 1903; by 1923, an outright ban was effected (Ponting 1994:91). This tax was sufficiently high to discourage wives or other relatives.

The first Chinese women who came to Canada were merchants' wives who were excluded from the head tax, prostitutes bought and sold by men, and "slave girls" or female servants imported to work as unpaid domestic labourers. Slave girls performed domestic work, thus freeing Chinese women to engage in piecework sewing at home, to work in tailor shops, laundries, restaurants, and small grocery stores. Women's labour, frequently unrecognized and unrenumerated, enabled Chinese businesses to succeed (Adilman 1984).

South Asians were also deterred from entering Canada. South Asian men began to arrive in the mid-1800s. Like the first Chinese settlers, Asian-Indian men left behind their families and friends. Racist immigration laws had the effect of banning Indian women from entering Canada until the 1917-1919 Imperial War Conference agreement legislated their entry (Doman 1984). The "Continuous Journey Stipulation" of 1908 allowed access into Canada only to those South Asians who had "come from the country of birth or citizenship by continuous journey and on a through-ticket, purchased before leaving the country of their birth or citizenship" (Simms 1993). Sometimes this policy had fatal ramifications. In 1914, 400 would-be Indian immigrants were denied entry to Canada because their freighter, the *Komagatu Maru*, had picked up passengers from different ports on their journey. For two months, the ship sat in a Vancouver port. During this time, one passenger died and several others became seriously ill because of the lack of food and water. Twenty-six others were killed in on-board skirmishes before the *Komagatu Maru* eventually returned to India (Elliott and Fleras 1992).

Underlying racist immigration policies and practices was the racist ideology of assimilation. Assimilationists suggest that those who emigrate to Canada ought to espouse the beliefs, emulate the culture, and epitomize the value systems of White Europeans. In a classic statement in 1928, then Prime Minister R.B. Bennett summarized Canada's position:

> We must still maintain that measure of British civilization which will enable us to assimilate these people (immigrants) to British institutions, rather than assimilate our civilization to theirs. (Ponting 1994:92)

Immigrant women have documented the many barriers they face in Canada, including social isolation, racial prejudice, employment difficulties, and work-family conflicts (Goudar 1989). Immigrant women have had more trouble than immigrant men in accessing social services and programs designed to assist in settlement and adaptation (Elliott and Fleras 1992). Lack of access to language training condemns them to menial, non-unionized, low-wage jobs. Each of these problems presents special difficulties for different groups of women.

Racial prejudice and discrimination against non-White people means that immigrant women are not all treated alike. Immigrant women from Britain, Western and Eastern Europe, and Scandinavia usually have little trouble phenotypically assimilating into Canadian culture because of their colouring. Their descendants will almost certainly be perceived as "real Canadians" because they will be White and lack a "foreign" accent. On the other hand, there are women of colour who immigrate to Canada and whose descendants will have difficulty assimilating because of their visually different phenotypical features. Ironically, native-born Canadians of Japanese or Chinese origin are often asked where they are from when, in fact, they are clearly as "Canadian" as White immigrants.

Now that the majority of immigrants to Canada are non-White, attitudes to immigration can be read as an index of racist sentiment. In 1987 and 1989, virtually half of Canadians expressed the view that too many people from different races and cultures had been allowed to live in Canada (Gregg and Posner 1990). A 1990 Angus Reid survey found that one-third of Canadians agree with the notion that Canadian society is being threatened by immigrants (59 percent disagreed), while one-quarter agreed (and 65 percent disagreed) with the ideas that "there should be more White immigrants taken into Canada and fewer non-White immigrants" (Ponting 1994). A poll conducted in February 1994 by Ekos Research Associates of Ottawa found that in cities with large immigrant populations, such as Toronto, "Canadians feel overwhelmed by the pace of change." In comparison with surveys from five years ago when researchers would only occasionally hear complaints of too many foreign languages being spoken on the subway or Sikhs wearing daggers in public, "Everyone in Toronto will mention these things now" in focus groups (The Globe and Mail 1994).

Immigrant women face persistent prejudice and stereotyping. The very word "immigrant woman" conjures up images of passive, sad-eyed, inarticulate, not-too-bright, dependent females with heavy, unintelligible accents. These ethnocentric images of "…backwardness, of a complete inability on our part to stand up (for ourselves)" (Bannerji 1993) are completely at odds with the reality of these women's lives. Far from being weak and passive, immigrant women are strong and active agents in creating new Canadian lives despite the continual resistance they encounter. They find the attitudes of White officials racist and ridiculous. In the words of one immigrant woman,

> …they tell me that these women, these "immigrant" women don't understand how to fight. I went to a meeting a couple of weeks ago where a woman from

Vietnam came and the questions they asked her were really amazing. This woman headed a huge army unit of missile operators, a detachment on top of a cliff. They had six American destroyers to their credit. These women lived on top of trees and operated missiles and they were trying to teach her about non-traditional occupations! (Fireweed 1989: 28)

Educational achievement among immigrants reveals a bifurcated distribution. Immigrants are more likely than non-immigrants to have a university education. In 1986, 12 percent of immigrants aged 15 and over had a university degree, compared with 9 percent of non-immigrants. However, a greater proportion of immigrants, 23 percent, also had less than Grade 9 education compared with 16 percent of non-immigrants (Badets 1990). Education levels differ for immigrant men and women as immigrant women are less likely to have formal education. Over 26 percent of immigrant women had less than Grade 9, compared with 16 percent of non-immigrant women and 20 percent of immigrant men (Badets 1990).

Differential education levels are reflected in occupational distribution. Immigrant women aged 25 to 44 employed full-time in 1985 earned an average of $20,400 compared with $21,300 for non-immigrant women (Badets 1990). Immigrant women are overrepresented in the manufacturing and processing occupations and the concentration is greatest for women most recently arrived (Elliott and Fleras 1992). Non-English speaking and non-White immigrant women are commonly recruited into three kinds of services and industries: private domestic and janitorial services by professionals; the lower strata of the service industries, including restaurants, janitorial and cleaning services, and the food industry; and the lower echelons of the manufacturing industries, including light manufacturing in textiles and garments, in plastic factories and in the retail trade (Ng 1993). While these jobs are often described as low-paying, unskilled, and dead-end jobs, a study by Roxanne Ng and Tania Das Gupta ( 1993) found that immigrant women demonstrated a wide range of general and interchangeable skills in order to procure these short-term, temporary jobs with their often irregular hours or shift work.

Immigrant women are three times more likely than their non-immigrant counterparts to be employed in product fabricating, mainly as garment workers and sewing machine operators. In 1986, 10 percent of immigrant women, compared with 3 percent of non-immigrants, were employed in these occupations (Badets 1990). Historically, Jewish, Italian, Chinese, South Asian, Greek, Caribbean, Portuguese, Polish, Vietnamese, and Eastern European immigrant women found their first job in the "rag trade" (Boroway, Gordon, and Lebans 1993).

Most unions organizing the textile and garment trade are historically weak (Arnopoulos 1979). The infamous 1912 Eaton strike by the predominately Jewish women who worked for the country's largest clothing factory was one of the first organized protests by women in the needle trades. Its failure was a result of anti-Semitic feeling in Canada. It was billed by the media as "only a strike of Jews" (Frager 1993). Since that time, union protection for female textile workers has been equivocal and weak.

The restructuring of the garment industry in the last fifteen years has further weakened women's labour protection. In an attempt to lower labour costs, companies now have women inside their own homes, homeworkers, who cut and assemble garments. Thirty Chinese homeworkers were interviewed by researchers with the International Ladies Garment Workers Union in Toronto. Many of these women were receiving an average wage of $4.50 an hour, a wage below the minimum one, and were working an average of 46 hours per week. They must provide their own equipment, such as sewing machines, receive no benefits or paid vacation time, are not protected by provincial Employment Standards Act legislation, and often enlist the help of family members, especially children, to help them meet their weekly quotas. All but one reported that they had turned to homework because they could not afford childcare. The International Ladies Garment Workers Union estimates there are about 2,000 homeworkers in Toronto in the garment industry alone. Their study concludes that women become homeworkers because they cannot find decent employment outside the home; they lack the skills required to compete successfully in the labour market; they face racial, ethnic, and gender discrimination; they lack affordable, accessible, high-quality child care; they are solely responsible for domestic labour and child care in their families; and there are few available social supports that facilitate their employment outside the home (Borowy, Gordon, and Lebans 1993).

Immigrant women are also relegated to low-paying jobs in clerical, service, and domestic sectors where submissiveness and complete obedience is expected (Elliott and Fleras 1992). In the early 1990s, the majority of domestic workers entering Canada came from the Caribbean, the Philippines, and Europe, including Britain (Ng 1993). Domestic work is socially isolated, alienating, and privatized, thus making it difficult to monitor or protect these workers. It is poorly paid and shares the generally low status accorded all domestic work. Numerous studies on domestic work confirm the exploitation of domestic workers (Arat-Koc 1989; Sivera 1988).

INTERCEDE, a national lobbying group serving domestic workers across Canada, has successfully lobbied the government for greater protection for domestic workers. Domestic workers are now able to apply for landed-immigrant status (permanent residency) from within Canada after living here for two years and are encouraged to attend skill upgrading and training courses that would enable them to secure other employment, a strategy that INTERCEDE says tends to favour younger women from European countries who have formal recognized education and to discourage older women, many of whom came from Caribbean countries and lack formal education. If a recent government proposal passes, nannies entering Canada will be required to have a minimum of grade 12 education. This legislation would prohibit women from the Third World coming to Canada as domestic workers (Ng 1993).

Immigrant women are often stigmatized by their accents. Within the education system and in receiving social services, immigrant women report insensitive and racist treatment on the basis of their accents and language. Even when they are able to read and write proficiently in English, their accents are often considered by mainstream society to indicate their inferiority. Native-born English-speaking Canadians do not take the time, literally and figuratively, to listen to what immigrant women are saying.

In the workplace, immigrant women report being spoken to in loud voices as if pure volume will make them better able to understand what is being said. These women are neither deaf nor stupid. Immigrant women are often denied information by those in positions of authority because their English is accented. They are often ridiculed behind their backs or told to come back "when you have learned how to speak English," or told to "get your husband to come back and deal with your problem" (Estable, 1986).

Immigrant women also report feeling stressed by their dual responsibilities of domestic and wage labour. Their paid jobs tend to be poorly paid, highly routinized and monitored. They described their domestic lives as difficult, hectic, anxiety-producing, and more intensified than their previous domestic duties in their countries of origin. Overnight they are forced to become consumers, find themselves more isolated from women's traditional communities, have new worries about their husband's job and children's activities, feel their domestic labour is devalued as it does not generate income, feel more dependent on their husbands for economic survival, and feel constantly pressed for money (Ng and Das Gupta 1993).

Are these immigrant women victims or heroines? Much of the immigrant women's literature portrays these women as dominated by triple oppression: victims of exploitative labour markets, racist societies, and domineering husbands. Such models provide little room for individual agency and may obscure how the women themselves respond to and interpret their experiences (Iacovetta 1992).

## WOMEN WITH DISABILITIES

To experience disability is to experience the frailty of the human body (Morris 1993). People are defined as disabled if they have any persistent physical, mental, psychiatric, sensory, or learning impairment; consider themselves to be, or believe that a potential employer would consider them to be disadvantaged in employment because of an impairment (Ontario Ministry of Citizenship 1991).

Three years after the end of the United Nations Decade of the Disabled (1983-1992), women with disabilities continue to experience serious social and economic disadvantages. Over 500 million people globally have disabilities, with what the United Nations terms a high concentration of disabled people in the developing countries (The Globe and Mail, 3 Dec. 1993). Canada has a population of 4.2 million people with disabilities. In 1991, almost 13 percent of Canadians reported they were disabled. Of these, about 50 percent are women. A large proportion of disabilities are age-related. An analysis of the 1986 Census data reveals that 4.4 percent of the population aged 15 to 24 was found to have disabilities, the figure rose to 39.5 percent of those aged 65 to 84. After age 85, nearly 73 percent of people have disabilities.

Persons with disabilities generally have lower levels of educational attainment than non-disabled persons as disability affects the level of education and training they receive (Human Rights Centre, March 1991). An Ontario survey of people with disabilities reveals that 21 percent have their education interrupted for lengthy periods, while equal numbers say they have to change schools or courses because of their disability (Ministry of Citizenship 1991).

Considerable barriers exist in formal schooling which limit the aspirations and attainments of women with disabilities. They are less likely to be encouraged by families and schools to obtain further education. Those who become disabled later in life are not encouraged to continue further education. Disabled women, especially in Africa, Asia, the Caribbean, and Latin America find it difficult to get even a basic education. In many countries, the limited educational opportunities which exist for disabled children usually are given to boys (Driedger 1993).

In a series of interviews she conducted with disabled university students, Karen Swartz, Coordinator of York University's Office for Persons with Disabilities, gathered the following comments from current students on the difficulties they face in getting to university.

> One problem at high school that didn't dawn on me until graduation night was that the teachers didn't encourage me to go to university at all. I was told that I wasn't smart enough and that I should just look at going to community college.

Another woman reports that teachers and fellow students frequently act as if women with disabilities do not, and should not, have educational aspirations.

> She would tell me you're never going to amount to anything. There wasn't acknowledgement from your peers or from your teachers and when people tell me I'm stupid every day of the week until doomsday, you begin to believe it.

Males and females with the same disabilities often receive different kinds of education. In higher education, females are channelled into traditionally female-dominated subjects and careers. Physical problems exist in the form of inaccessibility to buildings and transportation, and lack of suitable educational materials and methods. Schools promote able-bodied norms of behaviour and perpetuate inaccurate myths about the roles and abilities of women with disabilities. Attitudinal barriers constrain their participation in school life and thus limit their future family and employment choices by failing to create an atmosphere of acceptance of the capacity of disabled women to function, within the limits set by their disability, as normal school attenders.

With this type of discouragement, it is little wonder that disabled persons have higher rates of unemployment and that another large group have ceased looking for employment. A Statistics Canada 1985 Health and Welfare Activity Limitations survey found that the labour force participation rate of women with disabilities is especially low at 39 percent compared with 59 percent for disabled men. The likelihood of being employed is strongly related to the severity of the disability. Those with mild disabilities were most likely to be employed. Sixty percent of women with disabilities are not in the labour force. The unemployment rate for people aged 15 to 64 with disabilities that limited them at work— 19 percent for men and 22 percent for women—is double the national averages. Moreover, about one-quarter of women aged 15 to 64 with disabilities that limited them at work were employed as manual workers while the vast majority worked in clerical jobs (Ontario Women's Directorate 1993a).

People with disabilities do not have equitable access to training and education programs and are therefore restricted in their access to the labour force. Barriers include inaccessible work sites, washroom or cafeteria areas—problems for wheelchair users; lack of adequate transportation to the workplace; difficulty using public transport; biased attitudes of employers and co-workers, including false assumptions about what persons with disabilities are capable of doing (Ontario Women's Directorate 1993a). Moreover, they usually cannot obtain access to the physical and service supports they need in order to meet their disability-related needs as the result of a lack of commitment to and money for workplace accommodation (Todoroff 1993).

As reported to Karen Swartz,

> People didn't seem to have patience...you know, they would look at you as if it was your fault that they had to move out of your way...they would shoot you a dirty look because you were disrupting things for them.

Clearly women with disabilities face considerable social and psychological barriers in schools and at workplaces.

Women with disabilities face systemic discrimination in the labour market. Forty percent of all job discrimination complaints to the Ontario Human Rights Commission are lodged by people with disabilities. Compared with either disabled men or non-disabled women, women with disabilities earn the lowest wages in the lowest-paid jobs in industry, public administration, and the service sector. Unemployment for women with disabilities is higher than that for men with disabilities, hovering around 75 percent. Career paths are difficult, as many take up typically female jobs, such as secretary or receptionist, that are often linked with stereotypical images of physical beauty. Rehabilitation and job training programs often stream women with disabilities into home-based or part-time positions.

People with disabilities are generally poorer than the rest of the population, with 25.4 percent classified as living in poverty compared to 15.5 percent of all Canadians aged 15 or over. Survey respondents in 1985 reported gross incomes that were 46 percent lower than for non-disabled Ontarians aged 15 to 64. One-half of all disabled women in Ontario, and more than 60 percent of those unable to work, received 1985 incomes of less than $5,000. The average annual income for women with disabilities in 1985 was $7,700 while only 4 percent had incomes of $30,000 or more.

Women are traditionally defined by their roles as daughters, wives, and mothers. Women with disabilities are assumed unable to fulfill traditionally defined caretaking and partnership roles. Popular opinion does not expect these women to marry, to have intimate relationships with women or men, to bear children, or to be mothers. They are not expected to be "women." In fact, society encourages women to deny their disability. Denial of disability is socially sanctioned in that people who valiantly overcome their handicaps are idealized, and the model of good adjustment for everyone in society at large is healthy, physically fit, emotionally well-balanced, and mentally alert (Hillyer 1993:109). As one woman told Karen Swartz,

> I never really faced my disability before, I never wanted to look at myself in the mirror because when I was growing up, I had one person that kept insulting me and said I walked like I had stuff in my pants...because of that, I never wanted to look in the mirror and look at myself. When I got this operation, I thought that everything was going to be perfect and that I was going to walk perfectly. When I found out that it didn't, I was really depressed and angry about it.

Women with disabilities have the same hopes, fears, dreams, and desires as non-disabled women. Consistently, Canadian surveys reveal that adolescent women value intimate partnerships above careers, even though they expect to combine wage and domestic labour throughout adulthood (Duffy, Mandell, and Pupo 1990). While many women with disabilities build family relationships, too many are dissuaded from seeking partners, from bearing children, and believe sexuality is impossible (Driedger 1993). Social support and services are almost totally inaccessible for women with disabilities. Often living in isolation, they lack opportunities for meeting potential partners. Compared with non-disabled women, they are more likely never to marry, to marry later, and to divorce. When men become disabled, 50 percent of their marriages dissolve while for women who become disabled, the divorce rate is 99 percent. As single parents, they live alone in poverty. Constructed as dependent, they are treated as unable to fulfill the mothering role and have difficulty finding health-care providers willing to support their wishes for child bearing. Social workers usually deny their desires to adopt children. Lesbian disabled women are especially stigmatized (Stone 1990). They face discrimination in the community for establishing same-sex families, as well as managing whatever challenges their disabilities present.

Self-image, that internalized conception of self, is significantly influenced by our body image. Women are primarily defined by physical appearance, by gendered messages about how their bodies should look and behave. An attractive, marriageable woman is young, slim, White, medium height, and able-bodied. Women with disabilities, particularly non-White, older, heavy, tall ones are viewed as defective, unattractive, and unable to manage their own bodies.

The constant message that women with disabilities receive from peers, media, and social institutions tells them they are unlovable, undesirable, and unacceptable. For these women, their bodies become sources of embarrassment, anguish, guilt, and shame. Negative body images confirm feelings of inferiority, worthlessness, and inadequacy.

Negatively positioned as sexually unattractive women, women with disabilities experience ambivalence and confusion around their own sexuality. They are characterized as asexual, or, at best, as having inferior sexual desires. Over-protection by caregivers means young girls are often raised in ignorance of their own sexuality and denied access to information about sex, pregnancy, birth control, gynaecological procedures, abortion, and reproductive rights.

Women with disabilities are more likely than able-bodied women to be the victims of all forms of violence, especially sexual assault. Fifty-three percent of women born with disabilities have been raped, abused, or assaulted (Khosla 1993). Negative body images of disabled women as neutered, repulsive, and inferior objects are used by men as justifications for rape. Physical, verbal, and emotional assault are also common as is actual neglect. Dependence upon caregivers renders them susceptible to abuse, unassertive in resistance, and fearful of losing assistance. Often they are unable to defend themselves. One form of institutional abuse that disabled women experience is called "public stripping," in which the disabled person is physically displayed to others as a medical problem to be analyzed. No recognition is given to the violation of privacy and personal autonomy, and this leads to long-lasting psychological consequences for many who have experienced this kind of public stripping (Morris 1993). Sexual assault contributes to their low self-esteem.

A woman with a disability who is also an immigrant, a visible minority, an Aboriginal, or an elderly woman also experiences oppression as women, minorities, and the disabled. Aboriginal women with disabilities report extreme social isolation, especially in rural and northern communities. Visible minority and lesbian women report feelings of alienation, loneliness, depression, and extreme stress.

The dual expression of sexism and handicapism places women with disabilities in an extremely marginalized position. Feminist analyses suggest that the intersection of gender, race, sexuality, power, and violence combine to construct disabled women as "other." Yet, to date, the feminist movement has been curiously silent in taking up the concerns of women with disabilities.

Disabled women have had little opportunity to portray their own experiences within society or within feminism. This lack of voice makes it difficult for nondisabled feminists to incorporate their perspectives and to revolutionize theory. Rather than talking about disabled women as suffering from a "double disadvantage," a perspective some find unhelpful, disabled women's experiences must be placed at the centre of research and teaching.

## POOR WOMEN

Poor women's experiences and issues differ radically from those of non-poor women, yet the views of poor women have been ignored within feminist writings. This omission seems particularly telling when we consider how widespread the feminization of poverty is within Canada and how many women, at some point in their lives, will skirt or slip into poverty.

The "feminization of poverty" refers to the fact that women are particularly at risk of being poor. In many of the industrialized nations, women are more likely to be poor than men (Pearce 1984; Goldberg 1990). Over 15 percent of Canadian women and 11 percent of Canadian men lived in poverty in 1987. Women constitute 59 percent of the Canadian adults who are poor (National Council of Welfare 1990). Moreover, women are more likely than men to be among the "poorest of the poor," as female-headed, single-parent families fill the largest poverty gap—far below the poverty line an individual or family lives.

Women's impoverishment results largely from their position as women. A sex-segregated occupational sphere continues to exist in which women are channelled into "pink collar ghettos" with lower wages, less prestige, and less opportunity for advancement. Women's employment, at all levels, remains less well paid than men's with full-time women workers earning about 65 percent of male wages. Women still experience sexual and gender harassment in their jobs. They are less likely to be protected by unions than male workers.

Traditional gender ideologies still encourage women to focus their energies on marriage and motherhood, even when engaging in paid employment. These norms suggest women are primarily responsible for domestic labour and child care, meaning that women must wrap the demands of wage labour around their domestic responsibilities. Inadequate child care and parental leave policies and the constant juggling of domestic and wage labour demands lead women, often, to "choose" part-time, casual, or contract employment or to "choose" to spend time at home with their children. For these so-called personal "choices," women are often financially punished by having no pension, no steady income, and no opportunity to build up transferable skills or resources. When marriage ends in divorce, when women face years of widowhood, or when women opt for unmarried, single parenthood, their financial state is often precarious. Commenting on the irrelevancy of feminism to poor women, one woman talks about how feminism seems to threaten and confuse women's sense of their roles:

> Feminism seems to threaten the importance of women's role in the family, and it is the only role low-income women have. Jobs are just something to do until marriage, or afterwards, for extra money. Friends are okay, but there is still a lot of competitive feeling among women, so a firm basis of support does not always exist. Feminism does not seem even a safe thing to consider... (O'Connell 1986:12-13)

Analyses reveal that without access to male wages through the form of support payments or a male earner in the household, many women cannot adequately provide for their families (National Council of Welfare 1990:9). Because women have relatively lower incomes than men, people who depend on a woman's income will be relatively poorer (Ontario Women's Directorate 1992). Almost two-thirds of all working women in Ontario still make less than $20,000 each year, and only 8 percent make more than $40,000. In contrast, only one-third of Ontario men make less than $20,000 while three times as many men, or 26.7 percent, make over $40,000 (Ontario Women's Directorate 1992).

Sole-support mothers are far more likely to be poor than any other type of family. There were an estimated 272,000 poor families with children under eighteen headed by a female single parent under age 65 in 1991 (National Council of Welfare 1993). Sixty-one percent of single mothers are living under the poverty line. An appalling 96 percent of single mothers who had no employment earnings were living on just over $12,000 in 1991. Most of this money came from family allowances, unemployment insurance, social assistance, pensions, and the like (Khosla 1993). A 1991 survey by the Daily Bread Food Bank in Toronto found that 22.4 percent of sole-support mothers identified child-care responsibilities as the reason they were not working. Without access to child care, women cannot work (Khosla 1993).

Nearly 75 percent of never-married, single-parent mothers and 52 percent of women who head single-parent families because of death, divorce, or desertion are poor. The Economic Council of Canada's five-year survey of Canadian incomes found that when women are separated or divorced, their incomes drop by about 39 percent and thereafter rise only slightly. Three years after the marriage breakup, women's incomes are still 27 percent below their earlier level. In contrast, men's incomes rise by an average of 7 percent. Moreover, support payments are scanty. Only 68 percent of divorces involving dependent children (1989) resulted in a child-support order, and those orders averaged $250 per child per month (Economic Council of Canada 1992:49).

Elderly women, 65 and over, who are widowed, divorced, or never married are at great risk of being poor. Close to half of all women over 65 did not have enough to live on in 1993. Fewer than 50 percent of older women receive pension benefits (Khosla 1993). In 1990, 47 percent lived below the low income cut-offs. Moreover, impoverishment increases with age. Fifty percent of unattached women 75 or over are poor.

Immigrant women, minority women, and Native women face the double jeopardy of sexism and racism. Visible minority and immigrant women confront language barriers, low-wage work, and racism in their search for steady employment (National Council of Welfare 1990:118-27). Native women earn less than average wages, have lower than average labour force participation rates, and higher than average rates of unemployment (Abella 1984). Women with disabilities add prejudice against non-able-bodied persons to their attempts to search for work. Even though the majority of the disabled are poor, women with disabilities are poorer than men with disabilities (Ross and Shillington 1989; Barile 1992). When age is added into the variables of race, gender, and disability, the effect is disastrous for elderly women. Foreign-born elderly women in all marital categories have lower average incomes than their Canadian-born counterparts. Elderly women who are recent immigrants and/or who come from the Third World receive particularly low incomes (Boyd 1989).

Poverty exacts an enormous social, economic, and physical toll on women as it affects their sense of self, their relationships with their children and with others. Poor women are not likely to find the theorizing of feminist academics relevant to their daily struggle to make ends meet. Inadequate housing, especially in major cities, means that poor children live with sub-standard heating, too little hot water, improper ventilation, often unsafe conditions, and too little play space. There are New Brunswick children living in dwellings with mud floors, leaking roofs, and no running water (Spears 1991:A21).

Providing both enough food and nourishing food becomes a weekly challenge for poor women. Too many of their children get by on too little or low-quality, high fat-sugar content food (Kitchen et al. 1991:7). Infant death rates are higher for poor families. Native children have an infancy death rate five times higher than the rate among non-Native children. Native children are also much more prone to commit suicide than other ten- to nineteen-year-olds in Canada (Boyle 1991:99-100).

What psychological, emotional and cultural damage is done to poor women and their families? Fear, anger, isolation, frustration, and despair characterize their daily lives. Rather than experiencing efficacy, a sense that they can alter their situation, poor women sense defeat. Working poor women, those with low-paying jobs, work endless hours and still do not make enough money to support their dependents. Those without jobs battle welfare stereotypes and increasingly find themselves out of the mainstream. For both groups, women find they have to deny their children "treats" such as money for school teams or trips. "Luxury" items for themselves are non-existent (Duffy and Mandell 1994).

> If I say "no" to the children, they feel very depressed when they see other children taking things to school. The children feel very disappointed. They kind of lose love for you. They think that you don't love them. (Women for Economic Survival 1984:23)

What kind of effect does such a devastating observation have on poor women who fight every day of their lives to stay afloat? They feel not only inadequate as mothers but also dismissed by society. Since they do not see themselves reflected in television sitcoms, in magazine stories, or on billboard ads, poor women describe themselves as "observers of life," continually on the outside looking in. They find that the feminist movement's emphasis on getting women into the paid labour force and achieving better pay for women actually props up middle-class media images of women's lives. As one woman said:

> The majority of poor women haven't a hope of a "career" which is personally satisfying, financially rewarding or even pleasant. Mostly, we get jobs. And our jobs give us no prestige or power, very little pay and often are very bad for our health. Yet feminist theory continues to assume that all women want to work-for-pay because of the "personal satisfaction" we get from our "careers". (Pierson et al. 1993)

Their experiences, their fears, and their dreams rarely reach the attention of mainstream society. Poor women are virtually washed out of social consciousness by their invisibility. When they are thought about, it is solely in terms of their economic impoverishment, of their social location as "poor" women. Economic instability further marginalizes a group already stigmatized by factors of race, age, disability, and gender (Duffy and Mandell 1994).

Ontario's New Democratic Party has announced a $40 million plan to investigate welfare recipients for fraud, a scheme many estimate will end up costing more than will be recovered by the 300 investigators to be hired. The government concedes that fraud runs at less than 1 percent of the annual welfare bill. It is difficult to see Ontario's move, like Quebec's similar plan, as anything less than welfare bashing. It is precisely this type of negative portrayal that the poor attempt to overcome. In a moving plea to the non-poor, an individual writes:

> Think for a minute before you put us down. It hurts more than just shooting us with a gun. You do not know why we are on assistance. Consider the example of someone who works a job that you would never do in your life and who has been put out of work because his company's gone bankrupt. His unemployment insurance benefits have run out, so he has to be looking for work every day and has no luck finding a job. He goes on social assistance as the last resort to feed his children. Is he wrong? No! (*The Toronto Star* 1994)

## CONCLUSION

The four processes of erasure, denial, invisibility, and tokenism of differently situated women (Bhavnani 1993) have forced all feminists to rethink their theory, teachings, and politics. Theorists, for example, engage in lengthy academic battles in scholarly journals on the meaning and implication of shifting the feminist project to take account of difference. The category "woman," it is argued, has been rendered essentially meaningless by racialized critiques of difference. If every woman's experience of oppression is different, what unites all women?

Feminist teachers, for the most part, focus on less esoteric issues in Women's Studies classes. Adopting a poststructural, deconstructive stance has not precluded their challenge to economic, racial, sexual, class, ability, and age exploitation and oppression. Rather than seeing women's different experiences as reason to discard feminist pursuits, inclusive instructors see the task for Women's Studies as ensuring that feminism speaks both universally and specifically. In the classroom, we must pay attention to the manner in which our own practices create, sustain, and reinforce racism, sexism, and class oppression. We need to question how we "take up space" and silence others; how we "give up space" because, as immigrants, women, and possibly non-Whites, we have learned to be submissive (Ng 1993).

Finally, political agendas and practices have been recast, by recognizing that all women are racialized, gendered, and inscribed within unequal class relations. Analyses revealing the ways in which racism, classism, and sexism inform and structure the other challenge racially-unselfconscious feminisms that assume there are no differences amongst non-White and White women. History reveals that feminism emerged from a racialized and classed past, one that implicates White women in its historic and contemporary erasures.

White women cannot only be insensitive to the role race plays in the oppression of women of colour, but also often deny "white" as a racialized category and fail to problematize its privileges.

## BIBLIOGRAPHY

Abella, R.S. *Equity in Employment: A Royal Commission Report.* Ottawa, Ministry of Supply and Services, 1984.

Adilman, Tamara. "Preliminary Sketch of Chinese Women and Work in British Columbia, 1858-1950." In *Not Just Pin Money: Selected Essays on The History of Women's Work in British Columbia*, edited by Barbara Latham and Roberta Pazdro, 53-78, Victoria, British Columbia: Camosun College, 1984.

Agocs, Carol and Boyd, Monica. "The Canadian Ethnic Mosaic Recast for the 1990's. In *Social Inequality in Canada*, 2d ed., edited by James Curtis, Edward Grabb and Neil Guppy, 330-352, Toronto: Prentice Hall, 1993.

Anderson, W.W. and Rudolph W. Grant. *The New Newcomers: Patterns of Adjustment of West Indian Immigrant Children in Metropolitan Toronto Schools*. Toronto: Canadian Scholars Press, 1987.

Arat-Koc, Sedef. "In the Privacy of Our Own Home: Foreign Domestic Workers as Solution to the Crisis in the Domestic Sphere in Canada." In *Studies in Political Economy* 28 (Spring 1989): 33-58.

Arnopoulos, Sheila. *Problems of Immigrant Women in the Canadian Labour Force*. Ottawa: Canadian Advisory Council on the Status of Women, 1979.

ASEIN. "Breaking the Silence." In *Sharing our Experience*, edited by Arun Mukherjee, 101-108, Ottawa: Canadian Advisory Council on the Status of Women, 1993.

Badets, Jane. "Canada's Immigrant Population." In *Canadian Social Trends*, edited by Craig McKie and Keith Thompson, 7-11, Toronto: Thompson Educational Publishing, 1990.

Bannerji, Himani. *Returning the Gaze: Racism, Feminism and Politics*. Toronto: Sister Vision Press, 1993.

Barile Maria. "Disabled Women: An Exploited Genderless Under-class." In *Canadian Woman Studies* (Summer 1992): 32-33.

Berger, Carl. "The True North Strong and Free." In *Nationalism in Canada*, 21-44, Toronto: McGraw-Hill, 1966.

Bhavnani, Kum-Kum. "Talking Racism and the Editing of Women's Studies." In *Thinking Feminist: Key Concepts in Women's Studies*, edited by Diane Richardson and Victoria Robinson, 27-48, New York: The Guilford Press, 1993.

Boroway, Jan, Gordon, Shelly and Lebans, Gayle. "Are These Clothes Clean? The Campaign for Fair Laws and Working Conditions for Homeworkers." In *And Still We Rise: Feminist Political Mobilizing in Contemporary Canada*, edited by Linda Carty, 299-333, Toronto: Women's Press, 1993.

Boyle, Michael. "Child Health in Ontario." In *The State of the Child in Ontario*, edited by Richard Barnhorst and Laura C. Johnson, 92-116, Toronto: Oxford University Press, 1991.

Brand, Dionne. *No Burden to Carry: Narratives of Black working Women in Ontario, 1920's to 1950's*. Toronto: Women's Press, 1992.

Brand, Dionne. "A Working Paper on Black Women in Toronto: Gender, Race and Class." In *Returning the Gaze: Essays on Racism, Feminism and Politics*, edited by Himani Bannerji, 220-241, Toronto: Sister Vision Press, 1993.

Bristow, Peggy. "The Hour-A-Day Study Club," In *And Still We Rise: Feminist Political Mobilizing in Contemporary Canada*, edited by Linda Carty, 145-173, Toronto: Women's Press, 1993.

Brooks, Catherine. "Personal Interview with the Executive Director, Anduhyaun", 1993.

Cantryn, Ms."Native Women Are Divided, Vancouver, B.C. July 31, 1975" p.247 in *Canadian Women's Issues*. Volume 1.: Strong Voices. Ed. Ruth Roach Pierson, Marjorie Griffin Cohen, Paula Bourne and Philinda Masters. Toronto: Lorimer, 1993.

Cassidy, Barbara. "Personal Interviews with Navajo Women, 1994.

Doman, Mahinder. "A Note on Asian Indian Women in British Columbia, 1900-1935." In *Not Just Pin Money: Selected Essays on the History of Women's Work in British Columbia*, edited by Barbara Latham and Roberta Pazdro, 99-104, Victoria, British Columbia: Camosun College, 1994.

Doucette, Joanne. "Redefining Difference: Disabled Lesbians Resist." In *Lesbians in Canada*, edited by Sharon Dale Stone, 61-72, Toronto: Between the Lines Press, 1990.

Driedger, Diane. "Discovering Disabled Women's History." In *And Still We Rise*, edited by Linda Carty, 173-188, Toronto: Women's Press, 1993.

Duffy Ann; Mandell, Nancy; Pupo, Norene. *Few Choices*, Toronto: Garamond, 1988.

Duffy, Ann, and Mandell, Nancy. "The Widening Gap: Social Inequality and Poverty." In *Canadian Society: Understanding and Surviving in the 1990's*, edited by Dan Glenday and Ann Duffy, 49-85, Toronto: McClelland and Stewart, 1994.

Economic Council of Canada. *The New Face of Poverty: Income Security Needs of Canadian Families*. Ottawa: Ministry of Supply and Services, 1992.

Elliott, Jean Leonard and Fleras, Augie. *Unequal Relations: An Introduction to Race and Ethnic Dynamics in Canada*. Toronto: Prentice Hall, 1992.

Estable, Alma. *Immigrant Women in Canada: Current Issues*. Canadian Advisory Council on the Status of Women. Ottawa, 1986.

Fireweed. "We Appear Silent to People Who Are Deaf To What We Say." In *The Issue is "ism": Women of colour speak Out*, Volume 16:281, 1981.

Frager, Ruth. "Class, Ethnicity, and Gender in the Eaton Strikes of 1912 and 1934." In *Gender Conflicts: New Essays in Women's History*, edited by Franca Iacovetta and Mariana Valverde, 189-228, Toronto: University of Toronto Press, 1993.

Fuller, Mary. "Qualified Criticism, Critical Qualifications." In *Race, Class and Education*, edited by Len Barton and Stephen Walker, London: Croom and Helm Publishing, 1983.

Gabriel, Dolores. "Anger." In *Sharing Our Experience*, edited by Arun Mukherjee, 153-157, Ottawa: Canadian Advisory Council in the Status of Women, 1993.

Globe and Mail, Friday, 3 Dec. 1993.

Globe and Mail, Friday 11 March 1994.

Goldberg, Gertrude Schaffner. "Canada: Bordering on the Feminization of Poverty." In *The Feminization of Poverty: Only in America?*, edited by Gertrude Schaffner Goldberg and Eleanor Kremen, New York: Praeger, 1990.

Goudar, Ruth. "Adjusting the Dream." Saskatchewan Multicultural Magazine 8 (3)1989:5-8

Gregg, Allan and Posner, Michael. *The Big Picture: What Canadians Think About Everything*, Toronto: MacFarlane, Walter, and Ross, 1990.

Hamilton, Sylvia. "The Women at the Well: African Baptist Women Organize." In *And Still We Rise: Feminist Political Mobilizing in Contemporary Canada*, edited by Linda Carty, 189-206, Toronto: Women's Press, 1993.

Henry, Frances and Ginzberg, Effie. "Racial Discrimination in Employment." In *Social Inequality in Canada*, 2d ed., edited by James Curtis, Edward Grabb and Neil Guppy, 353-360, Toronto: Prentice Hall, 1993.

Hill, Daniel G. *Freedom Seekers: Blacks in Early Canada*. Agincourt: Book Society of Canada, 1981.

Hill, Daniel G. "Negroes in Toronto, 1793-1865." In *Ontario History*, Vol. 55 (1963).

Hillyer, Barbara. *Feminism and Disability*. London: University of Oklahoma Press, 1993.

Hodgson, Maggie, Nechi Institute on Alcohol and Drug Education, "Spirituality vs. Religion: First Nations Response to Healing of a Government's Decision to set Social Policy to Dictate Christianity as the solution to Assimilate Our People" p. 255 *Northern Lifelines*, 1993.

House of Commons, *Fifth Report of the Standing Committee on Aboriginal Affairs and Northern Development*. Ottawa: Indian Affairs and Northern Development, 1988.

Hrynyk, Dean. "Being Called Welfare Bum Really Hurts." *Toronto Star*, 27 March 1994. C5.

Human Rights Research and Education Bulletin. "People with Disabilities—On the Long Road to Integration." No. 21, (March 1991).

Iacovetta, Franca. "Making 'New Canadians': Social Workers, Women, and the Reshaping of Immigrant Families." In *Gender Conflicts: New Essays in Women's History*, edited by Franca Iacovetta and Mariana Valverde, 261-303, Toronto: University of Toronto Press, 1993.

James, Carl E. "Getting There and Staying There: Blacks' Employment Experience." In *Transitions: Schooling and Employment in Canada*, edited by Paul Anisef and Paul Axelrod, 3-20, Toronto: Thompson Educational Publishing, 1993.

Jamieson, Kathleen. "Sex Discrimination and the Indian Avt." In *Arduous Journey: Canadian Indians and Decolonization*, edited by Ponting, 112-136, 1986.

Khosla, Punam. *Review of the Situation of Women in Canada*. National Action Committee of the Status of Women, Ottawa, 1993.

Kitchen, Brigitte; Mitchell, Andrew; Clutterbuck, Peter and Novick, Marvyn. In *Unequal Futures: The Legacies of Child Poverty in Canada*, Toronto: Child Poverty Action Group and the Social Planning Council of Metropolitan Toronto, 1991.

Krosenbrink-Gelissen, Lilianne E. "The Native Women's Association of Canada." In *Native Peoples in Canada*, edited by James S. Frideres, 338, Toronto: Prentice Hall, 1993.

Monture, Patricia A. "A Vicious Circle: Child Welfare and the First Nations," *Canadian Journal of Women and the Law*. Volume 3, 1989.

Morris, Jenny. "Feminism and Disability" *Feminist Review*, No. 43 (Spring 1993): 57-70.

National Council of Welfare. *Poverty Profiles: Update for 1991*. Ottawa, (Winter 1993).

National Council of Welfare. *Women and Poverty Revisited*. Ottawa: Ministry of Supply and Services, 1990.

Native Child and Family Services of Toronto. *Native Family Well Being in Urban Settings: A Culture-Based Child and Family Services Model*. Toronto, 1990.

Ng, Roxanne. "Racism, Sexism and Immigrant Women." In *Changing Patterns: Women in Canada*, 2d ed., edited by Sandra Burt, Lorraine Code and Lindsay Dorney, 279-307, Toronto: McClelland and Stewart, 1993.

Ng, Roxanne and Das Gupta, Tania. "Nation Builders? The Captive Labour Force of Non-English Speaking Immigrant Women." In *Canadian Woman Studies 3*, no. 1: 83-85, 1981.

Ontario Women's Directorate. *Info Flash: A Fact Sheet on Women in Ontario*. No. 3, (March 1992).

Ontario Women's Directorate. *Women in the Labour Market: Focus on Women with Disabilities*, 1993a.

Ontario Women's Directorate. *Women in the Labour Market: Focus on Aboriginal Women*, 1993b.

Ontario Women's Directorate. *Focus on Racial Minority Women: Women in the Labour Market*, 1993c.

Ontario Ministry of Citizenship/Office for Disabled Persons. In *Statistical Profile of Disabled Persons in Ontario*. Volume 11, Toronto, Ontario, 1990.

Pearce, Diana. "The Feminization of Poverty: Women, Work, and Welfare." In *Urban and Social Change Review*, 11 (Feb. 1978): 28-36.

Penner, Holly. *Background Paper—Bill C-31: An Act to Amend the Indian Act*. Ottawa: National Association of Women and the Law.

Pierson, Ruth. *They're Still Women After All: The Second World War and Canadian Womanhood*. Toronto: McClelland and Stewart, 1986.

Pierson, Ruth. "The Mainstream Womem's Movement and the Politics of Difference." In *Canadian Women's Issues, Vol 1: Strong Voices*, edited by Marjorie Griffin Cohen, Paula bourne and Philindra Masters, 186-263, Toronto: Lorimer, 1993.

Ponting, J. Rick. *Arduous Journey: Canadian Indians and Decolonization*. Toronto: McClellan and Stewart, 18-56.

Ponting, Rick. "Racial Conflict: Turning the Heat Up." In *Canadian Society: Understanding and Surviving in the 1990's*, edited by Dan Glenday and Ann Duffy, 86-118, Toronto: McClelland and Stewart, 1993.

Reitz, Jeffrey G.; Calzavara, Liviana, and Dasko, Donna. "Ethnic Inequality and Segregation in Jobs." Toronto: Centre for Urban and Community Studies, University of Toronto, Research Paper No. 123, (1981).

Ross, David and Shillington, Richard. *The Canadian Fact Book on Poverty*. Ottawa: Canadian Council on Social Development, 1989.

Shadd, Adrienne. "300 Years of Black Women in Canadian History: circa 1700- 1980." *Tiger Lily*, Vol. 1, Issue 2(1987):4-13.

Silvera, Makeda. *Silenced*. Toronto: Williams-Wallace Publishers, 1988.

Simms, Glenda P. "Racism as a Barrier to Canadian Citizenship," *Belonging: The Meaning and Future of Canadian Citizenship*. Montreal: McGill-Queen's University Press, 1993.

Spears, John. "N.B. Seeks Answer to Childhood Poverty." *Toronto Star*, (May 31, 1991): A21.

Spelman, Elizabeth. 1988. *Inessential Woman: Problems of Exclusion in Feminist Thought*. Boston: Beacon Press, 1991.

Statistics Canada. *Canadian Social Trends: Employment Equity*. (Autumn 1991).

Statistics Canada. *Health and Activity Limitations Survey*. (1985).

Stone, Sharon. "Lesbian Mothers Organizing." In *Lesbians in Canada*, edited by Sharon Dale Stone, 198-208, Toronto: Between the Lines Press, 1990.

Swartz, Karen. Social Construction of Identity: Female University Students with Disabilities, 1994.

Thomson, Colin. *Blacks in Deep Snow: Black Pioneers in Canada*. Toronto: J.M.Dent and Sons, 1979.

Thornhill, Esmeralda. "Focus on Black Women!." In *Race, Class, Gender: Bonda and Barriers*, 2d ed., edited by Jesse Vorst, 27-37, Toronto: Garamond, 1991.

Todoroff, Milana. "You Think I Want to Make Fuck With You": Travelling With a Disability or Two." In *Canadian Woman Studies*, Volume 13, Number 4(1993): 28-30.

Toronto Star, Sunday, 3 April 1994.

Wagner, Sally Roesch. "The Iroquois Confederacy: A Native American Model for Non-Sexist Men." In *Iroquois Women: An Anthology*, edited by Wm. Guy Spitall, 219, Ohsweken, Ontario: Irocrasts, 1990.

Walker, James W. *A History of Blacks in Canada: A Study Guide for Teachers and Students*. Supply and Services, Hull, Quebec: Minister of State Multiculturalism.

Wall, Naomi Binder. "The Beautiful Strength of My Anger Put to Use: Women Against Poverty in Canada." In *And Still We Rise: Feminist Political Mobilizing in Contemporary Canada*, edited by Linda Carty, 279-298, Toronto: Women's Press, 1993.

Ward W. Peter. *White Canada Forever: Popular Attitudes and Public Policy Towards Orientals in British Columbia*. McGill-Queens University Press, Montreal, 1978.

Weaver, Sally. "First Nations Women and Government Policy, 1970–92: Discrimination and Conflict". Eds. Sandra Burt, Lorraine Code and Lindsay Dorney. Changing Patterns: Women in Canada 2nd Ed. Toronto: McClelland and Stewart, 1988.

Wendell, Susan. "Toward a Feminist Theory of Disability" *Hypatia*, Vol. 4, No. 2 (Summer 1989).

Williams, Dorothy W. *Blacks in Montreal, 1628–1986: An Urban Demography*. Cowansville, Quebec: Editions Yvon Blais, 1989.

Winks, Robin. "Negroes in the Maritimes: An Introductory Survey." *Dalhousie Review* (Winter 1968-69).

Women for Economic Survival. *Women and Economic Hard Times: A Record*. Victoria: Women for Economic Survival and the University of Victoria, 1984.

Young, Mary Jane. Epijig Ag Unjanua (Women and Their Children): A Research Project on Native Single Mothers Sponsored by the Advisory Council on the Status of Women. Youth Job Corps Project Number 141. 1992.

Young, T. Kue et al. The Effects of Housing and Community Infrastructure on Canadian Indian Reserves. Ottawa: Indian and Northern Affairs, 1991.

# WHAT MAKES LESBIANISM THINKABLE?: THEORIZING LESBIANISM FROM ADRIENNE RICH TO QUEER THEORY

*Kathleen Martindale*

## INTRODUCTION

This chapter tells a story about the rapid and exciting development of theorizing about lesbianism since 1980. This history is not for lesbians only; it deserves attention by straight, non-straight, and anti-straight readers. The writing discussed here asks: who is a lesbian, what does she do, and, most importantly, what makes lesbianism thinkable? The chapter begins by giving an overview of how the concepts of "lesbianism" and "sexuality" have been elaborated by historians and other thinkers. That overview provides a context for understanding the three key intellectual events that have shaped how those questions have been addressed by feminists and lesbians, categories that can overlap but do not necessarily do so. The key events are the publication in 1980 of an essay by the American poet-critic Adrienne Rich entitled "Compulsory Heterosexuality and

Lesbian Existence," the so-called "sex wars" within feminism from 1982 on, and the emergence of "queer theory" around 1990.

A few words need to be said about the difficulties of making the two key terms—"lesbian" and "theory"—intelligible. Despite the dominant culture's fascination with homosexuality, ignorance about gays and lesbians is, unfortunately, the norm. Most adults' "knowledge" about lesbians consists largely of what was "learned" from taunts and whispers heard in the schoolyards of their childhood. In spite of study after study about the need to confront heterosexism (that is, the assumption that heterosexuality is or at least ought to be the only legitimate sexual expression), universities are still doing little to educate students (Martindale 1992: 449-65). "Heterosexism" is a new word, designed to parallel other words such as "racism" and "sexism" that name and implicitly object to unjust discrimination against large but marginalized groups. "Heterosexism" is coming to be preferred as a more accurate term than the more common "homophobia," or fear and irrational hatred of gays and lesbians, because calling this sometimes lethal hostility a "phobia" seems to psychologize away the injustice. Michael Warner's recent coinage, "heteronormativity," a key concept in "queer theory," is even more useful because it makes it clear how heterosexist "normalcy" normalizes itself through making homosexuality "deviant" (Warner 1991: 3-17). While a few élite American universities have begun to offer graduate degrees in gay and lesbian studies and many more offer undergraduate courses in this emerging area, only women's studies, as a discipline, has a theoretical and political commitment to question the official academic treatment of lesbianism as a psychopathology. Because women's studies has a deep interest in exploring the relationship between gender, sexuality, and knowledge, learning about contemporary issues in lesbian culture is or ought to be crucial in all women's studies courses.

The question is where to begin? To the general population, lesbians are an invisible but despised sexual minority. Most North Americans claim they do not know any. As a result, for many readers putting the word "lesbian" side by side with the word "theory" might seem odd. If lesbians lead an existence almost as mythical and shadowy as unicorns, what status could "theory" by, for, or about them have as contributions to knowledge, and why should anyone in the "general population" care enough to inquire? It is the contention of this chapter that upheavals in theories about what a lesbian is and does are of interest not just to the minority of people who are either theorists or lesbians or both. That is, notions of what the word "lesbian" signifies reveal a lot about the limits and the limitations of being "women," a category in some ways as mysterious and problematic as "lesbian" (Riley 1988: 1). Anyone who is curious about the relationship between sex, sexuality, gender, and knowledge (and that takes in just about everyone) has a stake in lesbian theory.

Unfortunately, in Canadian culture many people are as afraid of theory as they are of lesbians! Theory sounds intimidating, but if you understand it as a universal human activity that we engage in all the time when we explain anything to or for ourselves, you may come to agree that you too have a stake in theorizing. Indeed, while you are reading and actively trying to make sense of this chapter, you are implicitly theorizing (Martindale 1991: 9-14). No writer, especially no theorist, expects readers to understand or agree with everything he or she says. While you read this chapter, concentrate on the broad outlines about the development of lesbian theory rather than on the names of the individual theorists. It doesn't matter if you don't know the theorists. It's the forest (the argument), not the individual trees (the names and biographies of the theorists), that matters. If you are interested in learning more about their writing, consult the bibliography. Because theory generally uses a specialized vocabulary, new or unusual words will be explained briefly when they are introduced. Endnotes will provide information about where readers can learn more about subjects touched upon here.

## WHERE DOES LESBIAN THEORY COME FROM?

Putting lesbian theorizing into a context means studying the history of lesbianism as a sexual practice, an identity, and a politics of same-sex female desire that parallels but is not identical to the history of feminism, since feminism is a theory of gender oppression rather than a theory of sexuality (Rubin 1984: 307). Thinking about lesbianism historically requires questioning what seems most obvious about "sex"—even when put in quotation marks. What constitutes "sex" (the act) or "sexuality" (the broader and more abstract category)? Just as, in this culture, women's inequality is common sense, so it follows that "sex" is natural, unchanging, and prediscursive. But sexual justice, like gender justice, is not an intuitively obvious idea, and in a culture where it is assumed that girls and women don't know much about sex and don't need to know more, feminist thinking about sexuality needs to rethink the basics.

In the model that lesbian and feminist historians have appropriated (not without controversy for doing so) from the writings of French historian and philosopher, Michel Foucault, and his English popularizer, Jeffrey Weeks, the relationship between "normal" and "deviant" sexualities is denaturalized, historicized, and deconstructed (Foucault 1980; Weeks 1985). Doing this is difficult for the same reason that becoming a feminist is difficult: it challenges the status quo. Common sense teaches us that sexuality is the deepest and most obvious truth about us: as such, it is hard to believe that sex has a history.

Even for those who believe that it is crucial to study lesbianism historically, there are profound disagreements about who or what counts and what the political implications of counting narrowly or counting loosely are for feminists and lesbians. Whereas the debate between historians of male homosexuality over essentialism (the contention that homosexuality is a transhistorical and transcultural phenomenon) and social constructionism (the claim that it is a historically and culturally specific aspect of late capitalist urban societies) has been largely won by those upholding the latter theory, lesbian theorists remain more divided. As to the basic question, did "lesbians" and "lesbianism" exist before the end of the nineteenth century, they differ, depending on whether they stress continuity between past and present definitions, or discontinuity. The former say yes, meaning they believe that lesbians have always existed and can be found in all cultures, while the latter say no, lesbians came into historical existence as a self-conscious group only toward the end of the nineteenth century in large Euro-American cities.

Those who stress continuity want to define lesbianism more inclusively, if less historically, as something other than a sexual practice of female deviants, outlaws, and lowlife (Grahn 1984; Faderman 1981). Wishing to escape the clinical definition of lesbianism as a set of sexual practices performed by unfeminine women, those who accept the continuity model find a perennial "lesbian continuum" defined by Adrienne Rich as inclusively as possible to mean "a range through each woman's life and throughout history—a woman-identified experience; not simply the fact that a woman has had or consciously desired genital sexual experience with another woman" (1980: 648). All women could potentially be placed on the continuum based on their love for women and their resistance, however weak, to "compulsory heterosexuality," that is, the ideologically and materially enforced insistence that women see themselves entirely as the complements of men and live under male control or risk severe sanctions ranging from social stigma to death (1980: 632-4).

In previous times and in different cultures, some of the women who were Beguines, or were in Chinese marriage-resisting communities, convents, brothels, and Native American unified households, might, in current shorthand, be considered lesbians. Adrienne Rich (19: 651) argues that all these belong on a lesbian continuum. From the sixteenth century onward to the late nineteenth century in Western Europe and North America, according to the continuity model, these women-loving women were mainly perceived and perceived themselves as respectable women of delicate, even noble feelings. They were known as "romantic friends."

Lillian Faderman's enormously influential cultural study of romantic friendship, *Surpassing the Love of Men: Romantic Friendship and Love between Women from the Renaissance to the Present* (1981) uses the abundant evidence of written documents such as poems, letters, journals and memoirs not only to argue that many middle-class and upper-class women in England, Scotland, France, Germany, and the United States frequently spent their emotional lives in passionate "romantic friendships" with other women, but also to argue that these relationships were seen as normal and even inspiring until their innocence was spoiled by the cataloguing propensities of the Victorian era sexologists from Havelock Ellis to Freud.

The twentieth century demarcation between heterosexual and lesbian women was unknown and would have been unthinkable, partially because those names as well as the technical sexological categories were not invented until late in the nineteenth century. Only as a result of the popularization of the ideas of the sexologists and doctors, which in Faderman's view was part of an anti-feminist backlash, were romantic friendships considered pathological and deviant, that is, lesbian (1981: 238-240).

In the earlier part of the century, when women were excluded from higher education, the professions, and well-paid work, most women were forced to marry. Because the Victorian insistence that "good" women be passionless and keep to the private rather than the public sphere, the evidence of feminist historians suggests that they experienced their deepest connections to other women rather than to men. Later in the century, when social change fostered by the growth of feminism allowed some women entrance to the public sphere, it became possible for educated women to remain unmarried and to enter the professions. These romantic friends, who were known legally as spinsters, often lived their feminist principles in long-term monogamous relationships termed "Boston marriages." While acknowledging that interpretation of these written documents is difficult, continuity theorists argue that most romantic friends probably did not engage in genital sex; but nonetheless, because of the depth of their feelings, they should be included among what twentieth century post-Freudians call lesbians.

Other sexual historians and cultural theorists, influenced by Foucault, believe that, historically speaking, the category and subcultural community of women we now call lesbian came into existence only toward the end of the nineteenth century as an outgrowth of and a reaction to capitalism, feminism, and the writings of the sexologists. In this view, lesbians arrived later on the world historical scene than did gay men because patriarchal notions made it impossible for women-loving women to have the self-consciousness and material means necessary to see themselves and be seen by others in terms of lesbian sexual identity. While female as well as male same-sex sexual relations have always occurred, those who argue the discontinuity model mainly regard the category "lesbian" as fitting at most only the last hundred years of Western culture.

The discontinuity approach taken by lesbian historians such as Judith Brown, Martha Vicinus, and Ann Ferguson restricts the label "lesbian" far more than that taken by historians like Adrienne Rich who assert lesbian continuity across history and cultures (Brown 1989; Vicinus 1982; Ferguson 1981). Since the former are materialist thinkers, they, unlike moralistic or utopian thinkers, stress the interaction between the work people do on physical things and the ways they do that with the relationships they enter into to survive; they demand, for lesbianism, a historical model that is more sensitive, to race, class, and ethnic differences, and therefore also more interested in expanding the notion of the sorts of women who should be studied as lesbians. Through searching nineteenth century and even earlier police reports as well as legal and medical scandals to find women-loving women who were other than White, bourgeois, and generally supportive of the dominant culture, these historians have traced an alternative history and culture of lesbians who, unlike the earlier romantic friends or the later middle-class and upper-class "New Woman" professionals of the early twentieth century, were rebels rather than ladies. These women, many of whom were genitally sexual, frequently supported themselves as prostitutes and transvestites or "passing women," becoming famous or infamous as pirates, soldiers, doctors, politicians, and artists.

Most recent lesbian theorists endorse the discontinuity model and use it to argue that none of the discourses involved in studying lesbianism from the nineteenth through the middle twentieth centuries was in itself simply conductive or hostile to its growth.[1] By contrast with this approach, which allows for contradictory reading practices, a commonsense approach to sexuality seems to have a greater immediate appeal: it provides the safety and comfort of familiarity. On the other hand, thinking about sexuality historically allows feminists to reconsider the relationship between sexual coercion and sexual choice and to imagine ourselves as agents in our lives who can build a future in which sexuality for all women is more a pleasure and less of a nightmare.

## WHAT'S IN A NAME?

"Thinking Sex" from a feminist perspective requires curiosity about the role that language plays in sexual history. Just as when, as children, we tried to find out about sex in a sex-negative culture, we can start this exploration by reading the dictionary, critically. A browse through *The Oxford English Dictionary*, a dictionary organized on historical principles, turns upside-down fundamental  assumptions about the relationship between sexual normality and deviancy and suggests how the power to name can be the power to control.

Feminist social historians who have appropriated the work of Michel Foucault and Weeks also tend to explore the sexual politics of words for sexual categories, but, unlike them, they have tended until recently (Sedgwick 1990 and Butler 1990) to be less interested in the binarism heterosexual/homosexual, and more interested in the ways women of all sorts transgress against the boundaries and the linguistic boundary keepers.

Theorists remind us that the word "heterosexuality" was not coined until 1901, some thirty years after sexologists, the men who studied sex "scientifically," used the term "homosexuality" (Penelope 1990: 11). The term "homosexuality" came first because the sexologists were primarily interested in cataloguing what they regarded as "perversities." They were far less interested in what they regarded as "normal", which for the sexologists was unremarkable. Just as a White male perspective is non-remarkable from a racist and sexist perspective, so also is heterosexuality. Heterosexuality is sexuality, just as heterosexual sex is sex.

But even that assumption demands scrutiny. Apparently the sexologists used the word "heterosexual" to denote deviancy, just as they had used "homosexual" and "lesbian" (Penelope 1990: 11). "Heterosexuality," too, originally named a mental disease, an excessive attraction to the opposite sex. Ironically, the study of heterosexuality, even feminist heterosexuality, still suffers by comparison to what is written about homosexuality. Very little has been written about how to theorize heterosexuality from a feminist perspective, but Canadian theorists have made significant contributions in this area. In 1985, Mariana Valverde devoted a section of her book, *Sex, Power and Pleasure*, to the crisis in heterosexuality (47-74). In 1990, Canadian feminists published a double issue of *Resources for Feminist Research* on the subject of "Confronting Heterosexuality."[2]

The history of the words used to name female homosexuals reveals both more mystery and political contentiousness than do those used to name same-sex loving men. Apparently, throughout linguistic history, there have been no words that were both non-euphemistic and non-insulting in designating women who loved or had sex with other women. Slang words of ancient but unclear origin such as "dyke" and "bull dyke" have generally been regarded as hateful taunts, but recently they have been proudly reclaimed by some lesbians (Grahn 194: 134-137).

Many women reject the comparatively more neutral term "lesbian" as clinical, irrelevant, or a bad eurocentric, classist, and patriarchal joke. To find out why, check your dictionary: the first meaning given is "of Lesbos," a Greek island, home of the poet Sappho; the second, is "of homosexuality *in women*" (emphasis mine), the practice of which means being "sexually attracted only by persons of his or her own sex," of which the ancient Greek poetess was "suspected." In their groundbreaking ethnographic study of working-class White and Black lesbian communities active in Buffalo, New York, from the 1930s through the late 1950s, Elizabeth Kennedy and Madeline Davis found that their informants very rarely used the word "lesbian" to refer to themselves; instead they used "butch and fem," or "butch and her girlfriend" (Kennedy and Davis 1993: 6-7, 68-69). "Lesbian" at this time and place mainly referred to women of a higher and a whiter social class, and thereby lends support to the Black lesbian poet-theorist Ekua Omsupe's recent claim that the term "without racial specificity focuses on and refers to White lesbian culture" (Omosupe 1991: 108). Kennedy and Davis, though with reluctance, feel compelled to use it throughout the book for lack of a better word.

Even the most academically respected work on sexuality by gay male historians such as Foucault and Weeks has had little to say about women and lesbians. Though they and their feminist and lesbian followers have treated changes in the meanings of words associated with sexual diversity and perversity as important evidence for their position that sexuality does have a history and is constructed in and through language, neither traces the history of the word "lesbian." Even the feminist historian Judith C. Brown, in her study of lesbian sexuality in medieval Europe, consigns most of her argument about the debates between lesbian essentialists and social constructionists to a footnote (1989: 499-500).

That footnote is as good a place as any to find an explanation of how controversies about how to identify female sexual deviants are connected with much larger questions of feminist and lesbian theory and sexual politics. Brown's footnote is full of the controversies whose analysis will structure the rest of this chapter. Following Foucauldian constructionism, the belief that lesbian and gay identities and subcultures are the historical creation of Western European and North American urban centres, Brown argues in the body of her text that it is improper to use the word "lesbian" for individuals or identities prior to Queen Victoria's reign: "Although the word 'lesbian' appears once in the sixteenth century in the work of Brantome, it was not commonly used until the nineteenth, and even then was applied first to certain acts rather than a category of persons" (Brown 1989: 73-74). But who exactly used the word? It is unlikely to have included many women (Frye 1990: 311).

In Brown's footnote, she suggests that the fight over who will define and hence map lesbian historiography has switched away from male theorists and toward lesbian poet-philosophers and feminist theorists whose theoretical prestige in this battle will decide how we will read the lesbian past. Should lesbianism be construed broadly, as a form of womanly bonding rather than a sexual practice, as Adrienne Rich does, or narrowly, as a self-conscious sexual identity, as Ann Ferguson does? How is lesbian history related to the history of feminism—as central or tangential? The next part of this chapter will focus on these questions.

## ADRIENNE RICH'S "COMPULSORY HETEROSEXUALITY AND LESBIAN EXISTENCE" (1980): POSSIBLY THE BEGINNING, BUT NOT ALL THERE IS TO SAY ABOUT LESBIAN THEORY

In the twenty years since the "second wave" of feminism swept over North America and Western Europe, lesbianism has been theorized as outside, then inside, and once again as outside the feminist "mainstream." What does lesbianism mean for feminism and vice versa? How have lesbians who are feminists theorized lesbianism as a sexual practice, an identity, and a political perspective? What has been the response within institutionalized feminism, particularly women's studies scholarship, to the increasing visibility of lesbians and to the growing prestige of lesbian theorizing within the academy? This chapter attempts to answer these questions by relating changes in the theorizing of lesbianism to the mapping and remapping of the relationship between feminism and lesbianism.

Adrienne Rich's essay, "Compulsory Heterosexuality and Lesbian Existence" appeared in 1980, just prior to the outbreak of the so-called feminist "sex wars," the resurgence of the right wing in North America, and the AIDS epidemic worldwide. This essay shows lesbian and feminist theoretical practices at a moment of consolidation and legitimation. If one article has overwhelmingly been chosen by feminist teachers to represent modern lesbianism in both introductory Women's Studies courses and more advanced courses in feminist theory, it is this classic by Adrienne Rich. Rich wrote her still widely anthologized poetic polemic with Women's Studies students and faculty in mind as her intended audience. She wrote to change minds: to decrease homophobia in the women's movement and in feminist scholarship and to build bridges between heterosexual and lesbian feminists (1986: 23-24). To accomplish these goals, Rich built on the ideological work of 1970s feminist culture which had transformed the image of lesbians from sexual outlaws to respectable citizens. Her chief stroke of brilliance in this rhetorical take-over was to make lesbianism natural, womanly, and feminist.

Legitimizing lesbianism this way is tricky. Obviously, it requires a rewriting of all the myths, popular and scholarly, about ugly, man-hating lesbians. Less obviously, it requires rewriting the twentieth century history of relationships between feminists, lesbians, and gay men. Given the revolutionary task she set herself, it is not surprising that Rich's argument is frequently contradictory, unsupported by evidence, or, at key points, incredible.

Rich argues that lesbianism is a choice. Lesbians are made, not born. In making this choice, women are not choosing a sexuality so much as they are choosing to resist patriarchy. Heterosexuality is not a choice: it is collaboration with the enemy in the interests of survival. Any resisting woman is entitled to take a spot on what she calls "the lesbian continuum," but the patriarchy will destroy her if she does so. Therefore, feminists make the best lesbians; lesbian/feminism is industrial-strength feminism (unlike earlier pre-feminist lesbians who were sex-crazed and therefore not really political). If all women became lesbians, the patriarchy would crumble.

"Compulsory Heterosexuality and Lesbian Existence" is what Katie King calls an "origin story," an interested tale about the relationship between lesbianism and feminism (1986: 65). Since Rich wants to unite them, to make lesbianism feminism's "magical sign," she forges the link visually as well as rhetorically—"lesbian/feminism." (Throughout this account of shifts in the relationship between these terms, I will use the typography that the theorist under discussion used at the time she wrote. Since there is no standard form, usage varies and probably reflects the relationship the writer believes exists between lesbianism and feminism. For theorists who are lesbian and feminists but not "lesbian feminist," I will use the term "feminist lesbian".) Since I want to re-examine the ways that link was forged and reforged and occasionally broken, my rewriting of Rich's and other origin stories about more recent twists in this relationship is also an interested tale.

My narrative reveals its interests by highlighting some features and down-playing, even ignoring, others. There are certain things you should know about my positionality: I grew up in a white, working-class, conservative family in New York City. I did some of the things that were expected of me as a young woman, including getting married, but I transgressed in other ways against my gender, race, class, and sexual orientation. I became an intellectual and a politi-cal activist: I came to feminism via the standard route for women of my age and radical political perspective—from the civil rights, anti-Vietnam movements, fol-lowed by infatuation/disillusionment with the New Left, then by feminist orga-nizing in Canada around reproductive rights. I became an academic feminist, a teacher of Women's Studies, around the time I came out as a lesbian. I believe that the tensions between feminism and lesbianism can be theoretically and politically productive.

Those tensions are suppressed in Adrienne Rich's article, because Rich sought to unify lesbianism and feminism and also because she saw lesbianism as a solution to the problems of female heterosexuality (Wilson 1986: 173). Because of what she forced underground, Rich's article is probably much more often cited for the memorable phrases she introduced into feminist culture than read as an extended argument.

While the latter part of the title is often forgotten and misquoted—per-haps because Rich's argument about the all-encompassing, trans historical and trans cultural nature of "lesbian existence" has been largely discredited by historians—the first and most shocking part of the title, the notion of "compulsory heterosexuality," has become a cornerstone of feminist and les-bian theorizing. Rich's insight that heterosexuality should be seen by all women as an institution, a frequently violent and always coercive social con-struction, rather than as a freely chosen natural state, has had some accep-tance in other academic disciplines such as literature, psychology, sociology, and cultural studies, and has even made its way into the larger world outside the academy. For many feminist readers, Rich is lesbian theory, but, since les-bian theorists have largely rejected her arguments, I'd like to use her article and its reception by scholars, teachers, and students as foreground in my pre-sentation of developments in lesbian theorizing from a variety of feminist perspectives from 1980 to the present.

While Rich's article is groundbreaking, nonetheless, with the passage of time, it has become more and more problematic both to scholars and to those who encounter it as the token lesbian text in otherwise heterosexist feminist courses. Rich's article frequently functions as a gesture of tolerance and inclusivity in response to the marginalization of lesbianism within institutionalized feminism and for the homophobic silences around these subjects in all too many classrooms. Rich's now dated text needs to be read and studied in light of later developments in feminist and lesbian theory; otherwise, it seems to tell a misleading and partial study about the relationship of feminism to lesbianism and vice versa.

Attendance on "Rich day" is usually smaller than usual; lesbian students stay away because they're sick of being tokenized; other students stay away because of homophobic logic: if you show interest in this text, you might be one. And since Rich bases her premise for the "lesbian continuum" on the evidence that sexualities are fluid rather than fixed, the essay can stir up homophobia in readers who are anxious to maintain their hold on heterosexual privilege. Speaking up in discussions of Rich can be an ethical and political dilemma for students known or presumed to be lesbian. They can stand to lose as much as or even more than their instructors in terms of classroom credibility, since if they engage in discussion they have implicitly come out and explicitly become the class expert, whose every word thereafter becomes "the lesbian" viewpoint.

A good place to begin addressing homophobia in the Women's Studies classroom is by de-tokenizing Adrienne Rich and treating lesbian theory historically. Just as feminist teachers have learned not to marginalize theoretical and other writings by and about women of colour, they need to reform their curricula, integrate material, and make their teaching anti-homophobic. This process demands recognizing that teaching one outdated lesbian article in isolation from other texts won't do.

## IS LESBIANISM MORE (OR LESS) THAN WOMAN-BONDING?: THE DEBATE BETWEEN ADRIENNE RICH AND ANN FERGUSON

Feminist scholars responded in various ways to Rich's controversial essay, and, in fact, the debate about it is still ongoing. One of the most important responses to Rich is that by the socialist-feminist lesbian Ann Ferguson. The debate between Rich and Ferguson, still unresolved, is crucial in understanding the directions that lesbian theorizing took during and after the sex wars and the role that theorizing played in the breakup of what Catharine Stimpson called the North American feminist "cultural consensus" (1988: 179-196). The ironic outcome of their debate is that, though Ferguson has the better and more historically grounded argument, and though later theorists have largely followed her lead in applying her methodology in asking similar questions about lesbian identity, her response has been forgotten, whereas Rich's polemic has become the primary text in the lesbian theoretical canon, that is, the works considered by experts to be "required reading," the classic texts.

Rich's article holds this pride of place because it creates an appealing idealist myth of the lesbian/feminist as a present-day freedom fighter against patriarchy who has a mystical connection to all the heroic women who have ever lived. In its scope and imaginative grandeur, Rich's article is a manifesto of lesbian modernism. ("Modernism" is a technical term in the intellectual history of the twentieth century, a way of making a cultural, philosophical, and social outlook whose exact meaning varies from discipline to discipline, but whose chief characteristics include an emphasis on the creativity of individual subjectivity in an urban and complex social reality where communication between human beings is difficult because of the breakdown of traditional and unified systems of understanding.) Through the bonds of women-identification, which she shares with non-lesbians, rather than through specific acts of sexual deviancy, which isolate her as a pervert, Rich's lesbian is a romantic though respectable figure. Naturalizing the lesbian, freeing her to float free from historical impurities and taints, linking her oppression to the oppression of all women, Rich makes lesbianism intelligible and seductive in heterosexual terms. That is, she desexualizes lesbianism.

Ferguson pricks the romantic bubble by finding Rich's vision ahistoric, exclusionary, and utopian (1981: 160). Unconvinced by Rich's totalizing claims for compulsory heterosexuality as the motor driving patriarchy and the lesbian continuum as the nesting place for all women (172), Ferguson questions Rich's definitional strategies and her broadly inclusive claims about lesbian identity (160-1). She does this by setting out five different definitions of lesbian identity, including Rich's and her own, that reflect changes in ways of being sexual and of thinking about sexuality.

The major difference between Rich and Ferguson is that Ferguson re-establishes the importance of the creation of "an explicit lesbian identity connected to genital sexuality" (160). Ferguson admits that no one definition will fit all cases (164, 166). The question of lesbian identity demands self-conscious reflexivity, must remain open-ended, and must be meaningfully grounded in material and cultural specificities. Hers is a far narrower and in many ways less romantic view of lesbianism, one not so easily assimilable into heterosexual feminism.

Nonetheless, unlike Rich, Ferguson does not put the lesbian into the vanguard position, and, unlike Rich, she acknowledges that significant political differences divide women. By underlining the implications of her own socialist-feminist perspective, one that stresses the interconnections between gender and other forms of difference, such as class and race in comparison to Rich's radical feminism that stresses gender as the primary form of social difference, Ferguson anticipates the drive to map and taxonomize the various feminisms, an activity that took up much intellectual energy of academic feminists throughout the 1980s. For these reasons, her essay prefigures the development of lesbianism in a postmodern mode. ("Postmodernism," like modernism, is a technical term whose most inclusive sense names the culture, philosophy, and sociopolitical outlook characteristic of the contemporary period of late capitalism. In comparison to "modernism," its meanings are far less stable and more contentious, but, by stressing fragmentation and multiplicity within and without the human subject, they have produced an extreme crisis of representation, value, and meaning.[3]

> At two places in her counter-argument, Ferguson asks who is excluded from or devalued by Rich's redefinition of lesbian existence. By doing so, Ferguson antici-pates the unrest among lesbians that led to the sex wars and other theoretical schisms that have divided feminists and lesbians for the last decade. Very point-edly, in contrast to Rich, she rejects any definitional strategy which seeks to drop the sexual component of 'lesbian' in favor of an emotional commitment to, or preference for, women tends to lead feminists to downplay the historical impor-tance of the movement for sexual liberation. The negative results of that move-ment...do not justify dismissal of the real advances that were made for women, not the least being the possibility of a lesbian identity in the sexual sense of the term. (164)

In other words, Ferguson implies that Rich's article is what Katie King called an "interested story" (1986) about lesbianism and feminism that marginalizes many lesbians, in particular working-class butch-femme lesbians, bar dykes, and sexual radicals.

Though many other theorists began to question Rich's key ideas as soon as she published her essay, any possibility that there would be time for a nice quiet discussion of Ferguson's respectful rejoinder to Rich was dashed by three events that changed feminist and lesbian discourses about sexuality: the rise of the right wing in North America and Britain, he outbreak of the AIDS epidemic, and the sex wars within feminism.

## THE SEX WARS

Since this chapter is structured around debates internal to lesbianism and femi-nism, I will concentrate most on what has been termed the sex wars. Of course, as writers address issues that are closest to us in time, especially those in which we have participated and have a stake in being right, it becomes harder to assess issues accurately and fairly. Though some of the hurt and hostility has gone out of the sex wars, old wounds still linger, even for those women who were not personally involved.

It is hard to be neutral about the sex wars. It is still important today for feminists and lesbians to sift through the meanings and significance of the debates over female sexuality that broke out in the early 1980s. Ultimately figuring out who was "right," or which side had the "more advanced" arguments, or even who "won" is not as important as understanding why the wars happened and what we can learn from them. Without these understandings, feminism and lesbianism, especially in North America, will continue to be stuck in the theoretical and political impasses created by these events.

Looking backward, every scholar who has discussed this period agrees that the ninth "Feminist and Scholar" conference held in 1982 at Barnard College in New York on the subject "Towards a Politics of Sexuality" marked the outbreak of the wars. The climate, however, had been heating up between lesbian-feminists and other lesbians for some time. In many ways, the sex wars were disputes about the meanings of lesbian life in large American cities in the 1970s, although they also troubled lesbian and feminist communities in England and Canada.

Janice G. Raymond has a celebratory but sorrowful view of a lesbian feminist paradise lost:

> There was a time when this movement called lesbian feminism had a passion, principles, and politics. Without romanticizing that period as the golden age of lesbian feminism, I would like to recall for us what that movement was and what it stood for.
>
> This movement was the strongest challenge to hetero-reality that feminism embodied. It challenged the worldview that women exist for men and primarily in relation to them. It challenged the history of women as primarily revealed in the family...It challenged that seemingly eternal truth that 'Thou as a woman must bond with a man,' forever seeking our lost halves in the complementarity of hetero-relations. It even challenged the definition of feminism itself as the equality of women with men. Instead, it made real a vision of the equality of women with our Selves. It defined equality as being equal to those women who have been for women, those who have lived for women's freedom and those who have died for it; those who have fought for women and survived by women's strength; those who have loved women and who have realized that without the consciousness and conviction that women are primary in each other's lives, nothing else is in perspective.
>
> This movement worked on behalf of all women...But then something happened. Women—often other lesbians—began to define things differently. (Raymond 1989: 152)

By contrast, Joan Nestle has a very critical view of what lesbian feminism suppressed:

> We Lesbians from the fifties made a mistake in the early seventies: we allowed our lives to be trivialized and reinterpreted by feminists who did not share our culture.

The slogan 'Lesbianism is the practice and feminism is the theory' was a good rallying cry, but it cheated our history. The early writings need to be reexamined to see why so many of us dedicated ourselves to understanding the homophobia of straight feminists rather than the life-realities of Lesbian women 'who were not feminists' (an empty phrase which comes too easily to the lips). Why did we expect and need Lesbians of earlier generations and differing backgrounds to call their struggle by our name? I am afraid of the answer because I shared both worlds and know how respectable feminism made me feel, how less dirty, less ugly, less butch and femme. But the pain and anger at hearing so much of my past judged unacceptable have begun to surface. (Nestle 1987: 105-106)

These visions from the inside, of how internal differences around the meaning and practice of lesbian sexuality (and in Nestle's case of class and ethnicity) were managed within "the" lesbian feminist community are compelling polemics. Just as theoretical and political developments within feminism, such as the evolution of radical feminism into cultural feminism and the rise of postcolonial and women of colour feminism, shattered the fragile unity of feminism in the singular, so these versions of lesbian life in the 1970s show how the onset of the sex wars divided lesbian from lesbian and led to the proliferation of lesbianisms, which in turn led to the theorizing and legitimating of more diverse sexual minorities who have an even more tenuous connection to feminism. The breakdown of the grand narrative of sexuality which offered two flavours—heterosexual and lesbian—ushered in the new age of postmodern sexuality that seemed to hold out the possibility of an endless variety of sexual expressions and an end to the policing of sexual boundaries.

But this is getting ahead of the narrative. What were the sex wars about? The immediate catalyst was the picketing and leafleting at the Barnard conference by "cultural feminists" who were politically offended by the presence of lesbian sex radicals at a feminist event (Faderman 1991: 251; the descriptor, "cultural feminist," is generally used derogatorily, but Faderman's usage is neutral to positive).

The demonstrators attempted to stop the conference, in part by having its funding removed, since they regarded the radicals' work as part of the backlash against feminism (Faderman 1991: 251; Snitow 1983: 39). The conference quickly became legendary, a symbol of divisions among feminists and lesbians; the fate of feminism itself seemed to hang in the hands of those who were there or wrote analyses of it. Needless to say, since the sex wars were fought largely by (White, American) academics and intellectuals over books and ideas and then hashed and rehashed in more books and scholarly articles, the whole affair might at first seem like a tempest in a teapot. Perhaps, as it recedes from view, that will by the way feminist history will regard it. Looked at from the vantage point of another decade, however, this highly cerebral and ironically disembodied struggle set the terms and the agenda for contemporary feminist and lesbian discourses on sexuality and sexual representation.

Scholars differ about the extent to which this was almost entirely a lesbian dispute over unconventional sexual practices such as sadomasochism, public sex, the use and production of pornography, and butch-femme role-playing that directly affected only a minority of a minority. Lesbian social historian Lillian Faderman, in her very successful study of twentieth century lesbian life in the U.S., *Odd Girls and Twilight Lovers* (1991), is of two minds about this.

In one of the most concise statements about the meaning of the wars, Faderman claims that "The lesbian sex wars of the 1980s between those lesbians who were cultural feminists and those who were sex radicals reflected the conflicting perceptions of the basic meaning of femaleness and lesbianism with which women have long struggled" (268-9). If she's right, then the issue is a large one, with a potential for involving a very large number of women, even though the number of actual combatants was small.

This reading of the wars' significance is, however, contradicted by the other claims, backed up by sexological statistics, surveys, and questionnaires, that structure her chapter on this period of lesbian history (253; 270). Unlike the other analysts, Faderman for the most part takes the sex wars at face value. They weren't about deeper issues such as the naturalness or constructedness of lesbian sexuality, relationships with heterosexual feminism, or representational politics; they were about what lesbians do in bed. Faderman concludes, based on her interview data, that the attempt by lesbian sex radicals to change lesbians' sexual behaviour failed, largely because lesbians, like other women, share the same female socialization which emphasizes tenderness, love, romance, and sexual safety above the pleasures and dangers of adventuring on the fringes, let alone outside the borders of sexual respectability (269-70).

If the sex wars are looked at less concretely, however, the immediate outcome was not what Faderman reports, namely that the cultural feminists, or the lesbian essentialists as she names them, won the battle and the sex radicals, or lesbian existentialists lost (269). Looked at in larger theoretical and historical terms, the sex wars are only the latest round in a 200 year-long struggle over the boundaries between normalcy and sexual deviance in which feminists have tended to play the role of regulators as well as the regulated (Weeks 1985: 217, 234; Burstyn 1985: 10-31).

That is the crux of the argument of lesbian sex radical and anthropologist Gayle Rubin, whose article, "Thinking Sex: Notes for a Radical Theory of the Politics of Sexuality," is the most cited and important piece in the very influential anthology of papers from the Barnard conference, *Pleasure and Danger* (1984: 267-319). If Adrienne Rich's essay, "Compulsory Heterosexuality and Lesbian Existence," is the first classic to have emerged from recent lesbian culture, then Gayle Rubin's article is the second. Using a Foucauldian analysis of modern sexual history, Rubin argues that the sex wars should be studied as a symbolic contest between feminists and sex radicals over what she calls a stratified and unitary sexual system.

Like Rich before her, Rubin is a powerful polemicist who is trying to legitimize and naturalize her preferred form of lesbian sexuality, in this case lesbian sadomasochism. Unlike Rich, who tried to do this by blurring the boundaries between heterosexuality and lesbianism, Rubin does it by attacking the very notion of sexual hierarchy (282). Feminists, especially lesbian feminists, have legitimized themselves as the respectable sex deviants by demonizing the sexual practices of other sexual minorities. By pathologizing feminist sexuality's "others" as extremists, Rubin argues, lesbian feminists normalize themselves, and thereby make their own position seem reasonable and respectable. Now that some historical distance has been put on the most inflammatory aspects of the rhetorical battles of the sex wars, this part of Rubin's argument has come to be regarded as far more significant than her sexual libertarianism (310).

While Lillian Faderman regards the adoption or rejection of "kinky" sexual practices for lesbians as a blip in the pattern of female sexual socialization, Rubin treats the sex wars as a crucial moment in the history of sexuality. The sex wars, like the period in the late eighteenth century when homosexuality was "invented," were a time of "sexual ethnogenesis" in which new sexual minorities were created and formed identities and communities (287). For those living through it, this moment is hard to read because anything having to do with sex is highly mystified in Western culture. "The wars over it are often fought at oblique angles, aimed at phoney targets, conducted with misplaced passions, and are highly, intensely symbolic". (297)

Rubin puts the sex wars within feminism and the ideological construction of AIDS as the "gay plague" into a historical and political context by relating them to other American "moral panics," such as the 1950s witch-hunts for homosexuals, communists, and "white slavers." Figuring out how fears and anxieties about sex are used to increase the power and the respectability of political reactionaries in the U.S. is particularly hard to analyze because political progressives, including feminists and lesbians, have tended to take a moralistic or trivializing attitude to sex rather than put their energies into developing an adequate theory of sexuality. Trying to develop one which she calls theoretical and sexual pluralism, Rubin argues that the sex wars should be perceived as a border skirmish in a much larger territorial conflict over sexual values and moral judgments (294; 309).

Rubin's article undoubtedly makes uncomfortable reading for most feminists. Not only does she resexualize lesbians, removing the halo of respectability that 1970s feminism had worked hard to create; she also unties the relationship between feminism as a theory of gender oppression and lesbianism as a sexual identity and practice. By prying apart the categories of gender and sexuality, Rubin began to lay the theoretical groundwork for a new disciplinary formation—lesbian studies—that runs parallel to, but does not overlap, Women's Studies.

Rubin uses her account of the sex wars to make a compelling argument that feminism should no longer be seen as the "privileged site of a theory of sexuality" (307). Feminism is of limited usefulness for lesbians and other sexual minorities:

> Feminist conceptual tools were developed to detect and analyze gender-based hierarchies. To the extent that these overlap with erotic stratifications, feminist theory has some explanatory power. But as issues become less those of gender and more those of sexuality, feminist analysis becomes irrelevant and often misleading. Feminist thought simply lacks angles of vision which can encompass the social organization of sexuality. The criteria of relevance in feminist thought do not allow it to see or assess critical power relations in the area of sexuality. (309)

Whereas in her earlier and extremely influential essay, "The Traffic in Women," she had suggested that the concept of a "sex/gender system" allowed the best ways of understanding the structural links between sex and gender (1979: 197-210), Rubin now repudiated her previous work. Her essay, "Thinking Sex," played a significant part in rupturing the fragile theoretical unity between heterosexual and lesbian feminists. Just as theoretical work by women of colour had shattered the feminist consensus by calling attention to hegemonic feminism's failure to theorize race and racism, so lesbian theorists began to challenge feminism's silences around sexuality and homophobia. Groundbreaking work by women of colour and lesbians (frequently overlapping categories) has led many feminists to wonder: just how well does feminism explain differences among women such as race, class, or sexuality? Is gender alone feminism's "primary contradiction"? By providing the theoretical foundations and justifications for another "gay/straight" split within feminism, Rubin's "Thinking Sex" essay should be seen as the opening round in a still ongoing legitimation crisis over sexuality that parallels the one over race in political and theoretical importance.

## BREAKING UP THE IMPASSE: THE SEX WARS AND POSTMODERN LESBIANISM

So far I've emphasized loss and rupture. Did the sex wars have nothing but disturbing effects? Must feminists and lesbians still take sides? By the mid to late 1980s, feminist theorists began to rethink the sex wars. By then, some of the heat had gone out of the conflict. Theorists took two major steps in working out what the sex wars signified for feminist theory and practice: they began to probe the conflict's underlying theoretical and political dynamic and they began to question what goes on when feminists play "sex cops" versus "sex criminals."

In 1986, lesbian film theorist Ruby Rich provided ways of breaking up the impasse around discussion of the sex wars, a descriptive phrase she herself coined (528). In her astute review essay of the most controversial texts, Ruby Rich wrote a new narrative about what had happened. Displaying a remarkable generosity of spirit toward all the combatants, she hoped her essay would allow interested readers to understand the trajectory of the sex wars so that new patterns might emerge and healing could begin in the troubled relationship between feminism and lesbianism.

Perhaps her wisest counsel was "we would do well not to make outlaws of each other" (549). Rich linked the tendency to insist that all feminists take sides in the sex wars, that they be "pro-sex" or "anti-sex," to earlier rifts in feminism over acceptable and unacceptable notions of romance and romanticism (548). Though historically feminism has been critical of romantic attitudes toward women, sex, and sexuality, romanticisms of various sorts have never been entirely suppressed. By means of this insight, Ruby Rich linked two apparently very different models for lesbian life: the romantic friendship model that prevailed among middle-class White women before the Freudian era, and the butch-femme model that organized erotic life among White and Black working-class lesbians in the period before Stonewall (pre-1969) as differing ways of expressing similar deep desires for romance.

By relating the sex wars to previous feminist struggles, especially earlier gay/straight splits, Ruby Rich provided a historical frame that allows readers to understand why sexuality, especially as inflected by race and racism, became an intense site of struggle in the 1980s.[4] Ruby Rich deconstructs the sex wars; that is, she asks what was missing, undone, or displaced in the feminist and lesbian books that were at the centre of the controversy. By proceeding this way, Rich was able to see patterns where other writers had seen only catfights or conspiracies and hence had gotten caught up in the awarding of praise or blame. Rich's analysis of the sex wars broke new ground and thereby enabled the writing of even more original and provocative analyses by Katie King (1986, 1990), Teresa de Lauretis (1990), and Julia Creet (1991).[5]

The most important omissions from discussion in the sex wars, according to Ruby Rich, were race, racism, class differences, homophobia, and a sense of humour! In the books and articles that were the focus of the controversy, even sex itself, sexual behaviour and practices, failed to get the attention paid to "sexuality," the abstract, generalized discursive production. Ruby Rich perceptively notices that, in each of these, a binary opposition is operating. That is, the frame in which the sex wars are understood makes one term seem more valuable or correct than the other which is accordingly seen as lesser in intellectual or moral value. As long as binary thinking limits the ways in which sexuality is theorized, then polarized positions will be taken up, feminists will occupy them, and all the participants will be stuck at a theoretical and political impasse.

By 1980, the anti-porn cultural feminists had taken the high moral ground by defending an earlier radical feminist and lesbian/feminist vision. This writing was at once politically engaged and intellectually accessible (Lederer 1980; Linden, Pagano, Russell, and Star 1982). Key sites for disseminating this point of view were women's studies programs and feminist scholarship. By contrast, the so-called pro-sex materialist feminists took up the theoretical vanguard position.

Lesbians and feminists could weather the increasing political and cultural repression of the 1980s by producing theoretically exciting books and articles. Rather than aiming their writing at the grassroots or the undergraduate Women's Studies classroom, they addressed their work primarily to other oppositional intellectuals, many of whom were doing feminist work in literary and cultural theory and the emerging field of lesbian and gay studies.

In terms of this binary opposition, cultural feminism was the past—feminism's old-time religion; post modern feminism/lesbianism was the future—feminism's new kid on the block. Feminist lesbian academics such as Catharine Stimpson explained how postmodern feminists and the sex wars broke up the American feminist cultural and political consensus on the nature and meaning of representation, particularly representations of female sexuality (1988: 179-196). Like Ruby Rich, Stimpson argues that the fights over sex are better understood as displaced disagreements over other issues. Rich believed they were disputes over romanticism; Stimpson claims they concerned representation. For both, sex is the pretext, the catalyst, for something larger or deeper that deepens the divisions among feminists and creates new positions that in turn require more complex taxonomies.

Stimpson locates the emergence of a new feminist subculture at an earlier and less controversial Barnard conference on the Scholar and the Feminist that predates the sex wars, the 1979 session on "The Future of Difference." What Stimpson terms "feminist postmodernism" (and she may have been the first to use the phrase) is a mix of "revisionary psychoanalysis, European post-structuralism, and feminism" (189). As a result, feminists had to choose: pure but old-fashioned, or trendy but difficult? In some senses, the sex wars became the text wars. If you didn't keep up with your reading, you couldn't play.[6]

Postmodern feminist lesbians, numerically a minority among North American feminists and lesbians, have become the theoretical élite. As much as their writing initially removed the heat from the sex wars, it also tended to keep them going by relocating them to another location, to the places where "high theory" is produced—élite universities and their academic journals, presses, and conferences. This location has meant a shift in terms of who produces feminist and lesbian theorizations of sexuality and who reads them.

The most celebrated of the theorists of lesbian sexuality since the sex wars, such as Judith Butler and Teresa de Lauretis, have tended to be cultural critics or philosophers rather than historians, psychologists, or social scientists and so questions about the difficulty of their writing and its "accessibility" have been complexly interwoven with questions about race, class, and political accountability. Ruby Rich noticed the process by which certain kinds of writing—theoretical texts written by "certified theorists" who were largely middle-class White women—had come to control what was theorized in the debate over sexuality and had relegated fictional as well as other historical, ethnographic, and autobiographical writing to an alternative theoretical economy (550-1).

Though Ruby Rich's remarks were made with respect to the American context, they apply very well to the way lesbian theorizing by francophones and by women of colour has been marginalized in Canada. With respect to the Canadian context, the unvoiced question as to what counts as a theory has great relevance. In fact, the way this chapter is structured offers an implicit answer. Writing by women of colour is often treated as "experiential" rather than as "theoretical" (Silvera 1991). Lesbians in Quebec who tend to use writing modes other than the formal academic essay are largely unread in English Canada. While Québécoise lesbian fiction/theorist and poet Nicole Brossard is the most widely known of "Canadian" feminist lesbian theorists outside the country, her writing is not often cited as "theory" in Canadian lesbian and feminist scholarship (Brossard 1988, 1991).

## POSTMODERN LESBIANISM AND "QUEER THEORY"

Though recent lesbian theorists agree that it is crucial for feminists to deconstruct binary models of female sexuality, they differ in the ways they relate lesbianism and other sexual minorities to feminism, in the degrees to which their work is enabled by feminist thought, and on whether their emphasis falls more on the intellectual or political effects of binary thinking on feminists and lesbians. For example, though they generally agree that binary thinking fuelled the sex wars and kept feminists at an impasse, some believe that out of the impasse over these debates came a more complex way of imagining sexual differences, such as the proliferation of sexualities beyond the simple "gay/straight" split (King 1990: 82-101). Katie King suggests that

> Situationally other differences that cannot be imagined as opposites may be as salient or more salient: race, class, nationality, language, religion, ability. All suggest that sexualities are too plural, too politically granulated to be named in a gay/straight division, as women have too many genders, sexes to be seen simply across such a "gay/straight" divide; indeed, any such centering of a gay/straight divide is in itself deeply divisive: mystifying the power dynamics feminists play with each other, and our accountabilities to each other. (83)

King's suggestion provides a point of entry for understanding what I am calling postmodern lesbian theory, especially with respect to how lesbianism and sexuality in general have been theorized in the emerging disciplines of lesbian (and gay) studies and in so-called "queer theory." Though what to call this theoretical enterprise is itself controversial, there is no doubt that lesbian theorists such as Teresa de Lauretis and Judith Butler are among its originators, along with the non-lesbian, Eve Kosofsky Sedgwick. Though their work uses feminist, poststructuralist and psychoanalytic analyses, they differ on whether theorizing lesbianism is central to their project and in how relevant feminism is to it.

Eve Kosofsky Sedgwick is the most celebrated and controversial of all queer theorists, perhaps because she argues in her book, *Epistemology of the Closet* (1990), that the binary opposition "homosexual/heterosexual" is central to every other important binary relation of knowledge and ignorance in Western twentieth century culture (11). Because her analysis is more focused on sexuality than on gender, Sedgwick calls it "antihomophobic" and indicates that it should not be taken as coextensive with feminism (27).[7]

Sedgwick rejects what she calls the minoritizing view of homosexuality (that lesbian and gay issues are of interest only to a minority) in favour of a universalizing view (that the production of the category of the homosexual minority is interesting to everybody because it constructs and normalizes the heterosexual majority, which would not make sense without it). Sedgwick thus prefers to identify herself as a queer or a pervert (1, 9, 59). By making queerness a theoretical perspective that is open to anyone regardless of her sexual experience or identity, she seems to have found a way of transcending the gay/straight splits within feminism. Sedgwick's writing has received much critical attention and has for many readers a great appeal because she rejects the boundary-keeping preoccupations and "normalizing/deviantizing" discourses that have driven feminist as well as most earlier lesbian and gay theory.

Judith Butler's book, *Gender Trouble: Feminism and the Subversion of Identity* (1990), has played a similar role in "queering" and querying the identity of lesbian and gay studies. Butler argues that constructing lesbianism as the vanguard position of feminism is a mistake that actually reinforces compulsory heterosexuality. Lesbian theorizing based on essentialist notions of identity is nothing more than a theoretically naive and politically disastrous reverse discourse. Butler solves the problems created for lesbian theorists by the binary oppositions of sex and gender by "denaturalizing" gendered and sexed identities and encouraging them to be seen as performances (128). Queer theorists can further subvert identities through the exploration of practices such as drag, butch-femme roles, cross-dressing, transsexuality, and the proliferation of erotic minorities, performed as self-conscious and voluntary parodies (137-141).[8]

By comparison with Butler and Sedgwick, Teresa de Lauretis, in her writing, offers a more materialist as well as lesbian approach to what has variously been called lesbian and gay studies or queer theory. Like them, de Lauretis deconstructs the binary "heterosexual/homosexual," but, unlike them, she connects the historic marginalization of lesbians from Women's Studies with the current possibility that lesbians will be the silent partner in the new enterprise of (lesbian and) gay studies. In essays about lesbian and feminist subjectivity and representation, de Lauretis has done more than any other feminist or lesbian theorist to break out of the theoretical paralysis induced and marked by either/or thinking—study sexuality or study gender; do antihomophobic or feminist analysis (1990, 1991).

Unlike Butler and Sedgwick, de Lauretis is concerned about what is missing, undone, or displaced from lesbian and gay studies, especially from what has been called "Queer Theory," a term she herself coined in 1991 but now rejects as politically problematic (1991, xvii).[9] Attentive to the politics of naming, de Lauretis chose "queer" because she thought it would be more inclusive than "the by now established and often convenient formula" "lesbian and gay" (iv). In discussing why she re-appropriated the previously hateful epithet, "queer," de Lauretis concisely mapped the development of lesbian and gay studies to date. Explaining the significance of shifts in the nomenclature of deviance from the medicinally flavoured "homosexual/ity" in the titles of books written in the '70s to the more positively affirming "gay," to the more inclusive "gay and lesbian," and then to the pro-feminist sequencing "lesbian and gay," de Lauretis observes that the whole range conceals the differences in power between the much more visible, moneyed, and older (White) gay male culture and its "others" (iv-vi).

De Lauretis therefore addressed the definitional tasks confronting the emergent field of lesbian and gay studies without denying their political urgency. She hoped that queer theory would produce a paradigm shift in the study of the intersection of the construction of gender and sexuality, "another way of thinking the sexual" (iv). She defines lesbian and gay sexualities as "an agency of social process whose mode of functioning is both interactive and yet resistant, both participatory and yet distinct, claiming at once equality and difference, demanding political representation while insisting on its material and cultural specificity" (iii). Unlike the other major queer theorists, de Lauretis refuses to ignore or displace feminist and lesbian perspectives on sexual representation.

Unlike Butler and Sedgwick, de Lauretis made it explicit that queer theory needs to be written both with and against the institutionalization, the accomplishments and the failures of other minority discourses, most obviously Women's Studies, but also African-American and other ethnic studies. Having learned from feminism's mistakes, de Lauretis seems to have recognized that queer theorizing has a responsibility to be both more attentive to its internal contradictions and more conscientious about not repeating the exclusionary practices of more established minority studies. De Lauretis insists that it is urgent that queer theorists not only interpret lesbian and gay cultures but talk back about the constructed silences in them (1991: 35, 38).

## CONCLUSION

Since the 1970s, the developing discourses of feminist and lesbian theory in English have run in parallel with each other, coming together in classic texts such as Adrienne Rich's "Compulsory Heterosexuality and Lesbian Existence" and pulling apart first during the sex wars of the early 1980s and then again with the rise of lesbian and gay studies in the late 1980s. As the sex wars within feminism made clear, feminist theorists have produced an impressive theory of gender oppression but have yet to devise an adequate theory of female sexuality. As a result, there has been no general agreement on the relation of feminism to lesbianism or to other sexual minorities. Many lesbians have insisted on a much more highly sexualized personal and theoretical presence since the sex wars. That, and continuing heterosexism within feminism, have led to another round of gay/straight splits in North America. Though the consequences of the sex wars at first seemed merely negative, another indication of feminism's failure to deal with differences among women in the mid to late 1980s, some lesbians broke out of the theoretical impasse by formulating a new way of relating lesbianism to feminism that refuses to centre or naturalize either discourse. This new theoretical approach could be called "postmodern feminist lesbianism." As with other postmodernisms, it is an eclectic mix of the old and the new, high theory and popular culture. The reappearance of older lesbian cultural expressions, such as butch-femme roles, usually as a parodic performance, is an example of postmodern lesbianism. Postmodern feminist lesbian theorists such as Judith Butler and Teresa de Lauretis have played a key role in the development of what is variously referred to as lesbian and gay studies or queer theory. It is theoretically exciting and politically engaged, connects the analysis of sexism with heterosexism and resists the marginalization of lesbians in feminist scholarship.

## NOTES

1   For example, Elaine Marks acknowledges that what she called the "Sappho model" of women's same-sex relationships in her 1979 article, "Lesbian Intertextuality," has been used since the ancient Greek poet's time mainly by and for men (353-371). The Sappho model has been used for purposes that are sometimes pornographic, apologetic, or lyrical, depending not only on genre, but on how each reader reads them, which Marks insists is inevitably contradictory and ultimately political.

2   So far, the most complete introduction to this subject is *Heterosexuality: A Feminism and Psychology Reader*, compiled in 1993 by British feminists Sue Wilkinson and Celia Kitzinger.

3   For more information on how feminists have considered the relationship between feminism and postmodernism, see Linda J. Nicholson's anthology, *Feminism/Postmodernism*.

4   For a very different view of how to do this, see Sheila Jeffreys' *Anticlimax: A Feminist Perspective on the Sexual Revolution* (1989). Jeffreys argues throughout her book that the sex wars were an American import, an attack on feminism on the part of lesbian sex radicals who were hoodwinked by discourse theorists and gay men into trying to destroy the movement.

5  Creet, a Canadian theorist who is a student of de Lauretis's, constructed an elegant psychoanalytic analysis of the role of fantasy in lesbian s/m fiction by expanding on an observation of Ruby Rich's. Rich had suggested that for the lesbian sex radicals, the debate over whether lesbian sadomasochism was feminist constituted a daughter's rebellion against feminism as symbolic and repressive mother (Rich 1986: 529; Creet 1991: 135-159).

6  For one of the most concise treatments of what the discursive and disciplinary shift required and what its political consequences have been for feminism, Stimpson quotes the art critic Lisa Tickner:

It was psychoanalysis that permitted an understanding of the psycho-social construc-tions of sexual differences in the conscious/unconscious subject. The result was a shift in emphasis from equal rights struggles in the sexual division of labor and a cultural feminism founded on the reevaluation of an existing biological or social femininity to a recognition of the processes of sexual *differentiation*, the instability of gender posi-tions, and the hopelessness of excavating a free or original femininity beneath the layers of patriarchal oppression. (189-190)

7  Sedgwick's discussion of feminist theory is casual and out of date, relegated mainly to footnotes. Lesbian theory is treated as a subdivision of gay theory and is regarded as relevant to her project only to the degree that it separates gender from sexuality and links lesbian concerns with those of gay males. (33, 37, 39)

8  Unfortunately, Butler, like Sedgwick and another "queer" theorist, Diana Fuss, author of *Essentially Speaking: Feminism, Nature and Difference* (1989) and editor of one of the most important anthologies in lesbian and gay studies, *inside/out: Lesbian Theories, Gay Theories* (1991), are all rather uninterested in most contemporary contributors to the development of lesbian theory. In her first book, Fuss claims that the major problem of lesbian theory is its failure to theorize male homosexuality; she is silent about the work of most lesbian theorists and under that heading names lesbian activists and cre-ative writers, rather than academics and scholars (100, 111).

9  In her introduction, de Lauretis explains that she was inspired to call this theorizing "queer" in reference to a New York conference she participated in 1989 entitled "How Do I Look? Queer Film and Video," rather than by the political action group, Queer Nation (xvii).

## BIBLIOGRAPHY

Adams, Mary Louise; Lenskyj, Helen; Masters, Philinda; and Randall, Melanie. "Confronting Heterosexuality." *Resources for Feminist Research/Documentation sur la recherche féministe* 19 (3 & 4), 1990.

Brossard, Nicole. *The Aerial Letter*. Translated by Marlene Wideman. Toronto: The Women's Press, 1988.

Brossard, Nicole. *Picture Theory*. Translated by Barbara Godard. Montreal: Guernica, 1991.

Brown, Judith C. "Lesbian Sexuality in Medieval and Early Modern Europe." In *Hidden From History: Reclaiming the Lesbian and Gay Past*, edited by Martin Bauml Duberman, Martha Vicinus, and George Chauncey, Jr. New York: New American Library: 67-75, 1989.

Burstyn, Varda. *Women Against Censorship*. Toronto: Douglas & McIntyre, 1985.

Butler, Judith. *Gender Trouble: Feminism and the Subversion of Identity*. New York: Routledge, 1990.

Case, Sue-Ellen. "Towards a Butch-Femme Aesthetic." *Discourse* 11 (1): 55-73, 1988-89.

Case, Sue-Ellen. *Performing Feminisms: Feminist Critical Theory and Theatre*. Baltimore: Johns Hopkins, 1990.

Creet, Julia. "Daughter of the Movement: The Psychodynamics of Lesbian S/M Fantasy." In *differences*: 135-159, 1991.

de Lauretis, Teresa. "Queer Theory: Lesbian and Gay Sexualities: An Introduction." In *differences* 3 (2):iii-xviii, 1991.

de Lauretis, Teresa. "Sexual Indifference and Lesbian Representation." In Case 17-39, 1990.

de Lauretis, Teresa. "Upping the Anti [*sic*] in Feminist Theory." *In Conflicts in Feminism*, edited by Marianne Hirsch and Evelyn Fox Keller, 255-270. New York: Routledge, 1990.

Faderman, Lillian. *"Odd Girls and Twilight Lovers: A History of Lesbian Life in Twentieth-Century America*. New York: Columbia, 1991.

Faderman, Lillian. *Surpassing the Love of Men: Romantic Friendship and Love Between Women from the Renaissance to the Present*. New York: William Morrow, 1981.

Ferguson, Ann; Zita, Jacquelyn N.; and Addelson, Kathryn Pyne. "On 'Compulsory Heterosexuality and Lesbian Existence': Defining the Issues." "Patriarchy, Sexual Identity, and the Sexual Revolution." *Signs* 7 (1): 158-199, 1981.

Foucault, Michel. *The History of Sexuality: An Introduction*. Translated by Robert Hurley. Vol. 1. New York: Vintage, 1980.

Frye, Marilyn. "Lesbian 'Sex.'" In *Lesbian Philosophies and Cultures*, edited by Jeffner Allen. Albany: State University of New York Press: 305-315, 1990.

Fuss, Diana. *Essentially Speaking: Feminism, Nature and Difference*. New York: Routledge, 1989.

Fuss, Diana. *inside/out: Lesbian Theories, Gay Theories*. New York: Routledge, 1991.

Grahn, Judy. *Another Mother Tongue: Gay Words, Gay Worlds*. Boston: Beacon, 1984.

Jeffreys, Sheila. *Anticlimax: A Feminist Perspective on the Sexual Revolution*. London: The Women's Press, 1990.

Kennedy, Elizabeth Lapovsky and Davis, Madeline D. *Boots of Leather, Slippers of Gold: The History of a Lesbian Community*. New York: Routledge, 1993.

King, Katie. "Producing Sex, Theory, and Culture: Gay/Straight Remappings in Contemporary Feminism." In *Conflicts in Feminism*: 82-101, 1990.

King, Katie. "The situation of lesbianism as feminism's magical sign: Contests for meaning and the U.S. women's movement, 1968-1972." *Communications* (9): 65-91, 1986.

Lederer, Laura. *Take Back the Night: Women on Pornography*. Toronto: Bantam, 1980.

Linden, Robin Ruth; Pagano, Darlene R.; Russell, Diana E.H.; and Star, Susan Leigh. *Against Sadomasochism: A Radical Feminist Analysis*. East Palo Alto, CA: Frog in the Well Press, 1982.

Marks, Elaine. "Lesbian Intertextuality." In *Homosexualities and French Literature*, edited by George Stambolian and Elaine Marks. Ithaca, New York: Cornell University, 1979.

Martindale, Kathleen. "Addressing Heterosexism in the Women's Studies Classroom." In *A Reader in Feminist Ethics*, edited by Debra Shogan. Toronto: Canadian Scholars Press, 449-65, 1992.

Martindale, Kathleen. "Articulating the Difficulties in Teaching/Learning Feminist Critical Theory." *Radical Teacher* 39: 9-14, 1991.

Nestle, Joan. *A Restricted Country*. Ithaca, New York: Firebrand, 1987.

Nicholson, Linda L., editor. *Feminism/Postmodernism*. New York: Routledge, 1990.

Omosupe, Ekua. "Black/Lesbian/Bulldagger." In *differences*. 101-111, 1991.

Penelope, Julia. "A case of mistaken identity." Review of Shane Phelan, *Identity Politics: Lesbian Feminism and the Limits of Community. Women's Review of Books*. vii (7): 11, 1990.

Raymond, Janice G. "Putting the Politics Back Into Lesbianism." *Women's Studies International Forum* 12 (2): 149-156, 1989.

Rich, Adrienne. "Foreword." In *Blood, Bread, and Poetry: Selected Prose, 1979-1985*. New York: W.W. Norton, 23-26, 1986.

Rich, Adrienne. "Compulsory Heterosexuality and Lesbian Existence." *Signs*. V. 631-660, 1980.

Rich, B. Ruby. "Feminism and Sexuality in the 1980s." *Feminist Studies* 12 (3): 525-61, 1986.

Riley, Denise. *Am I That Name? Feminism and the Category of "Women" in History*. Minneapolis: University of Minnesota Press, 1988.

Rubin, Gayle. "Thinking Sex: Notes for a Radical Theory of Sexuality." In *Pleasure and Danger: Exploring Female Sexuality*, edited by Carole S. Vance. New York: Routledge, 267-319, 1984.

Rubin, Gayle. "The Traffic in Women." In *Toward an Anthropology of Women*, edited by Rayna Reiter. New York: Monthly Review Press, 197-210, 1979.

Sedgwick, Eve Kosofsky. *Epistemology of the Closet*. Berkeley: University of California, 1990.

Silvera, Makeda. Ed. *Piece of My Heart*. Toronto: Sister Vision Press, 1991.

Snitow, Ann; Stansell, Christine; and Thompson, Sharon. "Introduction" to *Powers of Desire: The Politics of Sexuality*, edited by Snitow, Stansell and Thompson. New York: Monthly Review Press, 1983.

Stimpson, Catharine R. "Nancy Reagan Wears a Hat: Feminism and Its Cultural Consensus." In *Where the Meanings Are: Feminism and Cultural Spaces*. New York: Methuen, 179-196, 1988.

Valverde, Mariana. *Sex, Power and Pleasure*. Toronto: The Women's Press, 1985.

Warner, Michael. "Fear of a queer planet." *Social Text* 29: 3-17, 1991.

Weeks, Jeffrey. *Sexuality and Its Discontents*. New York: Routledge, 1985.

Wilkinson, Sue and Kitzinger, Celia. *Heterosexuality: A Feminism and Psychology* Reader. London: Sage Publications, 1993.

Wilson, Elizabeth. "Forbidden Love." In *Hidden Agendas: Theory, Politics, and Experience in the Women's Movement*. London: Tavistock, 1986.

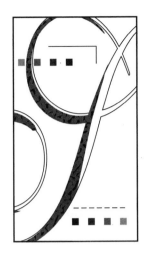

# PART 2

# WOMEN'S EXPERIENCES: ENGENDERING DIVERSITY

# AGING WOMEN AND STANDARDS OF BEAUTY

*Sharon McIrvin Abu-Laban and Susan A. McDaniel*

*Levity in words, and much more in actions, is unsuitable and a shame to them, considering their age, and stains their glory,...if aged women dress themselves like young girls, it exposeth them to reproach and contempt.*

> *A colonial American admonition quoted in Fisher, D.H.,*
> Growing Old in America, *New York: Oxford, 1978.*

## INTRODUCTION

In many ways, elders are devalued in our society, and older women are particularly disadvantaged. Aging has long been seen as a women's issue (Sommers 1976; Abu-Laban and Abu-Laban 1977; McDaniel 1988b, 1989a, 1989b; Posner 1977) and, compared to other research areas in the social sciences, from its beginning aging has had an unusual proportion of women researchers (Abu-Laban 1981). Several factors, including discrimination against aging women, as well as the caregiving responsibilities that fall to women with aged relatives (Kaden and McDaniel 1990; McDaniel 1992a; 1993b; McDaniel and McKinnon 1993), suggest ample reason for the centrality of women in age-related issues. Given this, researchers have pointed out that aging is a profoundly *feminist* issue (Russell 1987; McDaniel 1988b).

Women live longer than men, they live longer in disability and poverty, and they have to live out their last years marked by the demeaning labels given to older women. Gender and gender inequalities matter to aging, both societally and individually. How aging is interpreted and analyzed is also a feminist issue. It makes a difference whether gender inequities among the aged are seen in terms of accumulated injustices or as social problems resulting from women's greater longevity. Policies and public perceptions of what is socially problematic are filtered through the lenses of social analysts. Hence, the subordination of women that is aggravated in older age, the institutionalization of women's inequality, and the dominant patriarchal ideologies that support this need to be examined, questioned, and challenged.

Women are said to be older sooner than men. While aging is seen as empowering for many men, it is not seen to be so for women. *His* facial lines are seen as signs of character; *her* lines are signs of decrepitude and decreasing sexual attractiveness. In men, power in itself is thought to be sexually appealing, while in women, appearance is considered the *sine qua non*. Power can enhance women's appeal, but it is seldom sufficient in itself to establish that appeal. Appearance, in women, often is. This is the reason public figures such as Henry Kissinger and Ronald Reagan can be judged attractive or sexy as they age (as one U.S. poll reported), whereas playwright Lillian Hellman and Eleanor Roosevelt were not seen to be attractive as they aged and gained in influence and power. Oscar Wilde suggested, in a less than flattering statement both about women and society's expectations of them, that "A man's face is his autobiography; a woman's, her greatest work of fiction." For aging women, a lifetime of living under patriarchal structures is reflected in their day-to-day lives in older age, as well as in their relationship with their own bodies. This chapter examines the social and demographic characteristics of Canadian women in older age, gender-linked age inequities, and, given the stark reality of biological aging, the incremental effect of our cultural emphasis on female appearance.

## BRIEF HISTORICAL BACKDROP

It is often thought that the devaluing of women as they age is a relatively recent phenomenon that developed as a result of increases in life expectancy, particularly among women, and a youth-oriented culture. Although longevity has indeed increased, and there has been more attention paid to youth over the last 30 years, a number of myths about aging women and their families have led to a sentimental view of past family life. Most important among these is the myth of the large, caring families who lived together in large households, and had respect for their elders. Nett (1981) points out that

> ...contrary to the implication, past households, although notably different in some respects from present ones, appear to have been for the most part two-generational, not much larger than current ones with members sharing small

and somewhat crowded dwellings for all but the wealthy, not entirely economically self-sufficient, and experiencing frequent change of members and locale. (Nett 1981:248)

What, then, occurred with the older generation, if most families lived in two-generation households? Shorter life expectancy meant, of course, that fewer lived to see their grandchildren. Women's greater longevity, even then, often meant that women "outlived their usefulness," preventing adult sons from taking over the family farm. This frequent occurrence could result in a number of scenarios: mother becoming a boarder or tenant farmer on her own land, mother moving away to live with servants or as a servant (depending on her circumstances), or, in dire situations, aging mothers being turned away from the family farm and becoming the first of Canada's homeless. In each of these scenarios, the aging woman was treated with less than the mythical respect for elders.

Morton (1992), in a study of single mothers in working-class Halifax in the 1920s, finds that the vast majority of single-parent households at that time were headed by widows. This is also found by Bradbury in her study of nineteenth century Montreal (1989). The social concern was for the widow's "moral vulnerability, as sexually active women who now lived outside marriage and male supervision" (Morton 1992:92). Widows were seen as attractive and their virtue needed to be guarded through constant surveillance by neighbours. The Mother's Allowance Act of 1930 agreed to assist only those "who were in every respect a fit, proper, and suitable person to have the custody and care of her children" (Morton 1992:101). Thus, sexual impropriety, or its appearance, mattered greatly not only to the social standing of the widow but also to her material well-being. Morton reports the case of Emma Lawson, who, when her neighbours observed a man leaving her house late in the evening, had her mother's allowance suspended. Another widow, Lillian Kennedy, had her allowance permanently discontinued after an illegitimate birth, "her immoral behaviour reinforced by the fact that she had taken in boarders of 'undesirable character'" (Morton 1992:101).

Essentially, there is no clear relation between modernization (the so-called progress of time) and a degeneration in the status of older women. It is a myth that the past was the pinnacle of good treatment of older women and that we have slid downwards ever since. It is possible that in the past, older people were consistently regarded with respect only among the upper classes. If this is so, then older women today may not be treated as differently from their grandmothers and great-grandmothers as we tend to think. One parallel between older women in the past and those of today is that they tend to be valued more for their utility as mothers, wives, or potential sexual partners than for what they were, or are, as individuals (de Beauvoir 1970).

## AGING AND WOMEN'S DIFFERENTIAL LIFE EXPERIENCES

Aging is a profoundly different experience for women than for men, with much of the difference having more to do with the structural realities of women's lives than with individual differences or preferences. To understand why this is so, two factors should be explored. The first is the cause of population or demographic aging, which is the unintended result, not of increased life expectancy as is often thought, but of declining birth rates. As fewer and fewer young people enter a population, the average or mean age of that population tends to increase, even with no changes in life expectancy. But if life expectancy also increases, then the mean age of the population will increase at an even faster rate. In Canada over the past two decades, there has been a precipitous decline in the birth rate, so precipitous that it has been termed a "baby bust," compared to the baby boom of the late 1940s to the early 1960s. It is the decline in the birth rate that is the most important factor in the aging of Canada's population. For a more detailed explanation of population aging, see McDaniel (1986). Birth rates have declined largely as a result of changes in women's lives, particularly their dramatically increased labour force participation. This is another factor that makes population aging particularly a women's issue.

Second, women's experiences with the process of aging are different simply because women tend to outlive men. Any older population, such as that of North America, Europe, or Japan, will have many more women than men. This is particularly true at the older ages, where women outlive men by a considerable number of years. In Canada at present, there are twice as many women as men in the 85+ age group (McDaniel 1986:109). This ratio is actually increasing somewhat as greater gains are made in increasing life expectancy at age 85 and above. Old men are truly hard to find!

The life experiences of women as they age are shaped by their greater longevity for several reasons. For one thing, women, who still tend to marry men about two years older than they, can expect to be widowed, given the differential life expectancies of men and women. Even in early old age, at age 65-69 for example, less than 20 percent of men are widowers while almost one-half of women are (McDaniel 1988b). By age 80-84, over 80 percent of women are widowed while about 38 percent of men are. This large and significant difference has numerous ramifications in the lives of older women.

Women, as they become middle-aged and older, have much greater likelihood of experiencing the most traumatic of life's losses, the death of a spouse. In today's world, this often means that the spouse has died of a chronic illness after being sick over some extended period of time, perhaps with the woman acting as central caregiver (McDaniel 1989a; 1992b). The death of the spouse thus often entails loss of one's recent role in life and whatever prestige that involved as well as one's spouse. Marriage is more than an emotional bond: it is an economic union. After the death of her husband, a widow sometimes finds her standard of living reduced. This is true largely because many private pensions in Canada do not have any survivor's provisions. This was the case in approximately 78 percent of private pensions in Canada in the mid-1980s (McDaniel 1986), although this figure has now been somewhat reduced. The increase in survivor's benefits in private pensions has been countered, however, by a tendency at present for working people with benefits packages, still differentially men, to bargain away survivor's benefits for job security or better wage settlements. Many widows are not aware until after the spouse's death that they are limited in their pension entitlements. Women who live common-law, are single, or divorced, are often ineligible for any survivor's pensions at all. Women's greater longevity has other consequences too. Women who outlive their spouses and suffer grief at the death tend to be more prone to physical and mental illnesses. Together with their changed living arrangements as widows, these illnesses often cause family members to intervene. Older widows lose autonomy and independence much more often than married women or women who live on their own. The longer women live, the greater the likelihood that they will be institutionalized, either for health reasons (the longer one lives, the stronger the probability of failing health) or for social reasons (no one at home to help them out with activities of daily living). It has been estimated that more older women in Canada may be institutionalized for social reasons than for health reasons (Novak 1988:234).

Pensions structure women's experiences with aging differently than men's too. Those women who are entitled to anything more than Canada/Quebec Pensions or Old Age Security (Gee and McDaniel 1992: McDaniel and Gee 1993)—not a large proportion in any case because of the kinds of discontinuous work experiences that many women have—find that on retirement their pensions are often pro-rated for their greater longevity: the same sum in pension funds means less per month or year for a woman than for a man so that the pension might last to the estimated end of the woman's life. Pensions for women are not user-friendly. The presumption in many pension schemes is that women are not sole supporters of themselves and others but rather that they are spouses of someone with access to pension benefits, a presumption that simply is not borne out for many women. It is not surprising then that poverty among women in their older years, as for women of any age, is more common than among men. Women comprise 60 percent of all poor people in Canada, 70 percent of all poor people over age 65, and 83 percent of all poor unattached over age 65 (McDaniel 1988b). For aging women, poverty is a common experience indeed.

Mainstream literature on women and aging relies on assumptions that women's lives involve marriage, children, and men as well as happy family situations in both family of origin and family of choice. The many references to widowhood, caregiving by adult children, and family supports in the literature on aging suggest that women's lives are perhaps more homogenous than they, in fact, are. Unmarried women and women who have lived in non-traditional family lives have received very little research attention.

## ASSUMPTIONS AND PRESUMPTIONS ABOUT AGING WOMEN

The preoccupation in research literature on social support, particularly family support, has led, until very recently, to the presumption that families of older women exist and are in sufficiently close proximity to help out and that their support is positive and welcome. McDaniel and Gee (1993) make the point that current initiatives for changes in social policy in Canada often start with these presumptions. For example, much of the reasoning in regard to recent reductions in hospital stays and in funds for chronic care and recuperation facilities is based on the presumption that discharged hospital patients will have someone at home to care for them. Often this is not true, for any number of reasons. Family mobility and immigration is one factor. Others, often overlooked, include the fact that not all families are happy families, willing and able to care for aging parents. Much is known about family violence and other negative aspects of family interactions, yet when aging is discussed, too often these realities are forgotten as questions are asked about contact with adult children, the assumption being that this contact is good, welcome, and helpful. It well may not be for many older women. More older women are divorced or separated. These women may rely on non-relatives, ex-relatives or extended families for help and support, or may have few resources on which to call for help. Much more needs to be known and understood about the heterogeneity of women's experience with aging.

Another factor to consider is that in the mainstream aging literature, heterosexuality is the prevailing assumption. The experiences of aging lesbian women have been largely ignored. More attention has been devoted to visible minorities, such as ethnic groups and their experiences with aging, but even that attention has been acknowledged to be very scant indeed (Driedger and Chappell 1987).

The invisibility of lesbian women generally, and aging lesbian women in particular, works in contradictory ways both to conceal lesbians' experiences with aging and to reinforce prevalent stereotypes about lesbians. Concealment means that almost nothing is known about whether and how lesbian aging experiences differ from those of heterosexuals (Lee 1987). Stereotypical beliefs about lesbians and aging can prevail in the absence of evidence to the contrary. Heterosexist bias and homophobia work together to instil in lesbians a fear of discovery and subsequent persecution. The silence that is a result of their fear helps to reinforce the stereotypes about lesbians and seals the double standard.

In sociological literature, it often happens that lesbian experience is subsumed under public gay male subcultures. Berger's (1982) conclusion that lesbians are absent from public institutions of the gay culture—such as bars, nightclubs, and bathhouses—and therefore unavailable for sociological analysis, excludes lesbians of all ages, but older lesbians even more so. This is rather like stating that heterosexual women cannot be studied because they are not found in strip joints, sports bars and locker rooms. Older lesbians are overlooked not only because they do not participate in the "gay subculture" that attracts sociologists of deviance but also because they are subsumed by gerontologists under the category of aging women in general, where lesbian experiences tend to be reduced to the level of simple friendship or confidante relationships. Even the concept of a "lesbian community" tends to ghettoize lesbian experience and isolate it further from that of other women. Ethnic lesbian experiences are even more invisible.

The notion that lesbians might have better experiences with aging than heterosexual women, although not without possibilities, poses further questions. This idea rests on the premise that lesbians in their younger years have learned to cope with being society's outsiders and, in essence, have achieved a measure of crisis management that could serve them well as they age. Adaptive strategies involved in "coming out" could, in other words, be relied upon with aging. Lee (1987), however, finds no support in his study of older gays and lesbians that crisis management skills are cumulative. He suggests instead that this view is rather like "a new version of the Puritanical notion that suffering is good for you in the long run" (Lee 1987:53). His conclusion, based on life satisfaction scores of 47 gay men, is that "Sailing into a happy homosexual old age may be more a matter of steering clear of storms than of weathering them" (Lee 1987:57).

Generational conflict may be sharp and divisive among lesbians and gays because many contemporary elders who are gay or lesbian are part of the "pre-Stonewall" era,[1] when one's sexual orientation was strictly private and cautiously concealed. By contrast, for many in the post-Stonewall era, being gay or lesbian is of political and public moment. This has several important implications. One is that there are few gay role models—gay or lesbian elders or grandparents who can guide younger people on how to age well and gracefully. Another is the creation of a generation gap as older gays and lesbians react in fear and apprehension about the more public activities of younger gays and lesbians.

The post-Stonewall generation of lesbians may face another challenge. In "coming out," there is a need for the sort of crisis management discussed above that can prepare one for other crises, including the crisis of old age. On the other hand, coming out can have considerable costs too, including the loss of family

1 The Gay Liberation movement is usually said to have begun with the 1969 Stonewall Riot in New York City where gay men being rounded up by police at gay bars and bathhouses fought back. In Canada, 1981, a similar pivotal change occurred when 3,000 people protested the arrest in Toronto of 300 men as a result of police raids in gay baths.

contact and support. In later years, this can result in smaller networks on which to draw for support and aid as well as in cumulative stress. Little is known or understood about the effects that these losses of family contacts can have on elderly women, losses that do occur in the lives of many women.

## EMOTIONAL SUPPORTS

Women are socially central in a demographically aging society like Canada's, as well as structurally central. Their social roles and the expectations placed on them mean that women of all ages are more often placed in situations of looking after others (Connidis 1989; Gee and Kimball 1987; McDaniel 1989a; 1993c). In Canada, a disproportionate share of caring for the young, and old, and the poverty-stricken falls to women. Caring by women extends across the boundaries of race, ethnicity, class, sexual orientation, and (dis)ability—all but the rare woman become involved in caring for others in some way and to some degree at some point in their lives.

Caring is, of course, not something that women have a monopoly on, yet it seems that it is a defining requirement of femininity in our society (McDaniel 1992b). A caring woman is a feminine woman, embodying the madonna image of nurturing along with the self-sacrificing image of the woman who puts the needs of others, including the sexual needs of men, above her own interests and needs. Girls, as they become adult women, are socialized to care for others. Girls who do not care sufficiently are often labelled unfeminine, selfish, aggressive, or deviant, among other even less flattering labels. Learning to care, to be self-sacrificing and self-deprecating, is often the same as learning to be a good woman.

The socially sanctioned imperative to care extends well beyond adolescence. Kaden and McDaniel (1990) find in a study in Ontario that it is women (wives, daughters, and daughters-in-law, sisters, aunts, women friends) who are called upon most often to do the caring for older relatives and friends. It is also women in the paid labour force who do the caring work: day-care workers, nursing home staff, nurses generally, and others who care for the sick and disabled, often in low-paying jobs. Older people prefer to call on daughters and daughters-in-law rather than on sons or sons-in-law for needs, except financial ones.

In a national study of Canadians, McDaniel (1993a; 1993c) finds that it is usually women who are asked by both men and women for emotional support in times of stress or crisis. So reliant are older men on their spouses for emotional support that in situations where they are upset with their wife, almost one-quarter of older men report that they would have no one to call on for help. This compares with 16 percent of older women. Women tend to diversify choice of whom they might rely on for emotional support, drawing on siblings, adult children, friends, and professionals more than men do. Women of all ages, who are in positions to be asked for emotional support, may come to see themselves and be seen by others as more nurturing and caring than men. The pressures on women to continue in their caring roles, often considerable in these times of economic difficulty, have negative consequences on their well-being. Cutbacks to government programs, which differentially affect women as single parents, as health care and social services providers, and as family care providers, have further negative consequences for them. Women can burn out as a result of persistent and increasing expectations to be caring, to take on responsibility for the problems of others, and to put themselves and their own needs last. In such situations, women can develop a variety of stress-related problems that can eventually severely damage both their health and self-esteem.

## AGING WOMEN AND WELL-BEING

Much about well-being among mid-life and older women is not known, largely as a result of the inadequacy of traditional social science measures to tap into the concept. Well-being includes physical, mental, and social health and often involves more than the absence of disease or disability. Asking how satisfied people are with their lives or with specific aspects of their lives typically leads to the majority reporting few dissatisfactions. It is probably not true that everyone surveyed is happy and satisfied. It could be, in fact, that they are merely saying that compared to the wasted lives they see nightly on TV news programs, lives torn apart by war, disease, or famine, things could be worse. These results can be misleading at best.

Well-being is known to be as closely related to independence and autonomy as it is to physical health. Lack of control over one's life is well known to have adverse effects on emotional states, performance of tasks, subjective well-being, and on actual physiological indicators. Lack of control is precisely what many women experience at various stages of their lives as demands are placed on them by others, with women being seen more as mothers, wives, and daughters than as individuals with control and autonomy. No one has been assigned the role of enhancing the development and well-being of women beyond the stage of childhood. This, combined with the popularly held stereotype of women as dependent and passive social agents, means that women are often seen as lacking in control and in the benefits to well-being it offers.

Women, as they pass into old age, tend to lose more control and autonomy. Men do too, but less so. The reason is partly social: women are seen to be more social, more relational, more dependent, and more familial than men. Thus, it might be that women are seen as more needy and more likely to be diagnosed as having problems with activities of daily living than men are. This is what some have called the "Now, now dear" approach to aging women. This approach trivializes women's complaints by treating the women themselves like children.

It is also the case that women's structural circumstances make them more vulnerable to loss of control and autonomy. Women who outlive their husbands are more likely to find their lives influenced by other family members, by professionals, and by others. A couple tends to be more respected on both privacy and judgment. A long-time married couple share collective memories and can assist each other with their daily tasks. When one spouse dies, the collective memory may too, so that the remaining spouse, most often the woman, may be perceived as having lost her memory if only because she can no longer rely on her spouse for the details of the shared memories. Similarly, her physical well-being can be imperilled by the need to do tasks, possibly for the first time, that previously were done by her husband. Family members also tend to observe an aging widow more closely for signs of problems with memory or well-being, signs that all of us might show but that may not be taken with the same degree of seriousness when they appear among younger family members. One of the authors (McDaniel) conducted an experiment in a large Sociology of Aging class: she asked the students to keep track over a week's time of how often they forgot things. The results revealed that, according to the self-reports of the students, most could be potential candidates for a diagnosis of Alzheimer's! Had the students been older and emotionally vulnerable after the death of a spouse, it can easily be imagined that doubts might have been raised about their mental competency.

The cumulative weight of women's various social obligations means that women often blame themselves for "not coping," for not being well enough organized, or for not being sufficiently capable rather than simply acknowledging the social forces that impinge on them and constrain their lives. Self-censure can translate quickly into self-neglect (because we are not deserving of nurturing after all) or self-abuse (substance abuse perhaps—most often nicotine and caffeine, but sometimes prescription drugs, alcohol, and/or street drugs). Certainly, stress-related illnesses, depression, and anxiety are predictable problems for women. At the societal level, there is a potential growth not only in the feminization of social problems (inadequate mothering as the cause of crime) but in women-blaming. After all, the argument goes, women with their selfish demands got us into all these problems: too low a birth rate (which leads to population aging), work outside the home, demands for help in caring for children and older relatives, and altogether too many demands on the public purse.

In addition to the subjective aspects outlined above, several ascriptive aspects of well-being have also been identified. Women seen by gatekeepers as healthy (medical doctors, social workers, psychologists, etc.) are those who most closely fit the culturally preferred definitions of a good woman. Women who are married with children would fit the definition, White middle-class women even more so, and heterosexual women without doubt. Well-being for women, maybe particularly for aging women, is most surely obtained through this narrow definition of womanhood. Women of colour, women outside stable heterosexual relationships, and women without children are simply not often considered in prototypical definitions of well-being for women. Any definition of well-being that includes the concept of autonomy cannot be applied to all those women whose daily lives have degenerated into survival struggles with violent husbands, or to women who are so busy with their children and careers that physical (or mental) fitness is nothing but a dream, or to women who find themselves in any kind of role of subservience to others.

Social policy also has an impact on women's well-being, just as it does on their physical appearance. Compelling examples are provided of this by Gorlick and Pomfret (1993). They suggest that women on welfare, who have very limited access to non-essential health services, often find themselves, after years of raising children, with rotting teeth that have not been treated properly by routine dental care, with cheap eyeglasses that are far from flattering, and with weight problems (either obesity or emaciation) from years of trying to feed families without adequate income—leaving little for Mom to eat but pasta with a cigarette. Women, literally shaped in these instances by social policy, have limited possibilities for putting an end to their dependence on social assistance. The prospects for women of colour, Aboriginal women, women with disabilities, or lesbian women are even smaller. Aged women with out-of-date eyewear, bad teeth, overweight bodies, limited education, and whose only (or main) work experience is raising children on welfare (no matter how much credit they might deserve for creative budgeting), are not seen as good prospects for employment in a tightly competitive job market. Nor are these women seen to be developing their characters or physical attractiveness as they age.

## STANDARDS OF BEAUTY

As discussed above, women's aging differs from that of men because of the ways in which gender is constructed and inequities are defined, reinforced, and legitimated. Even though bodily changes are an expected part of human aging, they have different consequences for females compared to males. Physical appearance is a key indicator of aging and old age. Over time, one's appearance undergoes significant change and for aged women, particularly, these changes are subject to social judgments in some cases and social sanctions in others.

For the female child, to be assessed as "pretty" or "beautiful" is the highest accolade, one that usually makes her parents proud. They bask in the reflected praise and their daughter learns the lesson well. To be pretty is to be approved, liked, and rewarded. Notably, these evaluative terms that focus on the girl's facade are rarely applied to boys. Beauty is held out as an intrinsic goal for both girls and women. In infancy, females are judged by standards of "cuteness," and

"prettiness," and this shifts with age into standards of "beauty" and "glamour."
These beauty standards are societal creations, enshrined as ideals toward which
all females should strive. But, ironically, these standards of beauty are also
narrow, restrictive, and set impossible expectations for most females all of the
time, and by virtue of human aging, are impossible for all women at least some
of the time. There are major social consequences that stem from these unachiev-
able standards. Beauty norms are both prescriptive and proscriptive. They tell
women what ought to be, serve as mechanisms of social control, and are related
to women's access to economic security, social influence, health, and intimacy.
When women are reluctant to go swimming or participate in physical sport
because this would expose a body with less than prevailing standards of beauty,
when they want to stay home because of a "bad hair day" or lack of "anything
to wear" or because they've "gained too much weight," all these behaviour patterns reflect massively powerful controls over behaviour, with a proportional
impact on definitions of self and career opportunities. Appearance becomes a
measure of personal value. The socially created standards for appearance are far
from harmless decorative diversions. These standards have age, race-ethnic, economic, and sexual preference biases and, as such, they are anything but
optional. Although they present an illusion of choice, ("blue eye shadow or
green?") the "options" are both constrictive and controlling. Selected aspects of
these standards are discussed below.

## Beauty as a Constant

Beauty is often portrayed as some essential attribute that is readily apparent to
everybody. However, there can be little doubt that standards of beauty are
social and historical constructs that are linked to time and place, economics,
ethnicity, and power. This means that standards of beauty are neither constant
nor absolute. Not only do the standards change over time, but taste and judgment are always contingent upon the observer. The opulent, full-bodied figures painted by Peter Paul Rubens (1577-1640) stand in contrast to the slim
representations of women in the work of contemporary painters such as
Canadian Alex Colville or American Andrew Wyeth. Currently, as in the past,
that which is defined as feminine beauty may dramatically alter a woman's
natural appearance. While we may decry the whalebone corsets of earlier
times as "unnatural" attempts to rearrange women's bodies into an idealized
hourglass figure (some enthusiasts even removed one of their ribs to better
effect a wasp waist), this is only one example of countless attempts to rework
nature. Women's breasts, for example, have been subjected over the years to
various management strategies—brassieres are only one example. Devices to
reshape women in whatever image happens to be currently acceptable to
those with the power to define it have resulted in sometimes painful and

harmful contrivances. In some historical eras, breasts were exaggerated; in others, they were minimized. In classical Greece and Rome, female curvaceousness was "unattractive" and women wore restrictive bands to de-emphasize their breasts. Yesterday's "falsies," today's "padded bras," were first advertised in the nineteenth century during an era when the ideal woman was pictured as inordinately slender through the waist but ample and curvaceous in breasts and hips. By the 1920s, flat chests were again fashionable and again women used bands to restrict and flatten their breasts, with the goal of achieving the "boyish" figure, considered appropriate to the "flapper" look. "Push-up" padded bras were fashionable in the 1950s and today we have the yearly spectre of thousands of North American women seeking elective breast surgery in order to increase their bra size. The ways in which beauty ideals impact obviously change over time but there can be little doubt of their influences. Over a fifty-year period in this century the idealized image of women has moved from an hourglass to decidedly slimmer (Furnham, Hester and Weir 1990:744). Current efforts to surgically remove or add fat in strategic parts of the body are but a technologically upgraded version of the nineteenth century procedure to remove an "offensive" rib. Historical fluctuations in ideal size and weight are reflected as well in the average weights of Playboy centrefolds and Miss America contestants. Evidence indicates they too have become thinner over time (Smith 1990). In 1951, Miss Sweden was five feet seven inches tall and weighed 151 pounds (Garner et al. 1980). Some three decades later, in 1983, the woman selected as Miss Sweden was five foot nine (two inches taller) but she weighed a rather scant 109 pounds. Naomi Wolfe (1991:192) argues that contemporary models are some 22 to 23 percent slimmer than the average woman. The manifold historical variations in definitions of beauty suggest beauty is far from a constant.

## Beauty as Youth

Female children learn to worry about their appearance from an early age. Parents of newborn girls treat their babies differently from their sons. They tend to emphasize appearance, and instruction on the norms of femininity begins early. Beauty is emphasized for young girls both in their play and in their toys. An exercise kit (including an exercise mat, skipping rope, and exercise clothes) for girls ages five and up seeking early access to the body beautiful was advertised nationally "...not as a means of developing coordination, fitness, or athletic skill but as a way to 'work off that extra chocolate chip cookie'" (Unger 1993:331). Little girls worrying about the effects on their "figures" of too many cookies, exposed to numerous "perfect" female images, grow to be adolescents struggling to conquer their physical imperfections. A letter from a hopeful reader of a teenage beauty and fashion magazine asks:

"In one of your past issues you said models and movie stars look like they have perfect skin because of air-brushing. What exactly is that, and can I do it at home? Anne" (Sassy, October 1992:28; as cited in Williams, 1992)

Glorious images set an alluring standard. However, the skills of photographers have moved beyond the simple airbrushing of pores to digital photography involving the computerized redesign of female images along with the obliteration of "imperfections" (i.e., natural human variations). These female representations are unlike any living person, a kind of technological female impersonator. Beauty ideals can now exceed all previous expectations; at the extreme, the commercialized representations of women are neither human nor obtainable.

This beauty ideal is contingent on age; the discrepancy between "younger" and "older" women may come quite early and perhaps shockingly:

The young girl of 18 or 25 may well believe that her position in society is equal to, or even higher than that of men. As she approaches middle age, however, she begins to notice a change in the way people treat her. Reflected in growing indifference of others toward her looks and toward her sexuality (read 'toward her as a sex object'), she can see and measure the decline of her worth, her status in the world. (Bell 1970:75)

The harshness of expectations regarding appearance has been pointed to by a number of authors (Moss 1970; Nowak 1977; Preston 1975; Abu-Laban 1981, 1984). Susan Sontag (1972) puts it more bluntly, arguing that, socially, women are "girls as long as possible, who then age humiliatingly into middle-aged women and then obscenely into old women."

In the 1980s, Louise Arcand, the first woman in Canada to hold a telecast anchor position with a major French-language television station, filed an age discrimination suit against the CBC. After she had successfully anchored the increasingly popular dinner hour newscast of Montreal's Radio-Canada affiliate for three years, the position was taken away from the then 40-year-old Arcand and given to a 28-year-old woman. Louise Arcand was moved to radio and given a reduction in pay because the network wanted a more "youthful" look. Both the Canadian Human Rights Commission and the Quebec Labour Department criticized the unjust, discriminatory nature of the decision to move Arcand to radio with a reduction in pay, but neither agency had the power to restore her job or award her significant damages (Globe and Mail, 1992:C4).

Beauty norms affect the lives of both young and aged women. But the ways in which these impact in advanced age is of particular relevance. The younger women who play the "beauty game" may find it troublesome or painful or simply impossible, but there is even less of a level playing field in advanced age. It is a game where few old women are winners.

## BEAUTY AS THE RESULT OF DISCIPLINED EFFORT

Given the numerous pressures on women to "look good," there is an implicit message that those who don't measure up to some standard of attractiveness have "let themselves go." They haven't tried hard enough to become beautiful, and this is a uniquely feminine moral failing for which women may be condemned. It is as if, in some way, they have contaminated the landscape of patriarchy. (Lest this sound extreme, it might be asked how many women have rejected their female friends because they don't look good enough?) Brownmiller says that unattractive women can be seen as "not caring about themselves—or not taking care of themselves" (13-19). The pressures on older women to "keep up" are numerous. Women "...are exhorted to stay young and beautiful, to do things to their bodies to achieve this, and to wear make-up, hair products, and clothes to conceal their real age" (Itzen 1986:126). Because of its expense, clothing is a social hierarchy made visible. In some ways it is as if the medieval sumptuary laws are still in effect.[2] Despite the continued gender wage gap, women must spend much more to keep up appearances, refurbish their facade, and "take care of themselves."

Young girls learn early that beauty rituals and preparations take time, planning, and money. Even so, plastic surgeons admit that their clientele of teenagers has doubled just in the past five years (Alexander 1990). With parental support, young teens are turning to elective surgery to correct their "defects."

But it is especially for older women that cosmetic surgery is held out as a way to remedy physical imperfections that, in their case, are usually the result of the natural aging process. The range of bodily alteration possibilities increases yearly. These include breast augmentations, lifts and reductions, liposuction (fat removal) of any of a number of ample areas of the body, face lifts, brow lifts, eye lifts, nose alterations, lip reduction as well as lip enlargement, collagen injections, facial peels of various sorts, tummy tucks, derrière lifts and so on. In the United States there is a $20 billion-a-year cosmetic industry and a $300 million-a-year cosmetic surgery industry (Wolf 1991:17). It is estimated that in 1989, one in every 225 American women had elective (cosmetic) surgery (Morgan 1991).

In addition to the expense of elective cosmetic surgery that makes it almost inaccessible for most older women and its risks that increase with age, it should be noted that this type of intervention has its fads as well. In the 1960s, the preferred "eye style" for surgeons doing blepheroplasties (eye "lifts") was a wide-eyed Audrey Hepburn look. By the 1980s surgeons favoured a different look, a narrower Christie Brinkley "sporty eye." Similarly, rhinoplasties (nose "corrections") have changed over the years since the 1950s from a turned up "cute" nose to a purportedly less "operated on" more "serious" nose.

---

2 During the thirteenth to fifteenth centuries, laws, based on moral and religious arguments, attempted to control extravagance by limiting personal expenditures for clothing and other purchases.

Without the benefits of surgical intervention, the aging woman, on the other hand, has been characterized by one best-selling physician-author as metamorphasizing into a pitiable figure characterized by obesity and a coarse appearance, "not really a man but no longer a functional woman. These individuals live in the world of intersex" (Reuben 1969:292). A team of biologists suggests that "increasing lines and wrinkles in the skin and sagging flesh" affect feelings of worth but cosmetic surgery (rejuvenation) has become "increasingly popular in middle age and beyond, especially among women...(and undoubtedly)...has helped to revive or maintain a successful emotional and sexual relationship between some aging husbands and wives (as well as contributing to the possibility of a sexual relationship between older women and younger men)" (Rockstein and Susman 1979:163). Again, the pressure is on women to maintain the exterior image of beauty. And what if a woman doesn't? Not meeting the expectations of society regarding physical appearance may sometimes make a difference between life and death (Abu-Laban 1984). Sudnow's classic study of a hospital emergency room noted a sharp difference in response to a child patient and an aged female patient when both, at admission, presented virtually the same symptoms. An intern gave mouth-to-mouth resuscitation to the child, but he did not do the same procedure on the aged woman. When questioned, the intern explained the difference in emergency room treatment by saying "he could never bring himself to put his mouth to 'an old lady's like that'" (Sudnow 1967:101).

The models available for women generally, and aging women specifically, are often economically advantaged women who have tapped into the surgeon's skill. In a recent article, *Chatelaine*, Canada's leading women's magazine, lauded actress Elizabeth Taylor, purportedly the veteran of a number of cosmetic surgery procedures, as *"the most beautiful 61 year old on the planet"* (Gooden 1993) [italics added]. Unaltered sixty-one-year-olds are not held out as models; instead, the surgeon's creation is set up as a "style" to emulate.

## BEAUTY AS THE RIGHT SIZE

Ideal body sizes and shapes are part of the standards of beauty set by society. There is a general concern about what is too much or what is too little, but very rarely an acceptance of the body in its natural state, free of surgical or cosmetic intervention. For those who have "too much" there are diets, liposuction, guilt, and recrimination. For those with "too little" there is breast augmentation and, more recently, a reversal of liposuction that involves injections of fat or the placement of hopefully "harmless" substances into the body to change the contours in one manner or another. Failure to maintain a certain body size and weight carries an inherent stigma and can plague females from an early age. A

Canadian survey of Saskatoon high school students found 76 percent of girls indicating that they "diet," while 17 percent vomit and 12 percent use diet aids (Currie 1990:7). In the United States alone there is a $33 billion-a-year industry concerned with diets (Wolfe 1991:17).

Deprivatory dieting commonly has horrendous implications, including anorexia and bulimia. Hesse-Biber (1991) estimates that some 20 to 25 percent of college women control their weight by vomiting, diuretics, and laxatives. Dash (1993:30) estimates that one in five anorexics die from the problem. When dieting doesn't produce the desired effect, women may again turn to surgery. In the United States, liposuction, the removal of body fat, is now the most common form of cosmetic surgery. It is estimated that in 1989 an estimated 200,000 pounds of fat were surgically removed (Morgan 1991).

The contemporary preoccupation with larger breasts and narrower hips (not the typical female form although it is the typical shape of Barbie dolls) has contributed to the rising popularity of breast augmentation surgery. This is the second most common form of cosmetic surgery. In 1988 over 70,000 U.S. women had breast augmentation surgery. By 1990, this number had dramatically increased to 150,000 (Tavris 1992:33). The great majority of breast augmentations (80 percent) are done for elective purposes, not for post-cancer reconstruction. This has raised a host of questions regarding safety. The silicon gel Meme implant, now banned in Canada, was once hailed as boosting confidence along with cleavage. The first official acknowledgement of potential problems came in January 1991 when both Canada and the U.S. put a moratorium on its use because of concerns regarding surgical complications including auto-immune problems, rupture of the implant, allergies, tumors, and repeated surgeries to correct the "problems" induced by earlier surgery. The immense popularity of implants, another seemingly harmless beauty "option," can be noted on some celebrities whose newly enlarged, sometimes unusually spherical breasts placed inordinately close to the collar bone (if high is good, higher is better) have been described as surgeons' attempts to "better" nature by enabling their patients to closer approximate the elusive Barbie. Surgically-created breasts have in themselves the potential to create a physical ideal. As we become accustomed to "new and improved breasts," particularly those appearing on the rich and famous, a new standard of beauty in female anatomy can be imposed.

Women can be damned if they do follow beauty standards and damned if they don't. A 1992 sexual harassment case against the giant Seattle aerospace company, the Boeing Corporation, illustrates this problem. Part of Boeing's "defence" against the sexual harassment charge was to attack the credibility of the plaintiff (as had just happened successfully in the Clarence Thomas hearings and the William Kennedy Smith rape trial) by asking what she had done to encourage the crime. Boeing's lawyers argued that the fact that the plaintiff had had cosmetic surgery on her breasts denied the validity of the sexual harassment charge because it suggested that the plaintiff (who, it might be noted, was married) had had breast augmentation surgery "to encourage overtures from male workers at Boeing" (Guteck 1993:209).

Ironically, size also defines power in patriarchal societies—hence the emphasis on the "little woman" who looks up to "her man." As women age, they tend to gain some weight, become larger. In fact, there is evidence to suggest that it may be to a woman's advantage to gain some weight post-menopause. Among other benefits, increased body fat can contribute to the retention of natural estrogen. But the advantages of weight gain are seldom spelled out, much less the potential that larger size may carry an aura of influence. What does it mean to be "a woman of substance" or a "weighty presence"? Is there power in taking up more space, in older age, than is often allowed to women of any age?

## BEAUTY AS MONOLITHIC

The image of beauty that society presents to women is embodied in a female who is not only young and slim but also White (or "whitish"), heterosexual, and class advantaged. This is a monolithic image of appearance that reflects the prejudices of those who are in dominant positions in our society. For example, there is an ethnic/racial bias in the authoritative beauty ideal. Since Caucasians are a privileged racial group, the beauty messages that are aimed at females from childhood on reflect white privilege. Advertising imagery, therefore, reflects the status of the dominant group by using models who are tall and slim, with fair skin, light hair and eyes. This sets an ethnocultural racial standard that is northern European and thereby excludes most of the world's women (Abu-Laban 1991). The result is that as we find women in general dieting, grooming, and purchasing commodities to imitate the consumer icon, we also find visible minority women specifically using hair straighteners, or skin lighteners, or cosmetic surgery to "westernize" the eyes (that is, to alter epicanthic eye folds), rhinoplasty to alter noses, liposuction to change body shape, tortuous high heels to look taller. Sometimes (not always) these procedures are done in order to erase signs of racial or ethnic origin implicitly discredited by the media. There are ethnocultural variations in typical average height, weight, and patterns of fat distribution. Yet the standard of beauty to which all women in Canada are subjected is culturally specific. It fits a northern European standard that is narrow even for women of northern European descent. Even when ads portray models other than Caucasians, their features often send mixed messages—an Oriental woman with "corrected" eyes or an African woman of mixed background or straightened hair or wearing a wig. Interestingly, and still to be studied, some physical traits associated with aging are more common among specific ethnocultural groups and the evidence does not favour northern European women (Abu-Laban 1993). Sun damage is a major cause of skin aging: it causes wrinkling and loose skin. Darker, thicker-skinned women are less susceptible to sun damage, while women with a so-called "Scotch-Irish" complexion (i.e., with pale, thin skin) are more susceptible to damage from ultraviolet light and hence their skin is more susceptible to loss of tone and elasticity over time.

The cultural notions of beauty are related to class advantage. The presence or absence of money means differential access to the facade of "beauty." Ehrenreich and English (1978:108) describe the ideal beauty of the nineteenth century as sickly, "a beautiful invalid sensuously drooping on her cushions, eyes fixed tremulously at her husband or physician or already gazing into the Beyond." It is a description of beauty that is class dependent. Economic advantage allows time for beauty rituals and pays for the associated expenses. Those with marginal economic status cannot afford the luxury of leisurely draping over pillows, nor the discretionary time needed for cosmetic artifice; they cannot afford the clothing, whether haute couture or ready-to-wear, that demonstrates style and status; they cannot afford "corrective" cosmetic surgery (even though some cosmetic surgeons are offering loan plans for future-oriented women) and they certainly cannot afford the élite surgeons who reconstruct the rich and powerful. In other words, for most aged women, access to the techniques that preserve what is defined as beauty is severely limited.

The biases of heterosexism and heterosexual privilege also interact with societal beauty standards to castigate women who are or who are presumed to be lesbian. Thus, the woman who openly chooses another woman as an intimate partner is more likely to be considered by the larger society as unattractive or "unfeminine" or even a feminist. Unattractiveness may be imputed to those who reject tradition (for example, lesbians and feminists) because it is assumed that they choose to be "different" because they cannot be successful women in the usual sense, that is, by relying on their appearance (Jacobson and Koch 1978:169). Conversely, women judged as "highly attractive" are more likely to be seen as "feminine" and less likely to be seen as a lesbian (Unger, Hilderbrand, and Madar 1982).

In Laner's 1979 study of personal ads, 96 percent of lesbian women specified their own age in the ad compared to 76 percent of heterosexual women. But heterosexual women were more likely than lesbians to specify their age preference for a partner. Laner concludes that older age is less stigmatic among lesbians who are seeking a romantic partner. Yet Jeanette Auger (1990:33) suggests that "Lesbians and heterosexual women alike are vulnerable to the myth that after menopause they are no longer sexual or attractive." Supporting this, Barbara MacDonald, a lesbian feminist, observes about her own aging:

> "Sometimes lately...I see my arm with the skin hanging loosely from my forearm and cannot believe that it is really my own. It seems disconnected from me; it is someone else's. It is the arm of an old woman. It is the arm of such old women

as I myself have seen, sitting on benches in the sun with their hands folded in their laps; *old women I have turned away from.* I wonder how and when these arms I see came to be my own—arms I cannot turn away from. (MacDonald and Rich 1983:14) [italics added]

## BEAUTY AND POWER

Frequently, women defined as beautiful are seen as holders of power, albeit female "power" defined by patriarchal structures. The mistress of the ruler; the "beautiful" woman who marries upward, purportedly exchanging the rarity of her appearance for economic security; the "beautiful" woman who achieves career success that is then attributed (fairly or unfairly) to her appearance—all are seen as, in essence, "cashing in" on their looks.

In fact, women are often instructed on the art of appearance, with the implication that beauty pays off with material and emotional rewards. Given that patriarchy allows women few avenues to power, *to the extent that it exists*, beauty power is uniquely female. Advocates of this view present beauty as a facilitator, however painful the process. A book on beauty at the office advises women to wear

> classic expensive-looking pumps... *as high as you can tolerate.* Keep them at your desk *if they're too uncomfortable* to wear to and from work. Remember: To look feminine is in your favor. (Schrader 1981:28) [italics added]

In this view, beauty is power and using this "power" opens other opportunities, some perhaps morally questionable. "Being beautiful, intelligent, and in a career situation has its responsibilities—*you can leap-frog into positions of prestige*, but real power comes from ability and confidence; selection for your merit, not for your favours is what you want." (Schrader 1981:158 [italics added].

"Reverence" for youthful beauty has its bizarre aspects. In 1993, a sixty-three-year-old Pennsylvania judge dismissed charges against a 30-year-old female model accused of driving 122 mph in a 55 mph zone because in his view the story she told was more likely to be true because of her appearance. In the judge's words, she was not "fat and ugly" or "an ugly broad" (*New York Times* 1993). While appearance may seem like a power advantage, still another court case suggests women can be damaged regardless. Consider the decision made by a Canadian judge a few years ago. A twenty-three-year-old man, armed with a knife and furious because his "girlfriend" had ended their relationship, kicked in the door of her home, pushed her into her bedroom, locked the door, and then ripped out the telephone cord when her friend tried to phone for help. The man had a lengthy criminal record, including previous forcible seizure armed with a knife, theft, break and entry, possession of drugs, assault, etc. The assailant was given a six-month sentence. The judge's comments are reflective of the bind in which women find themselves with youthful "beauty."

> I could give him five years but I don't think under the circumstances of this case I'd be entitled to...he got mixed up with a silly little bunch of girls...a bunch of clucking females running around and they're all so scared they have to call the police...they're a free-floating type of female *young for their age, very nubile, very attractive surely*, but still impressionable, still stupid. You know women don't get much brains before they're 30... (*Chatelaine*, March 1978:58 and 118)

However our society describes beauty and femininity, these are not seen as improving with age. Susan Brownmiller (1984:236) notes: "Women who rely on a feminine strategy as their chief means of survival can do little to stop the roaring tide of maturity as they watch their advantage slip by."

The conception of beauty as power implies elements of trickery and deception. It is open to question how advantageous beauty may be, but it is clear that in our society the attribution of beauty is *contingent* on age and that as a form of "power" it is limited by time. Beauty is assumed to be a dwindling asset. Conceiving beauty as power means that aging women must do all they can to conserve, preserve, and hide the ravages of time.

Germaine Greer (1991:378), in her sixth decade of life, observes: "Only when a woman ceases the fretful struggle to be beautiful can she...at last transcend the body that was what other people principally valued her for, and be set free from both their expectations and her own capitulation to them." Greer argues that this in itself can be an emancipatory experience.

## CONCLUSION

By situating women's diverse experiences with aging and the standards of beauty in a social context, we have been able to put the labels and approbations often placed on aging women in perspective. The social context of prevailing gender inequities, inequities often exacerbated by age, helps us to identify the biases in perceptions and self-images of most (or at least many) aging women in Canada today. Most women have come to judge themselves by standards that favour White, middle, or upper class, and heterosexual women. However, most women, whether they fall within the favoured categories or not, can see that myths about how they should age and what they should look like may not at all coincide with their genuine needs, self-images, life experiences, daily realities, or structural circumstances.

Myths from both the past and present suggest that women preferably should not age at all or, if they really must, at least they should have the good sense not to show it, or feel it, or demand the respect that their hard-worn wisdom deserves. The role models of "older" women on television and in the movies are women who are indeed older (i.e., in their fifties) but certainly look not a day over 30 or 35. These are the models held out to women in mid-life who are often without the necessary resources and leisure to take "nips and tucks" or stick with the diet or exercise program of a Jane Fonda or a Cher.

We have also shown how the structural realities of aging women's lives impinge on them as they age, literally shaping them in certain ways. Choices women make as they age may be less individual choices or predilections than what society expects and demands. Standards of beauty and behaviour at certain ages are determined by women's structural situations and societal interests in making women, or individuals, bear the responsibilities (and guilt) about aging differently than the standards suggest. How many times do mid-life women find themselves the brunt of stories and jokes about aging— middle-age spread, flapping inner arms, crow's feet around the eyes, menopause, Alzheimer's, weight, etc.? Often, mid-life women refer to themselves in these ways.

This chapter emphasizes what others have stressed—the need to question the presumptions of a homogenous aging experience for women. The diversity of women's experiences with aging must be examined, whether good, or bad, or both. Yet acknowledgement of diversity must not mask the clear injustices that shape and constrain women's lives and women's capabilities to control their own lives as they age.

It is said that we all tend, as individuals, to become more of what we are as we age. This is also perhaps true for us collectively as we age. Gender inequities, present at any age, play out louder with age. The same could be said of class, ethnicity, race, (dis)ability, and sexual orientation. The interactions of these forces with age, combined with the invisibility of women other than White, middle-class, heterosexual women in much of the literature and social policy on aging means that the true nature of the inequities and realities of women's experiences with aging have yet to be explored.

## BIBLIOGRAPHY

Abu-Laban, Sharon McIrvin. "Aging Women and Gender Disequity in Canada." In *The Elderly Population in the Developed and Developing World: Politics, Problems and Perspectives*, edited by P. Krishnan and K. Mahadevan, 444-470. Dehli: B.R. Publishing, 1992.

Abu-Laban, Sharon McIrvin. "Family and Religion among Muslim Immigrants and Their Descendants." In *Muslim Families in North America*, edited by E. Waugh, S.M. Abu-Laban, and R. Quereshi, 6-31. Edmonton: University of Alberta Press, 1991.

Abu-Laban, Sharon McIrvin. "Les Femmes Agées: Problèmes et Perspectives." *Sociologie et Sociétés*. XVI:2, October, 69-78, 1984.

Abu-Laban, Sharon McIrvin. "Social Supports in Older Age: The Need for New Research Directions." *Essence.* 4(3):195-210, 1980.

Abu-Laban, Sharon McIrvin. *Traversing Boundaries.* Unpublished manuscript. Department of Sociology, University of Alberta, 1993.

Abu-Laban, Sharon McIrvin, "Women and Aging: A Futurist Perspective." *Psychology of Women Quarterly,* 6(1):85-98, 1981.

Abu-Laban, Sharon McIrvin and Abu-Laban, Baha. "Women and the Aged as Minority Groups: A Critique." *Canadian Review of Sociology and Anthropology.* 14(1):103-116, 1977.

Alexander, Suzanne. "Teens Cosmetic Surgery Fad Causes Dismay Among Experts." The Globe and Mail, 25 Sept. 1990. (original *Wall Street Journal*)

Auger, Jeanette A. "Lesbians and Aging: Triple Trouble or Tremendous Thrill." In *Lesbians in Canada,* edited by Sharon Dale Stone. Toronto: Between the Lines, 1990.

de Beauvoir, Simone. *Old Age.* Harmondsworth, England: Penguin, 1970.

Bell, I.P. "The Double Standard." *Transaction.* 8:75-80, 1970.

Berger, Raymond. "The Unseen Minority: Older Gays and Lesbians," *Social Work,* 27:236-242, 1982.

Bradbury, Bettina. "Surviving as a Widow in 19th Century Montreal," *Urban History Review* XVII (3):148-160, 1989.

Brownmiller, Susan. *Femininity.* New York: Linden Press/Simon and Schuster, 1984.

Chapkis, W. *Beauty Secrets—Women and the Politics of Appearance.* Boston: South End Press, 1986.

Connidis, Ingrid Arnet. *Family Ties and Aging.* Toronto: Butterworths, 1989.

Currie, Dawn. "Women's Liberation and Women's Mental Health: Towards a Political Economy of Eating Disorders." In *Women and Well-Being,* edited by Vanaja Dhruvarajan, 25-39. Montreal: The Canadian Research Institute for the Advancement of Women.

Doress, Paula Brown and Siegaland, Diana Laskin. *Growing Older.* Midlife and Older Women's Book Project: Boston, MA, 1987.

Driedger, Leo and Chappell, Neena. *Aging and Ethnicity: Toward an Interface.* Toronto: Butterworths, 1987.

Ehrenreich, Barbara and English, Deirdre. *For Her Own Good: 150 Years of the Experts' Advice to Women.* New York: Doubleday, 1978.

Fisher, D.H. *Growing Old in America.* New York: Oxford, 1978.

Furnham, A.; Hester, C.; and Weir, C. "Sex Differences in the Preferences for Specific Female Body Shape." *Sex Roles* 22:743-753, 1990.

Garner, David; Garfinkle, Paul; Schwartz, Donald; and Thompson, Michael. "Cultural Expectations of Thinness in Women." *Psychological Reports*, 47:483-491, 1980.

Gee, Ellen M. and Kimball, Meredith M. *Women and Aging*. Toronto: Butterworths, 1987.

Gee, Ellen and McDaniel, Susan A. "Social Policy for an Aging Canada," *Journal of Canadian Studies* 27(3):139-152, 1992.

Globe and Mail. "TV Anchor Filed Complaint Against CBC Over Age Discrimination." *Globe and Mail*, 15 August 1992, C4.

Gooden, Charmaine. "Knife Styles of the Rich and Famous." *Chatelaine Magazine*, (April 1993).

Gorlick, Carolyne A. and Pomfret, A and D. "Hope and Circumstance: Single Mothers Exiting Social Assistance," In *Single Parent Families: Perspectives on Research and Policy*, edited by Joe Hudson and Burt Galaway, 253-70. Toronto: Thompson, 1993.

Greer, Germaine. *The Change: Women, Aging and the Menopause*. New York: Fawcett Columbine, 1991.

Greer, Germaine. *Sex and Destiny*. New York: General, 1984.

Gutek, Barbara A. "Responses to Sexual Harassment." In *Gender Issues on Contemporary Society*, edited by Stuart Oskamp and Mark Costanzo, 197-216. Newbury Park, CA: Sage, 1993.

Hesse-Biber, Sharlene. "Women, Weight and Eating Disorders," *Women's Studies International Forum*, 14(3):173-191, 1991.

Kaden, Joan and McDaniel, Susan A. "Caregiving and Care-Receiving: A Double Bind for Women in Canada's Aging Society," *Journal of Women and Aging*, 2(3), 3-26, 1990.

Laner, M.R. "Growing Older Male: Heterosexual and Homosexual." *The Gerontologist*, 18:496-501, 1978.

Lee, John Alan. "What Can Homosexual Aging Studies Contribute to Theories of Aging?" *Journal of Homosexuality* 13(4):43-69, 1987.

MacDonald, Barbara and Rich, Cynthia. *Look Me in the Eye*. San Francisco: Spinsters, Ink., 14, 1983.

McDaniel, Susan A. *Canada's Aging Population*. Toronto: Butterworths, 1986.

McDaniel, Susan A. "Challenges to Mental Health Promotion Among Working Women in Canada," *Canadian Journal of Community Mental Health*, 12 (1), 1993b. Forthcoming.

McDaniel, Susan A. "Emotional Support and Family Contacts of Older Canadians," *Canadian Social Trends*, Spring, No. 28:30-33, 1993a.

McDaniel, Susan A. *Family and Friends 1990: General Social Survey Analysis Series*. Ottawa: Statistics Canada, 1994.

McDaniel, Susan A. "Getting Older and Better: Women and Gender Assumptions in Canada's Aging Society," *Feminist Perspectives*, #11, Canadian Research Institute for the Advancement of Women, 1988b.

McDaniel, Susan A. "Les femmes dans un Canada en voie de vieillissement: une approche feministe," *Cahiers québécois de démographie*, 18(1):137-156, 1989b.

McDaniel, Susan A. *Life Rhythms and Caring: Aging, Family and the State*. 23rd Annual Sorokin Lecture. Sorokin Series, University of Saskatchewan, 1992b.

McDaniel, Susan A. "Women and Aging: A Sociological Perspective," *Journal of Women and Aging* 1(1-3), Spring:47-67, 1986a.

McDaniel, Susan A. "Women and Family in the Later Years: Findings from the 1990 General Social Survey." *Canadian Woman Studies*, 12(2):62-64, 1992a.

McDaniel, Susan A. and Gee, Ellen M. "Social Policies Regarding Caregiving to Elders: Canadian Contradictions," *Journal of Aging and Social Policy* 5(1 & 2): 57-72, 1993.

McDaniel, Susan A. and McKinnon, Allison. "Gender Differences in Informal Support and Coping Among Elders: Findings from Canada's 1985 and 1990 General Social Surveys," *Journal of Women and Aging*, 5(2):79-98, 1993.

Morgan, Kathryn Pauly. "Women and the Knife: Cosmetic Surgery and the Colonization of Women's Bodies," *Hypatia*, 6(3):25-50, 1991.

Morton, Suzanne. "Women on Their Own: Single Mothers in Working-Class Halifax," *Acadiensis* XIX (2):90-107, 1992.

Nett, Emily. "Canadian Families in Socio-Historical Perspective," *Canadian Journal of Sociology* 6(6):239-260, 1981.

*New York Times*. "In This Courtroom, Beauty is Truth." March 1993, Section I, 20.

Novak, Mark. *Aging and Society: A Canadian Perspective*. Scarborough, Ontario: Nelson, 1988.

Posner, Judith. "Old and Female: A Double Whammy," *Essence* 2(1):41-42, 1977.

Reuben, David. *Everything you always wanted to know about sex (but were afraid to ask)*. New York: McKay, 1969.

Rockstein, Morris and Sussman, Marvin. *Biology of Aging*. Belmont, California: Wadsworth, 1979.

Russell, Cherry. "Aging as a Feminist Issue," *Women's Studies International Forum*, 10(2):125-132, 1987.

Schrader, Constance. *Nine to Five: A Complete Looks, Clothes and Personality Handbook for the Working Woman*. Englewood Cliffs, New Jersey: Prentice-Hall, Inc., 1981.

Smith, Jane E., Waldorf, V. and Trembath, D. "Single White Male Looking for Thin, Very Attractive...," *Sex Roles*, 23 (11/12):675-683, 1990.

Sommers, Tish. "Aging is a Woman's Issue." *Response* (March):12-15, 1976.

Sontag, Susan. "The Double Standard of Aging," *Saturday Review*. October, 55(39):29-38, 1972.

Sudnow, David. *Passing On: The Social Organization of Dying*. Englewood Cliffs, New Jersey: Prentice-Hall, 1967.

Tavris, Carol. *The Mismeasure of Woman*. New York: Simon and Schuster, 1992.

Unger, Rhoda and Crawford, Mary. *Women and Gender: A Feminist Psychology*. Philadelphia: Temple University Press, 1992.

Unger, Rhoda; Hilderbrand, M.; and Madar, T. "Physical Attractiveness and Assumptions About Social Deviance: Some Sex by Sex Comparisons." *Personality and Social Psychology Bulletin*, 8:293-301, 1982.

Williams, Deborah. *"Women and Beauty."* Unpublished term paper submitted to Professor S. Abu-Laban, Sociology 491, University of Alberta, Fall, 1992.

Wolf, N. *The Beauty Myth*. Toronto: Vintage Books, 1990.

# THE PSYCHOLOGY OF WOMEN

*Nikki Gerrard and Nayyar Javed*

*Psychology has nothing to say about what women are really like, what they need and what they want, especially because psychology does not know...psychology has looked for inner traits when it should have been looking for social context.*

*Naomi Weisstein (1971)[1]*

## INTRODUCTION

The psychology of women has emerged in the past twenty-five years as a response to what Weisstein identified above. It has been a discipline that has primarily used males as its reference and standard in research, theory, and practice. This "malestream psychology" (O'Brien 1981) is embedded in a patriarchal society that also uses male language, values, practices, and propriety as the standard. In this society, women are considered to be "other"—different, outside of, the exception to the rule. In this chapter we explore what this means, psychologically, for and to women and the ways and areas in which we have historically been cast as "other" in psychology. We also explore some new pathways in the psychology of women.

First, it is necessary to explore what psychology is, in general, why it exists, and what the different types of psychology are. The discipline of psychology focuses mainly on attitudes, behaviours, cognition, and emotions. Whether psychologists are working with rats or dogs or humans, the ultimate goal of traditional psychology is to predict and control any of these areas. Understanding is secondary to prediction and control. The two ends of a continuum of psychology are experimental and applied. Experimental psychologists do experiments with nervous systems, including the brain, of various animals. They wish to determine how these systems work and which stimuli produce which results. Applied psychologists, including clinical psychologists, want to use the knowledge found by experimental psychologists, as well as other sources of information, in some sort of practice with human beings, be they children or adults. This does not mean that applied psychologists can not do research. They frequently do. But their ultimate goal is to apply what they learn to the area of human attitudes, beliefs, cognition, and emotions.

There are numerous specializations in psychology including (but not limited to) the following: abnormal, clinical psychology, which uses abnormal, personality, and developmental psychology for the treatment of people with emotional distress or disorders; developmental psychology, which focuses mainly on children and adolescents; educational and learning psychology, which looks at cognition and intelligence; industrial and organizational psychology; personality psychology; physiological psychology; social psychology; and neuropsychology, which emphasizes the brain and nervous system. More recent specializations include more contextually-based psychologies: cross-cultural, community psychology, which is organized around social context issues in communities, and feminist psychology. It is the last specialization that has resulted in the broad and diverse field sometimes called the psychology of women.

## THE PSYCHOLOGY OF WOMEN

There are a number of different ways in which to explore the psychology of women. This chapter focuses on woman as "other" and explores "other" in two ways that are interwoven: woman as biologically determined to be "other"[2] (we develop and exist in predetermined ways, depending on our sex), and woman as socially constructed to be "other"[3] (we are the way we are because of society's rules, sanctions, stereotypes, and structures).

The concept of "other" affects people's diversity: rendering someone as "other" sets her or him up to be marginalized, trivialized, and/or dismissed. Thinking in terms of "other" "homogenizes" a whole array of specific characteristics; in other words, it destroys the specificity of something or someone. Imagine sorting some papers into two piles: one pile is about a specific subject and the "other" pile is everything else. The specific pile has many details and contains much information; the "other" pile becomes a blur of generalized, non-specific, mass. The "other" pile may be labelled as something neutral like "general", or labelled with a name (like "junk") that reflects a *value perception* of what it contains. In any event, the individual characteristics of the content of that pile become blurred, or even invisible. When people are put into an "other" category, they also become a blur of generalized, non-specific mass. When *value perceptions* of good or bad, right or wrong, which we have learned and adopted from our cultural environment, are ascribed to that group of people, their individual characteristics will be rendered invisible, feelings toward that group of people will be generalized, and they will be regarded as all alike because their specificity will have been lost in the grouping of them as "other". This leads to a belief that women, racialized people, poor people, old people, disabled people, gays and lesbians, are not only "other" but are often grouped, in their particular label, are all alike.

When this type of dichotomy is set up and there are two groups, the reference or standard group and the "other," this triggers a pattern of thoughts and practices that have far-reaching implications. This dichotomization is the beginning of oppression.

## THE THEORY OF OPPRESSION: PROCESSES, SOCIAL CONTEXT, AND LANGUAGE

Oppression is a form of thought and a process that is both socially constructed and located in a social context; that is, it occurs within but also beyond *individual* lives. Brittan and Maynard (1984) write that oppression results in the body becoming socially constructed as an object. They say that "'lived experience' of the body is subverted by 'objective' forces" (p. 13) and they give the example of sexual objectification:

> A woman's body is a gendered body. While she has her own feelings, perceptions, pain, her "lived experience" is mediated and worked upon by social and cultural powers which "objectify" her sense of bodily reality. (p. 13)

This means that a woman exists in many different ways at the same time. She is biologically female, she is an individual, and she is a person belonging to a socially constructed gender. For a woman, these different ways of "being" do not always exist in concert or in balance. When the "social and cultural powers" are stronger than her own sense of self, she is objectified. We, the authors, have felt this objectification, one of us as a woman, the other as a woman and also as a racialized person. It feels to us as if we are observing ourselves from some social and cultural perspective outside ourselves. The greater the loss of individual self and the greater the social appropriation of a woman's experience, feelings, and existence, the greater the objectification. This objectification is a crucial element of oppression.

The processes of oppression are described by Frye (1983):

> The root of the word "oppression" is the element "press". *The press of the crowd; pressed into military service; to press a pair of pants; printing press; press the button.* Presses are used to mold things or flatten them or reduce them in bulk, sometimes to reduce them by squeezing out the gasses or liquids in them. Something

pressed is something caught between or among forces and barriers which are so related to each other that jointly they restrain, restrict or prevent the thing's motion or mobility. Mold. Immobilize. Reduce. (p. 2)

She also says that these forces "are not accidental or occasional and hence avoidable, but are systematically related to each other" (p. 4). Objectification of the body and the systematic forces Frye refers to take place not just within one individual or during a single event. Frye writes:

One cannot see the meanings of these rituals if one's focus is riveted upon the individual event in all its particularity....It seems sometimes that people take a deliberately myopic view and fill their eyes with things seen microscopically in order not to see macroscopically. At any rate, whether it is deliberate or not, people can and do fail to see the oppression...because they fail to see macroscopically and hence fail to see the various elements of the situation as systematically related in larger schemes. (pp. 6-7)

The social context is reiterated by Brand and Sri Bhaggiyadatta (1986) in their work documenting people's experiences of racism:

There are two overriding themes common to all the interviews. The first is what we call a *culture of racism,* that is, the random and institutional ways in which racism pervades the lives of the speakers, and the second is the structuring of economic hardship or disadvantage by the use of racism. (p. 3)

All of these writers describe the systematic processes of oppression in a social context. Oppression *is* organized and reproduced in the social context by various practices and relationships in society. These practices and relationships are called "discourses."

Discourse refers to the obvious and not-so-obvious aspects of a topic. For instance, the discourse of psychology might be theory (what *is* psychology?), and practice (*how* is psychology practised?), but may also include how psychology is related to other aspects of our society (social control), and what the agenda, as in political power, of psychology theorists and practitioners may be? This list is not complete but is meant to give an idea of how widely and deeply rooted and interconnected a topic like psychology can be. It is also clear in this example that some aspects of psychology are visible but, others are invisible. One can see that not only concepts of psychology are reflected in the above discussion but also that various values are implied.

In her discussion about discourse, Farge (1988) says that discourses are far from value-neutral. She refers to Foucault and his belief that discourses have political agendas. Farge describes use of "the language of a discourse...to entrench itself as the commonsense [*sic*], the always/already known" (p. 17). The incorporation of discourse into the mainstream in the guise of "common sense" has direct application to how we conceptualize and practice oppression.

For example, in reference to racism, Brand and Sri Bhaggiyadatta write:

> The culture of racism is revealed through the received wisdoms about non-white people that exist in ordinary discourse. Many of the interviewees describe witnessing conversation and actions which isolated them and treated them as different, not "normal", or even not human. The distortion of information about non-whites is taken for granted; it is seen as "just plain common sense"!
>
> Errol Lawrence, in an essay, "*Just Plain Common Sense: the Roots of Racism,* defines it as follows:
>
> It is thought to represent the distilled truths of centuries of practical experience; so much so that to say that an idea is only common sense, is to appeal over the logic and argumentation of intellectuals to what all reasonable people know in their "heart of hearts" to be right and proper. Such an appeal can act at one and the same time to foreclose any discussion about certain ideas and practices and to legitimate them. (pp. 3-4)

Discourse has its own political agenda, and one of the products of discourse is to define common sense. This makes discourse very powerful.

The discourse of language is also important in relation to oppression. Language arises from the needs of people to survive in their world. This means that very early in life children learn how to speak in order to get what they want and need. This involves learning about power relationships and about who has power and who does not. A child may be whiny and demanding to her or his mother, in essence communicating that she or he does not think the mother has much power, and then turn to the father and be sweet and charming, deferring to the father's power or vice versa. Children learn to test out their own power by saying things and then seeing what reactions they get from listeners. The child's yelling "I will not!" in answer to someone's request is a common example of a child testing out how far she or he can go. When race and/or gender are inserted as variables in language development, power relations take on additional meaning. For example, until recently "he" and "his" were used to refer to any person, male of female, rendering females invisible. Who did that? Dorothy Smith (1987) would refer to the originators of such language as the "ruling apparatus." We often dichotomize "black" and "white" when expressing good and bad, right and wrong. Who did that? White people did. Hard or soft commonly refers to strong or weak. Whose values are apparent here? Male values.

Brand and Sri Bhaggiyadatta write that our culture is transmitted through language, and that language reflects the structures of society and the power relations in it. Brittan and Maynard refer to language as part of the practice of oppression. The interconnection between language and power is clear. Smith (1987) writes about the language that originated in positions of power in our society and the use of language as an important part of the relations of ruling. She says:

> The language of the everyday world as it is incorporated into the description of that world is rooted in social relations beyond it and expresses relations not peculiar to the particular setting it describes. (p. 156)

The forces of oppression are multidimensional. Racialized women are "other" because of gender and race; lesbians are "other" because of gender and sexuality; poor women are "other" because of gender and class. Those women who bear their "otherness" in more than one way suffer from multiple oppressions. These are interconnected in that the same elements of oppression occur: objectification, language, social context, processes. Multiple oppressions combine to form a warp and woof that entraps them and leaves them more vulnerable, psychologically, than if they were being oppressed because of only one form of "otherness." Oppressions are intertwined so that their tentacles reap damage through many entry points.

Oppression serves to marginalize those we consider to be "other," to devalue their specificity, and ultimately to dismiss them as insignificant, unimportant, invisible. This is the world of oppression constituted by processes, social context, and language in which we find ourselves as we examine the psychology of women.

## CONSTRUCTING WOMEN'S OTHERNESS: RESEARCH, THEORY, AND PRACTICE IN PSYCHOLOGY

Gender dichotomy has played a central role in psychology's location of women as "other of men." Psychology has invested extensively in according scientific validity to gender difference. According to Wine (1989), "No other discipline has invested more time, energy, and money in demonstrating that women are different than men and therefore inferior to men" (p. 80).

Traditionally, malestream psychology has been male centred in research, theory, and practice. Male bias in research has manifested itself in three ways according to Wine (1989): methodology borrowed from physics, that is, cause and effect without consideration given to a particular social context; a focus on gender differences in cognitive and other socially valued abilities; exclusive use of a White middle-class male sample. Moreover, it has ascribed research findings to all human beings irrespective of the difference in social context of women and other oppressed groups. Eichler (1988) lists, in addition to these issues, seven sexist problems in research generally. The first is androcentricity, which is having a male world view inform what, how, and why a researcher envisions a problem. The second is overgeneralization and overspecificity in which, respectively, the results of research on one sex are generalized to both sexes or language reflecting one sex is used when actually both sexes are involved. The third problem is gender insensitivity or ignoring the social importance of identifying gender as a variable in the research. Fourth, double standards imply different value measurements on behaviour, traits or situations that are differentiated only by gender. Another problem is sex appropriateness, the ascribing of non-biologically based realities as appropriate to one sex or the other. A sixth is familism, which conceptualizes the family, rather than the individual, as the smallest unit of analysis, and finally, sexual dichotomism, the total separation of the sexes, ignores overlapping similarities. Many of these problems become evident in the methodology chosen for the research.

All research uses some form of methodology. When Wine (1989) talks about a methodology borrowed from physics, she is referring to positivistic research that follows a cause and effect paradigm. The researcher is trying to prove that, in psychology, predictable, similar effects occur when a particular situation or stimulus exists or is introduced into the environment. An example would be that when most people hear a loud noise they become alarmed and ready for fight or flight. Another example is the use of surveys that tap a sample population's attitudes, beliefs, or behaviours when posed with a series of questions that pose scenarios or problems. Usually large numbers of people are tested and generalizations are made from the results and applied to a larger population. Typical quantitative techniques are used, such as surveys and experiments. This type of research is sometimes criticized as reductionistic; that is, it oversimplifies a situation and does not take into account the many variables that exist in the respondents' life experience or social context that may account for their answers. It also often does not allow a range of answers but requires a simple yes or no. The results may not give a true reflection of the sample population.

Research conducted more recently in women's psychology is following a research methodology called phenomenological research. This research methodology uses a small sample and focuses on understanding an individual's situation and the context in which she or he lives. Qualitative techniques are used such as in-depth interviewing and participant observation. There is no basis for generalizing the results of this research to a large population. The purpose is to fully document and analyze the informant's information and/or responses. This methodology is sometimes criticized for being too susceptible to the researcher's bias, using small sample size, and not being generalizable to a larger population. This methodology, however, does focus particularly on the social context and environment of the informer. For this reason it is favoured as a research methodology in women's psychology because, in the analysis, it reveals and integrates social oppression generally and the location of "woman as other" specifically.

Wine (1989) also refers to bias in sex differences research, perhaps the most blatant example of biased research. Wine (1985) critiques this research by drawing attention to the fact that sex differences research emphasizes difference rather than areas of overlap and uncritically accepts that areas in which males are alleged to be stronger are deemed more basic or essential: female strengths are deemed to be non-essential, simple ones.

In 1974 Macoby and Jacklin published their landmark book entitled *The Psychology of Sex Differences*. The authors reviewed research literature from 1966 to 1973 that had anything to do with sex differences. They re-evaluated the statistics used, gathered more information about the research, and re-assessed the validity of what the original author had said. They concluded that there was no evidence to prove most of the sex differences that had been accepted at that time. For instance, they debunked the following beliefs: girls are more "social" than boys, more suggestible than boys, girls have lower self-esteem, girls are better at rote learning and simple repetitive tasks while boys are better at tasks that require higher-level cognitive processing, boys are more analytical, girls are more affected by heredity whereas boys are more affected by environment, girls lack achievement motivation, girls are auditory while boys are visual. They agreed with research that had found that girls have greater verbal ability than boys and that boys excel in visual-spatial ability, mathematics, and aggression. Since then, even these conclusions have been challenged (see, for example, Caplan, MacPherson and Tobin 1985).

Another female scholar who challenged the whole field of sex differences research was Ruth Bleir (1988), a neuroanatomist who continually challenged the dominant paradigm in her field which said that parts of women's and men's brains are of different sizes and that this results in different cognitive abilities between the sexes. She not only revealed the faulty methodology in such research but also identified the systemic impact of this biased research. She referred to it as an "elaborate network of interdependent hypotheses" that "standing alone...has no independent scientific basis, but together, bolstered by each other, they create the illusion of a structure of reason, weight, and consistency" (p. 17). The history of this sex differences network is documented by Greenglass (1982) who also shows the impact of sex differences research on psychological development.

Within feminism there has been sex difference research. An example is Gilligan's (1982) work (discussed in more depth elsewhere in this chapter) which suggested a difference between girls and boys in moral development. Although motivated by laudable goals, such research has to be very careful that it does not reproduce biased research. No conclusion arising from sex difference research should be free of an analysis of the social context within which the subjects reside. Often it is the social context that accounts for the differences.

Male bias has also tainted psychology theory and practice. The written critique of sexism in psychology began almost a hundred years ago, but the bias was not labelled as sexism. Charlotte Perkins Gilman (1899, republished 1973) wrote a fictionalized account of what had actually happened to her at the hands of a psychiatrist who had diagnosed her as having hysteria, according to Friedan (1963) the most popular psychological diagnosis for women at the time. Gilman revealed the devastation she experienced as a result of the treatment—extreme isolation for long periods of time.

In 1963 the issue of women's unhappiness resurfaced, but with no name. In fact, Friedan described her own and other women's mental malaise as "the problem with no name." This malaise took the form of desperation and unhappiness in degrees ranging from moderate to extreme. To explain this phenomenon, Friedan pointed in part to psychology theory, particularly to what she called "The Sexual Solipsism of Sigmund Freud," which was characterized by his belief and practice in the "limitless subservience of women" (p. 113) and women's inferiority based on biological determinism; that is, penis envy. This was an example of how psychological theories claiming the accuracy and precision of physics theory have transformed patriarchal myths about women into scientific truths. Sigmund Freud, the father of Western masculinist psychology, "turned consistently to the mythology of the most patriarchal and sexist of civilizations, the Greek and the Roman, for psychological understanding" (Kaschak 1992, p. 57).

In representing Freud's psychoanalysis as a scientific theory of psychological development, masculinist psychology has attempted to conceal how he was influenced by such a mythology. Consequently, the assumptions about women's inability to individuate because they lack a "penis" and the absurdity of his oedipal theory remained unchallenged for a long time. His oedipal theory is based on what Freud described as a sexual attraction in children for the parent of the opposite sex. In fact, as Rush (1980) and Masson (1984) have pointed out, Freud's female patients told him about being sexually abused by their fathers but Freud refused to believe them. In turn, he developed his oedipal theory in which these tales of abuse are rationalized as "sexual fantasies" of children.

These assumptions in Freud's theory clearly reveal how women's oppression is reproduced in his theory. His ignoring of female abuse points out his bias which blinded him from seeing the abuse and led him to distort the reality.

Another psychological theory that reproduces women's oppression is object relations theory, an offshoot of psychoanalysis. Object relations continues reproducing women's otherness by focusing on gender difference in relational capacities and the development of a sense of self (Wine 1989). In object relations theory, an infant begins developing a sense of self through association with the mother's breast, which is described by Winnicott (1965) as an "object." Eichenbaum and Orbach (1983) highlight that these infants allegedly are in a one-way relationship—from the mother to the child—and so the lack of interactiveness of the relationship also constitutes it as a relationship with an object. Winnicott says that "with the recognition of the whole object [i.e., the mother as a whole] comes the beginning of a sense of dependence, and therefore the beginning of the need for independence" (p. 10) and thus the journey toward autonomy, individuation, and differentiation that object relations theorists (Winnicott,

Eichenbaum and Orbach, Guntrip 1961; Mahler, Pine, and Bergman 1975) believe must exist for healthy psychological development of self.

Given the importance these theorists place on this one-way relationship of mother to child, it is not surprising that Winnicott actually hinges the quality of the process of development on the mother. He writes, "Only if there is a good-enough mother does the infant start on a process of development that is personal and real" (p. 17).

A critical examination of this theory reveals many of the research traps identified above by Wine (1989) and Eichler (1988). The view of object relations theorists that the relationship is a one-way relationship reflects an androcentric view uninformed by females' lived experiences, a view which, as we show later in this chapter, has been challenged by other theorists (Kaplan 1991; Miller 1991; and Surrey 1991) who have developed an interactive model of psychological development that *does* take into account females' lived experiences. In addition, object relations theorists attribute such values to the breast-as-object that women are seen as the only possible caregivers. Do fathers have no place in this development of sense of self? When Winnicott states that the realization of the infant of the whole object results in dependence and *therefore* the need for independence, he is again being androcentric in his implied view that dependence must lead to a need for independence. There is no consideration that perhaps dependence (if it in fact develops) is not a bad thing. And finally, object relations theory generalizes a Eurocentric view to all people when, in fact, other cultures see dependence and connectedness as a very positive and desirable way of being.

One of the most well-known psychological theories in which women were constructed as "other" was Kohlberg's (1969, 1981) theory of moral development. His theory consists of six stages of moral development as they occurred in his subject population of eighty-four boys whom he followed for a number of years. He presented them with moral dilemmas and concluded that individuals who are morally evolved have a higher degree of differentiation. Therefore, in resolving moral dilemmas they are guided by a regard for rules and moral principles that take precedence over social relations. In other words, the relationship with others does not enter into the resolution of the moral dilemmas. According to Kohlberg's theory (1969, 1981), women do not go beyond stage four and therefore are incapable of achieving the same level of moral development as men are. Gilligan (1982), who worked with Kohlberg, became critical of his theory because, in using only boys for his research and then generalizing to girls, he ignored the core of women's identity (a feature that became the basis of her own research in women's moral development which we discuss later). She also points out that for Piaget, another well-known researcher theorist in psychological development, "girls are an aside, a curiosity to whom he devotes four brief entries in an index that omits 'boys' altogether because 'the child' is assumed to be male" (p. 18). Kohlberg and

Piaget are examples of icons in psychology whose theories have profoundly influenced the construction of "woman as other."

Virtually all psychology theory, whether traditional or feminist, has assumed heterosexuality as its reference. Homosexuality (gay or lesbian) is posited as "other." When Adrienne Rich (1980) wrote her groundbreaking article entitled "Compulsory Heterosexuality," she overtly challenged us to recognize that "heterosexuality, like motherhood, needs to be...studied as a *political institution....*" (p. 637), an institution very much a foothold of male dominance. Rich not only offered a critical analysis of heterosexuality but also reconceptualized woman-woman love as natural and normal. She suggests that the real threat to men in this case is that

> women could be indifferent to [men] altogether, that men could be allowed sexual and emotional—therefore economic—access to women *only* on women's terms, otherwise being left on the periphery of the matrix. (p. 643)

In place of compulsory heterosexuality, Rich proposed a lesbian continuum in which all woman-identified experience (though not necessarily real or imagined sex) could exist. The experience ranged from the "sharing of a rich inner life, the bonding against male tyranny, the giving and receiving of practical and political support" (p. 648-49) to an actual lesbian existence—the total rejection of a heterosexual way of life.

Challenging compulsory heterosexuality is still an issue in psychology. Recent efforts to "theorize heterosexuality" (see special issue on heterosexuality, *Feminism and Psychology*, 1992) reveal a vast diversity of thought. The special issue of this journal put forth *heterosexuality* as "other," for a change. In this challenge of the status quo the editors asked the following questions: "What is heterosexuality and why is it so common? Why is it so hard for heterosexuals to change their 'sexual orientation'? What is the nature of heterosexual sex? How does heterosexual activity affect the whole of women's life, her sense of herself, her relationships with other women, and her political engagements?" (p. 293) This total reversal of the usual questions asked (substitute "lesbian" for "heterosexuality" in the above questions) is a step toward deconstructing dominant malestream thought and "other" paradigms in psychology.

The above section has dealt primarily with psychological research and theory in constructing women's "otherness", but it is in the *practice* of psychology that the most direct damage is done. The diagnosing and labelling of women, followed often by a prescription of psychotropic medication, has rendered many women temporarily or permanently incapacitated.

## Psychiatric Diagnosis

As Caplan and Gans (1991) have noted, psychiatric diagnoses (see *Diagnostic and Statistical Manual of Mental Disorders-III-R*, [DSM-III-R], APA 1987) basically determine the normalcy or lack thereof of a person and the degree to which one so diagnosed is abnormal. Think about that for a minute. The very concept of normal exists only in relation to abnormal. What does "normal" mean? To establish the criteria for "normal," one has to establish boundaries beyond which one is "abnormal." In other words, one has to establish a reference or standard of that which is "normal" and then an "other" of that which is "abnormal". The currency of this diagnostic system is language—words that stand for complex events, systems, reactions. The mere naming of these complex phenomena is laden with values, beliefs, political agendas. But the very function of language, as Caplan (1985) writes, "is to help us understand our world, to help us to categorize the wealth of our experience", and Caplan acknowledges that the use and misuse of words affect the way people think." (p. 38) This becomes dangerous when language, in diagnosis, is used to explain something erroneously or to explain something that does not actually exist.

Classical examples exist of this mis-labelling or mis-diagnosing. In *The Myth of Women's Masochism*, Caplan (1985) points out that the diagnosis of "masochism" has been used to label women's learned behaviour of nurturance, selflessness, and endless patience as sick. When behaviour results in personal pain, there is no enjoyment; however, the label and definition of "masochism" implies that there is. Women behave in certain ways because after is unsafe not to: they are, in fact, employing survival behaviours. Violence against women is predicated on women as providers of service, a role that requires nurturance, selflessness, and endless patience. However, that aspect of the reality of women's lives is not mentioned in the diagnosis.

The interest of those in power, those who decide who is "other," in maintaining a diagnosis that labels women's behaviour discussed above as sick is demonstrated by the substitution, in 1986, of Masochistic Personality Disorder (in response to a major outcry from professionals and the public alike) with a new diagnostic category called Self-Defeating Personality Disorder. This new disorder continues to label women's survival behaviour as sick.

More recently Caplan and McCurdy-Myers (1992) have documented the subsequent entry of Late Luteal Phase Dysphoric Disorder (LLPDD) and Premenstrual Syndrome (PMS) into the *DSM-III-R*. These two so-called disorders label the emotional/physical changes that occur to women around the time of menstruation as sick. Mood swings referred to in these diagnoses are tied to physical changes occurring in the body as part of the menstrual cycle. It is important to note that emotional changes tied to physical changes in men are not labelled as sick. In a description of how categories are included in the *DSM*, Caplan (1991) points out that 86 percent of the American Psychiatric Association (the publishers of the *DSM*) are male. The connection between what is considered sick and what is not, on a gender basis, is beyond coincidence.

In reference to the earlier discussion of compulsory heterosexuality, it is of interest to note that the *DSM-III-R* has a diagnostic category called "ego-dystonic *homo*sexuality" (italics ours), characterized as "persistent and marked distress about one's sexual orientation" (p. 561) but no "ego-dystonic *hetero*sexuality." This is another example of homosexuals being treated as "other."

A final example of diagnosis used unfairly in malestream psychology with people who are considered "other" is reported in relation to racism within psychology. Various writers (see, e.g., Thomas and Sillen 1974; Guthrie 1976; and Mercer 1984) report racism against mental health patients of nondominant cultures. For example, common misdiagnosis of Black patients, disproportionate use of electroconvulsive therapy (ECT) with non-White patients, and the pathologizing of such natural reactions as anger and hopelessness, to a racist society, are well documented. Mercer writes that psychiatry (in collusion, we add, with psychology,)

> has played an active role in attempts to medicalise black resistances and define them not as aspects of a political struggle but as individualised, medico-psychological problems of "alienation" or "intergenerational conflict" or "identity crises". (p. 23)

The *DSM-III-R* is rampant with a lack of scientific research to support certain diagnoses, with methodologically flawed research, and with questionable validity of certain criteria (Caplan and Gans; Caplan 1991). The above examples point to the danger of diagnosis when the categories are unscientifically based, or biased based on such aspects as race, gender, and sexuality. Such misdiagnoses give the illusion of real sickness when, in fact, there is none. They ignore the social context of the lives of those who are "other" in relation to the dominant power group.

## Labelling

But what happens when someone is, in fact, diagnosed correctly? Sometimes that person becomes "labelled" and this labelling has its own form of destruction. Labels are the one or two words that arise from diagnoses and are given the power to describe complex phenomena in people's lives. People internalize these oversimplistic and reductionist labels. Our self-esteem is partly based on our self-image. When we are labelled, that self-vision may become flawed, inadequate, sick, and our self-esteem may drop. Labelling also tends to set up a self-fulfilling prophecy in which we behave in ways our "label" describes. The need for caution in labelling in psychology is emphasized by researchers who have shown that labelling can actually change the way one feels about one's self even though nothing has actually changed except that one has been labelled (Devadasan 1983).

Labels also limit our choices in a world in which others know about our labels. Years ago a candidate for the presidency in the United States had to withdraw from the race because he had, at one time earlier in his life, been diagnosed as depressed. That label stuck with him years later even though he was no longer depressed. When we hear a label, our mind presents a whole array of information, values, and beliefs about that label and we ascribe "good" or "bad" to the label and hence to the person. Labelling is a coding system in which we describe ourselves in a certain way and others in a different way. Used uncritically, insensitively, or inaccurately, labelling becomes dangerous. Diagnosis, then, often leads to labelling that can frequently lead to the prescription and use of psychotropic medication.

## Psychotropic Medications

According to Penfold and Walker (1983), 67 to 72 percent of all psychotropic medications go to women. Women receive two-thirds more prescriptions for antidepressants and more anti-anxiety drugs than men (Penfold 1991). In 1989, Health and Welfare Canada revealed that women used almost twice as many sleeping pills as men and two and a half times as many tranquilizers as men (Eliany, Giesbrecht, Nelson, Wellman, and Wrothy 1990). These drugs, besides trying to medicate away major reactions to women's various oppressions rather than end the oppression, are dangerous for a number of reasons. Addiction, use of the drugs in suicides, and long-term side effects are of major concern. Side effects include Parkinsonism, seizures, and tardive dyskinesia, a neurological disorder (Women and Mental Health Committee 1987).

## Electroconvulsive Therapy

Another physically intrusive treatment, one that is not actually a drug, is electroconvulsive therapy (ECT). This treatment, sometimes used as a treatment for depression, uses high-voltage electric shocks to the brain. Although studies for over forty years which have shown memory loss as a result of ECT (Janis 1948, 1950), ECT continues to be available as a treatment in most psychiatric wards. Twice as many women as men receive ECT (Women and Mental Health Committee 1987), partly because there are more women diagnosed as depressed, but Smith and Richman (1984) report that ECT is used more on women in other diagnostic categories as well. This is also consistent with observations made by Hollingshead and Redlich (1958) in which low-income mental health patients (disproportionately women) were given medication and ECT more commonly than those with higher incomes (more likely to be men) who more frequently received talk therapy.

Diagnosis, misdiagnosis, labelling, and the use of psychotropic medications and ECT are all attempts to bring those identified as "other" into line with whatever is deemed to be "normal." Whether cumulatively or individually, the construction of "otherness" in psychology research, theory, and practice has had a profound impact on women.

## THE PSYCHOLOGICAL IMPACT OF "OTHERNESS" ON WOMEN

The psychological impact of "otherness" on women manifests itself in many ways. Following are some examples in the areas of self-development, achievement, isolation, self-esteem, and relationships.

Women internalize "otherness" by defining themselves as the "other." Women live their otherness by giving up many needs, aspirations, and sense of self—in fact, their self-reality. Kaschak is of the opinion that gender training forces women to split themselves into unnatural categories. They grow up believing they really are the "other." They learn to have "selective awareness and selective expression" (Kaschak); for example, certain emotions such as anger are ignored. By giving up aspirations that conflict with their identity, they give up their sense of self. According to Kaschak, as the other of men, women live in paradoxes of which they are usually not aware. For example, "We constantly provide sustenance to men and children yet are considered weak and dependent" (Kaschak p. 5). Being expected to take care of others (especially those who need it the most) and rewarded for doing so, women get labelled as "co-dependent." This label, like many others, ignores how and why women become "co-dependent" (if there is, in fact, such a thing), and assumes women are sick.

Another psychological impact of "otherness" on women consists of representing women, in the way certain attributes are defined, as lacking or deficient in certain valued attributes. For example, our "lower achievement motivation" has been researched over and over again. Even many feminists believed the myth that women lack achievement motivation until the seminal work by Gilligan (1982). She theorized that women fulfil their achievement needs in relationship with others. Men, on the other hand, aspire to meet their achievement needs through success in the public and material world.

In malestream psychology, achievement is conceptualized around mastery in the material world (Vickers 1982; Yanico 1981; Zuckerman 1979). Lately, feminist psychologists have re-examined psychology's conceptualization of achievement, mastery, and autonomy—the very attributes women are perceived to lack. Travis, Phillippi, and Henley (1991) conducted two studies in which achievement was conceptualized as consisting of mastery *and* affiliative events. In these studies women viewed achievement as associated with mastery in personal and interpersonal activities. This confirms Gilligan's theory.

In our society women are forced to achieve vicariously (Stake 1979). Women give up their needs and aspirations to enable men—sons, husbands (and all male relatives in some cultures)—to succeed in life. This training for achieving vicariously begins at the moment of birth. Teaching is carried on by "behaviour of significant adults; by how an infant is held, touched, talked to, talked about; by the kind of toys considered appropriate; by colour coding of clothing and blankets. This emphasis on sex differentiation by both parents, father to a greater extent, increases with age..." (Kaschak p. 46.). Through this teaching an identity is forced upon women. For women, this identity is as a caregiver who is taught to avoid entering male territory: the only safe place for achievement is through relationship or vicarious means.

A third psychological impact of "otherness" is that it has created a deep sense of alienation that comes from a double bind. If women live their lives as the "other" in the ways described above, they are marginalized and labelled as "dependent," "deficient," and "masochistic." If they resist living such lives, they are seen as invaders and male-castrating bitches. Both of these paths have pain and suffering. Living an "otherness" engenders feelings of alienation, loss, and isolation.

Women go through this struggle feeling alienated from self. Fanon, an Algerian psychiatrist, writes about his feelings of alienation as a Black person: "I took myself far off from my own presence....What else could it be for me but an amputation, an excision, a haemorrhage that spattered my whole body with...blood" (in Bhabha 1992, p. 185). This alienation from self results in a pervasive and sometimes overwhelming sense of loss.

The loss of connection with self also results in a deep sense of isolation that is compounded by women's social location. As "other," women are exiled from the power positions in society. Social location restricts our options, exposes women to many dangers, and leads to exploitation and abuse in record numbers. The Badgely report (1984) indicated that in Canada, 53 percent of females have been victims of one or more unwanted sexual acts. The isolated nuclear family setting in Western culture places women in a position in which the abuse goes on in the privacy and secrecy of family life. Badgely also reported that 90 percent of abuse occurs with either a relative or friend of the family. Wife abuse also occurs in the privacy of the home; MacLeod (1987) estimates from her research that one in ten women is battered by her partner. Another source of isolation is job ghettos, where women are forced to endure exploitation and abuse and yet must remain silent because of the lack of options. These structural barriers are hard to break; therefore, an individual woman faces enormous odds in resisting her confinement.

The isolation multiplies for women, such as racialized[4] women, lesbians, disabled women, older women, whose "otherness" exists in more than one way.

The silence imposed on many such women engenders a deep sense of isolation because they cannot share their suffering and pain with each other or articulate them in society.

The loss of connection exists also in relationships with others. As women are bombarded in school, in the media, in private and professional lives with the "wisdom" of psychology theories, they feel more and more disconnected from those they love. As shown in the next section, recent critical analyses of these theories show that boys have been brought up to separate from their mothers, to get on with developing their "man-ness," to achieve, and to identify with their fathers (Chodorow 1978). Girls, who do not need to establish a gender identity discontinuous with the mother and are not scripted to achieve in patriarchal society, do not have the same pressures put upon them. Eventually, for girls, the pressure to separate and individuate comes partly from homophobia (Caplan 1981), which dictates that the relationship between mother and daughter cannot be too close lest it develop into a homosexual one, which, as we have shown, is a great fear in our society. Common clinical terms such as "enmeshed," "merged," and "fused" reveal psychologists' pathologization of close, connected relationships. The result is that women and their children feel isolated from each other and that women feel isolated from other women.

The psychological impact of "otherness" on women's self-esteem is confusing. Pop-psychology has capitalized on women's alleged low self-esteem. In the past few years books and audio-visual materials that have flooded the market target women consumers by convincing them that self-esteem depends on individual competency. Those who have self-esteem know the skills; those who lack self-esteem lack the skills, as if self-esteem has no relationship with the social context. As practicing psychologists, we have seen women clients who say they suffer from low self-esteem. This self-labelling that they have internalized from all these media messages and other mental health professionals causes them great anxiety. They believe they are responsible for this inadequacy. It appears that the label of low self-esteem, rather than low self-esteem itself, creates the anxiety, because, when they are questioned about their low self-esteem, they reveal that the anxiety of the label bothers them the most. Once the label is questioned, they feel better.

The research hypothesis that women have low self-esteem has, in fact, yielded mixed results. For example, Walker (1984) reports that battered women (whom you would expect to have low self-esteem) measured high on her self-esteem scale. She suggests caution in interpreting these results because these same women scored high on a depression scale. It appears that one can be depressed without having low self-esteem. We suggest that the issue of low self-esteem has been skewed by an androcentric bias in research, an observation supported by the research of Sanford and Donovan (1984). Nevertheless, the claim of low self-esteem in women has succeeded in contributing to women's perception of themselves as "other." This issue, like the others discussed, points out the need for new pathways in the psychology of women.

## NEW PATHWAYS IN THE PSYCHOLOGY OF WOMEN

New pathways in the psychology of women began with the realization among psychologists that women, as a homogenized group, had been marginalized as "other" in the theory, research, and practice of psychology. The landmark paper by Weisstein (1971) challenged psychologists to undertake a total reform in the methods of psychology. This section reviews some of the historical research that contributed to this awareness and demand for reform. Recent theories and research about the psychology of women is explored as well as new approaches to this issue. This section concludes with a discussion of psychology practice that is more inclusive, that strives toward inclusiveness, connectedness, and mutual empowerment.

Back in 1963, when Friedan criticized Freud's oedipal theory as discussed earlier in this chapter, there was no word that described oppression against women. Ehrenreich (1983) reports that the word "sexism" emerged in the 1970s as part of a consciousness and context that also included the terms "misogyny" and "male chauvinism."

It took researchers and practitioners a few years to define sexism within psychology. One of the first attempts was the landmark article by Broverman, Broverman, Clarkson, Rosenkrantz, and Vogel (1970), that reported on sex-role stereotypes in a population of seventy-nine clinical therapists, many of whom were psychologists. Their conclusions, based on questionnaire data, were that therapists' perceptions of a mentally healthy adult paralleled their perceptions of a mentally healthy adult *male*. There was *not* a positive correlation between a mentally healthy adult female and a mentally healthy adult person. This meant that a woman could be a mentally healthy female *or* a mentally healthy adult, *but not both*! In retrospect, what was then called psychologists' sex-role stereotypes was, in fact, sexism.

Ten years later, Davidson and Abromowitz (1980) reported on thirty-three studies conducted since 1970 about sex bias in clinical judgment. They concluded that the results were reminiscent of those reported by their predecessors. They identified a methodological problem in the research, namely that, because the subjects are getting wise to the questions, results are skewed. In more recent years, researchers have concluded that the questions asked in such questionnaires are, in fact, loaded with sex-role stereotypes of what constitutes male and female attitudes and behaviours (Widiger and Settle 1987).

By 1972, Chesler used the term "sexism" and went way beyond characterizing sexism in mental health systems as simply the existence of psychologists' (and others') sex-role stereotypes. She examined mental health systems, institutions, and women's lives and discovered not only prejudice and oppression but also abuse, ignorance, persecution, and hopelessness. By referring to statistics revealing gender differences in populations of psychiatrically institutionalized patients and in the diagnoses, she showed that women were overrepresented as patients and in such diagnostic categories as depression, neurotic, psychophysiological, schizophrenic, paranoic, and suicidal (p. 42). Chesler probed for answers to such questions as "Why?" and "What is happening here?" The answers revealed that the sources of psychological casualties were the mental health systems themselves *and* society as a whole.

Since Chesler's work, the theme of integrating psychology and society has developed. As we have pointed out in this chapter, psychology is an ideology and a male institution. In a Canadian context, the mislabelling of women in harmful and devaluing ways has been documented by The Women and Mental Health Committee of the Canadian Mental Health Association (1987). These committee members also raised the issue of sexual abuse of clients by psychologists. In an effort to emphasize the vulnerability of all women to societal and/or psychology abuse, the committee offered the reminder that "...no women belongs solely to any specific category of women. [A woman] experience[s] all...aspects of her existence simultaneously" (p. 66).

Miller (1986) reported that psychology and society were inextricably entwined in what she called the psychological order that encompasses women's lives. By re-examining and redefining words and concepts like power, conflict, domination, and subordination in the context of women's mental health, she gently but forcefully began to deconstruct the pillars of psychology theory and practice and to reconstruct them in a new and woman-positive way, basing her theories on women's everyday experiences. Although her method was new to psychology, this approach is justified, according to Storrie (1988), a sociologist,

> on the grounds that subordinated groups necessarily possess a usually painful familiarity with the relations that constrain and disadvantage them while those who benefit from this structured inequality remain blind to its essential features and to the work that sustains their privileges. (pp. 6-7)

Putting Miller's ideas into practice, Ehrenreich and English (1978) proposed guidelines for an alternative therapy "in which wisdom about daily life is not hoarded by 'experts' or doled out as a commodity but is drawn from the experience of all people and freely shared among them" (p. 324).

Having critically analyzed sex-role stereotypes among psychologists, sexism in mental health institutions, and fundamental psychological terms and concepts, feminists turned to the attitudes of psychologists to mothering and relationships. Prevalent throughout the latter critiques was the acceptance of the duality of women as individuals and as part of society. When Dinnerstein (1976) and Chodorow (1978) examined the social context and related psychological implications of mothering as it exists as an institution and an experience in our culture (Rich 1976), they drew conclusions about the impact of mothering on all of society—males and females alike. Both indicated that psychological issues arising from parenting, read "mothering", were a result of gender-unequal parenting embedded in our society. Chodorow stated that "women's mothering...creates a psychology of male dominance and fear of women in men" (pp. 218-19). As an alternative, she made the following suggestion: "The elimination of the present organization of parenting in favour of a system of parenting in which both men and women are responsible would be a tremendous social advance" (p. 219).

From mothering, feminist theories began to examine how relationships had been characterized in psychological theory and practice. They found a socially constructed image of pathology. Caplan (1981), for instance, illustrated the social construction of barriers between women. These barriers were the results of the psychological theories and popular wisdom discussed earlier in this chapter. Gilligan (1982) concluded from her research that commentaries on women and morality were based on an arbitrary judgment of "higher morality," a judgment that arose from a sample of males only and was based on abilities to differentiate in relationships. Gilligan (1982) found that morality in women develops from an ethic of care and relationships, whereas men's morality is based on an ethic of justice and rights. Women's masochism (discussed earlier in this chapter) was debunked by Caplan (1985) and identified as women's struggle to survive in a violent and misogynist society. Even depression was critiqued and renamed by Grinnell (1987) as "resting potential," a natural response to a disordered, hierarchical world. Siegel (1988) reframes "dependency" as interdependency and puts it in the context of being aware of and taking care of our own and others' human relational needs.

Currently, the critical analysis of sexism within psychology includes three strands. First is the finding and exposure of areas that still need to be exposed, as in Chesler's (1986) book about mothers in custody battles, Russell's (1986) research about incest survivors, and Caplan's (1989) struggle to help women overcome the stalemate that exists in many mother-daughter relationships.

Second are the new methodologies and frameworks that are emerging in all areas of psychology. As previously discussed, there is a move toward qualitative research as yielding a more accurate reflection of women's lives and the contexts in which they live. Refinement and reapplication of some old methodologies in new ways allow for subjectivity to be disclosed without interpretational validity problems. (See, for example, Kitzinger's and Rogers' 1985 research on lesbian identities using Q-sort methodology.) Feminist research methodologies have been developed by many scholars including Oakley (1981), Roberts (1981), Stanley and Wise (1983), Smith (1987), and Kirby and McKenna (1989). All address the traditional power imbalance between the researcher and the subject and advocate a more collaborative partnership between the two. Most feminist researchers realize the importance of locating themselves in the research and of cultivating a social action component to the research.

Theorists and practitioners are reframing, renaming, and redefining everything from developmental theory to family therapy to multiple-personality disorder (Bograd 1984, 1986; Hare-Mustin 1978, 1979, 1980, 1987; Rivera 1988; Robbins and Siegel 1985). They have moved from Showalter's (1974) ontogeny of imitation to a gynocentric focus (Wine 1985) that is woman-identified and woman-centred. One of the new frameworks is the new theory of women's psychological development emerging from the Stone Center of Psychological Development, Wellesley College (Kaplan 1991; Miller 1991; and Surrey 1991). This is called Self-In-Relation theory of psychological development. Its main tenets are the development of self through relationship. It diverges from object relations theory in that the emphasis shifts from separation to relationships as the basis for development. In fact, the major goal of development is relationship, *not* differentiation, autonomy, individuation, or separation as exists in the other theories. Self-in-relation theory is characterized by mutual empathy in which the mother and child *interact* and share feelings from which comes understanding and connection. Finally mutual empowerment, in which the mother and daughter attend to the feelings and well-being of the other. What develops is *the relationship between them* which is cared for by each of them. This happens even when the daughter is very young. From this empowerment comes the ability to act, both within and outside the particular mother-daughter relationship. Increased self-esteem and self-worth are directly connected to this reciprocal process of empathy, understanding and connecting, and empowerment. This is in sharp contrast to what is normally thought about close relationships in which closeness is pathologized.

Feminist therapy has emerged within the past twenty years as a model that takes into account all of these critical analyses but coming from a woman-positive perspective addresses sexism, individually and collectively, as a major part of the therapy (see, for example, Greenspan 1983; Laidlaw and Malmo 1991; Levine 1982; Sturdivant 1980). Details of feminist therapy practice are discussed later in this chapter.

The third strand of the critical analysis of sexism in psychology is the critical self-examination of those who have been at the forefront of the sexism critique. This introspection is mostly about the articulation of classism, heterosexism, and racism within psychology. In terms of class issues, Quinn (1974) notes that feminist psychology espouses middle-class values, and she criticizes it as individualistic and serving the needs of the privileged. Denny (1986) asks if poor women can benefit from feminist psychology or even survive it. She observes that most feminist psychologists are ignorant about the issues of non-middle-class women. Some conclude that feminist psychologists are homophobic (Burstow 1985; Kitzinger, Wilkinson and Perkins 1992).

An analysis of racism within women's psychology reveals emerging criticism. Calls for a more race-inclusive view of women in women's psychology have appeared in journals and texts. For example, Robinson (1985) writes:

> Black women, and the complexity of our lives must be included in the development of any psychological theory of women. As I read current theories, books or articles on the psychology of women or feminist therapy, I am constantly struck by the omission. Pertinent theory on Black women's psychological development is rarely included. (p. 135)

The practice of a woman-inclusive, diversity-inclusive psychology in which "otherness" disappears in favour of "richness" is only a dream. Alternative models in psychology include feminist therapy in which the following tenets exist: there is an effort to equalize power between client and therapist; the client is seen in the social context of constructed "otherness" and the problem is embedded in that context (that is, the personal is political); and social action is a valuable, if not vital, component of therapy. These basic tenets, if applied to all psychology research, theory, and practice, would transform it into a discipline of understanding and healing rather than a discipline of social control.

## CONCLUSION

Feminists have to be cautious about the risk of falling into traps in three areas: imitating malestream psychology that integrates the language of ruling which constructs our identity as "other"; making feminism another dogma; and excluding women whose "otherness" is multiplied by their skin colour, physical disabilities, class, age, and sexual orientation. An ongoing introspection, therefore, is necessary.

Acknowledging our vulnerability of remaining embedded in malestream psychology is crucial. In developing awareness to this vulnerability, we have to examine the language of ruling that has, for the purpose of our subordination, defined us as "other." Early feminists rebelled against being defined as "other"; however, at times, feminists themselves have fallen into a trap of accepting women's identity of "otherness" as given.

Examination of the earlier works of feminist psychologists reveals that they missed going beyond the language. For example, they dedicated their research efforts to explaining the reason women have lower achievement, motivation, fear of success and to exploring the whole issue of gender dichotomy. They continued examining women's psychology while lacking deconstructing definitions of the concepts which were applied, to women and men, for the purpose of creating gender dichotomy. However, Dorothy Smith's work here in Canada (1987, 1990) and the work of Black feminists in the United States (hooks 1989, 1991 and Davis 1981) challenged White feminists to rethink their approaches. In the

1990s we are seeing a shift in feminism toward examining how language is used in constructing and representing the reality of all oppressed groups, including women. Foucault sums up the description of language in maintaining power imbalance by stating "the history that bears and determines us has the form of a war rather than that of a language: relations of power, not relations of meanings" (quoted in Bannerji 1992, p. xxii).

Feminism has given women hope for changing their lives. Therefore many have strong sentimental attachment to it. While this attachment is valuable for feminism's evolution, it can create a sense of comfort that stops criticism. Critiquing feminism is essential for saving it from becoming yet another dogma. In fact, White, middle-class, heterosexual feminists have already been challenged by less privileged women for ignoring the reality of the less privileged women. Yoder and Kahn (1993) warn feminist psychologists: "The field of psychology of women clearly must avoid the trap of inadvertently creating a normative woman who is White, middle-class, heterosexual, young, physically able" (p. 847).

We have shown how malestream psychology has created a bleak landscape in which women have been constructed as "other." Our only hope is to be aware of the traps that await and beckon to us, and to continually evolve theories, research, and practices in psychology that include and represent all the voices that have traditionally been silenced. This will be the force that illuminates and creates change.

## BIBLIOGRAPHY

American Psychiatric Association. *Diagnostic and Statistical Manual of Mental Disorders-III-R.* Washington, DC: APA, 1987.

Badgley, R. *Report of the Committee on Sexual Offences Against Children and Youths.* Ottawa: Dept. of Supply and Services, 1984.

Bannerji, H. "Returning the gaze: An introduction." In *Returning the Gaze: Essays on Racism, Feminism, and Politics,* edited by H. Bannerji. Toronto: Sister Vision, Black Women and Women of Colour Press, 1992.

Bhabha, H. "Interrogating identity: The postcolonial prerogative." In *Anatomy of Racism,* edited by D. Goldberg. Minneapolis: University of Minnesota Press, 183-209, 1992.

Bleier, R. "The cultural price of social exclusion: Gender and science." *National Women's Studies Association Journal,* 1, 7-19, 1988.

Bograd, M. "Family systems approaches to wife battering: A feminist critique." *American Journal of Orthopsychiatry,* 54, 558-68, 1984.

———— "A feminist examination of family therapy: What is women's place?" *Women and Therapy,* 5, 95-106, 1986.

Brand, D. and Sri Bhaggiyadatta, K. *Rivers Have Sources, Trees Have Roots: Speaking of Racism*. Toronto: Cross Cultural Communication Centre, 1986.

Brittan, A. and Maynard, M. *Sexism, Racism and Oppression*. Oxford: Blackwell, 1984.

Broverman, I., Broverman, D., Clarkson, F., Rosenkrantz, P. and Vogel, S. "Sex-role stereotypes and clinical judgments of mental health." *Journal of Counseling and Clinical Psychology*, 34, 1-7, 1970.

Burstow, B. "Women and therapy" in *The Healthsharing Book: Resources for Canadian Women*. Edited by McDonnell, K. and Valverde, M., eds. Toronto: The Women's Press, pp. 112-115, 1985.

Caplan, P. *Between Women: Lowering the Barriers*. Toronto: Personal Library, 1981.

———— *The Myth of Women's Masochism*. New York: E.P. Dutton, 1985.

———— *Don't Blame Mother: Mending the Mother-Daughter Relationship*. New York: Harper & Row, 1989.

———— "How do they decide who is normal?: The bizarre but true tale of the DSM process." *Canadian Psychology*, 32, 162-170, 1991.

Caplan, P. and Caplan, J. *Thinking Critically About Research on Sex and Gender*. New York: Harper Collins, 1994.

Caplan, P. and Gans, M. "Is there empirical justification for the category of 'self-defeating personality disorder'?" *Feminism and Psychology*, 1, 263-78, 1991.

Caplan, P., MacPherson, G. and Tobin, P. "Do sex-related differences in spatial abilities exist?: A multilevel critique with new data." *American Psychologist*, 40, 786-799, 1985.

Caplan, P. and McCurdy-Myers, J. "Should 'premenstrual syndrome' be called a psychiatric abnormality?" *Feminism and Psychology*, 2, 27-44, 1992.

Chesler, P. *Women and Madness*. New York: Doubleday, 1972.

———— *Mothers on Trial: The Battle for Children and Custody*. New York: McGraw-Hill Book Co., 1986.

Chodorow, N. *The Reproduction of Mothering: Psychoanalysis and the Sociology of Gender*. Berkeley: University of California Press, 1978.

Davidson, C. and Abromowitz, S. "Sex bias in clinical judgment: Later empirical returns." *Psychology of Women Quarterly*, 4, 377-95, 1980.

Davis, A. *Women, Race and Class*. New York: Random House, 1981.

Denny, P. "Women and poverty: A challenge to the intellectual and therapeutic integrity of feminist therapy." *Women and Therapy*, 5, 51-63, 1986.

Devadasan, K. "Diagnostic labelling in psychiatric practice." *Indian Journal of Clinical Psychology*, 10, 103-105, 1983.

Dinnerstein, D. *The Mermaid and the Minotaur: Sexual Arrangements and Human Malaise.* New York: Harper & Row, 1976.

Ehrenreich, B. *The Hearts of Men: American Dreams and the Flight from Commitment.* Garden City, New York: Anchor Books, 1983.

Ehrenreich, B. and English, D. *For Her Own Good: 150 Years of the Experts' Advice to Women.* Garden City, New York: Anchor Books, 1978.

Eichenbaum, L. and Orbach, S. *Understanding Women: A Feminist Psychoanalytic Approach.* New York: Basic Books, Inc., 1983.

Eichler, M. *Nonsexist Research Methods: A Practical Guide.* Boston: Allen & Unwin, 1988.

Eliany, M., Giesbrecht, N., Nelson, M., Wellman, B., Wrothy, S. eds. *National Alcohol and Other Drug Survey 1989: Highlights Report.* Ottawa: Health and Welfare Canada; Minister of Supply and Services, 1990.

Farge, B. *Hostels for Single Women: Subjectivity, Discourse, and Social Regulation.* Doctoral Dissertation, University of Toronto, 1988.

Friedan, B. *The Feminine Mystique.* New York: Dell Publishing Co., 1963.

Frye, M. *The Politics of Reality: Essays in Feminist Theory.* Trumansburg, New York: The Crossing Press, 1983.

Gilligan, C. "Woman's place in man's life cycle." *Harvard Educational Review,* 49, 431-446, 1979.

———— *In A Different Voice: Psychological Theory and Women's Development.* Cambridge, Mass.: Harvard University Press, 1982.

Gilman, C. *The Yellow Wallpaper.* Old Westbury, New York: The Feminist Press, 1899, republished in 1973.

Greenglass, E. *A World of Difference: Gender Roles in Perspective.* Toronto: John Wiley & Sons, 1982.

Greenspan, M. *A New Approach to Women and Therapy.* New York: McGraw-Hill Book Co., 1983.

Grinnell, G. "Women, depression and the global folie: A new framework for therapists." *Women and Therapy,* 6, 41-58, 1987.

Guntrip, H. *Personality Structure and Human Interaction.* New York: International Universities Press Inc., 1961.

Guthrie, R. *Even the Rat Was White: A Historical View of Psychology.* New York: Harper and Row, 1976.

Hare-Mustin, R. "A feminist approach to family therapy." *Family Process,* 17, 181-94, 1978.

———— "Family therapy and sex-role stereotypes." *The Counseling Psychologist,* 8, 31-32, 1979.

—————— "Family therapy may be dangerous for your health," *Professional Psychology*, 11, 935-38, 1980.

—————— Gender and Meaning: The Construction of Metaphors for Our Times. In *New perspectives on gender and the construction of differences: Implications for working with women.* Panel presented at the annual meeting of the American Orthopsychiatric Association, H. Lerner (Moderator) Washington, D.C, 1987.

Hollingshead, A. and Redlich, F. *Social Class and Mental Illness: A Community Study.* New York: John Wiley & Sons, 1958.

hooks, b. *Ain't I A woman: Black Women and Feminism.* Boston: South End Press, 1981.

—————— *Talking Back: Thinking Feminist, Thinking Black.* Boston: South End Press, 1989.

Janis, I. "Memory loss following electric convulsive treatments." *Journal of Personality,*17, 29-32, 1948.

—————— "Psychological effects of electric convulsive treatments." *Journal of Nervous and Mental Diseases*, 111, 359-382, 383-397, 469-489, 1950.

Kaplan, A. "The 'self-in-relation': Implications for depression." In *Women's Growth in Connection: Writings from the Stone Center,* edited by J. Jordan, A. Kaplan, J. Miller, and J. Surrey. , 206-222, 1991.

Kaschak, E. *Engendered Lives: A New Psychology of Women's Experience.* New York: Basic Books, 1992.

Kirby, S. and McKenna, K. *Experience, Research, Social Change: Methods from the Margins.* Toronto: Garamond Press, 1989.

Kitzinger, C. and Rogers, R. "A Q-methodological study of lesbian identities." *European Journal of Social Psychology*, 15, 167-187, 1985.

Kitzinger, C., Wilkinson, S. and Perkins, R. "Theorizing Heterosexuality." *Feminism and Psychology*, 2, 293-324, 1992.

Kohlberg, L. "Stage and sequence: The cognitive-development approach to socialization" in *Handbook of Socialization Theory and Research.* Edited by D. Goslin, Chicago: Rand McNally, 1969.

—————— *The Philosophy of Moral Development.* San Francisco: Harper and Row, 1981.

Laidlaw, T. and Malmo, C. "Feminist therapy." *Canadian Journal of Counselling*, 25, 392-406, 1991.

Levine, H. "The personal is political: Feminism and the helping professions." In *Feminism in Canada: From Pressure to Politics,* edited by A. Miles and G. Finn eds. Montreal: Black Rose Books, 175-209, 1982.

Macoby, E. and Jacklin, C. *The Psychology of Sex Differences.* Stanford, Calif.: Stanford University Press, 1974.

Mahler, M., Pine, F., and Bergman, A. *The Psychological Birth of the Human Infant: Symbiosis and Individuation*. New York: Basic Books, 1975.

Masson, J. *The Assault on Truth: Freud's Suppression of the Seduction Theory*. New York: Farrar, Straus and Giroux, 1984.

MacLeod, L. . *Battered But Not Beaten: Preventing Wife Battering in Canada*. Ottawa: Canadian Advisory Council on the Status of Women, 1987.

McGrath, A. "Mental health services of women: Inadequate, unavailable, inappropriate, unaffordable." *Healthsharing: A Canadian Women's Health Quarterly*. 13, 27-30, 1992.

Mercer, K. "Black communities' experience of psychiatric services." *International Journal of Social Psychiatry*, 30, 22-27, 1984.

Miller. J. *Toward a New Psychology of Women, 2d ed*. Boston: Beacon Press, 1986.

———— "The development of women's sense of self." In *Women's Growth in Connection: Writings from the Stone Center*, edited by J. Jordan, A. Kaplan, J. Miller, and J. Surrey, eds. , 11-26, 1991.

Oakley, A. "Interviewing women: A contradiction in terms" in *Doing Feminist Research*, edited by H. Roberts. London: Routledge & Kegan Paul, 1981.

O'Brien, M. *Politics of Reproduction*. London: Rutledge & Kegan Paul, 1981.

Penfold, S. "The treatment of women in the mental health system." Keynote address at the Women and Mental Well-being Conference, Saskatoon, 1991.

Penfold, S. and Walker, G. *Women and the Psychiatric Paradox*. Montreal: Eden Press, 1983.

Quinn, A. "Insanity and control: A class trap." *Quest*, 1, 35-49, 1974.

Rich, A. *Of Woman Born*. New York: Bantam Books, 1976.

———— "Compulsory heterosexuality and lesbian existence." *Signs,* 5, 631-660, 1980.

Rivera, M. *All of Them to Speak: Feminism, Poststructuralism and Multiple Personality*. Doctoral dissertation, University of Toronto, 1988.

Robbins, J. and Siegel. R. eds. *Women Changing Therapy: New Assessments, Values and Strategies in Feminist Therapy*. New York: Harrington Park Press, 1985.

Roberts, H. *Doing Feminist Research*. London: Routledge & Kegan Paul, 1981.

Robinson, C. "Black women: A tradition of self-reliant strength." In *Women Changing Therapy: New Assessments, Values, and Strategies in Feminist Therapy*, edited by J. Robbins, and R. Siegel. New York: Harrington Park Press, 135-144, 1985.

Rush, F. *The Best Kept Secret: Sexual Abuse of Children*. Englewood Cliffs, N.J.: Prentice-Hall, 1980.

Russell, D. *The Secret Trauma: Incest in the Lives of Girls and Women*. New York: Basic Books, 1986.

Sanford, L. and Donovan, M. *Women and Self-Esteem.* New York: Penguin Books, 1984.

Showalter, E. "Is there a female aesthetic?" in *Women, Advocate and Scholar.* Proceedings of the Conference at Montclair State College, 1974.

Siegel, R. "Women's 'dependency' in a male-centered value system: Gender-based values regarding dependency." *Women and Therapy,* 7, 113-124, 1988.

Smith, D. *The Everyday World As Problematic: A Feminist Sociology.* Toronto: University of Toronto Press, 1987.

——— *The Conceptual Practices of Power: A Feminist Sociology of Knowledge.* Toronto: University of Toronto Press, 1990.

Smith, W. and Richman, A. "Electroconvulsive therapy: A Canadian perspective." *Canadian Journal of Psychiatry,* 29, 693-699, 1984.

Stake, J. "Women, self-estimates of competence and the resolution of the career/home conflict." *Journal of Vocational Behavior,* 14, 33-42, 1979.

Stanley, L. and Wise, S. *Breaking Out: Feminist Consciousness and Feminist Research.* London: Routledge & Kegan Paul, 1983.

Storrie, K. *The Everyday World As Problematic: A Bridge Between the Academy and the Community.* Paper presented at the First Annual Women's Studies Research Unit Conference, University of Saskatchewan, Saskatoon, 1988.

Sturdivant, S. *Therapy With Women: A Feminist Philosophy of Treatment.* New York: Springer Publishing Co., 1980.

Surrey, J. 'The "self-in-relation': A theory of women's development." In *Women's Growth in Connection: Writings from the Stone Center,* J. Jordan, A. Kaplan, J. Miller, and J. Surrey, 51-66, 1991.

Thomas, A. and Sillen, S. *Racism and Psychiatry.* New York: Brunner/Mazel, Publishers, 1974.

Travis, C., Phillippi, R., and Henley, T. "Gender and causal attribution for mastery: Personal and interpersonal events." *Psychology of Women Quarterly,* 15, pp. 233-249, 1991.

Vickers, J. "Memoirs of an ontological exile: The methodological rebellions of feminist research" in *Feminism in Canada: From Pressure to Politics.* Edited by Miles, A. and Finn, G., Montreal: Black Rose Books, 47-66, 1982.

Walker, L. *The Battered Woman Syndrome.* New York: Springer Publishing Co., 1984.

Weisstein, N. "Psychology constructs the female; or the fantasy life of the male psychologist (with some attention to the fantasies of his friends, the male biologist and the male anthropologist)." *Journal of Social Education,* 35, 362-373. Reprinted in *Feminism and Psychology,* 3, 195-210, 1971.

Widiger, T. and Settle, S. "Broverman et al. revisited: An artifactual sex bias." *Journal of Personality and Social Psychology,* 53, 463-469, 1987.

Wine, J. "Toward a feminist standpoint for psychology." *Popular Feminist Lecture Series.* Toronto: OISE Centre for Women's Studies, 1985.

———— "Gynocentric values and feminist psychology." In *Feminism: From Pressure to Politics 2d ed.*, edited by A. Miles, & G. Finn. Montreal: Black Rose Books, 77-97.

Winnicott, D. *The Family and Individual Development*. London: Tavistock Publications, 1965.

Women and Mental Health Committee. *Women and Mental Health in Canada: Strategies for Change*. Toronto: Canadian Mental Health Association, 1987.

Yanico, B. "Sex-role self-concept and attitudes related to occupational daydreams and future fantasies of college women." *Journal of Vocational Behavior,* 19, 290-301, 1981.

Yoder, J. and Kahn, A. "Working toward an inclusive psychology of women." *American Psychologist,* 48, 846-850, 1993.

Zuckerman, D. "The impact of education and selected traits on sex-role related goals and attitudes." *Journal of Vocational Behavior,* 14, 248-54, 1979.

## NOTES

1  Although originally presented as a paper entitled "Kinder, kuche, kirche, as scientific law: Psychology constructs the female" on October 26, 1968, at the Americal Studies Association at the University of California, Davis, this paper was published in 1971 and has been reprinted over forty times.

2  See, for example, Matlin M. (1993). *The Psychology of Women*, 2d ed. Orlando, FL: Harcourt Brace Jovanovich;,Williams, J. (1978). *Psychology of Women: Behavior in a Biosocial Context*, 3rd ed. New York: Norton; Walsh, M. (1987) *The Psychology of Women: Ongoing Debates*. New Haven, CT: Yale University Press; Greenglass E. (1982). *A World of Difference: Gender Roles in Perspective*. Toronto: John Wile & Sons; Lips, H. and Colwill, N. (1978). *The Psychgology of Sex Differences*. Englewood Cliffs, N.J.: Prentice-Hall.

3  This is called "essentialism" in some discourses. We prefer to talk about it as it exists, rather than use jargon.

4  Called "social constructionism", another term we will avoid in order to reduce jargon.

5  The term "racialized" has recently emerged within sociology and psychology and it reflects the social construction of race and challenges the biological concept of race.

# THE FEMINIST CHALLENGE: KNOWING AND ENDING THE VIOLENCE

*Ann Duffy*

## INTRODUCTION

Imagine any group of women, anywhere on the planet at any time in recorded history, discussing the impact of violence on their lives. Everywhere you would hear a litany of both abuse and fear of abuse. The lives of almost all women, regardless of class, caste and age, race and ethnicity, sexual orientation, ability or disability have been distorted by violence and the expectation of violence. Whether women are the actual targets of violence, live in fear of violence, or live with a commitment to transcend the violence, violence permeates their life experience and sense of self.

It is, accordingly, not surprising that at the heart of much feminist analysis and action is the issue of violence against women. It is an issue that unites feminists across other political lines and it is the issue that has been the source of some of the greatest successes and most profound failures of the modern women's movement.

## THE STICKS AND STONES: PHYSICAL AND SEXUAL VIOLENCE

Violence against women encompasses an enormous range of actions, actors, and social locations. Some researchers have defined the concept to include psychological and emotional violence as well as economic/financial and spiritual coercion (Canadian Panel on Violence Against Women 1993a:9). In this essay, the focus will be restricted to violence that has a physical and/or sexual manifestation. It must be emphasized, however, that other forms of violence, such as psychological and emotional abuse in wife battering, are extremely significant and prevalent. Indeed, survivors of wife assault frequently report that the emotional abuse is much harder to endure and transcend than the physical blows and injuries (DeKeseredy and Hinch 1991:18). Further, it is often, of course, impossible to fully separate emotional and physical violence. Physical and sexual attacks on women are frequently accompanied by vicious verbal tirades and persistent efforts to humiliate and dominate the victim. Nonetheless, here the emphasis will be on the physical and sexual manifestations of violence against women since it is this violence that has long provided the most irrefutable and graphic evidence of its presence and its impact.

Numerous behaviours are encompassed within this strictly physical and sexual conceptualization of violence. For example, within the sphere of intimate relations and family life, this violence includes infanticide, female genital mutilation, incest, child abuse, dating violence and date rape, dowry killings and bride burnings, wife abuse and marital rape, and intimate femicide. In society at large, this violence includes rape by strangers, sexual harassment (with a physical dimension) and rape of women workers, physical assaults on women in public situations, and murder of women by strangers.

## GROWING UP FEMALE: VIOLENCE IN THE FAMILY

> Don't tell. Your mother. She doesn't understand. Our secret. Every time you tell I'll hurt you worse. Remember that. This is so you'll remember to keep your mouth shut. This is so you'll do as you're told. This is because you're ugly. This is so you'll learn you are a woman. (Danica 1990:3)

A mass of research data now documents the extent to which women everywhere have been victimized by acts of violence. Historically and cross-culturally, there is considerable evidence that, particularly in the family, women have been targeted for victimization.[1] Indeed, many commentators have made the point that, for women and girls, the family is the most dangerous and violent institution in society.

## Sexual Abuse

Given the pervasive concern with the sexuality of young girls, with controlling and molding that sexuality, it is not surprising that much of the violence against girls and young women has been in the form of sexual abuse within the family. Historically, girls were a form of property within the traditional patriarchal family. As evident from the Talmud and Bible, the sexual misuse of children is embedded in Western traditions. For example, according to Florence Rush, Talmudic law allows for the betrothal of a female child of "three years and one day... *by sexual intercourse*" (emphasis added) (1980:18). From biblical times and until the late Middle Ages, child marriage[2] (when the girl was about age 12) was the norm and was generally seen as a property transaction between the father and the husband. Similarly, in biblical terms, child rape was a property crime against the father; the rapist, if unmarried, was required to marry his victim and pay a fine to her father. Within this historical tradition, with its implicit sexualization of female children and normalization of adult-child sexuality, it is not surprising that violence against many female children often takes the form of incest.

Since child sexual abuse has been acknowledged as a social problem in most Western countries only since the 1970s, the research base is relatively limited. There is some evidence that incest, predominantly the sexual assault of girls by older male relatives, has been a documented social problem since before the turn of the century (see Gordon 1986). However, the interesting findings presented by Freud, Kinsey, and others were dismissed by a society intent on both blaming the victim and ignoring the issue. Only with the advent of the modern women's movement and its explorations of violence against women were incest survivors empowered to come forward. In the late 1970s and early 1980s landmark memoirs—Katherine Brady's *Father's Days: a True Story of Incest* (1979) and Charlotte Vale Allen's *Daddy's Girl: a Very Personal Memoir* (1980)—established incest as a central feminist issue (Bagley and King 1990).

Rapidly expanding research has served to document the extent of this violence. Robin Bagley's ground-breaking national survey of child sexual abuse in Canada found that one in two females and one in three males had been victims of sexual offences (1984:193). Significantly, Bagley's work reaffirms the finding that suspected male offenders constitute the overwhelming majority (98.8 percent) of all offenders (1984:215; see also The Canadian Panel on Violence Against Women 1993:11). In subsequent research, Bagley and Young focused more specifically on female abuse. Based on 632 women randomly selected from community health clinic records, Bagley and Young found that 24 percent reported unwanted sexual acts before age 17 that involved at least contact with their genital area (1988). Diane Russell's breakthrough research using a probability sample of 930 San Francisco women (1986) focused more specifically on the issue of incest. She found 648 cases of child abuse before age 18: 16 percent of the sample reported being incestuously abused. Based on a review of this and other research data, Bagley and King conclude that *serious sexual abuse* in childhood (up to age 16 or 17) occurs in at least 15 percent of the female Canadian population and in at least 5 percent of the male population (1990:70).

The inescapable conclusion from these "conservative estimates" is that at least one in seven girls growing up today in Canada will be the victim of serious sexual abuse, that the perpetrator will in all likelihood be male and usually a male known to the victim and in some position of authority over the victim (such as stepfather) (Bagley and King 1990:56-77). The dramatic extent of the sexual abuse of female children in families has been further corroborated by the recent Women's Safety Project in which a random representative sample of 420 Toronto women (ages 18 to 64) were interviewed in depth about their experience of sexual and physical assaults. In this study, 17 percent (or one woman in six) reported at least one experience of incest[3] before age 16 (The Canadian Panel on Violence Against Women 1993a:11).

## Physical Abuse

In addition to sexual forms of abuse, female children will be as subject as their male counterparts to child physical abuse (and child homicide). A wide variety of research evidence confirms that child abuse is a significant social phenomenon. In 1987, for example, Ontario's child welfare agencies investigated 14,000 allegations of child abuse (more than double the 1983 case load of 6,383) (Maychak 1989:B2). In Canada as a whole, 220,000 cases of abuse were reported in 1986 (Rincover 1990:G2). Child abuse is the fourth most common cause of death in children under five years of age. A 1988 Gallup poll revealed that 14 percent of Canadians had *personal awareness* of a *serious* instance of physical abuse of children by a parent (Conway 1990:81-82). While both boys and girls are victimized by child abuse, it is important to note that boys are targeted when they are younger (under age 13) while girls are more likely to be physically abused when they are older (Gelles and Cornell 1990:54). In other words, boys grow out of their victimization while girls grow into it.

Feminist analysts would explain this pattern of victimization in terms of the traditional patriarchal family. Although women continue to be the primary caregivers in most families, most research concludes that men and women are equally likely to batter their children. However, it is argued that men batter their children as a reflection and statement of their power in the family, whereas women batter their children "because they have little power, except the power they can exercise over their children" (Cole 1985:26). For example, research reveals that the more violent a man is with his wife, the more violent she, in turn, is with her children (Straus 1983:229-230). It seems to follow that as boys mature, they grow into their patriarchal power and privilege and are therefore less subject to physical violence in the family. However, as girls mature, they remain the primary targets for both the enactment of power and the frustration of powerlessness.

As girls mature, they also move out of the family to explore intimate relationships with non-family members. In the process of dating and forming cross-gender friendships, many all too often replicate early experiences of violence and abuse. An impressive body of research, which dates back to the late 1950s, documents that in the dating process, many young women are subject to abuse and, in particular, sexual victimization. More than thirty years ago, Clifford Kirkpatrick and Eugene Kanin found that one in sixteen of the university women they surveyed had been subject to "aggressively forceful attempts at sexual intercourse in the course of which menacing threats or coercive infliction of physical pain were employed" (1957:53). Since that time, researchers have repeatedly reported that young men embrace notions of coercive sexuality; for example, in one study over half of male high school students said they believe it was acceptable for a boy to hold a girl down and force her into intercourse when, for example, she made him sexually excited (Malamuth 1981:152). Similarly, Neil Malamuth, Scott Haber, and Seymour Feshback found that 51 percent of a sample of college males said there was "some likelihood" they would rape a woman in a dating situation if they were assured they would not be punished (1980:130).

These coercive and rape-prone attitudes appear to be more than theoretical. Mary Koss and Cheryl Oros (1982) found that one in five men in a representative survey of 3,862 university students recalled "being in a situation in which they became so aroused that they could not stop themselves from having sexual intercourse even though the woman didn't want to." Approximately one in three of the women in this sample reported "being in a situation where a man became so sexually aroused that they felt it was useless to stop him even though the woman did not want to have intercourse." Slightly less than one in five women reported the threat of physical force being used in an attempt to force them to have intercourse, and one in seventeen revealed they had at some time been raped (456). Similarly, Karen Rapaport and Barry Burkhart (1982) also found that young men reported engaging in a wide variety of sexually coercive activities. More than half their male respondents had kissed or touched a woman against her will and approximately one in seven "acknowledged that they had had intercourse with a woman against her will."

The most recent research continues to reconfirm this pattern. A national survey of 6,159 U.S. college students found that "15.4 percent of women reported experiencing and 4.4 percent of men reported perpetrating since the age of 14, an act that met legal definitions of rape." The overwhelming majority of these rapes (none of which were reported to authorities) involved close acquaintances or dates (Koss 1989:163, 164). Similarly, Walter DeKeseredy's study of woman abuse in university dating relationships (the first major

Canadian study to address this issue) found that 11 percent of male respondents indicated that in the preceding twelve months they had engaged in minor physical abuse with a dating partner (such as pushing and slapping) and 6 percent used one or more acts of severe violence such as punching and kicking. Almost 3 percent indicated they had sexually abused their dating partner (1988:53-54).[4]

While the research record indicates that the clear majority of young women are not themselves the direct recipients of dating violence or date rape, violence is revealed as a significant feature in the sexual and social socialization of most Canadian young women.[5] If not personally involved, they are likely to know someone who has been subjected to physical or sexual violence. Concerns about victimization, often reinforced by parents, colour the experience of forming cross-gender relationships. Young women grow up in the shadow of interpersonal violence, a shadow that crosses their most intimate relationships. The violence supports a more generalized dating culture of coercion in which young women and men in Canada act out traditional gender roles. According to this script, men are to demand, pressure, harass, and joke while women are to avoid, give in, blame themselves, and feel guilty (Cairns 1993). Ironically, the ideology of romantic love tends to exacerbate the damage by encouraging young women to confuse physical and sexual aggression with romance. One study found that nearly one-third of respondents "interpreted violent premarital behavior as a sign of love" (Lloyd, Koval, and Cate 1989:129). In this cultural context, it is not surprising that issues of self-esteem, trust, and intimacy figure prominently for so many adult women (Steinem 1992).

## OUT OF THE FRYING PAN AND INTO MARRIAGE

> The bed was full of blood and I was scared, so scared. I didn't want to die, I didn't want to leave my children with him.... When they got the door open, my son Patrick jumped on the bed, and he was screaming, he was afraid, because of all the blood, it was everywhere. He kept screaming "Stop hurting my mother," "Why are you doing this?" (victim statement as reported in Crawford and Gartner 1992:150)

### Wife Abuse

For the overwhelming majority (94 percent) of Canadian young women, dating leads to marriage (Boyd 1988:87). Unfortunately, for a surprisingly large minority of Canadian women, love and marriage lead to abuse and violence. In 1993, Statistics Canada conducted a ground-breaking national study of male violence against women. In all, about 12,300 women 18 years of age or older were interviewed in depth about their experiences of physical and sexual violence since age 16. This random telephone survey revealed that more than one-quarter (29 percent) of ever-married women experienced violence "at the hands of a current or past marital partner" since age 16 (including common-law relationships). More than one-third of the victims of wife abuse were subjected to such serious abuse that they "feared for their lives."[6] Almost half (45 percent) of the violent episodes of wife assault resulted in physical injury to the woman and almost half (45 percent) of these injuries required medical attention (1993:4-6).[7]

This pattern of wife abuse is the enactment of a centuries-old tradition of violence against women in intimate relations. English common law (1767) encoded the rule of thumb by which it was permissible for a man to physically chastise his wife as long as he used a rod no thicker than his thumb (Ontario Women's Directorate: 1991). According to Sir William Blackstone's influential treatise, "The common law gave a husband almost unlimited power to control his wife's property; he was, in fact, the titled owner of all her property. He also controlled her person, and had the right to discipline her...'the husband...might give his wife moderate correction' just as he 'is allowed to correct his apprentices or children'" (Dranoff 1977). Historical research suggests that these rights were far from theoretical. For example, Nancy Tomes' examination of trial accounts in the *London Times* between 1841 and 1875 found that working-class women were subject to a "torrent of abuse" and that violent wife beating was so common that middle-class reformers introduced the Wife Beaters Act (1882) which gave magistrates the power to flog and publicly pillory men who battered their wives (1978:340).

Predictably, the common practice of wife abuse was transplanted to North America.[8] Even in the early 1800s there were states in the United States that specifically approved wife beating. For example, in 1824 the Supreme Court of Mississippi ruled that a husband had the right to "moderate chastisement in cases of great emergency." In 1874 North Carolina made wife beating illegal but urged that, if no great injury had been inflicted, it was "better to draw the curtain, shut out the public gaze, and leave the parties to forget and forgive." It was not until 1971 that Alabama acted to make wife beating illegal (Kurz 1993:259). In this context, it is not surprising to learn that the U.S. Senate judiciary committee estimates that 1.1 million U.S. women are battered by their husband or lovers each year (*The Toronto Star*, 3 Oct. 1991:A15).

In Canadian history, the English common law tradition and the notion that, upon marriage, women's legal identity was submerged into that of her husband meant that any notion of husbands injuring wives (through slander, rape, or violence) was unthinkable.[9] One cannot assault "oneself." When wives were given some property rights in the 1870s, they became able to sue their husbands for damage to their property but were still unable to take legal action against damage to themselves. If a husband broke his wife's nose and in the process shattered her glasses, she could only sue to recover the cost of the glasses. In

1975 Ontario became the first province to permit a wife to sue for personal injury compensation. The Napoleonic Code which influenced Quebec customs and laws also assumed the complete legal and social subordination of women to their husbands (Dranoff 1977:23, 12).

Within this social context, wife abuse was for generations simply experienced as part of everyday life. Just as many contemporary Canadians endorse spanking children, people saw violence between husbands and wives as an unfortunate, shameful, and very private aspect of married life.[10] It was not until the 1960s, with the growth of the modern women's movement, that wife battering was "named" and conceptualized as a serious social problem. It was not until 1974, with the ground-breaking publication of Erin Pizzey's *Scream Quietly or the Neighbours Will Hear* that the battered woman syndrome was firmly established in public discourse (Walker 1990). The 1980 publication of Linda MacLeod's *Wife Battering in Canada: the Vicious Circle* signalled to policy makers and the public at large that violence against wives was a social issue that was not going to go away.

## Marital Rape

The discussion and examination of wife abuse in turn generated new areas of concern. In particular, marital rape was identified as an important dimension of the violence against women in intimate relationships. Given the common law tradition that women belonged—lock, stock and barrel—to their husbands, it is not surprising that the notion of raping one's own wife was initially considered an impossibility. Women and men assumed that a wife owed her husband sexual access; throughout Canada and the United States, the law defined rape as an act committed on a female who is "not his wife." Just as a man could not rob from himself, he could not take by force that which already belonged to him (Finkelhor and Yllo 1985; Dranoff 1977).

By the mid 1970s, as feminists explored the nature of violence against women, marital rape was identified as an important part of the mosaic (Brownmiller 1975). Diana Russell's ground-breaking survey of a random representative sample of 930 women in San Francisco revealed that 14 percent of women who had ever been married had been raped by a husband or ex-husband (1982:2). By the late 1970s, feminists in Canada and the United States were demanding the removal of the marital rape exemption from the law.[11] In 1983, under Bill C-127, Canadian law was reformed and it became possible for wives to lay charges of sexual assault against their husbands (Cote 1984).[12] While very few legal cases[13] have been pursued following this change in the legislation, the research continues to suggest that marital rape is a significant component of violence against women. The 1993 Statistics Canada random national survey found that 8 percent of ever-married women 18 years and over disclosed that they had been sexually assaulted[14] by a current or previous partner. Underscoring the significance of sexual abuse in intimate relationships was the Women's Safety Project's random survey of 420 Toronto women which found that 50 percent of the women who reported physical assault[15] also experienced sexual assault in the same relationship (Canadian Panel on Violence Against Women 1993a:11).

## Intimate Femicide

Most recently, the examination of violence against women has been expanded to encompass the patterns of woman killing in marriage. Intimate femicide, often the deadly result of patterns of wife battering and marital rape, emerged by the 1980s as a persistent feature of the violence. Russell had briefly explored femicide in her San Francisco study—her research revealed that 11 battered women seemed to be in danger of being killed by their husbands or ex-husbands—but it is only in the last several years that Canadian researchers have explored in detail the numbers of wives who are murdered by their partners (Russell 1982:286-299). Canadian crime statistics reveal that every week two Canadian women are killed by their intimate partners (Canadian Panel on Violence Against Women 1993b:33). A study of intimate femicide in Ontario found that 551 women were killed by their current or estranged intimate partners between 1974 and 1990. Each year 30 to 40 women in Ontario are victims of intimate femicide. Indeed, whenever women are murdered there is a high probability that their partner is responsible (Crawford and Gartner 1992:vii). In Canada, women are much more likely than men to be killed by someone related to them through kinship, marriage, or common-law union; in 1986, for example, 62 percent of female murder victims and only 27 percent of male murder victims were killed by "intimates." The overwhelming majority of spousal homicides (79 percent) involve women as victims (Johnson 1990b: 286).

Many other women live in fear of being murdered. For example, The Women's Safety Project's random survey of Toronto women found that 25 percent of the women who were physically assaulted reported that their partners "explicitly threatened to kill them." In all, 36 percent of women who reported physical assault by their partners also reported that they feared they would be killed by their partners. For women who live apart from their abusers, the terror and intimidation may be accompanied by persistent stalking that sometimes does end with the woman's murder. While there are no official statistics on the number of women who are victimized in this way, a number of high-profile cases have suggested that this is an important aspect of violence against women. In 1993, the Canadian federal government responded to public concerns by passing a law that afforded stalked women some protection by creating the new offence of criminal harassment (Canadian Panel on Violence Against Women 1993a:11; 1993b:49).

Intimate femicide is not, of course, peculiar to Canada. Other countries, particularly those with very strong patriarchal traditions, have traditionalized wife murder. In India, for example, the dowry system, outlawed since 1962, still persists. When families of the groom believe they have been shortchanged by the bride's family, some resort to the practice of "bride burning." The unacceptable bride is typically eliminated by being doused with kerosene (a fuel commonly used in cooking in India) and set afire by her in-laws. The groom is, as a result, freed to marry again and obtain the dowry he desires. In New Delhi in 1975, 350 brides were burned to death; in 1978, the figure increased to 700 (*The Globe and Mail*, 5 June 1979:13). Attention from the Western media and the growth of women's liberation organizations in India have not stemmed the tide of killings. Analysts fear that as many as 11,000 young brides were killed or forced to commit suicide between 1988 and 1991. If anything, the problem seems to be increasing as more and more families demand large dowries when they take a daughter off the hands of her family. Official Indian government statistics record that 4,785 women were killed by their husbands for providing inadequate dowries. Currently 146 men are awaiting trial (Gargan 1994:A1, A7).

Wife killing has been similarly embedded in cultural traditions in some South American societies. Eva Blay, a Sao Paulo sociologist, argues, for example, that Brazilian men continue to consider women their personal property and when "their" women leave, the men feel they have a right to kill them. For centuries, Brazilian magistrates have condoned this behaviour by accepting that husbands, as a legitimate defence of honour, have the right to murder wives who are unfaithful. In several high-profile trials, men who have killed wives who have separated or threatened to separate from them have been exonerated or have received very light sentences by appealing to this principle. Since 1979 a variety of feminist organizations have protested this pattern of intimate femicide but to relatively little effect. Between 1979 and 1987, the number of women (of childbearing age) murdered each year in Brazil increased 400 percent (*The Toronto Star*, 3 November 1990:H6).

In sum, for women around the world, love and marriage do not provide protection from violence. Indeed, the research evidence repeatedly indicates that women are in greater peril in their home and in their close personal relationships than they are in the public domain. Newspaper headlines notwithstanding, women are much more subject to violent attack behind the closed doors of their home than on the streets of their city or the corridors of their workplace. A recent massive U.S. study based on 400,000 interviews conducted by the U.S. Bureau of Justice Statistics between 1987 and 1991 found that more than two-thirds of violent attacks on women were committed by someone they knew. Women are ten times more likely than men to be violently attacked by their spouse, ex-spouse, boyfriend, parents, or children (The Toronto Star, 31 Jan. 1994:A20). However, despite the perils of their private lives, women must also recognize public violence as an issue for women.

## PUBLIC PERILS AND STRANGER ATTACKS

> West Pakistanis had little money to wage war, so their soldiers were told to do whatever would best destroy the will of the people to resist, and would cost the least money. The thing they hit on was raping the women. They raped at least two hundred thousand Bengali women, and they did it purposefully, as a matter of military strategy. (Medea and Thompson 1974:32)
>
> Two weeks later, in a remote ditch along a stretch of dirt road in Burlington, Kristen's body was found—nude and face-down. Her long brown hair had been cropped short. She was sexually assaulted. The cause of death was asphyxiation. (Posner 1994:31)

Despite women and girl's vulnerability in their homes, it is, ironically, in public areas that women most frequently worry about their personal safety. For example, the Statistics Canada random survey of 12,300 women found that 39 percent felt worried when home alone in the evening but 60 percent were worried when alone in their area after dark, 76 percent when waiting for or using public transportation alone after dark, and 83 percent when walking alone to their car in a parking garage (1993:8). Many women are sufficiently fearful of public attack that they take precautions. Seventeen percent of the women surveyed carry something to defend themselves or to alert others, 31 percent avoid walking past groups of young men, 60 percent of women drivers check the back seat for intruders, and 67 percent lock the car doors while driving. Only 11 percent, however, have taken a self-defence course (1993:9). These fears and strategies are, of course, not completely unfounded since 23 percent of the women in this survey were subject to violent attack by a stranger (1993:2).[16]

## Male Victims of Crime

It is men, however, who are much more likely to be the victims of violent crimes in the public arena. For example, in the U.S. there are 40.5 victims per 1,000 males as compared to 24.8 victims per 1,000 females (*The Toronto Star*, 31 Jan. 1994:A20). Similarly, although Canada has much less violent crime, it is men who consistently constitute about two-thirds of all adult Canadian victims of homicide, typically outnumbering women murder victims by two to one.[17] Overall, men, as indicated in "official" crime statistics, are twice as likely as women to be the victims of violent crime (Johnson 1990a:279; 1990b:285). Indeed, violent crime, both in terms of victims and perpetrators, has long tended to be a male preserve.[18] Cross-culturally this appears to be a fairly consistent pattern (Crawford and Gartner 1992:83). Given the role of women in the patriarchal family, the traditional gender socialization of women into "femininity," and the historical exclusion of women from the social arena, this is to be expected.

Still, there are forms of public violence to which women are particularly subject, including sexual and physical harassment (particularly in the workplace) and sexual assault ranging from unwanted sexual touching to sexual violence resulting in wounding, maiming, or danger to the life of the victim. Also, the murder of women by strangers and the phenomenon of serial killers and rapists, although relatively uncommon, have attracted an enormous amount of public attention and deserve some consideration here.

## Sexual Harassment

Sexual harassment is another facet of the attack on women "named" by the modern women's movement. Previous to the rebirth of feminism in the 1960s, sexual harassment was persistently trivialized as harmless, even flattering, and an inevitable feature of "office politics." Feminists have ensured that sexual harassment has been recognized as a serious offence that impacts on a great many women. As a result, the issue has received considerable research attention and continues to benefit from it. While this offence is typically defined in relatively general terms such as "unsolicited, unreciprocated male behaviour that values a woman's sex role over her function as a worker" (DeKeseredy and Hinch 1991:103), it does encompass violent behaviours such as coerced sexual touching and rape.

Through the last two decades, sexual harassment has been revealed as a pervasive feature of women's public lives. Agencies and institutions ranging from the military to the ministry are all contexts for this form of violence against women. Repeatedly, research indicates that this is a widespread social problem. A landmark 1983 Canadian Human Rights Commission survey of 2,004 men and women found that 49 percent of women reported unwanted sexual attention (Ontario Women's Directorate 1990:1).

Similar findings have emerged around the world. Recent U.S. research indicates that at least 40 percent and as many as 85 percent of American women have experienced sexual harassment on the job (Lichtman 1993:13A). A Madrid survey found that 80 percent of employed women reported sexual harassment and 4 percent indicated they were subject to violent sexual harassment. In Holland, 58 percent of employed women indicated they had been physically or verbally harassed in the workplace. In a Tokyo survey of 6,500 women, 70 percent of employed women said they had been harassed while working and 90 percent had been molested during commuting; about 3 percent reported they were forced to have sexual relations at work (*The Toronto Star,* 7 Feb. 1992:F1). A survey by the European Community's executive commission found that 36 percent of employed women in France reported being harassed (*The Toronto Star*, 2 Dec. 1990:A12).

Predictably, certain kinds of workplaces are especially dangerous for women. Several studies have found that women who are nurses are subject to sexual harassment and physical abuse by co-workers, physicians, and, particularly, patients. A recent survey of nurses in Saskatchewan found that 81 percent reported verbal abuse, 54 percent physical abuse, and 39 percent indicated they had been sexually harassed. Although poorly documented in the research literature, women who work in the sex trade (prostitution, pornography, and so forth) have long been subject to physical and sexual violence by their customers and pimps (The Canadian Panel on Violence Against Women 1993b:42-44). In sum, extensive research literature demonstrates that for many women there are real dangers in the public domain, including the workplace. In a significant minority of cases, the violence contains a physical component. Research indicates that regardless of the form the violence takes, it has a dramatic impact on its targets and leads sometimes to attempted suicide, often to withdrawal from a work situation, and frequently to significant psychological effects such as depression, self-blame, and anxiety.

## Sexual Assault

Rape, since 1983 legally defined as sexual assault, is another form of violence against women that has been dredged from obscurity by the modern women's movement. Prior to the publication of ground-breaking analyses such as Susan Brownmiller's *Against Our Will: Men, Women and Rape* (1975) and Lorene Clark and Debra Lewis' *Rape: The Price of Coercive Sexuality* (1977), rape was trivialized by society, often humorously dismissed as just another example of "boys will be boys." Victims learned to blame themselves and to keep quiet. Predictably, official statistics on rape have, as a result, been so inaccurate as to be meaningless. As Clark and Lewis revealed, crime statistics often represented nothing more than how well the complainant fit the stereotype of an "appropriate victim." Women who were sexually experienced, unemployed, on welfare, unattractive, under the influence of drugs or alcohol, and so forth were very likely not to be "heard" by the police or the judicial system. In 1979, for example, 3,888 rapes and 8,167 assaults were reported to police. The police deemed only 68 percent of the rape complaints "founded," that is, the case, in the investigating officers' opinion, had sufficient legal merit to warrant criminal charges. Charges were actually laid in only 985 cases. It is estimated that in 1979 only 5 percent of rapists were convicted and that they served on average between two and three years in prison (Toronto Rape Crisis Centre 1985:69).

Predictably, when modern feminism focused attention on rape, the official statistical picture was transformed. Between 1962 and 1982 the number of rape charges laid in Canada almost tripled from three per 100,000 population to ten. Between 1982 and 1988, the rates almost doubled again. In 1988, per 100,000 persons, there were 91 sexual assaults, 4 sexual assaults with a weapon and 1 aggravated sexual assault reported in Canada (DeKeseredy and Hinch 1991:65-67). Even these dramatically increased figures probably underplay the dimensions of sexual violence against women. According to the Women's Safety Project, 51 percent of women have been the victim of rape or attempted rape. Even though 81 percent of these offences were perpetrated by men known to the women, the results still suggest that numerous Canadian women are violently assaulted by men who are unknown to them (The Canadian Panel on Violence Against Women 1993b:11).

## Female Homicide

Finally, a small number of women are the victims of stranger homicide. In 1988, for example, 202 women (373 men) were the victims of homicide in Canada. Of the 169 of these femicides which were solved, only 31 involved an attacker who was a stranger to the victim (97 were killed by someone with whom they had a domestic relationship and 41 were killed by an acquaintance) (Statistics Canada 1990:168-169). Since these cases are often highly publicized in the media, they tend to reinforce the erroneous impression that women are in greatest danger in the public domain and from attacks by strangers. As revealed above, nothing could be further from the truth.

## UNDERSTANDING THE VIOLENCE: FEMINIST THEORIES

> Without an understanding of male supremacy and female oppression, it is impossible to explain why the vast majority of incest perpetrators...are male and why the majority of victims...are female. (Herman and Hirschman 1993:47)
> The question of why men batter women can on one level be answered quite simply. Men batter women because they can. (Freedman 1985:41)

One of the great accomplishments of modern feminism has been the "naming" and exposure of the violence women endure. Much of the research record has been created and/or propelled by feminists. In the process, many aspects of the mythology that for centuries surrounded violence against women have been challenged and eroded. Commentators are much less apt to suggest that women enjoy violence and domination; few will now openly argue that victims of abuse invited the violence or in some way precipitated their own violation.

These achievements have been won not only by repeated documentation of the dimensions of the violence but also by a demystification and reconceptualization of the issues. Sexual violence such as incest (child rape), sexual harassment, and the rape of adult women is not about a few men's powerful, even uncontrollable, sexual urges, nor is it about a few foolish women who placed themselves in jeopardy. Rather, analysts over and over have made the point that rape and other forms of sexual violence are social phenomena having to do, not with sexual needs, but with the relations of power and domination between men and women in society. Rapists and incest perpetrators, for example, rarely are without some "legitimate" sexual outlet such as a wife. Frequently, their victims are selected because of their availability and powerlessness rather than because of their sexual desirability. An 83-year-old widow is beaten, raped, and robbed because she comes upon an intruder in her home; three sisters are victims of incest and abused sexually from the age of five until adulthood because their father had access to and power over them (Wilkes 1994:A1; Landsberg 1992:K1).

Repeatedly, feminist analysts have made the point that sexual violence is not about sexuality: it is about power. Historical analysis demonstrates this pattern of power and domination. For centuries, in groups and as individuals, as soldiers and civilians, ordinary[19] men have used rape to humiliate and subordinate women and to proclaim their masculine superiority and dominance to women and to other men (Brownmiller 1975). From this perspective, "'Rape' and other sexual violence is not simply an issue affecting individual women, but rather a social and political issue directly connected to imbalances of power between men and women" (Toronto Rape Crisis Centre 1985:63). In this sense, the violence is a reflection of the patriarchal tradition.[20] Women and children have long been considered the property, sexual and otherwise, of men. Many men grow up believing they have a right to assert these property rights in a wide variety of situations. Indeed, traditional male gender socialization often encourages men to be aggressive and to combine aggression and sexuality (DeKeseredy and Hinch 1991:82-83). Further, these various forms of violence and, perhaps more importantly, the fear of violence, perform an invaluable social control function for men and patriarchal traditions by encouraging women to tread lightly in the public domain, to restrict their activities, to accept whatever sanctuary marriage may offer, and to avoid challenging male preserves such as male-dominated jobs and social situations (see, for example, Kadar 1982).

Feminist analysis emphasizes that violence against women is a societal, not individual, problem. Put simply, the terror and abuse inflicted on women is a public issue, not a personal trouble. The patriarchal roots of Canadian society have encouraged many men to view a marriage licence as a "hitting licence" and to freely assert their dominion in the privacy of the home ("a man's home is his castle"). Violence between men and women in the family can then be understood as an expression of these power dynamics. Husbands use violence to proclaim or reassert their authority, to socially control behaviour of their wives or daughters; whereas women may use it as retaliation or as a means of protection. The socio-cultural context, which continues to assert that women are less important and less valuable than men, serves to perpetuate the violence (MacLeod 1986:38-39; see also Gagne 1992). Key social institutions, such as the legal and medical system, have long tended to privatize marital rape and wife battering. Other institutions and social organizations, such as the military, sports,[21] and university fraternities have functioned to reinforce male violence and aggressive sexuality (Kurz 1993).

Feminist perspectives that highlight the issue of power[22] relationships between men and women and the societal context of violence against women have received considerable corroboration in research literature. In particular, they have proven useful in explaining differences in violence rates between subcultures and cultures and between classes, races, and other social categories of women.

Peggy Sanday found that rates of rape vary across cultures (deflating any notions of men's biological predisposition to rape).[23] Societies in which women participated more fully in religious and cultural institutions and in which women's economic and reproductive contributions were formally recognized were characterized by less violence and rape against women (1981). Similarly, Kersti Yllo found that the amount of wife abuse reported in a random U.S. survey varied from one state to another. Specifically, she found that in states where women enjoy relatively high social status in terms of participation in professional and technical occupations, enrolment in post-secondary education, and representation in political office, they are particularly vulnerable to severe physical violence from their husband when they live in a husband-dominant family. Also, wife beating is more common in states where women are accorded a low social status and the wife dominates in the family. In other words, Yllo's research suggests that, when women's power in society at large is high, men have to resort to greater use of force in the family to remain dominant. Also, when women's power in society at large is low, men respond violently to what is regarded as women's illegitimate use of power in the family (1984).

A variety of other research tends to confirm the feminist position that violence against women is an historical and cultural phenomenon in which forms of male terrorism have been systematically employed to maintain the social subordination of women. For example, various information suggests that violence increases during periods of economic stress. Men who find themselves increasingly powerless and peripheralized in the economy exert power in the primary context remaining to them—the family. In 1991 for example, in the midst of a severe economic recession, there was a 33 percent increase over the previous year in the number of women killed by their partners (Toughill and Hall 1992:A3;

see also Spears 1991:F6). Extensive lay-offs in the steel industry in Hamilton and the recent collapse of the fisheries industry in Newfoundland have similarly been linked to increased reports of wife abuse (*The Toronto Star*, 8 Nov. 1993:A3).

Research also supports the notion that violence is a reflection of power struggles in the family. Consistently, wife abuse has been associated with low income and marital dissolution. It would seem that, when men cannot assert their dominion over the family through economic clout or when the foundation of their familial authority is challenged by the breakup of the marriage, they are much more likely to resort to the most direct and blunt expression of power—physical force and violence (Smith 1990). The women trapped in violent relationships tend to be unemployed or low wage earners—women who lack the economic power to fend for themselves and their children (MacLeod 1986:20-21). Women such as homeless women who are pushed to the economic perimeters of society are completely vulnerable to sexual and physical violence. Reports from shelter workers suggest that violence is an everyday occurrence for women living on the streets (The Canadian Panel on Violence Against Women 1993b:64).

Other populations of women, such as Native women, visible minority women, lesbians, young women and girls, disabled women, and older women, who are more likely to be socially and/or economically marginalized, appear to be particularly vulnerable to violence and abuse. Here again, it would seem that their heightened powerlessness in society translates into increased victimization both in public and private social contexts. Although research into the diversities of women's experience with violence is relatively recent, the evidence does appear to suggest that feminist analysis in terms of the impact of societal power relations is appropriate.

## Native Women

A recent survey of 104 Native women in Ontario found that 80 percent of respondents said they had been physically, sexually, or emotionally abused (84 percent by their husband). The 1989 report from the Ontario Native Women's Association also revealed that Aboriginal women face eight times the risk of family violence as non-Aboriginal women. Similarly, a 1985 study of Micmac women in Nova Scotia found that 70 percent reported being abused by their husbands. Research into intimate femicide indicates that Aboriginal women are at least six times more likely to be victims than non-Aboriginals (Fine 1990:A13; Crawford and Gartner 1992:68, 73).

Black women in North America have been likewise targeted for attack. In the United States, the history of slavery was intertwined with sexual violence against Black women. Black women, as slaves and later as part of a racially segregated society, were "open territory" victims whom White males could violate with impunity. This violence against Black women was rooted in and served to perpetuate the power relations between Blacks and Whites as well as between men and women. As Angela Davis comments (as cited in Collins 1993:99), "It would be a mistake to regard the institutionalized pattern of rape during slavery as an expression of White men's sexual urges.... Rape was a weapon of domination, a weapon of repression, whose covert goal was to extinguish slave women's will to resist, and in the process, to demoralize their men." Ironically, this tradition of violence and the embedded power relations translate today into the continued violation of Black women, generally by Black men, since "many Black men have internalized the controlling images of the sex/gender hierarchy and condone either Black women's rape by other Black men or their own behavior as rapists" (Collins 1993:102).

## Disabled Women

The powerlessness and vulnerability of disabled women have long been ignored and obscured. Women with disabilities have been rendered invisible by the use of gender-neutral terms such as people with disabilities or the disabled. Recent research suggests that disabled women are particularly vulnerable to violence. A survey of 30 women who attended the 1988 Action femmes handicapées conference found that 37 percent said they had been abused by their parents, 17 percent by medical personnel, 17 percent by their spouses, and 17 percent by caregivers. Similarly, 40 percent of the women who responded to the 1989 DisAbled Women's Network survey reported they had been abused or assaulted (Barile 1992/93:40-41; see also McPherson 1991).[24]

## Lesbians

Lesbians appear also to be subject to heightened rates of institutional and interpersonal violence. Though little has been documented in terms of "lesbian bashing," research suggests this is a common occurrence. A study of 1,000 lesbians in Quebec found that 10 percent indicated they were victims of socio-economic, psychological, and professional abuse because of their sexual orientation. Popular ideology has long legitimated the sexual assault of lesbians ("all she needs is a good lay") (The Canadian Panel on Violence Against Women 1993b:73). Further, living in a pervasively hierarchical and homophobic society may translate into violence and abuse within lesbian relationships (Ristock 1991; Renzetti, 1992).

## Elderly Women

The intensified vulnerability of older women may be a complex reflection of their economic plight, increased physical frailty, ageist attitudes in society and the institutionalization and/or social isolation of many elderly women. Further, since women tend to predominate in the population of the elderly, particularly among the aged, it is to be expected that the victims of violence among Canadians over 65 would be more commonly female. Research into elder abuse, a relatively new field in family violence literature, tends to suggest that, in terms of abuse in domestic settings and by informal caregivers, elderly women are more likely to be physically abused than elderly men and that the abuse is more severe when directed against women (McDonald et al 1991:11; see also The Canadian Panel on Violence Against Women 1993b:61-62).

## Young Women

Young women are also particularly subject to male coercion and abuse because of their social and economic powerlessness. Since the early 1970s, the sexual assault literature has consistently documented the predominance of young women as rape victims. According to official rape statistics, the "typical" sexual assault victim is a young woman aged 15 to 25 (Duffy 1983). The pattern persists today with 51 percent of all sexual assaults targeting women between the ages of 16 and 21 (The Canadian Panel on Violence Against Women 1993b:83).

Finally, there are many women who are caught at the intersection of these various identities: young, Native, poor women or older, visible minority, disabled women, and so on. Of course, many of the patterns tend to reinforce one another. Women who work as live-in domestic servants are often visible minority women who are young and possess few economic resources or alternatives. Native women are often economically marginalized in Canadian society. In short, for many women their private and public powerlessness is compounded. The emerging research suggests that these women are particularly subject to violence.

## All Women

These power-based differences in the societal assault on women are important to acknowledge and explore. They not only lend support to a sociopolitical analysis of violence but also underline that some populations of women may be in greater need of assistance and/or may require support that is particularly tailored to their special needs. However, it must also be noted that all women, regardless of class, colour, race/ethnicity, ability, age, or sexual orientation are subject to violence. Not only waitresses but also female medical students are subject to attack and abuse (Priest 1994:A3). The wives of prime ministers, sports celebrities, doctors, lawyers, and corporate chieftains have all been subject to wife battery. Daughters of executives, religious ministers, and university professors have been victims of incest and rape. A former prime minister of Japan was publicly accused by his wife of being physically abusive; in January of 1994 a warrant for the arrest of the husband of the 47-year-old heiress to the Scripps newspaper fortune was issued when she was found bludgeoned to death; in the 1980s an ex-Miss America claimed that for years she had been a victim of incest by her corporate executive father; early in 1994 a professor of nursing at McMaster University in Hamilton was stabbed to death reportedly by her husband; senior government officials and crown attorneys have come forward to lay complaints of sexual harassment and assault. No amount of economic, social, or class-based privilege can absolutely protect women from violence in a patriarchal society.

## THE FEMINIST FIGHT AGAINST VIOLENCE

> Louise Armstrong (1990) in a recent article entitled "Making an issue of Incest" gives her assessment of where we have gone over the last ten years in our responses to incest. She writes about the intentions of the women's movement: "In breaking the silence, we hoped to raise hell.... We hoped to raise a passion for change. Instead what we raised was discourse and a sizable problem-management industry". (Ristock 1991:77)

By challenging individualistic and sexual explanations of violence against women and by exposing the societal and power dimensions of the issue, feminist analysts have accomplished the herculean task of dragging anti-woman terrorism out of the closet. As the abundant research literature cited above attests, modern feminists have repeatedly and exhaustively documented the nature and pervasiveness of this violence. Most recently, feminists are examining the particular vulnerability of certain groups of women in certain life situations and/or during certain historical and economic periods.

These theoretical insights and research discoveries have resulted in political action in the community. A myriad of services have been created for the victims of violence, a wide variety of educational initiatives have been undertaken, and numerous efforts at legal and judicial reform have been pursued. A network of 200 shelters (transition houses) for battered women in Canada provides not only short-term accommodation (usually no more than six months) but also legal and social support and guidance for victims of wife abuse. The shelters also generally provide a telephone hotline for women seeking support and information and offer educational services on the issue of wife abuse to the community at large. Provincial and federal governments have supported these efforts by running media campaigns against wife abuse. The British government, for example, recently ran a poster campaign with the heading "He gave her flowers, chocolates and multiple bruising" (*The Toronto Star*, 24 January 1994:C3). A number of Canadian communities now provide individual and group counselling for abusive males. It is currently estimated that there are about 35 self-help groups for male abusers (Payne and Payne, 1993:50)[25] (see, for example, the Design for a New Tomorrow program in the Niagara region).

The legal system has been made more responsive to "domestic violence." Police are increasingly being required to prioritize women's complaints of assault as life-threatening calls and to lay charges whenever there are reasonable grounds regardless of whether the victim consents or not (Deverell 1993:A5). Further, women who, as a result of years of abusive violence, kill their husbands are now able to use the "battered woman's defence" in Canada's courts (as well as in the United States and Britain). The law now recognizes that, even when women are not in immediate threat of violence, they have a right to seek to protect themselves and their children (Swainson 1993:A15.

A national network of 62 sexual assault centres now provides support and counselling for women who are survivors of sexual violence.[26] This support may include accompanying women who pursue legal responses as well as providing support for women who years after the event are seeking to come to terms with their abuse. Many centres provide various ancillary services such as support groups for incest survivors and public education. In addition, a number of hospitals have established special programs and facilities for treating the victims of sexual assault. Some feminist groups have been successful in introducing into the school curricula such issues as dating and sexual assault (for example, the Lincoln, Ontario, Board of Education, P.S. We Care Program).

Numerous feminist organizations have successfully lobbied for changes in the legal response to violence against women and increased public education and awareness on the issue. These organizations include the National Action Committee on the Status of Women, LEAF (the women's legal, educational, and action fund); shelter and sexual assault centre networks; and union groups such as the B.C. Federation of Labour, along with profeminist men's groups such as Men for Change and the White Ribbon Campaign. As a result of various efforts, since 1983 rape/sexual assault is legally defined in terms of the level of violence that accompanied the attack, not its sexual nature. This same legislation removed the marital exemption so that it has now been possible for over a decade for women to charge their husbands with sexual assault. Also, this legislative initiative and others have sought to eliminate much of the personal inquisition that was inflicted on women who laid rape charges. The 1991 "rape shield law" reduces the opportunities for the defence attorney to put the victim's sexual past on trial. It also expressly and narrowly defines "consent" so that rapists will find it much more difficult to present a defence based on "mistaken consent." Under the new law, although judges may allow the victim's past sexual behaviour into testimony, there are strict guidelines determining its admissibility (Vienneau 1991:A14).

Incest survivors have benefited from legislation that removes a deadline on civil liability cases and supports special provisions for children who testify in sexual assault trials. The Supreme Court of Canada recently removed some of the obstacles for incest survivors who wish to sue their abuser. Rather than timing limitations from the time the child becomes an adult, the Court ruled that the time limit on legal proceedings is activated only when the child, usually as an adult in therapy, begins to appreciate the harmful effect of the childhood incest (Payne and Payne 1993:66). The Supreme Court of Canada has also eased the difficulties in prosecuting child sexual abuse cases by endorsing the view that children should be allowed to testify by videotape and from behind screens (*The Toronto Star*, 19 Nov. 1993:A4). This pattern of support is reflected in the court's acceptance of the uncorroborated testimony of a three-year-old girl in convicting a man of sexual assault (*The Toronto Star*, 5 Dec. 1993:A18).

It is interesting to note that it is men's groups that have successfully launched several education and public awareness campaigns. The White Ribbon Campaign, initiated by a group of men in the wake of the Montreal Massacre, encourages men to express their concern about the violence against women (Rebick and Kaufman 1991:A23). This response to the December 6, 1989 killing of 14 women (apparently as an expression of anti-feminist fury) is "the first time anywhere in the world that men have acted collectively against violence against women" (Steed 1992:D1). In addition, several Canadian men's groups are working to introduce into the schools curricula that will challenge traditional conceptions of masculinity and denounce male terrorism against women. Finally, one of Canada's largest male-dominated unions, the United Steel Workers of America, voted unanimously to accept violence against women as "our problem," to work with national and provincial women's organizations to distribute information, and to participate in joint events and fund raising (Papp 1992:A17).

Canada is, of course, not alone in these accomplishments. In Australia, for example, the movement for battered women's shelters emerged in 1974 when a group of Sydney feminists took over several derelict houses and offered accommodation to abused women and their children. By 1987, the Australian government was funding 163 women's refuges which, daily, were providing housing and assistance to 2,500 women and children (Hopkins and McGregor 1991:11). Germany has established 140 state-funded shelters which provide services to 24,000 battered women each year (Anderson 1991:93). In 1990, Italy opened its first battered women's shelter. Sweden has established more than a hundred shelters for women, and charges against batterers are laid without the victim's consent. Governments in Norway, Belgium, Denmark, and, to a lesser degree, Greece, have also funded shelters for survivors of wife abuse.

It is certainly no exaggeration to conclude that the feminist struggle to end violence against women has been a worldwide phenomenon that, in the last thirty years, has dramatically altered the lives of millions of women. The accomplishments cited above are by no means an exhaustive list of the breakthroughs achieved. The institutional and social structure of Canada and of many other countries has been effectively challenged and compelled to respond to women's pain. The struggle, however, is far from over.

## CONTINUED RESISTANCE AND FUNDAMENTAL FAILURE

The breakthroughs and victories have been persistently plagued by continued resistance and backlash. The tendency to stereotype, blame and harass survivors of abuse is, for example, alive and well. A 1992 survey concluded that almost 30 percent of Ontarians believe a woman is partly responsible for partner abuse and 40 percent have little sympathy for a woman who stays in an abusive relationship (Toughill and Hall:A3). Indicative of these sentiments, a New Brunswick professor recently came forward to argue that "date rape" simply reflects the necessity of sexual activity for boys (*The Toronto Star*, 5 Jan. 1994:A3). In response to a "No Means No" anti-rape campaign on campus, male Queens University students displayed signs in their residence windows such as "No Means Harder," "No Means Dyke," "No Means Tie Me Up," and "No Means More Beer" (Ainsworth 1989:A1). A national U.S. newspaper recently ran a front-page story on the "growing number of men filing sexual harassment charges against female bosses" and a bestselling book is written exploring the sexual harassment of a man by his female boss (Lawlor 1994:A1).[27] A young woman who in 1991 was instrumental in exposing the sexual harassment of female U.S. naval officers at the Tailhook convention resigned her commission in 1994, explaining, "The physical attack on me by the Naval aviators at the 1991 Tailhook convention and the covert attacks on me that followed have stripped me of my ability to serve" (Taylor 1994:A5).

In light of these continuing social realities it is not surprising that the overwhelming majority of women choose not to report violent incidents to the police or to use social services. For example, the recent Statistics Canada survey found that only 14 percent of violent acts were reported to the police and only 9 percent of victims used social services (1993:7). Even the under-utilized help available is not economically secured. Funding for many of the centres and programs remains tenuous, particularly in protracted periods of economic recession such as the early 1990s. As a result, many of these services are dependent on volunteer and unpaid women's labour.

Despite reforms in the legal system, judges continue to make comments that trivialize the violence or blame the victim. In one case a judge ruled that a woman provoked her live-in boyfriend to punch and kick her by scratching his newly painted car; another judge termed a sexual assault involving a 15-year-old girl "humorous"; in another case a (female) judge was lenient to a man who sexually assaulted a young woman because he "spared her virginity." This tendency to minimize the damage inflicted on the targets of violence is, in turn, reflected in sentencing patterns. An individual convicted of sexual assault will receive a sentence averaging between 45 (in P.E.I.) to 270 days (Quebec) (*The Toronto Star*, 26 Nov. 1993:A14). In recent years there has been a fairly concerted effort to undermine the testimony of adult survivors of child abuse on the grounds that the "recovered memories" are in fact part of the "false memory syndrome" in which overly enthusiastic therapists plant ideas of child abuse in their patients' minds (see, for example, Laframboise 1993:A19).

Numerous additional examples might be cited. The battles against the violence appear endless, and front-line workers despair at having to provide bandaid support to an endless stream of victims while fighting endless skirmishes with the victim-blaming and stereotyping forces. Ironically, the very research that had documented the depth and breadth of the problem also reveals its continued intractability. Although the damage is now more publicly visible, the violence against women has not been reduced. Efforts to attack the roots of the problem, for example to demand a redefinition of masculinity and to sever the connections between maleness and the militaristic,[28] capitalist state are, at best, in their infancy.

Imagine a group of women, anywhere in the world, at any time in the future, freed of both the violence and the threat of violence; women who grow up confident, free and strong; women who never see their mothers beaten or their friends raped or their sexuality rendered as pornography; women who travel in their community and in their world without fear, without countless automatic calculations of their vulnerability; women who need not constantly hone their strategies for avoiding private and public danger. Imagine the still unimaginable—women without violence.

# BIBLIOGRAPHY

Ainsworth, Lynne. "Male students mock anti-rape campaign." *The Toronto Star*. 2 Nov. 1989: A1, A36.

Anderson, Doris. *The Unfinished Revolution: The Status of Women in Twelve Countries*. Toronto: Doubleday, 1991.

Anderson, Karen. "A Gendered World: Women, Men, and the Political Economy of the Seventeenth-Century Huron." In *Feminism and Political Economy: Women's Work, Women's Struggles*, edited by Heather Jon Maroney and Meg Luxton. Toronto: Methuen, 1987.

Bagley, Christopher and King, Kathleen. *Child Sexual Abuse: the Search for Healing*. London: Tavistock/Routledge, 1990.

_____ and Young, L. "Depression, self-esteem and suicidal behaviours as sequels of sexual abuse in childhood: research and therapy." In *Child maltreatment: expanded concepts of helping*, edited by G. Cameron. New York: Lawrence Erlbaum, 1988.

Barile, Maria. "Validation as Prevention for Women with Disabilities." *Women's education des femmes* 10 (Winter 1992/93): 40-41.

Boyd, Monica. "Changing Canadian Family Forms: Issues for Women." In *Reconstructing the Canadian Family: Feminist Perspectives*, edited by Nancy Mandell and Ann Duffy, 85-109. Toronto: Butterworths, 1988.

Brownmiller, Susan. *Against Our Will: Men, Women and Rape*. New York: Bantam Books, 1975.

Brush, Lisa D. "Violent Acts and Injurious Outcomes in Married Couples: Methodological Issues in the National Survey of Families and Households." In *Violence Against Women: The Bloody Footprints*, edited by Pauline B. Bart and Eileen Geil Moran, 240-251. Newbury Park: Sage, 1993.

Cairns, Kathleen V. "Sexual entitlement and sexual accommodation: Implications for female and male experience of sexual coercion." *The Canadian Journal of Human Sexuality.* 2 (Winter 1993): 203-213.

*Changing the Landscape: Ending Violence—Achieving Equality—Executive Summary. Canadian Panel on Violence Against Women*. Ottawa: Minister of Supply and Services Canada, 1993a.

*Changing the Landscape: Ending Violence—Achieving Equality—Final Report*. Canadian Panel on Violence Against Women. Ottawa: Minister of Supply and Services Canada, 1993b.

Cole, Susan G. "Child Battery." In *No Safe Place: Violence Against Women and Children*, edited by Connie Guberman and Margie Wolfe, 21-40. Toronto: The Women's Press, 1985.

Collins, Patricia Hill. "The Sexual Politics of Black Womanhood." In *Violence Against Women: The Bloody Footprints*, edited by Pauline B. Bart and Eileen Geil Moran, 85-104. Newbury Park: Sage Publications, 1993.

Conway, John F. *The Canadian Family in Crisis*. Toronto: James Lorimer and Company, 1990.

Cote, Andree. "The New Rape Legislation: An Overview." *Status of Women News*. November, 1984: 8-12.

Crawford, Maria and Gartner, Rosemary. *Woman Killing: Intimate Femicide in Ontario, 1974-1990*. Women We Honour Committee, 1992.

DeKeseredy, Walter S. and Hinch, Ronald. *Woman Abuse: Sociological Perspectives*. Toronto: Thompson Educational Publishing Inc., 1991.

_____. *Woman Abuse in Dating Relationships: The Role of Male Peer Support*. Toronto: Canadian Scholars' Press Inc., 1988.

Deverell, John. "Police use new protocol to help wife abuse victims." *The Toronto Star*. 12 Dec. 1993: A5.

Dranoff, Linda Silver. *Women in Canadian Life: Law*. Toronto: Fitzhenry and Whiteside, 1977.

Dreiger, Diane and D'Aubin, April. "Discarding the Shroud of Silence: An International Perspective in Violence, Women and Disability." *Canadian Woman Studies* 12 (Fall 1991): 81-83.

Duffy, Ann. "Women, Youth Culture and Coercive Sexuality." Paper presented at the Family Life Conference, York University, April 1983.

Dworkin, Andrea. *Woman Hating*. New York: E.P. Hutton, 1974.

Fine, Sean. "Study of native women says 80% have suffered abuse." *The Globe and Mail*, 19 Jan. 1990: A13.

Finkelhor, David and Yllo, Kersti. *License to Rape: Sexual Abuse of Wives*. New York: The Free Press, 1985.

Frank, Jeffrey. "Violent Youth Crime." *Canadian Social Trends* 26 (Autumn 1992): 2-9.

Freedman, Lisa. "Wife Assault." *In No Safe Place: Violence Against Women and Children*, edited by Connie Guberman and Margie Wolfe, 41-60. Toronto: The Women's Press, 1985.

Gagne, Patricia L. "Appalachian Women: Violence and Social Control." *Journal of Contemporary Ethnography* 20 (January 1992): 387-415.

Gargan, Edward. "Dowry disputes bring murder to middle-class homes." *The Globe and Mail*, 1 Jan. 1994: A1, A7.

Gelles, Richard J. and Cornell, Claire P. *Intimate Violence in Families*. 2d ed. Newbury Park, 1990.

Gordon, Linda. "Incest and resistance: patterns of father-daughter incest, 1880-1930." *Social Problems* 33 (1986): 253-67.

Goldner, Virginia; Penn, Peggy; Sheinberg, Marcia and Walker, Gillian. "Love and Violence: Gender Paradoxes in Volatile Attachments." *Family Process* 29 (December 1990): 343-363.

Greer, Germaine. *Sex and Destiny: The Politics of Human Fertility*. London: Secker & Warburg, 1984.

Griffin, Susan. "Rape: The All-American Crime." *Ramparts*. 10 (September 1971).

Herman, Judith with Hirschman, Lisa. "Father-Daughter Incest." In *Violence Against Women: The Bloody Footprints*, edited by Pauline B. Bart and Eileen Geil Moran, 47-56. Newbury Park: Sage Publications, 1993.

Hopkins, Andrew and McGregor, Heather. *Working for Change: The Movement Against Domestic Violence*. Sydney: Allen & Unwin, 1991.

Hosken, Fran. *The Violence of Power: The Genital Mutilation of Females*. 1978.

Johnson, Holly. "Violent Crime." In *Canadian Social Trends*, edited by Craig McKie and Keith Thompson, 276-281. Toronto: Thompson Educational Publishing, Inc., 1990a.

_____, "Homicide in Canada." In *Canadian Social Trends*, edited by Craig McKie and Keith Thompson, 282-286. Toronto: Thompson Educational Publishing, Inc., 1990b.

Kadar, Marlene. "Sexual Harassment as a Form of Social Control." In *Still Ain't Satisfied: Canadian Feminism Today*, edited by Maureen Fitzgerald, Connie Guberman and Margie Wolfe, 169-180. Toronto: The Women's Press, 1982.

Kirkpatrick, Clifford and Kanin, Eugene. "Male Sex Aggression on a University Campus." *American Sociological Review* 22 (February 1957): 52-58.

Koss, Mary P. "Hidden Rape: Sexual Aggression and Victimization in a National Sample of Students in Higher Education." In *Violence in Dating Relationships: Emerging Social Issues*, edited by Maureen A. Pirog-Good and Jan E. Stets, 143-168. New York: Praeger, 1989.

_____ and Oros, Cheryl J. "Sexual Experiences Survey: A Research Instrument for Investigating Sexual Aggression and Victimization." In *Journal of Consulting and Clinical Psychology* 50 (June 1982): 455-457.

Kurz, Demie. "Social Science Perspectives on Wife Abuse: Current Debates and Future Directions." In *Violence Against Women: The Bloody Footprints*, edited by Pauline B. Bart and Eileen Geil Moran, 252-269. Newbury Park: Sage, 1993.

Laframboise, Donna. "Falsely accused's lives are shattered." *The Toronto Star*. 15 Nov. 1993: A19.

Landsberg, Michele. "Wife abusers rarely get the treatment they need." *The Toronto Star*. 5 July 1991: F2.

Landsberg, Michele. "Don't force the victims of sex assault to stay silent." *The Toronto Star*. 8 Feb. 1992: K1.

Lawlor, Julia. "Women gain power, means to abuse it." *USA Today*. January, 1994: A1.

Lichtman, Judith L. "How can we fight harassment." *USA Today*. October 14, 1993: 13A.

Lloyd, Sally A.; Koval, Jame E. and Cate, Rodney M. "Conflict and Violence in Dating Relationships." In *Violence in Dating Relationships: Emerging Social Issues*, edited by Maureen A. Pirog-Good and Jan E. Stets, 126-142. New York: Praeger, 1989.

Lundberg-Love, Paula and Geffner, Robert. "Date Rape: Prevalence, Risk Factors, and a Proposed Model." In *Violence in Dating Relationships: Emerging Social Issues*, edited by Maureen A. Pirog-Good and Jan E. Stets, 169-184. New York: Praeger, 1989.

MacLeod, Linda. *Battered But Not Beaten: Preventing Wife Battering in Canada*. Ottawa: Canadian Advisory Council on the Status of Women, 1986.

MacLeod, Linda. *Wife Battering in Canada: the Vicious Circle*. Ottawa: Supply and Services Canada, 1980.

Malamuth, Neil M. "Rape Proclivity Among Males." *Journal of Social Issues*. (Fall 1981): 138-157.

_____; Haber, Scott and Feschbach, Seymour. "Testing Hypotheses Regarding Rape: Exposure to Sexual Violence, Sex Differences and the 'Normality' of Rapists." *Journal of Research in Personality* 14 (March 1980): 121-137.

Maychak, Matt. "Extra funds to fight child abuse ruled out." *The Toronto Star.* 21 July 1989: B2.

McDonald, P. Lynn; Hornick, Joseph P.; Robertson, Gerald B. and Wallace, Jean. *Elder Abuse and Neglect in Canada.* Toronto: Butterworths, 1991.

McPherson, Cathy. "Tackling Violence against Women with Disabilities." *Canadian Woman Studies* 12 (Fall 1991): 63-65.

Medea, Andrea and Thompson, Kathleen. *Against Rape.* New York: Farrar, Straus and Giroux, 1974.

Morra, Norman and Smith, Michael D. "Men in Feminism: Theorizing Sexual Violence." *The Journal of Men's Studies* 2 (August 1993): 15-28.

Ontario Women's Directorate. "Wife Assault: Dispelling the Myths." Pamphlet. September, 1991.

_____. "Sexual Assault: the Sexual Harassment of Women." Pamphlet. November, 1990.

Papp, Leslie. "Steelworkers take stand on violence against women." *The Toronto Star.* 29 May 1992: A17.

Payne, Julien D. and Payne, Marilyn A. *Dealing with Family Law: A Canadian Guide.* Toronto: McGraw-Hill Ryerson Limited, 1993.

Pizzey, Erin. *Scream Quietly or the Neighbours Will Hear.* London: Penguin Books, 1974.

Posner, Michael. "A Town in Limbo: Will St. Catharines ever get over the sex slayings?" *Chatelaine,* 67 (February 1994): 29ff.

Priest, Lisa. "Medical students at U of T report harassment." *The Toronto Star.* 1 Feb. 1994: A3.

Queen, Stuart A. and Habenstein, Robert W. *The Family in Various Cultures.* 4th ed. Philadelphia: J.B. Lippincott Company, 1974.

Rapaport, Karen and Burkhart, Barry. "Collegiate Rape." *Psychology Today.* 17 (September 1983): 76.

Rebick, Judy and Kaufman, Michael. "Ending violence against women is a 'men's issue'." *The Toronto Star.* 5 Dec. 1991: A23.

Renzetti, Claire. *Violent Betrayal: Partner Abuse in Lesbian Relationships.* Newbury Park: Sage Publications, 1992.

Rincover, Arnold. "Child abuse has many disturbing definitions." *The Toronto Star,* 29 Sept. 1990: G2.

Ristock, Janice L. "Beyond Ideologies: Understanding Violence in Lesbian Relationships." *Canadian Woman Studies* 12 (Fall 1991): 74-79.

Russell, Diana E.H. *Rape in Marriage*. New York: MacMillan Publishing Inc., 1982.

Sanday, Peggy. "The socio-cultural context of rape: A cross-cultural study." *Journal of Social Issues*. 37 (1981): 5-27.

Simone, Rose. "Women often mutilated but it's not often big news." *The Spectator*. Thursday, January 20, 1994: A13.

Smith, Michael D. "Sociodemographic risk factors in wife abuse: Results from a survey of Toronto women." *Canadian Journal of Sociology*. 15 (1990): 39-58.

Spears, John. "Women's group wants inquiry into killings." *The Toronto Star*. 21 Feb. 1991: F6.

Statistics Canada. *Women in Canada: A Statistical Report*. Ottawa: Minister of Supply and Services, 1990.

Steed, Judy. "Michael Kaufman has message for men." *The Toronto Star*. 24 Sept. 1992: D1, D5.

Stephens, William N. *The Family in Cross-Cultural Perspective*. New York: Holt, Rinehart and Winston, 1963.

Straus, Murray A. "Ordinary Violence, Child Abuse and Wife-Beating." In *The Dark Side of Families: Current Family Violence Research*, edited by David Finkelhor et al. 213-234. Beverly Hills: Sage Publications, 1983.

Strong-Boad, Veronica. *The New Day Recalled: Lives of Girls and Women in English Canada: 1919-1939*. Markham: Penguin Books, 1988.

Swainson, Gail. "Free killers of abusive spouses, NAC urges." *The Toronto Star*. 30 Sept. 1993: A15.

Taylor, Joe, "Principal in Tailhook scandal resigns." *The Buffalo News*. 11 Feb. 1994: A5.

Tomes, Nancy. "A 'Torrent of Abuse': Crimes of Violence Between Working-Class Men and Women in London, 1840-1875." *Journal of Social History*. 11 (Spring 1978): 328-345.

Toronto Rape Crisis Centre. "Rape". In *No Safe Place: Violence Against Women and Children*, edited by Connie Guberman and Margie Wolfe, 61-86. Toronto: The Women's Press, 1985.

Toughill, Kelly and Hall, Joseph. "Bad economy blamed in rise of women slain by partners." *The Toronto Star*. 3 Nov. 1992: A3.

Vienneau, David. "Rape law will give definition of consent to sexual activity." *The Toronto Star*. 12 Dec. 1991: A14.

Walker, Gillian. "The Conceptual Politics of Struggle: Wife Battering, the Women's Movement, and the State." *Studies in Political Economy*. 33 (Autumn 1990): 63-90.

Wilkes, Jim. "Willowdale widow, 83, beaten, raped in robbery." *The Toronto Star*. 6 Jan. 1994: A1.

Wolf, Margery. "Chinese women: Old Skills in a New Context." In *"Women, Culture and Society,* edited by Michelle Z. Rosaldo and Louise Lamphere, 157-172. Stanford, CA: Stanford University Press, 1974.

Yllo, Kersti. "The Status of Women, Marital Equality, and Violence Against Wives." *Journal of Family Issues.* 5 (September 1984): 307-320.

## NOTES

1 Both male and female children have been victimized in the family. However, evidence does suggest, at this time, that female children have been and continue to be more likely victims than their male counterparts. One possible explanation for this gender discrepancy in the victimization of children may be that many boys already are seen to embody some of their future status as men so that there is some reluctance on the part of victimizers to invite later reprisals. The powerlessness of girls, however, is never fully mitigated by their adult status and so there is less to fear, perhaps, in terms of future ramifications.

2 Child marriage was legal in India as late as 1955 and it is reported to persist unofficially. Similarly, the marriage of girls under age 16 was outlawed in Israel in 1950 (Rush, 1980).

3 Here, researchers defined incestuous abuse as "any kind of exploitative sexual contact or attempted sexual contact that occurred between relatives, no matter how distant the relationship, before the girl turned 16 years old" (Canadian Panel on Violence Against Women 1993b: 37).

4 The significance of these patterns of violence is also borne out by research into resultant injuries. Though both young women and young men report engaging in dating violence, young women are four times more likely to report sustaining moderate to severe injury as a result (Sugarman and Hotaling 1989: 10).

5 Predictably, women who have been victimized as children, for example as the victims of childhood or adolescent sexual abuse, are at increased risk for date rape (Lundberg-Love and Geffner 1989: 175).

6 Women's fear for their lives is, perhaps, most understandable when taking into consideration that violent attacks often occur during pregnancy. One Canadian study found that 30 percent of assaulted wives were pregnant when beaten and 40 percent of the women indicated that the abuse became more severe when they were pregnant. Another Canadian study found that 50 percent of assault victims were pregnant during the abuse (Canadian Panel on Violence Against Women 1993b: 34). The first Canadian general survey of pregnant women (a study of 548 pregnant Ontario women) found that 7 percent reported being hit, choked, slapped, punched, kicked, or injured with a weapon, mostly in the abdomen. As a result of this study, doctors and prenatal care workers are being asked to routinely inquire about domestic violence (*The Toronto Star*, 9 Dec. 1993: A15). Predictably, many women miscarry as a result of the abuse. In this sense, they already know the abuse is lethal.

7   Considerable research indicates that women are not necessarily passive victims in wife abuse situations. For example, a national U.S. survey found that wives and husbands were equally likely to report that they hit, shoved, and threw things in relationship disputes. In other words, both partners acted violently. However, women were much more likely than men to report that they had been injured in these conflicts (Brush 1993). Even when both husband and wife are injured, the wife's injuries are usually three times as severe as her husband's (Kurz 1993: 258).

8   Research suggests that, at least for some native Canadian societies, one of the many dubious contributions from the European conquest was the introduction of women's subordination as enforced by coercive familial relations (Anderson 1987).

9   The legal position apparently continues to be informed by cultural norms. Frequently a wife has been the object of humour. An example is the ditty: "A woman, a horse and a hickory tree/The more you beat 'em the better they be." As many will recall, the serious introduction of the issue of wife abuse into the Canadian House of Commons was met on one recent occasion with peals of laughter. There have been persistent efforts in the academic and scientific literature to muddy the issue by referring to the "battered husband syndrome" and "spousal abuse" with the implication that the violence is mutual and the consequences shared. For example, *The Toronto Star* reported a University of Manitoba survey that found "39 percent of women admit they abuse spouse" (1992: A18). Contrary to the impression conveyed in the article, this finding of physical violence on the part of both husbands and wives is routine and does not obliterate the greater likelihood that women will be seriously injured in domestic conflicts and that wife abuse is a centuries-old tradition embedded in a larger cultural pattern of violence against women.

10   Strong-Boag's research into the lives of Canadian women in the early 1900s confirms that, as young girls and as wives, many women were forced to endure violent abuse in shamed silence (1988: 10, 97-98).

11   It is interesting to note that the first wave of feminism (the so-called suffrage movement) had identified coerced sex in marriage (and, as a consequence, coerced childbearing) as an important feminist concern in the late 1800s (Finkelhor and Yllo 1985: 3-4).

12   Change came somewhat more slowly in the United States. As late as January 1985, 27 American states still allowed marital exemption for husbands accused of raping a wife with whom they were currently living (Finkelhor and Yllo 1985: 140).

13   In 1991 British courts imprisoned a man for raping his wife. This was the first such conviction where the assailant was living with his wife at the time of the offence (*The Toronto Star*, 20 Apr. 1991: A13).

14   The Statistics Canada survey defined "sexual assault" in terms of the Conflict Tactics Scale; that is, respondents were asked if their partner "forced you into any sexual activity when you did not want to by threatening you, holding you down, or hurting you in some way" (1993: 5).

15   In all, 27 percent of the research population indicated that they were physically assaulted in an intimate relationship (Canadian Panel on Violence Against Women 1993a: 11).

16  Since many women are subject to multiple victimization—that is, they are victimized on more than one occasion and/or by more than one attacker—they may have been the victim of both stranger and acquaintance violence. For example, almost 60 percent of women who have been sexually assaulted (ranging from unwanted touching to sexual violence resulting in wounding, maiming, or endangering the victim's life) have been attacked more than once (Statistics Canada 1993: 3).

17  Predictably, the overwhelming majority of homicide suspects (85 percent in 1986) are male (Johnson 1990b: 284).

18  In recent years there have been only minor changes in the male dominance of violent crime. For example, in 1990-91 males comprised 82 percent of youth accused of a violent offence. However, females have minimally increased their representation. In 1986-87 women were 15 percent of those accused in all categories of violent youth crime; in 1990-91 this had increased to 18 percent (Frank 1992: 6).

19  To underscore that it is typical, average men who engage in rape, Susan Griffin entitled her landmark (1971) essay, "Rape: The All-American Crime."

20  The concept of "patriarchy" is central to feminist analyses of violence. Patriarchy refers to the societal institutionalization of male dominance over women in the family and throughout society in general, particularly in terms of the economic domination of women. While patriarchal societies do not, necessarily, render women powerless or lacking in "rights, influence and resources," women tend always to have "less" than men. Within this social context, men's violence against women is explicitly or tacitly legitimated and/or tolerated. Even though in Canada the family patriarch has been steadily replaced by the patriarchal state, the gender inequality between men and women has persisted (The Canadian Panel on Violence Against Women 1993b: 14).

21  A Quebec sociologist, Nathaly Gagnon, has undertaken an in-depth study of the relationship between sports events and family violence. Anecdotal evidence (from some U.S. women's shelters and hospitals) has revealed an increase in domestic violence when major sports events (such as the Super Bowl) are staged. Gagnon will explore the possibility of connections between the sports culture, masculinity, and violence (*The Toronto Star*, 7 Feb. 1994: E3).

22  For an example of the centrality of "power" to feminist analysis in the area of wife abuse, see Virginia Goldner et al's "Love and Violence: Gender Paradoxes in Volatile Attachments" (1990).

23  Currently there is some debate in feminist circles as to whether "radical" feminists believe that men are inherently (biologically) violent and domineering. Certainly some early feminists were prepared to develop this line of analysis (see, for example, Laurel Holliday 1978). Clearly, this position has implications for men's role in modern feminism; in short, men who were, by nature, violent, would have no place in a movement to liberate women. However, many feminists, including "radicals," do not subscribe to this deterministic view and accept that masculinity is socially, not biologically, dictated. From this feminist perspective, it is possible to end the violence against women by dismantling traditional male socialization practices and the supportive societal (institutional) structures. Pro-feminist men could be "comrades" in this enterprise (see, for example, Morra and Smith 1993).

24  Predictably, disabled women in countries with a strongly patriarchal tradition are particularly subject to private and public violence (see, for example, Driedger and D'Aubin 1991).

25  Landsberg reports 54 battering men's programs in Ontario alone (costing the province about $1 million a year). She expresses concern that there is no accountability of these groups to, for example, the local battered women's shelter (1991: F1).

26  A recent increase in funding for sexual assault centres in Ontario has meant an expansion of facilities in that province.

27  Ironically, the figures cited in the newspaper article indicate that 85 to 90 percent of sexual harassment complaints are lodged by women.

28  While the Canadian military is in a period of retrenchment, the militaristic tone of the U.S. culture and its hegemonic conception of masculinity has a strong impact on Canadian society.

# MEN IN FEMINISM: REINTERPRETING MASCULINITY AND FEMININITY

*Norman Morra and Michael D. Smith*

## INTRODUCTION

This chapter explores three issues of gender relevant to North American society. First, it discusses whether men can and should contribute to feminist social theory. Next, it examines how the gender identities of men and women have changed over the past several decades. Third, it analyzes critically one of society's most sensitive problems: men's sexual violence against women. Feminists disagree on whether men have the right to engage in feminist studies, but pro-feminist men can be instrumental as theoreticians, researchers, and activists in the field of feminism. Presently, some of these men are assisting feminists in trying to unravel the complexities of sexual violence. Men who actively support feminism have the ability to mediate conflicts between men and women; they can also act as the catalyst in finding a solution to the problem of violence against women. Above all, they perform the task of teaching other men about feminism's most basic principle: women are free agents with the capacity to forge their individual destinies.

## MEN'S INVOLVEMENT IN FEMINISM

Feminists, for the most part, are sceptical about accepting men's contributions to women's issues. The few men who attempt women's studies, whether in theory or research, come under the scrutiny of both men and women. Members of the wider public sometimes perceive men who study feminism as either gay or failures in conventional pursuits such as sports or business (Reinharz 1992). Although some feminists view men's involvement in Women's Studies as positive, others think that being a man, in the biological sense, should exlude men from supporting feminist causes. Poststructuralist-feminist Chris Weedon (1989) questions this line of reasoning and criticizes the "hostility" that radical-feminist writers such as Daly (1979) and Griffin (1986) have toward theory. According to Weedon (1989: 1-11), feminists who believe in an "essential womanhood" tend to regard theory as just another "masculine form of discourse" that marginalizes women. Elaine Showalter (1987) labels men who theorize about feminism self-serving and accuses them of masquerading under the guise of "critical cross-dressing."

Literary critic Terry Eagleton, according to Showalter, is a prime example of how a male scholar can artfully "borrow the language of feminist criticism" to further his own career. Showalter claims that Eagleton, in spite of his intellectual strengths, has two failings: he ignores the ideas of feminist literary critics and is unable to empathize with the *voicelessness* of women.

Eagleton, because of his masculine bias, cannot understand why the eighteenth century fictional heroine, Clarissa Harlowe, in Richardson's *Clarissa*, did not speak out against her rapist. Showalter challenges Eagleton's interpretation of Clarissa's silence with the one offered by feminist literary critic, Terry Castle. Showalter reasons that Castle can understand Clarissa's silence because, as a woman, she too has suppressed her own voice in a male-dominated society. Castle attributes Clarissa's silence, and the silence of women in general, to the repressive or "hermeneutic violence" that men have imposed on women throughout history. Women who have dared to criticize men publically have felt the backlash of masculine vindictiveness. Showalter concludes that "Eagleton's phallic feminism seems like another raid on the resources of the feminine in order to modernize male dominance" (p. 129).

Other, mainly radical, feminist writers, such as Hartsock (1985), Kelly (1989), Kremer (1990), and Eichler and Vandelac (1991) argue that men cannot experience the realities of women's lives. Consequently, men should refrain from contributing to feminist studies as both students and teachers. Feminist research, for these writers, is research done for *women by women*. Moreover, men who study feminism are intruding into a discipline that exceeds their scope. Eichler (1991) undertook a large-scale study of academics who taught feminist studies courses in Canada. She and Vandelac found that 112 of the 892 teachers in this field were men; 79.3 percent of the 112 men were full professors who held tenure. In light of their position in the professional hierarchy, these men often had first choice in selecting the courses they desired to teach. This meant that junior women, committed as they were to feminism, were unable to secure positions in Women's Studies. Many consider these men as a result of their inability to understand women's experience, as more hindrance than help to feminists. Hence, men who try to teach feminist studies in Canadian universities unwittingly "disempower and silence the very women for whom the course was designed" (Eichler 1991: 70).

In the radical feminist argument, no man can understand what women experience in the biological sense. Certainly men are unable to know what women go through at menstruation or during childbirth from conception to delivery. Men's understanding of women's lives differs markedly from women's interpretation of their own reality. Nonetheless, women and men do have similar life experiences. Elisabeth Badinter (1989) argues that gender is not as bipolar as some might think. She emphasizes that everyone is a blend of masculine and feminine, with likenesses outweighing the differences. If this were false, then the typifications used in making sense of everyday phenomena would be of little value. Women and men share much in life that is positive: eating, exercising, travelling, and receiving satisfaction after finishing a difficult task such as writing an essay. Even negative experiences, such as watching the media images of violence in Bosnia or the Los Angeles police beating of Rodney King, affect most of us in the same horrific way.

As with some women, some men also suffer the violence and humiliation from other men. Michael Kaufman (1987) points out that men who tend to harm others usually first experience physical cruelty themselves as boys. Alice Miller (1990) explains how a youthful Hitler and others of his generation in Germany learned to accept corporal punishment with unflinching determination: they learned from their fathers that regular beatings were essential in their learning that unquestionable obedience to authority was necessarily "for their own good." Profeminist men consider the desire for power over others to be the most damaging aspect of masculine behaviour. In the context of violence against women, some men know that their peers will, under some circumstances, reward them for using intimidation and brutality. The reward consists of support for their wrongdoing and reinforcement of their masculinity (DeKeseredy and Schwartz 1993). Above all, the respect that these men earn from their peers assures them a position in the hierarchy of male dominance.

In short, men as well as women have experienced repression, battering, and sexual abuse, albeit not in equal amounts. If theory grounds itself in experience, then profeminists and feminists should be fighting one battle against a similar enemy—the power of [.....] Profeminist men believe that violence is fruitless and that being *hu*[.....] ouraging others to develop their full potential or self-actualizatio[.....] fear, is life's ultimate goal (Maslow 1968). Men who cannot acc[.....] wn weaknesses and who believe that power over others is commen[.....] deceiving themselves. This is the starting point of profeminism.

## PROFEMINISTS AGAINST PATRIARCHY

Profeminist men believe that no man or men should have unlimited economic and political power over others. Because the term patriarchy has various connotations such as the power of the father over his household, of men over other men, and the legitimation of authority in society, it is frequently difficult to define. Carole Pateman (1988) describes how patriarchy no longer restricts itself to a few men but has become the prerogative of men as a whole.

> Patriarchy ceased to be paternal long ago. Modern civil society is not structured by kinship and the power of fathers; in the modern world, women are subordinated to men *as men*, or to men as a fraternity. The original contract takes place after the political defeat of the father and creates modern *fraternal patriarchy.* (p. 3)

Pateman argues that marriage, for instance, is by law a social contract that binds two consenting people. But Pateman asks how this is possible when, traditionally, the law regards the contracting parties in marriage as socially unequal. Society believes that women have always been subservient to men. Only recently, during the marriage ceremony, have women had the right to refuse to swear to "honour and obey" their husbands for life. Marriage represents the first institution of repression for it establishes itself not on equal partnership but in the belief that men are superior to women. Profeminist men, as well as feminists, are struggling to end master-slave relationships and achieve a more balanced and equitable social order. So long as people accept responsibility for their actions and acknowledge the rights of others, all women and men should be able to express themselves as they so wish. In this respect, both the women's and men's movements have mutual goals.

Feminists argue that men on the basis of their gender have silenced women throughout history, but men in dominant positions have done the same to less powerful men of different races, ethnicity, or religion. Pateman argues that the "fraternal patriarchy" prevails but that some men dominate large numbers of men who differ according to race, religion, and opposing ideological beliefs. The aspect of the father who punishes his underlings still persists. Max Weber (1978: 227) argued that patriarchy is linked with power, and power becomes legitimate through a blend of rational-legal authority and tradition or "the sanctity of age-old rules." The ruthless practice of "ethnic cleansing" occurring today in Bosnia and Hitler's "final solution" over fifty years ago indicate how small cliques of powerful men can silence defenceless majorities.

One of the darkest moments in Canadian history involved the treatment of Japanese-Canadian men during the Second World War. The federal government removed 800 of these Nisei, Canadian citizens by birth, from their families in British Columbia. The government refused to accept their oath of allegiance, expropriated their homes and businesses in British Columbia, then transported them to detention camps in northern Ontario to work as loggers. From 1942 to

1946 the Canadian government denied the wives and children of these men the right to visit them. Although the Canadian government has given some belated financial compensation to Japanese-Canadian families for their suffering, it has not erased the criminal records of the men who resisted incarceration (Oiwa 1991).

Men also know what it means to experience brutality and sexual violence at the hands of other men. There are examples of this every day in the media. The testimonies of men who endured beatings and sexual abuse as boys at the Mount Cashel Orphanage in Newfoundland and St. Joseph's Training School in Quebec prove that men too can feel the dehumanizing effects of sexual violence. Canadian history tells us that the abuse of power in political and religious institutions has done irreparable harm to innocent men. The examples of the detained Japanese-Canadian men and the sexually abused boys affirm that men in positions of power can do violence against powerless men.

## MEN OF THE PAST: ENDING THE MACHO MYTH

In the past, men tended to share an orientation commonly known as machismo. Machismo is a masculine stereotype with two basic traits: an exaggeration of male heterosexuality and a refusal to accept women as equals. Although it seems unthinkable that women should not have freedom of speech, control over their own resources, and immunity from sexual harassment, some men still refuse to accord women these basic rights. Arthur Brittan (1989) terms belief in the superiority of men "masculinism." Men who consider women as their inferiors also claim special powers and advantages for themselves. In trying to preserve their dominance over women, macho men do not hesitate to intimidate women in our institutions, including the home, workplace, schools, and politics.

Masculinism struggles to persist in popular culture: movies, literature, and advertising portray men as dominant over women. Movie producers realize that violence is a saleable commodity; film directors use macho screen stars such as Sylvester Stallone, Arnold Schwarzenegger, and Jean Claude Van Damme to attract moviegoers. These Hollywood heroes demonstrate to their audience that "real" men settle disputes, not by means of communication, but by brutality such as punching, kicking, and using weapons. The message that these movies give to children is subtle: in confrontations, all dialogue ends; lashing out in full fury is the appropriate response.

Although these are stereotypical examples of violent men, their ability to influence boys in search of a masculine identity cannot be underestimated. Macho heroes show that the use of power to control others is acceptable if it reaffirms their own sense of solitary masculinity. Inevitably, these fictional heroes seldom "get the girl" because this implies establishing a meaningful relationship with someone who is supposedly weaker than themselves. Fearing intimacy, they draw boundaries to distance themselves from those they perceive as threatening their manhood.

## NEW MASCULINITIES

Despite the presence of masculinism in our culture, an alternative type of masculinity is emerging. Boys and men who do not use violence to downgrade women no longer fall into the category of "sissy." Many men today reject violence as a means of settling disputes. Many of the newer generation of men consider the macho persona to be an unrealistic stereotype. For instance, nonviolent screen stars such as Dustin Hoffman and Alan Alda portray characters who choose not to fight or dominate others. Both Hoffman and Alda are examples of actors who in real life criticize hypermasculine behaviour and support women's liberation (Alda 1989). Their speaking out in favour of feminist issues, such as a woman's right to control her own body, has diminished neither their status as performers nor their public appeal.

These modern men espouse ideals of equality and nonviolence and serve as the model for the new type of masculinity. Hoffman and Alda do not represent all men, but they are media personnages who are telling today's men that using violence does not confirm a man's masculinity. In this sense, men's identities are evolving from the traditional macho type that values power over others to a more compassionate type of masculinity.

The transformation of masculine identity is gradual and has continued for a period of twenty-five years. Barbara Ehrenreich (1983) locates the beginning of the change in masculinity with the work of psychoanalysts Abraham Maslow (1968) and Fritz Perls (1969). According to Ehrenreich, it was Maslow's process of "self-actualization" and Perls' gestalt therapy that strongly influenced a generation of women and men after World War Two. These exponents of existential humanism, along with social philosophers Herbert Marcuse (1962) and Paul Goodman (1960), blamed the aimlessness of the baby boomers (people born between 1945 and 1950) in large measure on the absurdly restrictive gender roles endemic to North American capitalist society. Existential humanism proposes that people are basically good and can lead fulfilling, harmonious lives if they dare to break with the conformity of their times. Before making this break, they must understand their own feelings, strengths, and weaknesses. Perls (1969) advised young people to discard stoic behaviour such as suffering in silence. He urged people to touch one another physically and emotionally. Contrary to the common belief that men who cried were weak or feminine, gestalt therapy told men that admitting weakness was the first step in making oneself whole.

Marc Fasteau (1974) and Warren Farrell (1975), two pioneers of the men's movement, tell us that most men prior to the 1960s, believed that suppressing their emotions was honourable and manly. The key theme for Farrell and Fasteau was men's liberation from the confining aspect of the macho stereotype. The belief that men must be sound financial providers and sexual athletes was unrealistic: the pressure of keeping up this facade led to men dying prematurely from strokes and heart attacks. What is equally tragic is that boys never got to know the gentler side of their fathers' personalities. Because fathers were often engrossed in their careers, they failed to teach their sons the importance of showing tenderness to women. Fasteau, and later Robert Bly (1990), contend that men must first learn to communicate their feelings to other men before they can be affectionate toward women and children. Bly maintains that older men in our culture must follow the example of pre-literate societies and combine rituals, myth, and poetry to instruct boys how to treat others with respect. If boys learn respect for others during puberty, they will grow to be caring adults. This theme of fulfillment and liberation is at the heart of the men's movement, then and now.

Today's younger men appear less reluctant to express their hidden feelings, especially to their friends. For example, young men are no longer secretive about expressing their insecurities or self-doubts. In a recent study, Reid and Fine (1992) administered self-disclosure questionnaires to 16 heterosexual men. They found that younger, unmarried men revealed intimate personal details of their lives to their male and female friends equally. Older, married men were less eager to communicate their feelings to anyone except their wives, although they occasionally confided in a few close male friends. Reid and Fine studied only a small number of men, but they make the point that men are starting to open themselves up emotionally to others.

The identities of women are also changing. Many men and women now learn through education and their interpersonal relationships that traditional social roles no longer entirely define feminine identities. Women still internalize the roles of sister, mother, or girlfriend, but these roles do not completely exhaust the meaning of femininity. Philosopher Simone de Beauvoir (1961) clarified this point prior to the women's liberation movement of the 1960s and 1970s. De Beauvoir's classic work, *The Second Sex*, published in 1949, laid the foundation for future feminist texts. In analyzing women's revolt against patriarchy—the social system whereby men dominate women—she analyzed three elements that men themselves had long enjoyed but denied for women: sexual, intellectual, and economic freedom. Later, feminist Kate Millett (1970) developed de Beauvoir's earlier themes by deconstructing the mythical conception of sexuality that prominent male authors such as Henry Miller and Norman Mailer held. Both these male novelists reflected the masculine perspective that considered it a man's prerogative to sexually dominate women.

Some male writers viewed women as persons and not solely as sexual servants. According to de Beauvoir, Stendhal was the first male novelist to describe women as free subjects capable of forging their own destinies. Stendhal created heroines who formed the prototypes of twentieth century feminists who, in the 1960s, sought their own sexual emancipation. De Beauvoir concedes that some men do understand the meaning of feminism and praises Stendhal for his insights about women's innermost thoughts and passions. She marvels that a man could be "at once so deeply romantic and so decidedly feministic" (p. 232). His female characters reject the patriarchal values of their time by refusing to acknowledge the superiority of men. The Countess of Sanseverina, in *The Charterhouse of Parma* (1944), asserts her free will by overturning the moral barriers, prejudices, and double standards of nineteenth century French society. She scoffs at her powerful husband and rebuffs his threats to prevent her from acting independently. By amorously pursuing the much younger Fabrizio, who is already engaged to a young woman, the countess places her own passion before the sanctity of marriage (Sartre 1957).

The countess' single-mindedness and self-determination resembles that of Atwood's twentieth century heroine, Zenia, in *The Robber Bride* (1993). Zenia's contempt for conventional behaviour surpasses that of the countess. Atwood's character, a mixture of vamp and feminist, shows her disdain for monogamy by having affairs with the husbands of three of her friends. Since Atwood's strength as a novelist rests on her ability to understand women's emotions, this makes Stendhal's earlier achievement even more striking.

The example of Stendhal and his ability to empathize with women illustrates that tension between profeminists and tradition is not entirely new. Present-day profeminist men who are supportive of women's liberation share with nineteenth century men such as Stendhal, philosopher John Stuart Mill, and poet Robert Browning the desire for women's escape from patriarchy. Both Mill and Browning were married to creative and articulate women writers: Harriet Taylor Mill and Elizabeth Barrett Browning. It was these women who taught their husbands about women's plight under patriarchy. More and more men are starting to realize the significance of contemporary women's redefinition of their roles and relationships. Profeminist academic men such as Pleck and Sawyer (1974), Brod (1987), and Kaufman (1987) have taken up the difficult task of trying to persuade men that both women and men need freedom to develop their potential as persons.

## CULTURAL ASPECTS OF GENDER IN A CHANGING WORLD

Theorist William Goode (1992) argues that women have broken away from the role of nurturer and that this has shocked men into realizing that women can no longer provide them with unconditional emotional support. As Goode puts it, there is "no feminine riddle at all: women are as complex as men are, and will always escape the confinements of any narrow set of roles" (p. 294). Feminists face the challenge of persuading women to construct their self-concept not just according to the conventional roles in society. What has been in place for centuries takes time to dissolve. Ehrenreich and English (1979:11) refer to this archaic set of roles as the "old order" of an ironclad patriarchy.

For centuries men have set down fixed gender roles and laws in Western society to uphold patriarchal supremacy. Some feminists believe that men universally suppress and punish women. Cultural feminist Mary Daly (1978:39) argues that "patriarchy is itself the prevailing religion of the entire planet." If patriarchy is a religion, as Daly asserts, then religion also influences patriarchy. In some cultures the synthesis of religion and state has tragic consequences for women and children. In the Pakistani region of Peshawar, for instance, the Islamic law of purdah allows Afghanastani men to sell their young daughters in marriage to the highest bidder. No woman leaves her home without being escorted by a male relative. Women in need of medical treatment are forbidden to visit male doctors. Women, including widows, who engage in extra-marital relations face imprisonment or execution (Moghadam 1993: 220-251).

Men in our society seem increasingly aware that their own choices and commitments often conflict with archaic masculine values. The growing men's movement and proliferation of literature about men suggests that they are now re-evaluating the idea of having power over others. Patriarchy, whatever benefits it has alloted men, has also forced them to assume certain obligations. Traditionally, men were often the sole supporters of spouses and children. Many men now consider it a burden to be responsible for the financial support of a family. Men have learned, both through their parents' unhappy marriages and their own, that the struggle for power inevitably leads to a winner loses scenario. According to poet Robert Bly (1990), it is by using myth and poetry that men will understand that power over others is harmful and that true masculine strength abides in creativity and tenderness toward others. If older, wiser men fail to teach younger men to love themselves first, they will be unable to care for others, including women and children.

Mitigating circumstances such as a wife's death or divorce force some men to raise children alone, but few choose to be single parents. Shirley Hanson (1986: 141) reports that some studies show that men, for the most part, successfully adapt to the role of a single parent after they have already lived with a woman in a marital relationship. Men, in these instances, provide their children with better than adequate physical and emotional support. Hanson refers to a study by Ann Marie Ambert (1982) comparing the difficulties and degree of satisfaction reported by single parent men and women who raised children. Ambert found that men were often better at showing appreciation for their children's efforts and often received greater satisfaction as a single parent than did women.

Many men, however, are unprepared to do what large numbers of women have been doing for decades: raise children by themselves during a child's formative years. This indicates that men who want to be fathers in the context of the nuclear family still need women for the procreating, nurturing and raising of children.

Men construct their identities through their meaningful interactions with both women and men. They know that the situations of today differ markedly from those of their fathers. Even though in the past a man's sexuality defined his gender, this never gave him his true position in society. It was *merit*— what men accomplished—that ultimately proved their masculinity. Nevertheless, achievement was still not enough: men had to demonstrate resoluteness or grit both in their work and with family members.

Although some men still choose to be unsentimental and emotionally unexpressive, others have rejected these traits as confining and unrealistic. This openness is not an entirely new phenomenon. Karen Hansen (1992) cites examples from the late nineteenth century of both men and women in the New England states showing less inhibition with persons of the same gender. Hansen suggests that the shortage of housing resulted in separate living quarters for men and women; in these circumstances dependency on others for resources and emotional support became acceptable. Relationships between men were mostly social because war and work segregated them from women. When male bonding took place, it appeared less macho and more indicative of "rowdy joyfulness" (p.46). The rise of industrialization and the stress on productivity ended this innocent camaraderie. The puritan ethic affiliated with capitalism served to discourage open displays of affection between men and women. The emphasis on production and progress, coupled with middle-class propriety, condemned displays of sentimentality between men.

Economic conditions such as inflation make it necessary for both men and women to work if families wish to stay above the poverty line. Women's wages are essential to a family's material survival. Men are now seldom the main financial supporter of the family, and women now fill jobs that many had previously considered dangerous, strenuous, or unfeminine. They work in the public sector as firefighters, soldiers, police officers, and in a variety of other hazardous occupations. In her study of female rookie police officers, Hunt (1987) showed that women risk injury in the line of duty to gain the respect of their male peers. Hunt further argues that female officers, more so than their male peers, learned to willingly use excessive force to protect themselves and the public.

## ESSENTIALISM: ITS HARMFUL EFFECTS

Essentialist thinking, in respect to sexuality, interprets personal identities as being interwoven with biological inheritance. According to this logic, men's natures are aggressive and women's passive. Classifications such as feminist and masculinist tend to confuse when they divide gender into two clear-cut categories. Clatterbaugh (1990) points to one conservative writer on gender, George Gilder, who has adopted this approach in explaining sexual violence as the product of a character trait inherent to all men. More progressive men writers contend that gender identities are neither ascribed nor static but evolve through unique choices in relationships with men and women (Pleck 1981; Brittan 1989; Messner 1992). Identity depends upon both choices and our interaction with others. If conservative writers, men and women, regard gender categories only as concrete social facts and not as "social currents," as Durkheim (1966, p.8) had likewise proposed, then two problems arise. First, boundaries are tightly drawn up setting *them* apart from *us*, thus turning gender into a battleground, similar to apartheid. Second, the issue of sexual violence will stay unresolved.

Although the category "man" is a biogenetic term relative to the male reproductive faculty, it also connotes strength indicative of power over others. Some men believe they have an inherent right to possess this power. The belief, however, that all men, by virtue of their sex, have free access to power and privilege, is erroneous. It is true that men by and large do not understand the terror of sexual violence and harassment, but some do experience, because of their own shortcomings, a self-imposed violence of sorts. By refusing to acknowledge their feelings of vulnerability and fears of inadequacy (supposedly feminine traits), they fail to open themselves up to the affection of others. More frequently, in their attempt to keep their power over other men intact, men hurt each other in the context of schools, sports, bars, police work, and like settings. Violent men rely on episodes of bad temper and the loss of self-control as a form of justification for harming others whom they perceive as challenging their manhood. The spouses and friends of these men are often the ones who suffer the effects of this explosive behaviour.

Gay men also have continually experienced violence in the forms of taunting and bashing. This is something traceable to the discriminatory attitudes that straight men learn in our society. There are heterosexual men who consider the beating up of gays as commendable because it serves to reinforce their own sexual identity. In a culture such as ours, those men who are unwilling to fight back receive little sympathy and are often considered deserving of the beatings they receive. The law, in its reluctance to protect those it disfavours, regards the problem of violence directed at gays as one of minor concern. This anti-gay bias perpetuates itself within the taken-for-granted structures of the family, educational system, the military, peer groups, and the media (Comstock 1991; Kinsman 1987).

Another common feature men share with women is the reality of low-paying and unrewarding jobs. Again, this notion of privilege, that men on the whole fill powerful white-collar occupations, is propaganda put forward by the media (Harris 1992:226). To the contrary, a large percentage of men work within the service sector, in unskilled jobs, with little hope for any advancement in their standard of living. If the American dream is finished, then it has expired for both men and women.

## WOMEN, STATUS, AND POWER

There are examples of women occupying dominant positions in a variety of fields long considered male domains. Marge Schott, the owner of the Cincinnati Reds professional baseball team, exerts as much authority over her managers, coaches, and players as do any of her male peers in the National League. In light of her one-year suspension from the game for using racist slurs regarding her players, Schott has also demonstrated her ability to take her punishment as well as any man would under similar circumstances. The cantankerous Schott also draws as much attention from the media as any superstar male athlete.

Pamela Churchill Harriman, widow of the late tycoon and politician Averell Harriman, currently reigns as the influential matriarch of the Democratic party in the U.S. In a recent documentary, PBS illustrated the extent of her power. Through its description of the meteoric rise of then presidential candidate, Bill Clinton, it showed how heavily Clinton's initial success depended upon both Harriman's endorsement and her multimillion-dollar contribution to his campaign. Harriman, a former journalist, is an especially interesting character: besides chairing the Democratic party, she holds a postgraduate degree in economics from the Sorbonne and is on the board of directors of several key American corporations. Clinton has shown his gratitude to Harriman by appointing her to the prestigious post of U.S. ambassador to France *(Who's Who in America* 1992).

Although the financial independence of Schott and Harriman is tied to the fortunes amassed by their deceased husbands, one must not ignore the significance of these women's personal capabilities in maintaining their positions of power in the male-dominated realms of professional sports and politics. Interestingly, wealthy, powerful men such as George Steinbrenner, Donald Trump, Ted Turner, Conrad Black, and the late Howard Hughes, whom the media depict as "self-made,",built *their* commercial empires out of the substantial inheritances handed down to them by their fathers.

Dorothy E. Smith (1979) classifies women's work as physically demanding, as existing in a "bodily mode." Men's work, in contrast to the drudgery of women's labour, is often coolly intellectual: this she terms an "abstract, conceptual mode." Smith argues that women as a class have been physically and intellectually enslaved and that their self-concept, that of the nurturer, is inseparable from the menial work they perform on a daily basis. Men, privileged from birth, perceive themselves as free agents. It is this gratuitous freedom that grants men the right to appropriate women as their slaves. Both capitalism and patriarchy have maintained this oppression by keeping women not only subservient but also alien to their own bodies and minds. Women can free themselves only by means of a radical deep-seated refusal to define themselves according to the traditional dominant male discourse.

What confounds the notion that women as a class suffer universal economic deprivation through masculine oppression is the historical fact that women, too, have exerted power over men and other women. In 1990, federal Justice Minister Kim Campbell, later Canada's first woman prime minister, denied the Mohawks at Kahnawake their aboriginal rights during the Oka land dispute (York and Pindera 1992). Campbell refused to negotiate with the Mohawks and accused them of violating the "rule of law." Canadian governments in the past had used this questionable tactic to deny Aboriginals the vote in federal and provincial elections as well as to forbid them from leaving their reserves without official permission. Lawyers from Queen's University Faculty of Law attacked Campbell's interpretation of Canadian law and argued that her handling of the Oka situation was an attempt to quash a minority group's plea for equality.

Consider also pre-Civil War slavery in the U.S. south where White women, as powerful mistresses, treated Blacks as property. Davis (1983) and hooks (1984) point out that most White women today, including feminists, have ignored the needs of both underprivileged Black women and minorities. At present, in South Africa, the dominant status accorded White women over Black men continues unabated (Brittan 1989). If masculine identities vary not only in respect to how they are socialized but also on the basis of privileges accorded by their class position, then women's are shaped in the same way (Pateman 1988).

If suffering is common to working men and women under capitalism, as Marx professed, then how can one subsume all men as the enemy? To dichotomize class, itself an economic reality, into an arena of male-female sexual politics, misappropriates Marx's philosophy of liberation for all oppressed workers (Marx 1990:230). Surely Marx's meaning of alienation applies to all underclass workers regardless of gender. For Marx, suffering was something that the "immense majority" of people endured under capitalism. If this struggle for economic and spiritual survival is a joint venture encompassing the entire subordinate class, then it seems logical that a concerted effort by both women and men would be all the more feasible in defiance of patriarchy.

During the nineteenth century, prominent writers such as Marx, Engels, John Stuart Mill, Ibsen, Flaubert, and Robert Browning were willing to face societal disapprobation for their profeminist sentiments. One would be hard-pressed to find within English verse a more antipatriarchal poem than Browning's *"My Last Duchess."* Perhaps the writings of these few men signified the beginnings of a transition, albeit a slow one, in the attitudes men hold toward themselves and others. There are modern men who value the liberation of both women and men and envisage this occurring in a symbiotic fashion (Kaufman 1987; Thorne-Finch 1992). It is the writings of only a particular handful of progressive feminist writers that offer us a positive assessment of male collaboration, not only in regard to activism (hooks 1984) and theory (Harding 1986) but also in the study of sexual violence (Sanday 1981, 1990; Scully 1990).

## FEMINISM—WHO HAS THE VOICE?

Difficult as it may be, by avoiding the temptation to categorize persons according to ascribed statuses of race, gender, and age, theorists can safeguard their work against the pitfall of oversimplifying an issue. Declaring "all men are the enemy" or "all men hate women" places women of colour and ethnic minorities in an awkward position. Because of the shared bond between activist men and women in opposition to society's dominant oppressors, Black feminists have rejected one of the fundamental tenets of radical feminism—the exclusion of male comrades. Black women have realized for some time how fatal and counterproductive such a strategy can be since it foils their efforts in their battle to achieve basic civil rights. Feminist bell hooks (1984) explains this particular concept:

> This affirmation of bonding between black women and men was part of an anti-racist struggle. It could have been part of a feminist struggle had women's liberationists stressed the need for women and men to resist the sexist socialization that teaches us to hate and fear one another. They chose instead to emphasize hate, suggesting that it could not be changed. (p. 70)

Hooks correctly ascribes socialization as vital in the formation of prevalent male attitudes toward women. While this concept is apparent to some, radical feminists such as Andrea Dworkin continue to isolate male sexual desire as the main reason men objectify and control women. Men, according to Dworkin, are driven to dominate women by their biology: sexual intercourse is one pernicious way of keeping women in line. Dworkin (1987:139) sees intercourse, sexual and social, as a form of masculine existential theft, something that robs women of "the potential for human choice by men who love to hate us."

The ground shared by both hooks and Dworkin rests upon the primary and motivating principle of feminism: women's emancipation within patriarchal structures. If both theorists claim women's right to their own bodies and to the resources society offers, then a more solid platform for the new nonpatriarchal order must be constructed.

So far we have discussed how some feminists view the potential of men's roles in the fight against racial and economic injustice. We turn now to the part men are capable of playing in the advancement of feminist theory. Should feminists, in light of the hard-fought ground they have gained, share their theoretical advances with their male oppressors? This question may seem ludicrous to radical feminists. Dworkin (1988) advocates not simply an intellectual defence of the feminist vanguard but a *physical* one whereby women collectively "form a barricade with our bodies." What further perplexes the issue, particularly in respect to rape, are the pronouncements of Camille Paglia who refuses to categorically condemn all men as potential perpetrators of this violence. Paglia (1992) believes theoretical knowledge about sexual violence must be withdrawn from the context of Women's Studies and placed within the broader sphere of philosophy.

> Look—ethics has *always* condemned such abuses. You do not have this endless series of atrocities through history. Men have always protected women. Men have given women sustenance. Men have provided for women. We must look back and acknowledge what men wave done for *women*. (p. 273)

Feminist philosopher Sandra Harding (1986) in her essay "Is There a Feminist Method?" discusses the dilemma of who is justified in researching feminist theory. Harding's introduction to this volume of essays concerning feminist methodology is notable for its attempt to reclaim a sense of reason in this matter. For Harding, feminists can benefit from the inclusion of the male researcher because the masculine perspective, foreign to women's outlook, acts as a counterpoint to feminist theory. This counterpoint prevents feminism from imploding and serves to accentuate the reality of the feminine experience.

Harding argues that anyone who shows a genuine concern for women's struggles ought to be heard. Legitimate theory should appeal to reason and reflect the basic desire for the advancement of feminism. While accepting women's experiences as *primary* in feminist discourse, Harding (1986) nevertheless advises against any exclusive and unilateral study of feminism by women alone.

> It is sometimes falsely supposed that in using women's experience rather than men's as an empirical and theoretical resource feminism expresses a kind of relativism. It is sometimes also falsely imagined that men cannot make important contributions to feminist research and scholarship. (p. 10)

The problem with encapsulating woman as a unified totality is that just as all men are not abusive toward women, neither are all women sympathetic to feminism. Aware that gender cannot provide the sole criterion for contributing to feminist theory, Harding offers the example of one "misogynous" woman writer, Phyliss Schlafly, who staunchly rejects feminism. As a Harvard Law School graduate and advocate of the New Right ideology in the U.S. Republican party, Schlafly has resolutely opposed, for over two decades, the Equal Rights Amendment bill guaranteeing women paid maternity leave and subsidized child day care (Faludi 1991). These basic provisions have been legally in place in most European countries for well over ten years.

The ubiquitous Schlafly is visible on numerous television talk shows where she exhibits a remarkably composed manner. She renders, with some zeal, her uncanny version of how feminism contributes to the perpetuation of many of society's ills such as unemployment, teenage crime, and the breakdown of family values. It is her view that feminism, with its emphasis on liberation, has encouraged women to allow the family to disintegrate. Schlafly's (1977) argument, as expounded in her book *The Power of the Positive Woman*, remains unaltered over the years. She believes a woman's freedom is found in a return to the traditional family in which the husband and children assume priority and the woman's career takes second place. In using actress Katharine Hepburn as her model for younger women in America, Schlafly tries to show that women can still be "strong-minded" and independent but still believe in the family and behave patriotically. Schlafly's claims are undeniably ultraconservative and attempt to keep patriarchy secure against feminism.

## EARLIER STUDIES ON SEXUAL VIOLENCE

Before the 1970s, sociologists regarded rape as a taboo subject. In focusing on drug addiction and delinquency, earlier scholars neglected equally important issues such as violence against women and child abuse (Stanko 1990). Social scientists generally believed that rape was a psychological disorder rather than a sociological problem. Rapists were either mentally ill or unable to control their excessive sexual urges (Scully and Marolla 1993). Hesitant to analyze violence toward women, sociologists of the 1950s and 1960s contributed little to our present understanding of sexual violence. Since most cultures consider rape to be a crime second only to murder, the lack of research conducted during these two decades seems puzzling today.

In the early 1970s, however, sociologists began to study sexual violence in earnest, and their findings formed the basis for our present knowledge about this subject. Amir (1971), Brownmiller (1975), and Russell (1975) were the first to examine and publish some of the most remarkable data about rape. Both Amir and Brownmiller studied men from lower-class backgrounds and concluded that they were more likely to commit forcible rape than middle- or upper-class males. Amir examined the records of the Philadelphia police department for two years—1958 and 1960. The records showed that the police had charged mainly lower-class Black men between the ages of 15 and 24 with the crime of forcible rape. Brownmiller, a journalist, focused on men who raped in historical settings such as war; she also analyzed homosexual rape in prison. For Amir and Brownmiller there seemed to be a definite correlation between violence and subculture. Accordingly, these theorists hypothesized that rapists were usually poor, uneducated men. Both Amir and Brownmiller argued that men who raped readily used violence to degrade their victims and gain for themselves a distorted sense of power. Also, Amir and Brownmiller found that these men raped not only one on one but also in groups. This new evidence of group rape, a phenomenon sociologists had never previously examined, reinforced Amir and Brownmiller's thesis that rape, in the same instance, could denigrate women and help to bond men.

Russell (1972) in turn rejected the subcultural claim by using the self-reports of women from all levels of society. Using a woman-centred approach (women interviewing women), Russell learned that it was not uncommon for husbands, friends, and acquaintances to rape and batter women. Russell (1982) later interviewed 930 women in San Francisco and found that 14 percent had experienced beatings and rape by their husbands. In sum, the Russell, Amir, and Brownmiller studies proved that rape was really far more widespread than many had suspected. Few women in today's society are free from the threat of sexual violence. Scully and Marolla (1993) maintain that, in spite of the evidence garnered by Russell, Amir, Brownmiller and subsequent sociologists, many still believe that rapists suffer from psychopathological defects.

Today's women cannot fully appreciate the gains they have made in areas such as civil rights and equal pay so long as they are fearful of male violence. To answer this complex question, a coalition between feminists and profeminist men must first take place. Until both groups show a willingness to remove the barriers separating them, women will continue to fear for their safety. It is vital for both factions to set aside their differences and openly discuss the subject of sexual violence. Once this dialogue takes place, we will begin to understand and eventually resolve this problem. Unless both sides pool their theory and research, the reality of sexual violence will continue to pervade the lives of women.

## MEN'S CONTRIBUTION TO FEMINISM AND THE STUDY OF RAPE

Radical feminism, especially, argues that men as a category are the prime cause of sexual violence and the suppression of women's power. Radical feminists state that men must first stop their violence before any cooperation between women and men can materialize (Dworkin 1987, 1988; Hanmer and Saunders 1984; Kelly 1988; Stanley and Wise 1983). In order to end sexual violence, one must understand its complexities, in relation not only to its victims but also to its perpetrators. Focusing on those men who abuse, batter, and rape can provide some insight about the motives underlying much of this behaviour. Moreover, it is difficult to understand violent men without also examining the rituals of bonding that help to formulate, support, and reinforce the macho identity. Deconstructing this particular identity and the systems sustaining it should make it possible to eliminate one of the main factors responsible for the damage men inflict on women (Miedzian 1991; Smith 1991).

The problem of sexual violence and its eventual dissolution extends beyond the scope of academic analysis into the domains of law and the media. Preventing the continuation of crimes such as rape requires an entire societal commitment, and for any meaningful development to occur there must first take place an empathic, rational, open-ended discourse among all engaged parties, regardless of their political position (Habermas 1984, p. 108).

Much of the traditional theory about crime and deviance has had little to do with rape as a cultural phenomenon. One landmark statistical study, Amir's (1971) *Patterns in Forcible Rape*, points to the high numbers of multiple or group offenders involved in rapes. Of the 646 cases listed in the police records of his Philadelphia study, there were 1,292 offenders: a ratio of two attackers to one victim. His data showed that 71 percent of those offenders had engaged in gang rape (Amir 1971:200). Radical feminist Susan Brownmiller (1975) acknowledged Amir's remarkable finding in her depiction of rape within a variety of ordinary and extraordinary situations. Amir's study is pivotal for two reasons: it was the first quantitative analysis of group rape, work previously neglected by sociologists; and it channeled our attention away from the psychological to the explicit social and cultural factors conducive to its occurrence. An examination of Brownmiller's passages on the gang rape by American soldiers in Vietnam make it clear how important a role these factors play in understanding why some men choose to rape.

Anthropologist Peggy Reeves Sanday (1981, 1990) is another feminist who has contributed to our understanding of group rape by both tribal males in pre-literate societies and fraternity brothers in American universities. Of the 156 tribes that Sanday studied in her earlier work, one of the most interesting was the Mundurucu who inhabit the isolated rain forest of South America. Through her analysis of rituals of bonding among the Mundurucu men, Sanday shows how the hunters cooperate with females in the economic functions of the tribe but occupy separate living quarters, refusing to socialize with their assertive and independent women. Ritualistic gang rape is used both as a way of maintaining dominance over women and as a form of religious offering to the gods. In controlling the sexuality of women, symbolized as "sacred trumpets" capable of speaking directly to the gods, the men feel they are appeasing their deities' wrath (Sanday 1981:37-40).

In her more recent work, *Fraternity Gang Rape*, Sanday (1990) shows how the enactment of rituals in college fraternities helps reinforce the societal attitudes supportive of men's dominance over women. Although distantly removed from the Mundurucu, both culturally and spatially, the fraternities share striking similarities with them. In presenting her argument, Sanday states that the magnitude of this social problem moves beyond feminism and that consequences of this problem affect everybody. If the larger social order, of which the fraternity is one part, allows this problem to continue, then it should be accountable for its laxity. Also, pornography, readily accessible to society at large, plays a big part in fraternity subculture and thus affects the way fraternity brothers perceive women. Sanday argues that the same male-dominated legal system that allows the pornography industry to flourish also grants preferential treatment to these privileged young men when they rape. The central theme in much of pornography is that women exist exclusively for men's immediate sexual gratification. She appeals for harsher penalties for rape and for a debunking of the cultural myth that portrays male sexuality as an uncontrollable urge, which, if suppressed, might lead men to rape (Sanday 1990).

How does a woman researcher gain access to the empirical data necessary in unearthing the factors motivating gang rape? Sanday's recording of what is spoken and performed within a particular subculture was made possible by the narratives of the survivors, witnesses, and particularly the perpetrators of these crimes. Also assisting her in her analysis were the observations of those sorority sisters who frequented the fraternity parties that served as a preamble for these rapes. But the in-depth knowledge of campus party culture, including the rituals such as the "circle dance," "beaching," scapegoating, "purifying the fag," and the ritual circumventing the act of rape itself, "pulling train," could only have been garnered with the help of empathetic men infiltrators with whom the fraternity brothers felt some kinship. Anyone choosing to divulge the secret hazing rituals of the fraternity was leaving himself open to physical retaliation (Sanday 1990).

The element of secrecy, allegiance to the fraternal order, and of both in private and during the initiation rites, is one aspect of masculine bonding that the women researcher could record only with the collaboration of certain men. Perhaps it is this realization that prompted Sanday (1990:xii) to acknowledge that "These men have taught me that feminism is a way of thinking and not a matter of gender."

In contrast to these profeminist men are the sorority sisters at a large southern university who aided the men in the act of rape through their procurement of an unsuspecting sister. This feminine ritual, "little sister rush," served to ingratiate these particular sisters to the fraternity brothers. This ritual entailed the intentional abandonment of a naive sister, who, having consumed too much alcohol, blacked out at one of the fraternity parties. The sisters knew that the fate awaiting this woman, when all outsiders had left the house, was subjection to systematic gang rape (Sanday 1990, pp.101-110). For whatever her reason, Sanday does not call these women rapists, despite the fact the law specifically states that a woman may also be guilty of rape if she is implicit in procuring a woman for men to violate (Amir 1971, p. 24).

Another feminist, Diana Scully, believes that the key to understanding sexual violence lies not in dwelling upon the suffering of the woman but in fathoming the phenomenological world that men encounter. Her choice to make the rapist the centre of her studies is in opposition to radical feminism's belief that women concern themselves exclusively with the pain that women experience through male violence (Hanmer and Saunders 1984). Scully (1990) sees the attention paid to the victim as necessary and compassionate, but argues that overemphasizing the woman's plight often leads, unfairly, to blaming the victim. It also takes us away from our attempt to understand the experiential world of the rapist—the way he perceives himself and others as persons.

What Scully discovered, along with her assistant, Joseph Marolla, during their ten-year study of incarcerated rapists within ten U.S. prisons, was that these men perceived women as enjoying physical domination. Many of the rapists shared a self-image marred by a tendency to self-aggrandizement and a deluded perception of being irresistible to women. They believed they possessed inordinate sexual prowess and a masterful technique with women. One rapist, in denying the severity of his act, described his technique to Scully (1990:112) in this way: "If I thought a broad was dominant, I had to use strength. If she was passive, I'd still use strength, but not as much."

Scully's research helps us gain access to the perceptions of those men who inflict physical suffering on women for the purpose of enhancing their own mis-construed self-esteem. If the majority (77 percent) of her interviewees felt no shame or remorse for their actions, then perhaps this says something about how they have been taught to perceive themselves and others. In denying responsi-bility for their actions and disregarding the consequences, rapists are deluding themselves. There is no rationale to absolve them of the seriousness of their actions. Whatever constitutes the moral code of each rapist, how he interprets and internalizes society's norms and how he regards others depends very much on whether he has learned self-esteem. Self-awareness and respect for others is one crucial aspect of the socialization process that we must continually stress. If little attempt is made to reshape the rapist's self-concept, then there is no way to alter his behaviour.

## SUMMARY AND CONCLUSION

Feminists are divided on the question of accepting men as colleagues in areas such as racial and class inequality as well as sexual violence. Radical feminism remains steadfast in its conviction that women and men, when theorizing about feminist issues, adhere to separate perspectives. Other feminists reject this stance claiming instead that the contribution of men is relevant, often necessary, for the advancement of feminist praxis and theory.

This chapter has undertaken the difficult task of deconstructing some incon-sistencies in the work of particular feminists and, in pursuing this route, has tried to clarify some misconceptions concerning men. Research in both women's and men's studies should be open to any student who has a genuine interest in bringing about a more harmonious coexistence between men and women.

Unquestionably, men are the main perpetrators of violence against women, so it is men who must find a way to dismantle the mechanisms responsible for this violence. To achieve a positive alliance with others, men have to fathom their own changing identities, but this depends very much upon reciprocity with women. Profeminist men realize it is their task to teach other men that both masculine and feminine identities are evolving and that the personal growth of men is inseparable from that of women. Feminism's role in this process is invaluable, but, if it should close down the lines of communication vital to the creation of more compatible masculinities, then this can be only envisaged as disheartening.

## BIBLIOGRAPHY

Alda, A. "What every woman should know about men." In *Men's Lives*, edited by M. Kimmel and M. Messner, (294-95). New York: Macmillan Publishing, 1989.

Ambert, A. M. "Differences in children's behaviour between custodial mothers and custodial fathers." *Journal of Marriage and the Family*, 44, 73-86, 1982.

Amir, M. *Patterns in Forcible Rape.* Chicago: University of Chicago Press, 1971.

Atwood, M. *The Robber Bride.* Toronto: McLelland and Stewart, 1993.

Badinter, E. *The Unopposite Sex.* New York: Harper and Row, 1989.

Bly, R. *Iron John: A Book about Men.* New York: Addison-Wesley, 1990.

Brittan, A. *Masculinity and Power.* Oxford: Basil Blackwell, 1989.

Brod, H. "The case for men's studies." In *The Making of Masculinities*, edited by H. Brod, (39-62). Winchester: Allen and Unwin, 1989.

Brownmiller, S. *Against our Will.* New York: Bantam Books, 1975.

Clatterbaugh, K. *Contemporary Perspectives on Masculinity.* Boulder: Westview Press, 1990.

Comstock, G. D. *Violence against Lesbians and Gay Men.* New York: Columbia University Press, 1991.

Connell, B. *Gender and Power.* Stanford, CA: Stanford University Press, 1988.

Daly, M. *Gyn/ecology.* Boston: Beacon Press, 1978.

Davis, A. *Women, Race and Class.* New York: Vintage, 1983.

De Beauvoir, S. *The Second Sex.* New York: Bantam Books, 1961.

Dekeseredy, W. and Schwartz, M. "Male peer support and woman abuse: an expansion of Dekeseredy's model." *Sociological Spectrum*, 13 pp. 393-413, 1993.

Douglas, J. D. *Creative Interviewing.* Beverly Hills: Sage Press, 1985.

Durkheim, E. *The rules of Sociological Method.* New York: The Free Press, 1966.

Dworkin, A. *Intercourse.* New York: Free Press, 1987.

Dworkin, A. *Letters from a War Zone.* London: Secker and Warburg, 1988.

Eichler, M. and Vandelac, L. "An awkward situation: Men in women's studies." *Atlantis,* 16(1), 69-91, 1991.

Ehrenreich, B. *The Hearts of Men: American Dreams and the Flight from Commitment.* New York: Doubleday, 1985.

Ehrenreich, B. and English, D. *For Her Own Good.* New York: Doubleday Books, 1979.

Faludi, S. *Backlash: The Undeclared War Against American Women.* New York: Crown Publishers, 1991.

Farrell, W. *The Liberated Man.* New York: Bantam Books, 1975.

Fasteau, M. "Why aren't we talking?" In *Men and Masculinity,* edited by J. Pleck and J. Sawyer , 19-21. Englewood Cliffs, NJ: Prentice-Hall, 1992.

Goode, W. "Why men resist." In *Rethinking the family,* edited by B. Thorne and M. Yalom , (pp. 287-310). Boston: Northeastern University Press, 1992.

Goodman, P. *Growing Up Absurd.* New York: Vintage Books, 1960.

Habermas, J. *The Theory of Communicative Action* (Vol.1). Boston: Beacon Press, 1984.

Hanmer, J. and Saunders, S. *Well-founded Fear.* London: Hutchinson, 1984.

Hansen, K. "Our eyes behold each other: Masculinity and intimate friendships in antebellum New England." In *Men's Friendships,* edited by P. Nardi, 35-58. Newbury Park: Sage Publications, 1992.

Hanson, S. "Father/child relationships: Beyond Kramer vs. Kramer." In *Men's Changing Roles in the Family,* edited by R. Lewis and M. Sussman, 135-150. New York: Haworth Press, 1986.

Harding, S. "Is there a feminist method?" In *Feminism and Methodology,* edited by S. Harding, 1-14. Bloomington: Indiana University Press, 1986.

Harris, I. "Media myths and the reality of men's work." In *Men's Lives,* edited by M. Kimmel and M. Messner , 2d. ed., 225-231. New York: MacMillan, 1992.

Hartsock, N. *Money, Sex and Power: Toward a Feminist Historical Materialism.* Boston: Northeastern University Press, 1985.

Hunt, J. "Normal force." In *Deviance: The Interactionist Perspective (5th ed.),* edited by E. Rubington and M. Weinberg, 132-141. New York: Macmillan, 1987.

hooks, b. *Feminist Theory: From Margin to Center.* Boston: South End Press, 1984.

Kaufman, M. "The construction of masculinity and the triad of men's violence." In *Beyond Patriarchy,* edited by M. Kaufman, 1-29, Toronto: Oxford Press, 1987.

Kaufman, M. *Cracking the Armour.* Toronto: Viking Press, 1993.

Kelly, L. *Surviving Sexual Violence*. Minneapolis: University of Minnesota Press, 1988.

Kinsman, G. *The Regulation of Desire*. Toronto: Black Rose Books, 1987.

Kremer, B. "Learning to say no: Keeping feminist research for ourselves." *Women's Studies International Forum*, 13 (5) 463-467, 1990.

Marx, K. 1990. *The Communist Manifesto. In Karl Marx: Selected Writings* edited by D. McLellan, 221-247. Oxford: Oxford University Press, 1990.

Maslow, A. *Toward a Psychology of Being*. New York: Van Nostrand, 1968.

Messner, M. A. "Boyhood, organized sports, and the construction of masculinity." In *Men's Lives 2d ed.*, edited by M. Kimmel and M. Messner, 161-76. New York: MacMillan, 1992.

Miedzian, M. *Boys Will Be Boys*. New York: Doubleday, 1991.

Millett, K. *Sexual Politics*. New York: Doubleday, 1970.

Moghadam, V. *Modernizing Women: Gender and Social Change in the Middle East*. London: Lynne Rienner Publishers, 1993.

Paglia, C. *Sex, Art, and American culture*. New York: Vintage Books, 1992.

Pateman, C. *The Sexual Contract*. Stanford: Stanford University Press, 1988.

Perls, F. S. *Ego, Hunger and Aggression: The Beginning of Gestalt Therapy*. New York: Vintage Books, 1969.

Pleck, J. *The Myth of Masculinity*. Cambridge: MIT Press, 1981.

Reid, H. and Fine, G. "Self-disclosure in men's friendships: Variations associated with intimate relations." In *Men's Friendships*, edited by P. Nardi, 132-152. Newbury Park: Sage Publications, 1992.

Reinharz, S. *Feminist Methods in Social Research*. New York: Oxford University Press, 1992.

Russell, D. E. H. *The Politics of Rape: The Victim's Perspective*. New York: Stein and Day, 1975.

Russell, D. E. H. *Rape in Marriage*. New York: Macmillan, 1982.

Sanday, P. R. *Female Power and Male Dominance: On the Origins of Sexual Inequality*. Cambridge: Cambridge University Press, 1981.

Sanday, P. R. *Fraternity Gang Rape*. New York: New York University Press, 1981.

Sartre, J. P. *Existentialism and Human Emotions*. New York: Wisdom Library Publishing, 1957.

Schafly, P. *The Power of the Positive Woman*. New Rochelle: Arlington House, 1977.

Scully, D. *Understanding Sexual Violence*. Boston: Unwin, 1990.

Scully, D. and Marolla, J. "Riding the bull at Gilley's: Convicted rapists describe the rewards of rape." In *Violence Against Women*, edited by P. Bart and E. Moran, 26-46. Newbury Park: Sage Publications, 1993.

Showalter, E. "Critical cross-dressing: Male feminists and the woman of the year." In *Men in Feminism*, edited by A. Jardine and P. Smith, 116-135. New York: Routledge, 1989.

Smith, D. E. "A sociology for women." In *The Prism of Sex: Essays in the Sociology of Knowledge*, edited by J. Sherman and E. Tonton Beck, 135-187. Madison: University of Wisconsin Press, 1979.

Smith, M. D. "Male peer support of wife abuse." *Journal of Interpersonal Violence*, 6(4), 512-519, 1991.

Stanko, E. *Everyday Violence*. London: Pandora, 1990.

Stanley, L. and Wise, S. *Breaking Out: Feminist Consciousness and Feminist Research*. London: Routledge and Kegan Paul, 1983.

Thorne-Finch, R. *Ending the Silence*. Toronto: University of Toronto Press, 1992.

Weber, M. *Economy and Society*. G. Ross and C. Wittich, Berkeley: University of California Press, 1978.

Weedon, C. *Feminist Practice and Post-structuralist Theory*. Oxford: Basil Blackwell, 1990.

*Who's Who in America 92-93*, Vol. 47. New Providence: Marquis, 1992.

York, J. and Pindera, L. *People of the pines: The Warriors and Legacy of Oka*. Toronto: Little, Brown and Co., 1992.

PART 3

# RESTRUCTURING INSTITUTIONS: CHALLENGES AND CONFLICTS

# THE PARADOX OF FEMINIST ENGAGEMENT WITH LAW

*Mary Jane Mossman*

## INTRODUCTION

> Historically, feminists in Canada and other Western market societies have placed
> great emphasis on law as an important vehicle for establishing formal equality
> between men and women.... [However,] in light of the contradictory effects of
> reform, some feminists have raised the question of whether expending effort and
> resources to achieve piecemeal, ad hoc legal changes is ultimately worthwhile.
> Are feminists simply 'running hard to stand still'? (Chunn and Brockman 1993)[1]

Chunn and Brockman's question neatly captures the paradox of the
Canadian legal system for feminists: a legal system that feminists have used regularly and often successfully to advance women's claims, but which has, perhaps
just as often, rejected or undermined such claims, thereby confirming the limits
of law and legal processes in the achievement of broader feminist goals. Thus
law, as an institution, both facilitates change and poses barriers to change (Smart
1986). It may also provide different opportunities and create different barriers
for women claimants not affluent enough to pursue legal rights through litigation, or disadvantaged by race or ethnicity (Razack 1993).

This paradox has led some feminists to conclude that law, as an institution shaped by prevailing social and political ideology, cannot be useful in

the achieving of feminist objectives (Fudge 1989; 1987). By contrast, others have suggested that, in spite of these dangers, feminists cannot ignore it altogether because of the power of law in Western societies (Thornton 1991). This theme of the paradoxical relationship of law and feminist objectives is therefore fundamental to a feminist analysis of current law and public policy in Canada.

In addition to focusing on law as an institution, however, a feminist analysis must also take account of the role of women in the legal profession. Since lawyers (and judges) are responsible for applying and interpreting the law, their perceptions of law and their understanding of their roles within the legal system are important in their practical applications of legal principles. Because the past two decades have witnessed a "revolutionary" change in the composition of the legal profession (Abel 1988), women are now legal counsel and judges, not just claimants, in larger numbers than ever before in history (Mossman 1988). In such a context, a feminist analysis of law must ask whether significant numbers of women in the legal profession can make a difference in terms of feminist legal claims (Menkel-Meadow 1992; Mossman 1988b). This question must also take into account the differing experiences among women lawyers, and the impact of race, ethnicity, class, disability, and sexual orientation on women's perceptions of their lawyering roles.

This essay provides an overview of women and the law in Canada in three stages: first, the early twentieth century when women struggled to achieve legal recognition for fundamental claims to participate in public life; second, the early years of "second wave feminism" in the 1960s and 1970s when several women pursued important "test case" legal claims and simultaneously others began to enter law schools in record numbers; and finally, the period since the mid-1980s when women's relationship to law has been substantially dominated by equality claims and the Canadian Charter of Rights and Freedoms, a period in which women have entered the legal education process in numbers at least equal to the number of men.

In discussions of law and lawyers in these three periods, feminist themes reoccur regularly: themes about public and private life, about definitions of equality (formal or substantive), and about the idea of difference (both as between men and women, and among women). This paper will examine these themes by focusing both on women as litigants and on women as lawyers in these three historical periods. In doing so, this analysis of law and public policy focuses on the fundamental issue for feminism: the paradox of law's role in both facilitating and impeding changes in the interests of women. Thus, the concluding discussion addresses this fundamental issue and the dilemmas it will continue to present to Canadian feminist lawyers in the future.

# EARLY TWENTIETH CENTURY CLAIMS: PARTICIPATION IN PUBLIC LIFE

"Nineteenth-century law provided an almost perfect example of a formally patriarchal institution" (Backhouse 1991). Until the last years of the century, when, in 1897, Clara Brett Martin became the first woman lawyer in the Commonwealth, women were entirely excluded as actors in the legal system: women could not vote, and they were not eligible to be legislators, judges, or jurors. Although suffrage became an issue in the latter half of the nineteenth century in Canada, it was only in the 1890s that feminists began to find support from liberally minded men and women "who rallied to them not so much because of any enthusiasm for women's rights but more out of a general interest in community betterment" (Strong-Boag 1986).

Even so, it was not until 1916 that legislation entitling women to vote was enacted in Manitoba, Saskatchewan, and Alberta, with British Columbia and Ontario following suit in 1917 (Burt 1988).[2] Moreover, even this legislation did not enfranchise all women: prior to 1960, Aboriginal women (and men) in Canada were entitled to vote only if they gave up their Indian status, a status defined by the federal *Indian Act*. However, by section 12(1)(b) of this legislation, an Aboriginal woman became automatically "enfranchised" if she married a White man (Ng 1988). Yet, while feminists in the early part of the twentieth century identified the need to challenge women's exclusion from participation in public life and supported a number of legal claims with this objective, it was only in the 1970s that Aboriginal women's claims to equality in marriage were tested in the Supreme Court of Canada.

Indeed, women's legal claims in the early twentieth century can be characterized primarily as efforts to establish the civil or political status of women. Such claims were based on the idea of women's equality, defined as having access to the same status as men in terms of citizenship; in this way, suffrage for women was fundamental to the recognition of women's equality. Asserting such rights challenged the orthodox nineteenth century ideology that rigorously separated men and women into public and private spheres of life, even though it did so without any demands for consequential changes in the roles of women and men respectively. Thus, from our perspective, the legal claims in the early twentieth century reveal two important characteristics: they define women's equality entirely in terms of men's existing rights and responsibilities and they assert, although not without controversy, women's rights to participate in public life. By contrast with later claims, the early cases do not assert complex ideas of equality nor do they confront the (complementary) need for men to accept some responsibility for private life. These conclusions are evident in two cases about the entry of women into the legal profession and also in the now-famous *Persons* case about women's rights to become members of the Canadian Senate.

When Clara Brett Martin became a lawyer in Ontario in 1897, her request for admission was determined by the governing body of the legal profession in Ontario (Backhouse 1985). By contrast, Mabel Penery French's petition to be admitted to the legal profession in New Brunswick in 1905, after she had completed all the necessary training, was heard by judges in open court as was her subsequent application for admission as a lawyer in British Columbia in 1912: thus judges decided that it was not possible for women to be lawyers. Only after legislative amendments were enacted in both provinces did French become a member of their respective legal professions and the first woman lawyer in both New Brunswick and British Columbia (Yorke 1993; Mossman 1988; Mullins 1986).

Annie Macdonald Langstaff's application to become a lawyer in Quebec after she had graduated from the faculty of law at McGill University, was also heard by the court there in 1915, but when the court decided that women could not be lawyers, there was no subsequent legislative action. Consequently, she remained an employee in a law office, but not a lawyer, until her retirement in 1965 at the age of 78 (Baines 1988; Gillet 1981). In other Canadian provinces, women were admitted as members of the legal profession as a result of legislative action between 1915 and 1941 (Harvey 1970-71); in the latter year, Quebec admitted women as lawyers but, because Annie Macdonald Langstaff did not have an undergraduate university degree as well as a law degree, she was not eligible to be a member of the legal profession in Quebec even under the 1941 legislation (Baines 1988).

In terms of a feminist analysis of law, the arguments used by the judges for both French and Langstaff are as important as their particular results. The issue of their entitlement to become lawyers depended on an interpretation of common law principles (including the doctrine of precedent which required subsequent decisions to be consistent with earlier ones) and the language of provincial statutes governing the profession. In French's case, Judge Barker therefore quoted from *Bradwell* v. *Illinois*, a decision in 1872 in the United States which had denied Myra Bradwell's application to become a lawyer and which had affirmed the idea of "separate spheres" for men and women as "founded in the divine ordinance as well as in the nature of things" (Friedman 1993).[3] Another judge in French's case suggested that she should not be trying to compete with men and that women should "attend to their own legitimate business" (Mossman 1988; 1986).

These comments confirm the judges' acceptance of separate spheres for men and women, just as their decisions reinforced women's ineligibility, on the grounds of sex, to participate in the public sphere as members of the legal profession. The view that such activity was not appropriate for women was even more apparent in Langstaff's case in 1915. In interpreting the statutory language governing the legal profession, language that referred to lawyers by masculine pronouns, Judge Saint-Pierre stated that it was necessary to interpret this language in terms of the "context and purpose of the whole act" and continued:

> Now, taking that rule as a guide, who would presume to assert that ... in the Acts dealing with the *organization of the police force or of the fire brigad*e, the pronoun 'He' should be construed as including the female as well as the male sex?
>
> A woman may be as brave as any man, and scenes which are in the present time, daily depicted to us, show that many of them are proving their usefulness as nurses on the field of battle; but the physical constitution of woman makes it plain that nature never intended her to take part along with the stronger sex in the bloody affrays of the battle field.
>
> I would put within the range of possibilities though by no means a commendable one, the admission of a woman to the profession of solicitor or to that of avoué, but I hold that to admit a woman and more particularly a married woman as a *barrister*, that is to say, as *a person who pleads cases at the bar before judges or juries in open court, and in the presence of the public*, would be nothing short of a direct infringement upon public order and a manifest violation of the law of good morals and public decency. (Emphasis in original)

Such language by confirming the boundaries of public and private life based on sex, strongly insulated the public sphere from women's entry. In such a context, claims of sex equality necessarily emphasized that women, for purposes of legal rights and responsibilities, were the same as men. Indeed, it was the courts' conclusion that women were different from men because of sex that resulted in these decisions denying their claims and thus confining them to the private sphere. In this way, arguments about equality and about the public/private division were closely linked in this early period, both for the courts and for the women who challenged the limitations imposed on them by the law because of sex (Mossman 1988; 1986).

Yet, at the same time as these courts were denying women's claims to become lawyers, legislatures in most provinces were routinely amending relevant statutes to permit women's entry to the legal profession. Thus, in assessing law from a feminist perspective, it is important to take account of both legislative and judicial actions, especially when they offer such contrasting responses to women's claims. While it is likely that legislatures in early twentieth century Canada included male members who held more progressive views than those who sat as judges, there were also inherent institutional barriers to more reformist action on the part of courts. Traditionally, legislatures have been the "makers" of laws and courts have merely "interpreted" them; on this basis, judges in early twentieth century Canada eschewed responsibility for implementing major societal change, including the entry of women to the public sphere; courts as legal institutions were therefore unlikely to be responsive to new claims but deferred to legislatures to identify and respond to needed changes. Such a stance also means that, as legal institutions, the role of courts was one of preserving the status quo.

This conclusion suggests that it was not useful for women wanting societal changes to make claims before judges and courts. And yet feminists did continue to do just that, and sometimes they were successful. In the celebrated *Persons* case, for example, five women from Alberta (Emily Murphy, Nellie McClung, Louise McKinney, Henrietta Muir Edwards, and Irene Parlby)[4] challenged the federal government's refusal to appoint women to the Senate (Dranoff 1977). In the end, the highest appeal court decided that the language in the British North America Act, which authorized the appointment of "qualified persons" as members of the Senate of Canada, included both male and female persons. Indeed, the court started from a presumption that the word "persons" included both males and females and held that "the burden is upon those who deny that the word includes women to make out their case." Nor was the court deterred by the absence of precedents of women performing such public roles. As the court stated:

> The fact that no woman had served ... such an office is not of great weight when it is remembered that custom would have prevented the claim being made or the point being contested. Customs are apt to develop into traditions which are stronger than law and remain unchallenged long after the reason for them has disappeared.

Simply stated, the court decided that "women were persons" (Baines 1988; Mossman 1986).

Thus, by contrast with the cases concerning women's entry into the legal profession, the *Persons* case recognized their equality with men and their right to participate in public life. At the same time, there is all too little explanation for the differing approach on the part of the judges in the *Persons* case. Thus, while the outcome was successful for those asserting women's rights, the decision did not signal a fundamental shift in the courts' approach to such questions nor did it change the fundamental role of courts as the "interpreters," not the "makers," of law (Sachs and Wilson 1978).

An assessment of this decision is also complicated by the fact that it was handed down by the Judicial Committee of the Privy Council, a group of judges in the English House of Lords who formed Canada's highest court of appeal for some cases until 1949 (although appeals to the Privy Council in criminal cases had been abolished earlier). The "Alberta five" had appealed to the Privy Council after a unanimous decision of the Supreme Court of Canada holding that the word "persons" in the BNA Act, interpreted in accordance with views prevailing in 1867 when it was enacted, could not include "women" (Dranoff 1977). Thus, recognition of the women's claim in the *Persons* case occurred only because Canada had not finally emerged from a more colonial phase in its legal institutions (Baines 1988).

The other aspect of this case which is important for a feminist assessment of law is the assertion by all the judges (in both the Supreme Court of Canada and the Privy Council) of the law's neutrality. In the Supreme Court of Canada, for example, Chief Justice Anglin specifically stated that the court was "in no wise concerned with the desirability or the undesirability of the presence of women in the Senate, nor with any political aspect of the question submitted"; instead, the court was to focus only on the law and its interpretation. In the Privy Council, the court also stated that it was not "deciding any question as to the rights of women" but only the interpretation of the BNA Act. For the women, by contrast, their claim was clearly political and important in the establishment of women's rights. Thus, even though the claim was successful in the *Persons* case, the judges simultaneously denied any role for courts in the struggle for women's rights and asserted instead the courts' role as one of neutrality and objectivity in the interpretation of the law.

Overall, therefore, these cases in the early twentieth century reveal the connections between the definition of equality rights for women (generally defined as the same rights enjoyed by men) and women's challenges to overcome the barriers to their entry to public life. They also show, in relation to legislatures, the relatively more conservative approach of the courts and the judges to new claims such as those involving women's rights. More significantly, even these early cases demonstrate the paradoxical relationship of the law both as a means of facilitating change and also as a barrier to change. In part, this paradox is the result of the judges' claims to neutrality and objectivity, claims they asserted at the same time as they failed to explain the *real* basis for their decisions. In this way, the "power of the law" to define reality for women was revealed as both symbolic and very real indeed (Smart 1989).

In spite of the relatively more responsive action of legislatures to claims by women to become lawyers the paradoxical nature of law in the courts applies to legislative action during this early period. In the several decades before and after the turn of the century, the process of industrialization in Canada transformed both work and family relationships, and legislative action formed an important part of this process of change. Some of these legislative changes, such as the *Married Women's Property Acts* (initially enacted in Ontario in 1859) conferred new legal rights on women. Yet, while such legislative changes sometimes benefited women, they also had inherent limitations. In practice the range of occupations for women remained limited to lower-paying jobs (Lowe 1986), and the courts frequently defined the extent of new rights quite narrowly (Backhouse 1988). Moreover, legislative interventions which strengthened women's rights in relation to men (often their husbands) tended as well to increase the amount of state regulation of women and other dependents (Chunn 1993; Ursel 1992). Similarly, the absence of accessible divorce and of legislation guaranteeing equal pay for women's work inhibited women's equality both at home and at work. Thus, the legislative sphere, as well as the courts, showed the paradox of legal institutions in relation to feminist goals: they both facilitated and impeded change in women's interests.

Part of the reason for this paradox may have been the diffusion of feminist issues that seemed to occur in the early part of this century perhaps because of the rate of changes occurring in economic life (Chunn 1993). In spite of the relative success of the suffrage movement and its appeal to a wide-ranging set of progressive groups, feminism in the 1920s "could not mobilize its sympathizers under any single banner" (Strong-Boag 1986). In such a context, the legal success of the *Persons* case is important: in making women eligible for appointment to the Senate, it symbolized women's changed legal status. At the same time, it is clear that some perplexing questions remained, even after the *Persons* case, about the limits of feminist engagement with law.

## "SECOND WAVE" FEMINISM AND THE LAW: NEW BEGINNINGS

The cases about the admission of women as lawyers at the turn of the century did not challenge the fundamental nature of law nor suggest alternative ways of practising as a lawyer. For the first women lawyers, the goal was conformity to the (male) norms of law practice and existing legal principles. Indeed, this necessity to conform to traditional practice was demonstrated by the need for early women lawyers to "choose" whether to practice law or to marry and have a family. "As the early women lawyers married and had children, they dropped out of visible practice in droves" (Backhouse 1991). Perhaps for this reason, very few women entered law practice until the early 1970s. As Backhouse has commented, "women looking [at the profession] from outside were not enthusiastic [and] voted with their feet, steering remarkably clear of the male-dominated legal profession" (Backhouse 1991). For women other than White women, moreover, the legal profession was remote: although an Asian-Canadian woman graduated from law school in Ontario in 1946 (Law Society of Upper Canada), the first Black woman lawyer in Ontario was admitted only in 1960, and only in 1976 did the first woman from the First Nations graduate (Backhouse 1991).

In spite of their small numbers, however, there were some women lawyers whose work during the period before World War Two and in the decades immediately thereafter contributed to new beginnings. This was the "second wave" of feminist engagement with law. Thus, in 1951, the same year in which Nellie McClung died, the Ontario legislature enacted Canada's first equal pay legislation, in part as a result of the efforts of Margaret Hyndman, a practicing lawyer since 1926 who had also been counsel for the Canadian Association of Consumers in the *Margarine Reference*, the case which permitted the sale of margarine in Canada (Mossman 1986b). Hyndman's male law partner represented Dorothea Palmer, a nurse arrested in 1936 and charged under a provision of the Criminal Code for advertising birth control information in her work on behalf of the Parents' Information Bureau. Her trial lasted four months and, even though the Criminal Code provision was not repealed until 1969 she was acquitted because she had acted in the public interest (Atcheson, Eberts, Symes and Stoddart 1984).

In 1960, another lawyer, Judy LaMarsh, became the first woman appointed to the federal cabinet by a Liberal government (Ellen Fairclough in 1957 was the first woman federal cabinet minister). LaMarsh was responsible in 1966, as minister of health and welfare, for the creation of the Canada and Quebec Pension Plans (Armour and Staton 1990; Dranoff 1977). In 1968, the federal government also enacted comprehensive divorce legislation for the first time in Canada. Prior to 1968, divorce laws were based on earlier versions of English legislation and varied from province to province. Moreover, for married couples in Quebec and Newfoundland, an Act of Parliament was required because there was no applicable divorce legislation (Dranoff 1977).

The most significant contribution to the agenda of second-wave feminism in Canada was the Report of the Royal Commission on the Status of Women in 1970. Although the report did not have a separate chapter on law, many of its recommendations were directed to needed legislative reforms in family law, tax and child-care allowances, social assistance, immigration, and criminal law. In this way, the Royal Commission report implicitly accepted the need for legal action as a significant component in achieving changes in the interests of women (Abner, Mossman and Pickett 1990).

In retrospect, the definition of equality adopted by the report was crucial, reflecting again the "sameness" standard of the earlier period. Thus, for example, the commissioners stated their acceptance of the principle that:

> Women and men, having the same rights and freedoms, share the same responsibilities. They should have an equal opportunity to fulfil this obligation. We have, therefore, examined the status of women and made recommendations in the belief that there *should be equality of opportunity to share the responsibilities to society as well as its privileges and prerogatives.* (Emphasis in original) (Report on the Status of Women 1970)

The idea that equality required that everyone (both men and women) have *exactly* the same rights and responsibilities in law reflected the pervasiveness of the "sameness" standard of equality. By contrast, some human rights lawyers had begun to argue that law should aim to achieve "equality of results or outcomes" for men and women and that, in order to achieve equality of results, the differing situations of the sexes might thus require different, not the same, treatment. To an extent, the Royal Commission report's recommendations showed an understanding of the need for "different" or "special" treatment for women, particularly in relation to pregnancy. Since men could not become pregnant, women's equality would not be achieved using a "sameness" standard. Instead, it was necessary to recognize women's differing (or "special") needs during pregnancy, such as maternity leave and arrangements for nursing infants.

The "special treatment" recommendations in the Royal Commission report were strongly criticized in one commissioner's dissenting report. As he argued:

> It was the duty of the Commissioners to make recommendations aimed at the removal of [sex] discrimination. This they have done. But, in some cases, they have gone on to make recommendations which would introduce new kinds of discrimination, not only between men and women but also between different classes of women. These recommendations I cannot support. In a just society, you do not eliminate one injustice by creating another.

The Royal Commission report thus joined in the debate about whether legal equality meant "equal treatment" (the "sameness" standard) or "treatment as an equal" (which required courts to take account of women's differences, both biological and economic). This debate increasingly influenced feminist litigation in the 1970s, and especially under the Charter of Rights and Freedoms, contributed to the transformation of equality doctrine (Abner, Mossman and Pickett 1990).

One of the important cases at the beginning of the second wave was *Murdoch* v. *Murdoch*, in which Irene Murdoch brought a claim to share in one-half the property owned by her husband when they separated after 25 years of marriage. Mrs. Murdoch claimed an interest in the property on the basis of her contribution of money and labour; in particular, she claimed that she had been actively involved with her husband in all of the work of managing large ranch properties in Alberta: "haying, raking, swathing, moving, driving trucks and tractors and teams, quietening horses, taking cattle back and forth to the reserve, dehorning, vaccinating, branding, anything that was to be done... just as a man would" (Dranoff 1977). All the same, Irene Murdoch's claim was denied in the Supreme Court of Canada on the basis that applicable legal principles did not entitle a wife to share in property owned by her husband. In a dissenting opinion, however, Mr. Justice Laskin characterized her contribution of labour as "extraordinary" and concluded that it would be inequitable to deny her an interest in her husband's property.

This case captured public interest across Canada, with newspapers like The Toronto Star emphasizing the Royal Commission's recommendation for law reform to recognize "the concept of equal partnership in marriage" so that future Irene Murdochs would not be "left out in the cold with less than $60 a week to show for a quarter-century of labour" (Mossman 1993). By 1980, every common law province (all provinces except Quebec) had enacted legislation amending the arrangements for sharing property between a husband and wife at the time of separation or divorce. (Interestingly, the common law reform legislation borrowed from the idea of "community property" within marriage, a system of property-sharing for married couples that is common in civil law jurisdictions, including Quebec.) Significantly, these new legislative provisions characterized married partners in terms of "equality," a concept that ensured that women and men would be treated as if their circumstances were the same. With the benefit of hindsight, many feminists now recognize that the reform legislation in common law provinces was fundamentally flawed since it assumed that men and women had equal access to economic self-sufficiency. None of the legislative schemes originally took into account, for example, that women in Canada earn (on average) about two-thirds of men's earnings, and there was little recognition that women frequently became the custodial parent at marriage breakdown, a circumstance that further limits their ability to engage in full-time work outside the home. As Chunn has argued, family law based on liberal egalitarianism "continues to help reproduce and sustain women's inequality" (Chunn 1993; Abner, Mossman and Pickett 1990). In legal terms, the problem with the legislation was its use of a "formal" rather than "substantive" equality approach. In this way, the law regarded men and women as "formally" equal at divorce; however, the substance of their economic situations was often very different, and women were frequently substantively disadvantaged. As well, some women were excluded from the application of these legislative arrangements altogether: women in families with little or no property received no benefit from this reform legislation, and Aboriginal women were excluded because the Supreme Court of Canada decided in 1986 that the legislation did not apply to Indian lands (Turpel 1991).

In the mid-1970s, Aboriginal women challenged the discriminatory provisions regarding status on marriage for Indian women under section 12(1)(b) of the *Indian Act*. They were undoubtedly encouraged by the successful outcome in *R. v. Drybones*, a case in which the Supreme Court of Canada found that provisions of the *Indian Act* contravened protections in the *Canadian Bill of Rights*, the federal statute that guaranteed to individuals (in relation to claims involving federal law only) the right "to equality before the law and the protection of the law." The Aboriginal women demonstrated the severe consequences of section 12(1)(b) which resulted when an Aboriginal woman married a non-Indian: she had to leave her parents' home and reserve, dispose of any property on the reserve, and was prohibited from inheriting property left to her by her parents; moreover, her children could not be recognized as Indian and, even if she separated or divorced or was widowed, she could be prevented from returning to live on the reserve (Jamieson 1978). Thus, lawyers for Jeannette Lavell and Yvonne Bedard (including Margaret Hyndman) argued that section 12(1)(b) of the Act constituted sex discrimination and contravened the Bill of Rights. In the Supreme Court of Canada, five judges denied their claims (four judges dissenting), on the basis that the *Canadian Bill of Rights* was not intended to guarantee that the substance of the law did not discriminate but only that it would be applied in an even-handed way by its administrators (Atcheson, Eberts, Symes and Stoddart 1984). After a number of other cases, including a petition by Sandra Lovelace to the United Nations in 1977, the federal government repealed the section of the *Indian Act* in 1985 (Baines 1988; Atcheson, Eberts, Symes and Stoddart 1984). Thus, once again the reform occurred as a result of legislative action after unsuccessful appeals to the courts.

The *Canadian Bill of Rights* also proved unhelpful for women in Stella Bliss' case concerning unemployment insurance and maternity leave. Bliss claimed unemployment insurance benefits shortly after the birth of her child in 1976. However, the Unemployment Insurance Commission disallowed her claim on the basis that she had to apply for pregnancy benefits, not regular unemployment benefits; however, because the qualifying period for pregnancy benefits (in terms of weeks worked prior to unemployment) was longer than that for regular benefits, Bliss was not eligible for pregnancy benefits. When her case was eventually heard in the Supreme Court of Canada in 1978, the court denied her claim, stating that she was not discriminated against because she was a woman but because she was pregnant; thus "the discrimination arose not because of law, but because of nature" (Atcheson, Eberts, Symes and Stoddart 1984). In 1983, the federal government repealed the provisions at issue in Bliss' case and amended the Canadian Human Rights Act to provide that under the Act, "discrimination because of pregnancy is discrimination on a prohibited ground." In relation to Bliss and the cases under the *Indian Act*, however, Baines has suggested that the judiciary "effectively emptied the guarantee of sex equality in the *Canadian Bill of Rights* of any meaning" (Baines 1988), just as judges had earlier upheld the idea of separate spheres for men and women.

In 1973 the long saga of Henry Morgentaler's involvement with the criminal justice system in relation to abortion began when he was charged in Quebec under the therapeutic abortion section of Canada's federal legislation, the Criminal Code. Section 251 permitted abortion on the recommendation of a hospital's therapeutic abortion committee in the interest of "the life or health" of the mother. A jury found Morgentaler not guilty, but the Quebec Court of Appeal overturned the acquittal and substituted a verdict of guilty, sending the case back to the trial judge for sentencing. The trial judge sentenced him to 18 months in jail, and eventually the Supreme Court of Canada dismissed an appeal from this sentence. While serving his sentence, Morgentaler was brought to trial on another set of charges and was again acquitted by a jury. Meanwhile, public dissatisfaction with the role of the Court of Appeal resulted in amendments to the Criminal Code preventing the appeal court from substituting a guilty verdict after a jury has decided to acquit. Relying on this amendment, the federal minister of justice set aside the guilty verdict against Morgentaler and ordered a retrial instead. The jury once again acquitted him and he was released from prison, having served 10 months of the 18-month sentence. After the provincial election in 1976 when the Parti Quebeçois was elected, the Quebec minister of justice advised Morgentaler that "qualified physicians performing abortions under proper medical conditions would no longer be prosecuted in Quebec" (Atcheson,

Eberts, Symes and Stoddart 1984). This action meant that women in Quebec could obtain abortions from qualified physicians in abortion clinics as well as in hospitals, and thereby ensured wider access to abortion as well as improved safety for women seeking abortions. As became evident, however, these new arrangements in Quebec did not preclude subsequent legal action in other provinces.

Other legal claims during the early part of the second wave of feminist activity included a challenge under human rights legislation on the part of seven Jamaican domestic workers. They had been permitted to enter Canada under a special agreement that provided for the entry of women who were "single, widowed, divorced, without minor children." After they had been in Canada for a number of years, however, the federal government commenced deportation proceedings against them on the ground that they had not disclosed that they had dependent children at the time of entry and that they had therefore provided false and misleading information. The women maintained that they had been so advised by officials of the Jamaican government and that the deportation proceedings were motivated by racism. Eventually, however, they were deported but were then allowed to reenter Canada six months later. Their case also received public sympathy because the women had been in Canada for several years (Atcheson, Eberts, Symes and Stoddart 1984). Significantly, however, the plight of foreign domestic workers continues; they remain less protected as workers and vulnerable in terms of immigration arrangements (Macklin 1992; Arat-Koc 1989).

In the employment context, there were a number of important cases in the 1970s. Two women managers at Bell Canada—Elizabeth Kennedy and Patricia Harris—filed claims under federal equal pay legislation that were successful initially but were then overturned by the federal Court of Appeal. However, the cases received wide publicity and helped to establish a climate in Canada "sympathetic to the idea of equality for women in the workplace" (Kates 1990). As Margaret Hyndman, counsel for Kennedy and Harris, suggested, "[The] ultimate result, of course, was a disappointment but looking back one can't help feeling that it was another step forward" (Kates 1990).

Another equal pay case was filed in 1979 with the Canadian Human Rights Commission on behalf of women employed by the federal government as food service and laundry workers. The case claimed that these women should have pay equal to that of custodians, protective personnel, and building workers who were predominantly men. Even before a tribunal hearing, the case was settled when the Treasury Board agreed to pay $17 million (an average of $5,000 each) to 2,300 female employees. Similarly, Canadian National paid $80,000 to seven women workers who claimed that they had been discriminated against in relation to entry-level jobs and also offered them satisfactory jobs. A Montreal-based organization, Action Travail des Femmes, also filed a complaint with the

Canadian Human Rights Commission claiming systemic discrimination on the part of CN. "Systemic" discrimination occurs when a system that looks even-handed on the surface is applied to persons with differing characteristics so that the outcome or impact is discriminatory. The determination of discrimination results from the impact, not the existence, of an intention to discriminate (Atcheson, Eberts, Symes and Stoddard 1984). Several years later, the systemic discrimination complaint against CN reached the Supreme Court of Canada where it was among a group of important decisions advancing women's interests at the end of the 1980s.

Thus in the early years, second-wave feminist legal action was somewhat more successful in claims under human rights legislation than under the *Canadian Bill of Rights*. In some cases, the specificity of the language of human rights legislation seemed more useful in achieving results for women than the more general language of the *Canadian Bill of Rights*. In addition, the "neutral" stance of the courts and their role in interpreting, not making, law also impeded women in their use of courts to achieve legal changes. For both these reasons, the overall result of women's legal claims was somewhat uneven in this period. However, some successful cases were nonetheless extremely useful in creating publicity about women's struggles for equality and illustrate the ways in which court action may be useful both for achieving specific results and also for creating public support for political action.

The complexity of the law's impact was also evident in cases like *R. v. Pappajohn*, a 1980 rape case in which the accused was convicted. In making its decision, the court adopted a legal principle that failed to take sufficient account of women's experiences of rape. In *Pappajohn*, the court held that a man did not commit the offence of rape if he had a mistaken, but honest, belief that the woman had consented to sexual intercourse. Because there was no evidence that the accused in *Pappajohn* had had such a mistaken but honest belief, he was convicted. However, feminists criticized the legal principle adopted by the court because it seemed to enshrine in law what men frequently wanted to believe: "that a woman's refusal to consent to sexual acts could be ignored and that their [men's] own aggression was socially acceptable" (Atcheson, Eberts, Symes and Stoddart 1984). In this way, the *Pappajohn* decision fuelled feminist reform activity; in 1983, the Criminal Code amendments restricted the scope of the defence of mistaken but honest belief about a woman's consent. Once again the process of reform in the law of rape did not end here but resurfaced with another set of legal issues for the next phase of feminist engagement with law.

As is evident, therefore, these cases at the beginning of the second wave of feminist activity generally reveal a much broader set of issues than the cases in the early part of the twentieth century. Clearly, the spectrum of women's interests represented by legal claims before courts and tribunals widened in the years after World War Two and especially during the 1970s. In addition, the cases at the beginning of the second wave also demonstrated a preoccupation with the private sphere as well as the public and incorporated economic issues as well as concerns about political status. As has been suggested, "the cases which came forth in the 1970s reflect[ed] an increasing consciousness of the importance to women of ensuring their economic autonomy" (Atcheson, Eberts, Symes and Stoddart 1984). This preoccupation is, moreover, as apparent in the equal pay and property cases as in those involving domestic workers and Aboriginal women. Even in the latter case, section 12(1)(b) clearly assumed women's economic and social dependence on men. Thus, claims during this period that focused on issues relating to the private sphere as well as public life did not challenge these categories and the ways they can be used to frustrate women's legal claims.

In these cases also, there was a preoccupation with ideas about equality, particularly in the interpretation of the *Canadian Bill of Rights*. In general, the courts adopted a narrow definition of equality that precluded success for women's claims in cases concerning the *Indian Act* and the *Unemployment Insurance Act*. By contrast, some equality claims were recognized in relation to human rights legislation, but the approach of courts and tribunals continued to be constrained by ideas of sameness that used men as the norm (Eberts 1985).[5] Indeed, in cases like *Murdoch*, women seemed to be asking the court to treat them like men. On the other hand, feminist criticism of cases like *Pappajohn* suggested that women's experiences in expressing their sexuality were not the same as men's. Moreover, the domestic workers case showed that women domestic workers could have interests separate from, and perhaps even opposed to, those of other women in the paid work force, the domestics' employers.

Thus, the cases in this period revealed the inherent complexity of ideas about legal equality and challenged feminists to expand this concept in ways that could further the goal of women's status in a myriad of differing contexts. These cases had demonstrated the need to formulate legal theories that would take account of women's specific circumstances (economic and social as well as political). Perhaps to a lesser extent they had also shown a need to understand the differing experiences of women in different circumstances. And, as the Canadian political process moved closer in the early 1980s to entrenching constitutional guarantees of equality, feminist lawyers who had been involved in these cases prepared to engage in the equality debate in the political context.

## THE 1980s: EQUALITY, THE CHARTER, AND BEYOND

By 1980, women had been entering law schools in ever-increasing numbers for more than a decade. In Quebec (which has a civil law system), from 1979 at L'Université Laval and from 1981 at L'Université de Montreal women students constituted over 50 percent of the total number of entering students. *The Globe and Mail* reported in 1986 that, in law schools in other Canadian provinces that have "common law" systems, at the University of Windsor women constituted just over 50 percent of the first-year class while the entrance rates for other common law schools in Canada hovered around 35 percent to 45 percent (Mossman 1988).

During the preceding decades, some women had been appointed as judges. When Helen Kinnear was appointed to the Ontario County Court in 1943, she was the first woman in the British Commonwealth to serve on a court at this level (Dranoff 1977). However, it was only in 1969 that the first woman was appointed to a Superior Court in Canada: in that year, Quebec appointed Rejanne Laberge-Colas to the Quebec Superior Court. Six years later, in 1975, Bertha Wilson, with her appointment to the Ontario Court of Appeal became the first woman member of a provincial appellate court. In 1982, Justice Wilson was also the first woman appointed to the Supreme Court of Canada followed by Justice Claire L'Heureux-Dubé in 1987 and Justice Beverley McLachlin in 1989.

Women lawyers and women law students organized the first National Conference of Women and the Law in 1974 in Windsor and it gradually emerged as the National Association of Women and the Law. At the 1974 conference, the Treasurer of the Law Society of Upper Canada, Sidney Robins, announced that the Law Society would discipline lawyers who discriminated against women in the legal profession (Dranoff 1977). Courses in women and the law appeared in law school calendars in the mid-1970s, developed in most cases by women law academics who wanted to explore the law's potential for changing the status of women. Just a decade later in 1985, *The Canadian Journal of Women and the Law* was established by women law academics and practitioners. This coincided with the appearance of similar journals in a number of U.S. law schools (Mossman 1985). Also in this period, a few women were elected to the governing bodies of provincial law societies, although the first woman president of the Canadian Bar Association was elected only in August 1992 when Paule Gauthier from Quebec became president of the CBA; in August 1993, she was succeeded as president of the CBA by Cecilia Johnstone from Alberta.

As numerous provincial studies showed, the circumstances for women lawyers were often more difficult than for their male colleagues, especially in terms of prestigious work and salary levels. Indeed, the Canadian Bar Association's Task Force on Gender Equality, reporting in 1993, recommended substantial changes to ensure that women lawyers have equality with their male colleagues:

> Women have gained entry to the profession in increasingly large numbers, but their entry has been marked by struggle rather than enthusiasm. This cold reception is accentuated for Women of Colour, Aboriginal women, women with disabilities and lesbians. True access to the profession will require a transformation in the profession itself. (Canadian Bar Association 1993)[6]

By the 1980s, by contrast with earlier decades, women were increasingly numerous and active members of the Canadian legal profession both in private practice and in government policy-making positions. Many took an active part in the debates about constitutional reform preceding repatriation in 1982 and were unstintingly involved in lobbying about the wording of the equality section of the *Canadian Charter of Rights and Freedoms* (section 15) and the negotiation of a specific sex equality guarantee (section 28) (Baines 1988; Kome 1983). The language of these two sections of the *Charter* reflects women's efforts to entrench more effective constitutional guarantees. Thus, section 15 provides:

> 15(1) Every individual is equal before and under the law and has the right to the equal protection and equal benefit of the law without discrimination and, in particular, without discrimination based on race, national or ethnic origin, colour, religion, sex, age or mental or physical disability.
>
> 15(2) Subsection (1) does not preclude any law, program or activity that has as its object the amelioration of conditions of disadvantaged individuals or groups including those that are disadvantaged because of race, national or ethnic origin, colour, religion, sex, age or mental or physical disability.

Like other constitutional guarantees in the *Charter*, section 15 guarantees may be limited according to "such reasonable limits prescribed by law as can be demonstrably justified in a free and democratic society" (section 1), but the wording of section 28 made its guarantee of sex equality available regardless of any other provisions of the *Charter*:

> 28 Notwithstanding anything in this Charter, the rights and freedoms referred to in it are guaranteed equally to male and female persons.

The negotiation of the *Charter* guarantees, like the suffrage movement almost 100 years earlier, was a collective and highly-focused campaign, a campaign in which women who were lawyers played some of the key roles as advisers and strategists (Kome 1983). Unlike in the suffrage campaign, however, the negotiation of wording for sex equality guarantees was a somewhat more speculative process. As Baines has stated:

> [Sections 15 and 28] do not explain the meaning of sex equality. That meaning is no more self-evident from these Charter provisions than it was from the Canadian Bill of Rights sex equality provision. The Charter does not preclude the gender bias that permeated most of the 'persons' cases and all of the Canadian Bill of Rights cases. This puts an enormous burden on women before they even begin to litigate the Charter sex equality cases. (Baines 1988)

What was needed, therefore, was a means of influencing the courts' interpretation of these constitutional provisions in ways that better accorded with (all) women's interests.

Although the *Charter* came into effect in April 1982, the equality provisions of section 15 were not in effect until three years later in 1985. Federal and provincial governments were thereby granted a three-year period in which to review their statutes and enact appropriate amendments to bring them into conformity with the requirements of the equality section. For women lawyers who had lobbied for the *Charter* language on sex equality, the three-year period offered an opportunity for strategic research and planning. Thus, as early as November 1982, a group of women lawyers, law academics, and law students met to form the nucleus of the Charter of Rights Educational Fund, a network of interested women who together produced an overview of the statutory laws then affecting women, laws that might be challenged under section 15 (Razack 1991). Perhaps more importantly, this work, in the process of "auditing" existing statutes, offered an opportunity for discussions about appropriate interpretations of "equality." Some of the women involved in the CREF project also worked tirelessly on other related projects, organizing conferences for discussion and information, arranging consultations with American feminist lawyers and scholars who had conducted test case litigation concerning sex equality, and generally lobbying governments and constitutional experts. As they subsequently described it, these women lawyers wanted to "manipulate the system to accommodate women's needs, using ways with which [they] were most at home" (Razack 1991).

The result of this activity was the creation of the Women's Legal Education and Action Fund, a research and litigation organization with a mandate to initiate, and to intervene in, cases affecting women. Since 1985, LEAF has intervened in a large number of cases including *Andrews* v. *The Law Society of British Columbia* in 1989, the leading case in the Supreme Court of Canada defining "equality." In that case, the court adopted a purposive approach to the definition of equality (an approach that interpreted the equality guarantee so as to achieve the legislative purposes defined by the *Charter*), holding that equality analysis required consideration of the existence of comparative disadvantage. As Lynn Smith has explained, the court's approach added a "third dimension" to the traditional analysis of equality guarantees:

> Canadian courts no longer limit their analysis to whether the claimant and the treatment are sufficiently similar to or different from selected comparators. Instead, the Court will consider whether the claimant is a member of a group which has experienced persistent disadvantage on the basis of a personal characteristic, such as those named in section 15, and whether the questioned classification continues or worsens that disadvantage. (Smith 1992)

In this way, Canadian equality jurisprudence has taken a different (and arguably more successful) approach by contrast with principles developed in the United States. Moreover, in the context of women's claims, the Canadian approach shows how the definition of equality has also changed significantly by contrast with the approach used in the cases litigated in the early part of the twentieth century. This change has also occurred because the role of courts has changed, at least to some extent, with the entrenchment of constitutional guarantees in the *Charter*. Because courts have been authorized by the constitution to declare legislation invalid when it is inconsistent with *Charter* guarantees, the courts now have a more assertive role than previously (Russell 1982), a role that has arguably influenced the relative success of women's legal claims in recent years.

After the *Charter*, and even before the *Andrews* case was decided in 1989, there were a number of important decisions for women. One was the Supreme Court of Canada's decision in *Action Travail des Femmes* v. *CNR* in 1987 concerning the interpretation of the *Canadian Human Rights Act* in relation to workplace discrimination. Responding to the systemic discrimination complaint filed by Action Travail des Femmes, the court held that the company's actions clearly constituted systemic sex discrimination against women employees and that the human rights tribunal had jurisdiction to make its remedial order: that CN hire at least one woman in four for nontraditional categories of work until women constituted 13 percent of those working in nontraditional categories at CN (the objective of 13 percent corresponded to the national average of women in non-traditional work in Canada). According to the court, "specific hiring goals ... are a rational attempt to impose a systemic remedy on a systemic problem." In this way, the Supreme Court of Canada recognized that discrimination could occur without intent to discriminate and confirmed that it was necessary to look at the results or impact of apparently neutral employment policies.

In the same year the court decided three cases ("the trilogy") concerning women's rights to request continuing financial support from their former husbands after divorce. In all three cases, the women had signed agreements limiting their rights to claim such support, but they had then experienced financial difficulty and all three were facing, or were already receiving, welfare. In these cases, the Supreme Court of Canada reviewed all the issues carefully and concluded that it was important to encourage spouses to settle their affairs privately by contract, an objective that could be achieved only if the court recognized and enforced such private contracts. The court decided therefore that it would interfere with these contracts only in rare circumstances. According to Madame Justice Wilson, the court should intervene only if a spouse could show "a radical change arising out of the economic relationship of the spouses during the marriage."

In one of the cases, *Richardson* v. *Richardson*, the wife had left her employment as a secretary just before the birth of her second child and had then worked only part time on a few occasions. The court's decision confirmed that she should be regarded as economically "self-sufficient" even though she had child-care responsibilities and had been out of the work force for several years at a time when secretarial skills had substantially changed to include word processing. The court's approach thus characterized the spouses as independent and equal for purposes of determining financial support, an approach that appeared inconsistent with statistical evidence about the disadvantaged position of women in the paid work force in Canada (Bailey 1989-90; Cossman 1989). Moreover, the equality approach adopted by the court wholly failed to consider "the inequality of bargaining power which is the *leitmotif* of these cases" (Bailey 1989-90).

Thus, *Action Travail des Femmes* (recognizing the substance of women's inequality in nontraditional workplaces) and *Richardson* (confirming women's *formal* equality within the family) posed once again the problems of defining equality for women in the legal system. Are women the "same" as men or "different" from them? Should the court interpret equality in terms of substance or only form? That is, should the court assume that women and men are the same (equal as a matter of "form") or should the court take account of the circumstances of women's lives that make their experiences (in terms of reproduction, participation in the paid work force, social and sexual norms, or other expectations) substantially different from those of men? Indeed, is it possible for legal principles to reflect the complexity of women's specific circumstances—sometimes similar to those of men, sometimes different from them—but always flowing from social arrangements as well as biological needs? These questions were at the heart of *R. v. Morgentaler*, another important decision for women in Canada in 1988 in which Madame Justice Wilson suggested a need to define women's equality in a new way.

In *Morgentaler*, the Supreme Court of Canada decided, in relation to charges against Dr. Morgentaler in Ontario, that the provisions of the *Criminal Code* regarding "therapeutic" abortion procedures were unconstitutional. The court held that the *Criminal Code* provisions were not consistent with the requirements of section 7 of the *Charter* (regarding the right to life, liberty and security of the person). In her decision, Justice Wilson stated that the history of human rights from the eighteenth century onward was primarily the history of men struggling to assert their dignity against the power of the state, and that the struggle for women's rights thus far had therefore been one of trying to eliminate discrimination, to achieve a place for women "in a man's world," and to develop legislative reforms to place women in the same position as men. However, she emphasized that the struggle for women's rights had not (yet)...

> been a struggle to define the rights of women in relation to their special place in the societal structure and in relation to the biological distinction between the two sexes. Thus, women's needs and aspirations are only now being translated into protected rights. The right to reproduce or not to reproduce which is in issue in this case is one such right and is properly perceived as an integral part of modern woman's struggle to assert *her* dignity and worth as a human being. (Emphasis in original)

Moreover, she acknowledged that it was "probably impossible for a man to respond, even imaginatively, to [the dilemma of an unwanted pregnancy]" not only because no man has had such an experience but also because no man could imagine it subjectively. These comments clearly underlined Justice Wilson's recognition of the need for a new definition of equality, one that could capture the nuances of women's lives, and demonstrated her willingness to search for legal principles to accommodate both women's as well as men's experiences (Martin 1987-88).[7]

In the three areas of work, family, and sexuality, the Supreme Court of Canada demonstrated its continuing dialogue about the meaning of equality in the years after section 15 came into force. By 1989, when the court decided the first case under section 15, the *Andrews* case, two other cases involving women's employment rights under human rights legislation had also reached the highest court. In *Janzen* v. *Platy Enterprises Ltd.*, the court held that sexual harassment constituted sex discrimination under Manitoba human rights legislation and awarded the complainants—waitresses in a restaurant—their lost wages as well as "exemplary damages" (special compensation for their predicament). The court held liable both the employee who had sexually harassed the complainants and also their employer. This latter point thus established a legal responsibility on employers to ensure that none of their employees is sexually harassed. In the second case, *Brooks* v. *Canada Safeway Ltd.*, the issue of pregnancy leave entitlement was reconsidered, and the outcome in *Bliss* a decade earlier was reversed. Both these decisions established important legal principles for women in the paid work force (Mossman 1993b).

Some decisions, however, continued to raise concerns about the unevenness of legal developments. In the 1990 decision, *R.* v. *Lavallee*, for example, the Supreme Court accepted the validity of evidence of the "battered women's syndrome" as the basis for a claim of self-defence, exonerating a woman who had murdered her battering spouse. While this decision was obviously important for its willingness to take into account differences in the experiences of women and men in relation to violence and self-defence, it may also have had unintended side effects. One such effect results from the court's reliance on the evidence of an expert to define the experience of a battered woman; in doing so, the court implicitly rejected the validity of a woman's own statements about such experiences, at least in the absence of expert confirmation. In addition, the legal principle used by the court required the accused woman to establish that she had been a victim of persistent violence so that she had acquired a "learned helplessness" in the relationship with her batterer. Such a principle reinforced the view of women as victims and powerless. Thus, although the outcome in the case allowed the woman's experience to be considered in the interpretation of the substantive law, the principle adopted in *Lavallee* nonetheless confirmed women in the stereotypical role of victim requiring expert evidence to establish the facts of her situation for the court. In this way, the case demonstrated how law both facilitates reform and is at the same time a barrier to achieving it.[8]

Two other cases must be mentioned. One again concerned a former wife's entitlement to financial support after divorce. In *Moge* v. *Moge*, the Supreme

Court reconsidered its earlier views about formal equality set out in the trilogy of cases (including *Richardson*). Madame Justice L'Heureux-Dubé's decision for the court outlined the difficult financial circumstances experienced by many women after divorce: the "feminization of poverty" problem, characterized by low wages in the paid work force and relatively more extensive responsibilities for child care. She justified an award of continuing support to Mrs. Moge by recognizing the need for a more substantive definition of equality:

> [The Divorce Act] recognizes that work within the home has undeniable value and transforms the notion of equality from the rhetorical status to which it was relegated under a deemed self-sufficiency model, to a *substantive* imperative. In so far as economic circumstances permit, the Act seeks to put the remainder of the family in as close a position as possible to the household before the marriage breakdown. (Emphasis added)

Yet the earlier approach in the trilogy of cases regarding financial support was not rejected for cases where the spouses had signed separation agreements; thus, the court's approach in *Moge* was confined to cases where the parties had not reached their own agreement. However, the distinction between cases of private agreement (*Richardson*) and those in which the court makes an initial order for support (*Moge*) may not justify such contrasting legal principles—principles which in one case deny subsequent variation and in the other make it fully available. Certainly, the feminization of poverty does not occur only for those cases where there is a court order. Such a case thus once again reflects the unevenness of legal principles that simultaneously facilitate some changes and act as a barrier for others.

The contrast between formal and substantive equality was also evident in contrasting judgments in the Supreme Court of Canada in *R. v. Seaboyer; R. v. Gayme*, two sexual assault (rape) cases involving the constitutional validity of *Criminal Code* provisions restricting the admissibility of evidence about the victim's prior sexual conduct. The majority of judges decided that these provisions wrongly curtailed the accused's right to a free trial. In her decision for the majority judges, Justice Beverley McLachlin held that the Code provisions were too broad and that the constitutional right to a fair trial for the accused outweighed the interests in protecting the privacy of a witness. By contrast, Justice L'Heureux-Dubé, on behalf of the two dissenting judges, held that the provisions of the Code did not impair the accused's right to a fair trial because evidence of a victim's sexual reputation was unreliable and thus would not affect the fairness of the trial of the accused. In so deciding, she relied on social science studies about the prevalence of myths about rape that render the evidence of the victim's sexual reputation especially dangerous as part of the trial; as she stated, "this baggage belongs to us all."

Nonetheless, the majority decision meant that the provisions protecting the victim's sexual reputation were eliminated from the *Criminal Code*. This result led to pressure from women lawyers and others for further amendments to the Code. In the consultative process for the new law, women workers from rape crisis centres worked with women lawyers to make recommendations that resulted in a new definition of consent from the subjective experience of women (McIntyre forthcoming). In particular, efforts were made in the reform process to incorporate the experiences of women in differing contexts, such as women of colour, disabled women, and lesbian women. The court decision that failed to recognize women's experiences in the context of sexual assault became a cata- lyst in 1992 for remedial legislative action that was informed by (differing) expe- riences among women. However, since courts will continue to interpret the new laws, the work of influencing interpretations that recognize substantive equality for women will need to continue.

The most recent court decisions have revealed ongoing tension about the meaning of equality in the "public" context of work and the "private" contexts of family life and sexuality. The recent legislative process to create amendments to the *Criminal Code* provisions regarding sexual assault also demonstrated efforts to consider differing experiences among women, an approach that has only recently been recognized as important in the legal system. While it is clear that women as lawyers have been significantly involved in these recent legal cases concerning women's lives, it remains difficult to characterize their overall achievements as successful or otherwise. On this basis, the paradox of feminist engagement with law remains a continuing challenge and an issue for women lawyers as well as for other women activists.

## THE PARADOX OF FEMINIST ENGAGEMENT WITH LAW

The use of equality litigation as a strategy for advancing women's interests remains controversial. Although women have used the *Charter* to establish their equality claims, a 1989 study showed that men had used *Charter* sex equality arguments more often and more successfully than women (Brodsky and Day 1989). As well, there have been cases where *Charter* claims have actually removed benefits expressly conferred on women. An egregious example was the removal of welfare benefits for single mothers by a Nova Scotia court (*A-G Nova Scotia* v. *Phillips*) because the legislative scheme failed to meet the test of formal equality for men and women. The court preferred to remedy the problem by declaring invalid the legislation providing benefits to single mothers rather than ordering the extension of welfare benefits to eligible male single parents (Fudge 1989). Such decisions not only confirm the dangers of equality guarantees that are interpreted in terms of formal equality but also demonstrate the paradoxical support of law for women's equality claims.

This paradox is also revealed by an assessment of the meaning of such court decisions for women's daily lives. Since each court decision confirmed or denied only the rights of parties to the litigation, specific rights and obligations flowed from the decisions only to individual parties and left the broader impact of such decisions in practice much harder to assess. Thus, although in *Janzen*, employers were held to be liable for workplace sexual harassment the decision did not create a broadly based and effective monitoring process for workplaces. A woman facing such harassment must file another individual complaint to obtain the appropriate remedy from a lax or recalcitrant employer. The same process is needed for a woman who wants to enforce the rights to pregnancy benefits required by the court's decision in *Brooks*. Similarly, nothing in the *Lavallee* decision extends emotional or other support to the large number of women in battering relationships. All the case decided was that a battered woman who kills her partner (a small number of women in such relationships) may use the battered woman's syndrome to claim self-defence and thus avoid being found guilty of murder.

More generally, *Charter* equality arguments have not been particularly useful in enforcing economic equality rights. For example, it has been suggested that the *Charter* is not very useful in challenging legislative restrictions in provincial welfare schemes for women receiving welfare assistance (some of the poorest women in Canada) (Abner 1989). As well, in the context of issues about financial support after divorce, "the trilogy" used a formal equality approach that did not permit the Supreme Court of Canada to take account of the differing economic circumstances of men and women at the end of a marriage. Although the court's decision in *Moge* did recognize the feminization of poverty in relation to divorce, it did not overturn the approach of the earlier trilogy cases but merely confined their application to those spouses who had negotiated separation agreements. In this way, *Charter* litigation seems to offer little in terms of broadly based remedial policies directed to alleviating women's relatively poorer economic circumstances.

Beyond *Charter* litigation, women's access to courts and the legislative process generally is also detrimentally affected by women's relative lack of economic resources (Mossman 1990). There is no doubt that the impact of women's claims in the last decade has resulted primarily from initiatives and interventions on the part of the Women's Legal Education and Action Fund. In this sense, the establishment of legal principles responsive to women's legal needs has been accomplished in large measure by the work and organization of women lawyers, academics, and law students (Razack 1991). While LEAF's activity clearly demonstrates the importance of having women in the legal profession as a means of accomplishing legal changes for women, its cases have tended to reflect the perspectives of the women lawyers who have been actively involved. More recently LEAF has reached out to less well-represented communities of women, particularly grassroots organizations, a strategic approach necessitated by the fact that women lawyers are not themselves (at least yet) broadly representative of the larger women's community in Canada.

In addition to LEAF litigation, other important litigation for women continues in the 1990s, frequently sponsored by women with the financial or fundraising resources necessary for pursuing lengthy and time-consuming legal claims. For example, the recent claim by a woman lawyer, Elizabeth Symes, to deduct her child-care expenses as "business expenses" necessary to enable her to practice law raised important issues about women's experiences as full-time workers who are also parents, issues not traditionally experienced by men who are both workers and parents. Clearly, the position of women lawyers often differs substantially with that of their male colleagues with child-care responsibilities in terms of societal expectations (Mossman 1992) and the trial judge in the case accepted that many of the expenses currently accepted as "business deductions" for income tax purposes reflect patterns of men's lives more than those of women. The trial judge's decision permitted the deduction of child-care expenses as "business deductions," but this decision was overturned by the Federal Court of Appeal. Moreover, in late 1993, the Supreme Court of Canada confirmed the decision of the Federal Court of Appeal, both women members of the Supreme Court dissenting from this conclusion. According to Justice Claire L'Heureux-Dubé, the cost of a nanny should be regarded as much a legitimate business expense as male-dominated activities such as cars, wining and dining clients, or joining a golf club.

Yet the *Symes* case also presented a strategic dilemma for feminist lawyers and activists. Since the success of this claim would permit only self-employed women to claim such child-care expenses as business expenses, it did not address at all directly the more general need to create an appropriate, broadly based child-care policy in Canada. Indeed, some feminists expressed concern that claims of such women lawyers might succeed at the expense of claims on the part of other women, including both women employees (especially those on minimum or low wages) and domestic workers who care for children (Macklin 1992). Thus, the case did not address directly the more general need to create an appropriate, broadly based child-care policy for working parents, especially women, in Canada. In the context of scarce governmental resources, the fear that a successful outcome in the *Symes* case would actually impede the creation of a more broadly based child-care scheme for all parents (and especially mothers who are also paid workers) was a serious, if speculative, concern. Such a case thus starkly reveals another paradox of feminist engagement with law: not only are women "running hard to stand still" (Chunn and Brockman 1993; Smart 1989), but it seems that the claims of some women may potentially undermine those of others.

At the same time, the educative value of a case such as *Symes* is undeniable. The case, by drawing attention to the personal dilemmas of so many women who are both mothers and workers, has arguably contributed to much more widespread concern about these issues and has clearly focused pressure for both political and legal changes. In this way, the failure of the *Symes* claim in the Supreme Court of Canada may result in much broader legislative action, just as the failure of Irene Murdoch's claim to share in one-half of her husband's property at divorce was the catalyst for widespread legislative reform. In both cases, of course, the perseverence of these women claimants in the legal process may thus benefit many other Canadian women personally and politically, a fact that should not be minimized. In this way, an assessment of the benefits of feminist engagement with law remains paradoxical.

In this context especially, women lawyers appear to be at the same time privileged women and also harbingers of important feminist activity designed to influence broader movements for legal change. Moreover, as the Canadian Bar Association's Task Force on Gender Equality in the Legal Profession in 1993 suggested, the unequal treatment of women lawyers within the legal profession undermines the confidence of all women that the justice system is fair (Canadian Bar Association 1993). In such a context, however, feminist lawyers need to continue to ask hard questions about women and also about law. In spite of their increasing numbers in the profession, women lawyers remain less well-positioned than their male colleagues so that their resources must be carefully and strategically deployed on behalf of women in many differing circumstances. In this way, the debate about feminist engagement with law remains both vital and necessary for women lawyers as for other feminists. As Nicola Lacey has argued:

> Any political theory which does not recognize that power relations within society are relevant to the attainment of social justice is dodging what is in fact a central question: indeed, just this kind of evasion is at the root of political theory's failure adequately to take on board questions of gender. (Lacey 1992)

Thus, the paradox presents a challenge for both current and future feminist engagement with law. For women who are both lawyers and feminists, it remains the central paradox of both their work and their lives.

## NOTES

The research assistance of Michael Gardner, LL.B. 1993 and Susan Saltzman, LL.B. 1994 is warmly appreciated, as is the excellent technical assistance of Hazel Pollack.

1   The phrase "running hard to stand still" was coined by Carol Smart in her analysis of the uneven development of laws affecting women in the United Kingdom (Smart 1986).

2   The federal government passed the *Wartime Elections Act* which enfranchised some women by giving the vote to close relatives of members of the armed services; the *Military Voters Act* also gave the vote to women who were themselves in active service. In 1918, the federal government granted full female suffrage in federal elections. In

Nova Scotia, legislation in 1918 entitled women to vote, in New Brunswick in 1919, and in Prince Edward Island in 1922; in Quebec, women were not entitled to vote until 1940.

3 Although it is not unusual for Canadian courts to look to the United States for arguments in legal cases, Canadian courts are never required to reach the same result as courts in other legal jurisdictions. On this basis, Judge Barker's reliance on the U.S. case was unnecessary. In addition, by 1905 several U.S. states, including Illinois, had admitted women as members of the legal profession (Weisberg 1982; Sachs and Wilson 1978).

4 Emily Murphy and another woman magistrate had been challenged on the basis that they were disqualified from holding the public office of magistrate, but an Alberta court in 1917 decided that women were entitled to hold public office in that province (*R. v. Cyr*). Subsequently, when she became president of the Federated Women's Institutes of Canada in 1919, Murphy inspired a resolution requesting the Canadian government to appoint a woman to the Senate of Canada. Throughout the 1920s, lobbying continued without success. Thus, eventually Emily Murphy chose to seek an interpretation of a constitutional matter under the BNA Act. She needed five persons to launch this action.

The four other women included Nellie McClung, well known for her writing and speaking and a member of the Alberta legislature from 1921 to 1926. She was the mother of five children, one of whom (Mark) worked as a researcher for the Royal Commission on the Status of Women report in 1970. Henrietta Muir Edwards was 78 years old when the women launched their action in 1927 and a long-time and respected advocate of issues about the status of women. She had been active in organizing the Montreal Working Girls' Association in 1875 and had worked in the suffrage movement and influenced passage of the *Dower Act* in Alberta. Irene Marryat Parlby was a member of the Alberta Cabinet for 14 years and sponsored and supported many legislative reforms for women and children. She had also been president of the United Farm Women of Alberta in 1916. Louise Crummy McKinney was one of the first women to sit in a legislature in the British Empire and had been active in the Women's Christian Temperance Union. Elected to the Alberta legislature in 1919, she was influential in getting the *Dower Act* passed and was active in militant farm politics in Alberta (Dranoff 1977).

5 Concurrently, feminist lawyers in the United States were debating the relative merits of two differing approaches to legal equality ideas: the "sameness" approach which assumed that women were in all relevant respects the same as men and thus should be subject to the same rights and responsibilities; and the "difference" approach which argued that women were different from men in some ways (including at least their reproductive capacity) which needed to be accommodated by legal principles. These differing approaches were challenged by a number of legal issues: the drafting of women for military service, the existence of statutory rape offences for men but not for women aggressors, and arrangements to accommodate pregnant workers. For good examples of this literature, see Littleton 1987; Williams 1982; and Scales 1980-81.

6   The CBA Report examined several areas of legal practice in terms of equality goals. The report also addressed, as a general issue, the need for the legal profession to better integrate work and family life. As the report stated emphatically:

> In gaining entry to the legal profession women have demonstrated their creativity and energy in forging a place for themselves in an inhospitable environment. The challenge, however, has not diminished as numbers have grown: 'as women have entered the work force, both women and the workforce have changed. What still have to change are the work*place* and men' (Canadian Bar Association 1993, quoting Hochschild (with Machung) 1989).

7   Dr. Morgentaler has not escaped criminal prosecution since 1988 in spite of the decision of the Supreme Court of Canada. He was charged with breaching Nova Scotia legislation which effectively precluded the use of abortion clinics in that province. In 1993, the Supreme Court of Canada decided once again that he was not guilty because the provincial legislation was unconstitutional.

8   A similar analysis can be made about the court's decision in *R.* v. *Butler* upholding the obscenity provisions of the Criminal Code in relation to the Charter. The court adopted a test for obscenity that took into account the detrimental impact on women of pornographic material, but such a test has negatively affected some lesbian women's literature. The outcome has therefore been subjected to further scrutiny by feminist lawyers (Busby forthcoming).

# BIBLIOGRAPHY

Abel, R. "The Contradictions of Professionalism." In *Lawyers in Society*, edited by Abel, R. and Lewis, P. University of California Press, 1988.

Abner, E. "The Merits of the Use of Constitutional Litigation to Unravel the Fabric of the Feminization of Poverty." LL.M. Thesis, Osgoode Hall Law School, 1989.

Abner, E., Mossman, M.J. and Pickett, E. "No More Than Simple Justice: Assessing the Royal Commission Report on Women, Poverty and the Family." 22 Ottawa Law Review 573, 1990.

Arat-Koc, Sedef. "In the Privacy of Our Own Home: Foreign Domestic Workers as Solution to the Crisis in Domestic Sphere in Canada." 28 Studies in Political Economy 33, 1989.

Armour, M. and Staton, P. *Canadian Women in History: A Chronology.* Green Dragon  Press, 1990.

Atcheson, E., Eberts, M., Symes, E., and Stoddart, J. *Women and Legal Action.* Canadian Advisory Council on the Status of Women, 1984.

Backhouse, C. " 'To Open the Way for Others of my Sex': Clara Brett Martin as Canada's First Woman Lawyer." 1 Canadian Journal of Women and the Law 1, 1985.

Backhouse, C. "Married Women's Property Law in Nineteenth-Century Canada." 6 Law and History Review 211, 1988

Backhouse, C. *Petticoats and Prejudice: Women and Law in Nineteenth-Century Canada.* The Osgoode Society and Women's Press, 1991.

Bailey, M. *"Pelech, Caron* and *Richardson."* 3 Canadian Journal of Women and the Law 615, 1989-90.

Baines, B. "Women and the Law" In *Changing Patterns: Women in Canada,* edited by Burt, S., Code, L. and Dorney, L. McClelland and Stewart, 1988.

Brodsky, G. and Day, S. *Canadian Charter Equality Rights for Women: One Step Forward or Two Steps Back?* Canadian Advisory Council on the Status of Women, 1989.

Burt, S. "Legislators, Women and Public Policy." In *Changing Patterns: Women in Canada,* edited by Burt, S., Code, L. and Dorney, L. McClelland and Stewart, 1988.

Busby, K. "Leaf and Pornography: Litigating on Pornography and Sexual Representations." Canadian Journal of Women and the Law. Forthcoming.

Chunn, D. "Feminism, Law and Public Policy: 'Politicizing the Personal' " in *Reconstructing the Canadian Family,* 2d ed., edited by Mandell, N. and Duffy, A. Butterworths, 1993.

Chunn, D. and Brockman, J. " 'Running Hard to Stand Still?' - Future Directions for Studying 'Gender Bias' in Law" In *Investigating Gender Bias: Law, Courts and the Legal Profession,* edited by Brockman, J. and Chunn, D. Thompson Educational Publishing, Inc., 1993.

Cossman, B. "A Matter of Difference: Domestic Contracts and Gender Equality" 28 Osgoode Hall Law Journal 303, 1990.

"Crossing the Bar: *A Century of Women's Experience* 'Upon the Rough and Troubled Seas of Legal Practice' in Ontario. Law Society of Upper Canada. Museum Exhibit, 1993.

Dranoff, L.S. *Women in Canadian Life: Law.* Fitzhenry and Whiteside, 1977.

Eberts, M. "Sex and Equality Rights" in *Equality Rights and the Canadian Charter of Rights and Freedoms.* Carswell, 1985.

Friedman, J. *America's First Woman Lawyer.* Prometheus Books, 1993.

Fudge, J. "The Public/Private Distinction: The Possibilities of and Limitations to the Use of Charter Litigation to Further Feminist Struggles." 25 Osgoode Hall Law Journal 485, 1987.

Fudge, J. "The Effect of Entrenching a Bill of Rights upon Political Discourse: Feminist Demands in Sexual Violence in Canada." 17 International Journal of the Sociology of Law 445, 1989.

Gillet, M. *We Walked very Warily: A History of Women at McGill.* Black Rose Books, 1981.

Harvey, C. "Women in Law in Canada." 4 Manitoba Law Journal 9, 1970-71.

Hochschild, A. with Machung, A. *Second Shift: Working Parents and the Revolution at Home.* Viking, 1989.

Jamieson, K. *Indian Women and the Law in Canada: Citizens Minus*. Canadian Advisory Council on the Status of Women, 1978.

Kates, C. " 'Identical or Substantially Identical': Bell Canada and the Struggle for Equal Pay 1967-1976". 4 Canadian Journal of Women and the Law 133, 1990.

Kome, P. *The Taking of Twenty-Eight: Women Challenge the Constitution*. Women's Educational Press, 1983.

Lacey, N. "Theories of Justice and the Welfare State." 1 Social and Legal Studies 323, 1992.

Littleton, C. "Reconstructing Sex Equality." 75 California Law Review 1279, 1987.

Lowe, G. "Women, Work and the Office: The Feminization of Clerical Occupations in Canada, 1901-1931." In *Rethinking Canada: The Promise of Women's History*, edited by Strong-Boag, V. and Fellman, A.C. Copp Clark Pitman Ltd., 1986.

Macklin, A. "Foreign Domestic Worker: Surrogate Housewife or Mail Order Servant?" 37 McGill Law Journal 682, 1992.

Martin, S. "*Morgentaler* v. *The Queen* in the Supreme Court of Canada." 2 Canadian Journal of Women and the Law 422, 1987-88.

McIntyre, S. "Redefining Reformism: The Consultations that Shaped Bill C-49." In *Confronting Sexual Assault in Canada: A Decade of Legal and Social Change* edited by Roberts, J. and Mohr, R. University of Toronto Press. Forthcoming.

Menkel-Meadow, C. "Excluded Voices: New Voices in the Legal Profession Making New Voices in the Law." 42 University of Miami Law Review 29, 1987.

Menkel-Meadow, C. "Mainstreaming Feminist Legal Theory." 23 Pacific Law Journal 1493, 1992.

Mossman, M.J. "'Otherness' and the Law School: A Comment on Teaching Gender Equality." 1 Canadian Journal of Women and the Law 213, 1985.

Mossman, M.J. "Feminism and Legal Method: The Difference it Makes." 3 Australian Journal of Law and Society 30, 1986.

Mossman, M.J. *"Unequal Access: Women Lawyers in a Changing America."* Review of R. Chester. 2 Canadian Journal of Women and the Law 178, 1986, 1986b.

Mossman, M.J. "'Invisible' Constraints on Lawyering and Leadership: The Case of Women Lawyers." 20 Ottawa Law Review 567, 1988.

Mossman, M.J. " Portia's Progress: Women as Lawyers—Reflections on Past and Future." 8 Windsor Yearbook of Access to Justice 252, 1988, 1988b.

Mossman, M.J. "Shoulder to Shoulder: Gender and Access to Justice." 10 Windsor Yearbook of Access to Justice 351, 1991.

Mossman, M.J. "Work and Family in the Legal Profession: Re-thinking the Questions." CBA National Conference of the Task Force on Gender Equality in the Legal Profession, 1992.

Mossman, M.J. "Family Law: Cases and Materials." Osgoode Hall Law School, 1993.

Mossman, M.J. "Feminism and 'Re-visioning' Law: Toward a General Theory." In *Femmes et Droit*, edited by Dumont, H. Les Editions Themis, 1993, 1993b.

Mullins, C. "Mabel Penery French" 44 Advocate 676, 1986.

Ng, R. "Immigrant Women and Institutionalized Racism." In *Changing Patterns: Women in Canada*, edited by Burt, S., Code, L. and Dorney, L. McClelland and Stewart, 1988.

Razack, S. *Canadian Feminism and the Law.* Second Story Press, 1991.

Razack, S. "Exploring the Omissions and Silences in Law Around Race." In *Investigating Gender Bias: Law, Courts and the Legal Profession*, edited by Brockman, J. and Chunn, D. Thompson Educational Publishing Inc., 1993.

Report of the Royal Commission on the Status of Women. Information Canada, 1970.

Russell, P. "The Effect of a Charter of Rights on the Policy-Making Role of Canadian Courts." 25 Canadian Public Administration 1, 1982.

Sachs, A. and Wilson, J.H. *Sexism and the Law.* Free Press, 1979.

Scales, A. "Towards a Feminist Jurisprudence." 56 Indiana Law Journal 375, 1980-81.

Smart, C. *Feminism and the Power of Law.* Routledge, 1989.

Smart, C. "Feminism and Law: Some Problems of Analysis and Strategy." 14 International Journal of the Sociology of Law 116, 1986.

Smith, L. "Adding a Third Dimension: The Canadian Approach to Constitutional Equality Guarantees." 55 Law and Contemporary Problems 211, 1992.

Strong-Boag, V. " 'Ever a Crusader': Nellie McClung, First-Wave Feminist." In *Rethinking Canada: The Promise of Women's History*, edited by Strong-Boag, V. and Fellman, A.C. Copp Clark Pitman Ltd., 1986.

Thornton, M. "Feminism and the Contradictions of Law Reform." 19 International Journal of the Sociology of Law 453, 1991.

*Touchstones for Change: Equality, Diversity and Accountability*, Canadian Bar Association, 1993.

*Transitions in the Ontario Legal Profession.* Law Society of Upper Canada. 1991.

Turpel, M.E. "Home/Land." 10 Canadian Journal of Family Law 17, 1991.

Ursel, J. *Private Lives, Public Policy: 100 Years of State Intervention in the Family.* Women's Press, 1992.

Weisberg, D.K. "Barred from the Bar: Women and Legal Education in the United States 1870-1890." In Women and the Law Vol.2, edited by Weisberg, D.K. Schenkman, 1982.

Williams, W. "The Equality Crisis: Some Reflections on Culture, Courts and Feminism." 7 Women's Rights Law Reporter 175, 1982.

Yorke, L. "Mabel Penery French (1881-1955): A Life Re-Created." 42 University of New Brunswick Law Journal 2, 1993.

## LIST OF CASES

### Early Twentieth Century Claims: Participation in Public Life

*In re French* (1905), 37 N.B.R. 359

*Re French* (1910-12), 17 B.C.L.R. 1

*Langstaff* v. *Bar of Quebec* (1915), 47 R.J.Q. 131;
      and (1916), 25 R.J.Q. 11

*Bradwell* v. *Illinois* 16 Wall 130 (U.S. 1872)

*Reference re Meaning of the Word "Persons" in s. 24 of the BNA Act*, [1928] S.C.R. 276; *Edwards* v. *A.G. for Canada*, [1930] A.C. 124

*R.* v. *Cyr*, [1917] 3 W.W.R. 849

### "Second Wave" Feminism and the Law: New Beginnings

*Canadian Federation of Agriculture* v. *AG of Quebec*, [1951] A.C. 179.

*R.* v. *Palmer*, [1937] 2 D.L.R. 609 (Ont. Mag. Ct.); [1937] O.W.N. 37; [1937] 3 D.L.R. 493 (C.A.)

*Murdoch* v. *Murdoch* (1973), 41 D.L.R. (3d) 367

*R.* v. *Drybones*, [1970] S.C.R. 282

*Attorney General of Canada* v. *Lavell; Isaac et al.* v. *Bedard*, [1974] S.C.R. 1349; (1974) 38 D.L.R. (3d) 481

"Views of the Human Rights Committee under Article 5(4) of the Optional Protocol to the International Covenant on Civil and Political Rights" 1 Canadian Native Law Reporter 1, 1982.

*Bliss* v. *Attorney General of Canada* (1977), 16 N.R. 254 (Fed. Ct.); [1979] 1 S.C.R. 183 (S.C.C.)

*R.* v. *Morgentaler* (No. 5) (1973), 14 C.C.C. (2d) 459; (1974), 42 D.L.R. (3d) 444 (Que. Q.B.) and

*Morgentaler* v. *The Queen*, [1976] 1 S.C.R. 616; (1975), 53 D.L.R. (3d) 161

*Re Lodge et al. and Minister of Employment and Immigration* (1978), 86 D.L.R. (3d) 553 (Fed. Ct.); [1979] 1 F.C.R. 775; (1979), 94 D.L.R. (3d) 326 (Fed. Ct. of Appeal)

*Bell Canada* v. *Palmer*, [1973] F.C. 982; Re: Bell Canada and Palmer (1974), 42 D.L.R. (3d) 1 (F.C.A.)

*Action Travail des Femmes* v. *CNR* (1987), 76 N.R. 161

*R.* v. *Pappajohn*, [1979] 1 W.W.R. 562; (1979), 45 C.C.C. (2d) 67 (B.C.C.A.); Pappajohn v. The Queen, [1980] 2 S.C.R. 120

## The 1980s: Equality, the Charter, and Beyond

*Andrews* v. *The Law Society of British Columbia* (1989), 56 D.L.R. (4th) 1

*Richardson* v. *Richardson* (1987), 7 R.F.L. (3d) 255

*R.* v. *Morgentaler*, [1988] 1 S.C.R. 30

*R.* v. *Morgentaler* S.C.C. Unreported.

*Janzen* v. *Platy Enterprises Ltd.* (1989), 59 D.L.R. (4th) 352

*R.* v. *Lavallee* (1990), 108 N.R. 321

*R.* v. *Butler*, [1992] 1 S.C.R. 452

*Moge* v. *Moge* (1992), 145 N.R. 1

*Re Seaboyer and the Queen; Re Gayme and the Queen* (1991), 66 C.C.C. (3d) 321 (S.C.C.)

## The Paradox of Feminist Engagement with Law

*A.G. Nova Scotia* v. *Phillips* (1986), 34 D.L.R. (4th) 633; *Reference re Family Benefits Act (N.S.) Section 5* (1986), 75 N.S.R. (2d) 338

*E.C. Symes* v. *Canada* S.C.C. (Unreported. [1991] 2 C.T.C. 1 (Fed. Ct. of Appeal); [1989] 1 C.T.C. 476 (Fed. Ct.)

*Brooks* v. *Canada Safeway Ltd.* (1989), 59 D.L.R. (4th) 321

# WOMEN'S WORK AND FAMILY LIVES

*Marion Lynn and Milana Todoroff*

## INTRODUCTION

There have been several technological, social, and economic changes in Canada over the past three decades that have transformed how we organize our lives in families and in wage labour. Reduction in family size, increased longevity, and increased labour force participation of married mothers are three such changes. The overall effect of these demographic trends has been greater flexibility in family forms and structures. Common-law marriages, divorce, gay/lesbian families, single-parent families, and step-parenting families are all now more socially acceptable and statistically common (Eichler 1988; Transition, Sept. 1993). Not only has the male breadwinner, nuclear family household become statistically unusual, but heterosexuality, which has formed the central basis for family establishment, has also been publicly and actively challenged. Lesbian women have created families and households as have gay men, and they are demanding recognition of these.

Women have always worked. What has changed during the past few decades in Canada is that women now comprise almost half of the full-time and part-time labour force, that they have entered occupational categories that had previously been closed to them, and that, like men, they are entering and staying in the paid labour force for most of their adult lives. In spite of these shifts, the majority of working women are still found in only a few occupations—the lowest paid with the fewest opportunities—and those women who have entered previously male-dominated occupations still earn less money than their male colleagues.

In this chapter, we critique what Eichler calls the four biases in the literature on families. These biases result in families being analyzed from a perspective that is monolithic, conservative, sexist, and microstructural. As a result, researchers talk about "family" as though all families and households are the same: changes from a male breadwinner, nuclear family household are viewed as problematic; relative positions of power and privilege of males and females in families are ignored; and the assumption is made that we can analyze family forms and dynamics without examining the broader social context (Eichler 1988, 2).

As well, we critique assumptions about women's work, assumptions suggesting women participate only marginally in the paid labour force and that their role as homemakers cannot be considered "real work." The dominant conceptions of work tend to make women's contributions to both household and public production invisible. In pushing these boundaries of how we define work and of how we understand what women do, we provide evidence that Canadian women have always been productive members of both family and community, supporting themselves and frequently contributing at least half of the family income (Baker 1990; Bradbury 1993).

We suggest that women's lives in family relations and productive work can be understood only within a framework of fluidity, flexibility, and struggles for freedom. One of the impediments to a clearer understanding of shifting and complex arrangements of women's lives in contemporary structures of family and work is the assumption that there is some fixed, ideal standard. This standard supposedly acts as a beacon, drawing people to it and enabling us to evaluate and judge that which is normal and deviant, positive and problematic.

In this analysis we acknowledge the powerful impact of economic forces in shaping people's lives. However, an economic analysis is overlaid with both a feminist and a postmodern critique. A feminist critique looks at restrictions and differential power relations because of sex and gender both in families and in the paid labour force. Postmodernism provides one framework within which to critique the limitations of universalism and essentialism and to consider the significance of the standpoint or location of the speaker. In this way, we can evaluate the validity of representation of the experience of the subjects under study.

To demonstrate the degree to which diversity and fluidity have always existed, we begin with an examination of the various histories of women's lives in families and in work in Canada. As well, this historical perspective shows the degree to which women have been active agents in shaping their relationships and in struggling for equality and freedom.

We then move into a detailed analysis of women's roles in the current Canadian labour force and look at the particular organizational factors that separate men and women, treat women as less worthy, and keep them marginalized. As well, we examine the various ways in which women have tried to redress this imbalance and show that these struggles result in more success for some women than for others.

The final section outlines some of the multiple and changing ways in which people are currently constructing their family systems and relationships. These include single-parent families, gay and lesbian families, and extended family arrangements. None of these is set out as problem free; neither is any one of them seen as the model others should follow but as viable alternatives.

We conclude with a suggestion that, in fact, the fluidity, flexibility, and struggles for freedom found within what Judith Stacey (1990) calls the contemporary, postmodern family are part of an ongoing process of changes in work solidus family intersections.

## HISTORICAL AND CROSS-CULTURAL EXPERIENCES

History reveals a variety of family forms and relationships that have co-existed in Canada. These include the egalitarian household economy of the Huron Indians, the interdependent roles of early settlers, the "split household families" of Chinese and Italian immigrants, and the female-headed households of English hosiery workers. Then, as now, there has been no neat and easy division between the "public" sphere of "productive" male work, and the "private" supposedly unproductive work of women in the home.

Prior to European colonization, North American Native women enjoyed respect, autonomy, and a central position in work and family systems. One example of this egalitarian culture is found among the seventeenth century Hurons of Ontario. The Hurons traced descent, rights, and titles to property within a clan through the female line. Housing and food production were under the control of the women. An older woman and her female descendants shared space and food in a longhouse; a man moved into the longhouse of the woman he married and was forced to leave if she no longer wanted to be married to him. Within standards established by the entire community, women had control over their sexuality, their children, and whom they would marry and remain married to. Men were frequently away for long stretches of time, engaged in hunting, warfare, or trading with other nations. The women were responsible for cultivating the crops and ensuring an adequate food supply. Within the systems in which women produced food, clothing, and housing, and reproduced the clan by childbirth and rearing, relationships among women provided economic security as well as family and clan stability (Anderson 1991; Bourgeault 1989; Horn 1991).

Aboriginal cultures and social systems were decimated by colonial powers: patriarchal systems of male dominance were imposed by both the British and the French. However, residuals of a more egalitarian structure still exist among the Aboriginal families, and Native women are politically engaged both locally and nationally. Grandmothers and other elders are still highly respected in many communities (Castellano et al. 1989). The Native Women's Association of Canada refused to be silenced by the all-male Assembly of First Nations in the constitutional debates (Native Women's Association of Canada 1992). Native women are actively involved in re-empowerment of themselves and their people (Maracle 1993).

Early days of Canadian colonization produced a form of interdependent relationships between men and women in both family and work systems among most other members of the working classes as well. Prior to nineteenth century industrialization, for European settlers, American Black immigrants, and native communities, Canada was primarily an agrarian-based household economy in which the place of residence and the place of work were the same. All family members—the father, mother, and children as well as others—contributed to economic production and the well-being of the family. The division of labour in this system was differentiated by age and gender. Mothers taught daughters skills such as weaving, butter-making, and canning; sons learned skills of harvesting and animal husbandry from their fathers. Many girls and women engaged in all forms of labour. The majority of people lived on farms and worked at a variety of jobs including farming, fishing, logging, and fur trading. Households produced their own clothes, food, heat, and lodging (Gaffield 1990).

The move from a household economy to a wage-labouring one, in which people were paid a wage for what they produced, led to changes in family structures and relationships. Economic changes occurred slowly and in stages. As the production of goods, such as cloth, moved from households to factories, women and children still did some parts of the process, such as spinning, done in the home, while the men worked on other parts of the production process in the factory. Pregnancy and child care were seen as female tasks and responsibilities which made it difficult but not impossible for women to work outside their homes. Men, unencumbered by domestic responsibilities, were "free" to work in factories and gradually became associated with public, wage-labouring activities. Some highly skilled male workers, by demanding a "family wage" large enough to support a dependent wife and children, further restricted women's access to decent-paying work. The ideology of a family wage entrenched both domestic and wage-labour occupational segregation by sex (Benenson 1991).

Within working-class families, wives and children still contributed to the family economy. However, women who had primary responsibility for the family found their work being devalued and paid less than men's whether in their homes or in factories. "Work" became defined as that which resulted in a wage, while domestic labour, child care, clothing and food preparation were hidden, trivialized, and devalued. Although most women and children provided both income and services, they were viewed as dependents in a family consumer economy because their economic contributions were ignored (Bradbury 1993).

Racism, colonialism, and nationalism embedded in Canada's laws and policies have helped shape the history of family and work patterns for women and men. A "split household family" is one family form resulting from immigration policies in the late 1800s and early 1900s. For example, Chinese men brought to Canada to build railroads were kept marginalized both economically and socially. Government policies such as the Chinese Immigration Act of 1923 with its $500 head tax prevented the Chinese-Canadian men from forming family households based on marriage and children (Li 1988; Ng 1989; Chinese Canadian National Council 1992). Similarly, wives and children of Black American porters working in Canada were prohibited from joining their husbands and fathers prior to the 1940s (Calliste 1989). The internment of Japanese-Canadians during World War Two fractured their families and communities in irreparable ways and destroyed successful businesses of Canadian men and women of Japanese descent that had taken years to develop (Kogawa 1981; Omatsu 1992).

Since women immigrated to the North American continent over a 300 year period, their roles and responsibilities in families and in domestic and wage work defy easy categorization. The nineteenth century English ideology of the "cult of domesticity," which suggested that a woman's rightful and biologically natural place was in the home, bore little resemblance to the reality of women's daily lives. Whether they came from France as "les filles du roi" (Landry 1992) or as Armenian picture brides (Kraprielan 1986) or as Finnish domestic workers (Lindstrom-Best 1988), women immigrants played an important economic role in establishing families and supporting themselves and their children.[1]

Women worked as farmers, teachers, journalists, and nurses. They worked in factories and in stores. They organized trade unions and engaged in labour struggles. In 1912 a strike was carried out by the International Ladies' Garment Workers Union against the T. Eaton Company (Frager 1986). In nineteenth century working-class Montreal, women as domestic workers kept pigs, cows, and boarders which combined with the wages of family members working in the factories and workshops of the city to create a family economy (Bradbury 1984).

Twentieth century immigration to Canada continued to create diversity and add to the multiple facets of women's family and work lives. Many Italian immigrants spent long periods of their lives in split family households. Some Italian men came to Canada a decade ahead of their wives and children. Back in small Italian villages, wives of Italian-Canadian workers ran farms and engaged in paid labour in order to keep their families and communities together.

> The little hamlets... were run by women: the young men had left, only very old men remained. They (women) did all the manual labour, tilled the soil, built the homes, erected the schools, taught the children, tended the sick, delivered the babies. (Sabia 1987)

When these women came to Canada, they performed crucial economic roles within the family. They grew vegetables in the backyards, took sewing and tailoring work that was paid by the piece into their homes, and cared for up to four generations of family members. Along with contributing to the domestic economy, by 1961 40 percent of Italian women in Toronto were in the paid work force (Iacovetti 1987; Sabia 1987).

British women hosiery workers who immigrated to Paris, Ontario at the turn of the century also combined domestic duties with paid labour. Investigation of their lives suggests yet another permutation of the family/work interaction during early Canadian industrial capitalism. These women came from a particular economic and historical time in England during which men's work was neither reliable nor highly paid, and marriage was not seen as an option to provide either financial or social security for women. These highly skilled women workers also came from a tradition of confidence in their own economic abilities and were used to setting up households by themselves and with other women, independent of marriage and men. They did not subordinate wage labour to marriage and family. Rather, they were workers first and perhaps wives and mothers second. Further, these women were the ones who sponsored friends and family to emigrate, and helped these new immigrants to become established in both jobs and households (Parr 1990).

As this historical overview indicates, women's family lives have never been easily separated from the broader economic system. As Joy Parr (1990) notes, "family" and "work" are neither separate nor fixed categories but intersect in both straightforward and complex ways. Another example of this interrelationship is recorded in Luxton's (1980) study of married women who were deliberately excluded from paid employment in a one industry town; this factory system shaped women's economic dependence and thus the men's dominance within marriages and families. As Luxton so eloquently puts it, "the 'long arm of the job' stretches from the workplace into the bedroom and exerts its grip on the most intimate part of marriage" (Luxton 1980, p.55).

In another study, Duffy, Mandell, and Pupo (1989) conclude that women's so-called "choice" to be a part of the paid labour force is in fact not really her own but is contingent upon factors outside of her control. These include the needs of the family, the age and number of children, the career demands or lack of employment of her husband, and the availability of work in her community. Thus the work/family balance is fluid in that a woman who is a part-time worker today might be a full-time worker or full-time homemaker tomorrow. Economic factors as well as stages of the life cycle affect women's work in the family and in the paid labour force.

Judith Stacey (1990) suggests that current families fit a category she calls "the postmodern family." In her longitudinal study of women and their families in California's Silicon Valley, Stacey outlines some of the parameters of the postmodern family. One case study exemplifies this family form. Pam, initially married to a professional man, was part of a "traditional" middle-class marriage until factors such as further education, job opportunities, and feminist consciousness led her to question family and marital relations. She eventually divorced and lived as a single parent for some time while she pursued a professional career. Then she lost her job and married a man who worked in the trades. She eventually became friends with her ex-husband's second wife, since the two women shared child care and kinship functions. Thus her class status, employment history, family status, and relationships with other family members, in-laws, and ex-in-laws changed considerably over the years (Stacey 1990 and 1993).

What this background from both historical and contemporary lives of women in work and family relationships shows is the degree to which, although political economic systems shaped their lives, women in turn have been active participants in the labour force and in family systems. In the following sections we focus on current issues for women, first in the labour force and then in family systems.

## WOMEN IN THE CURRENT CANADIAN LABOUR FORCE

### Labour Force Participation

The "labour force participation rate" is based on official government statistics and therefore on state-determined categories and assumptions about "work." It refers to the percentage of all women between 15 and 65 years of age who are paid for their work and who are employed either full time, part time, seasonally, are self-employed, or listed as unemployed (those who are currently not working but who have actively looked for work within the past four weeks). It does not include people who have given up looking for work, who do volunteer work, or who are retired; nor does it recognize the work that women do in the home.

In 1901, less than two in ten (16 percent) women over 15 years of age and over were working for wages. Since the Second World War, women's participation in the paid labour force has increased substantially with a particularly high rate of increase during the 1960s. In 1961, 29 percent were in the work force compared to 40 percent by 1971 and over half of all women over 15 by 1981. By 1991, the labour force participation rate for women was 58 percent; almost six in ten women were working outside the home for wages (Krahn and Lowe 1993).

This general outline of women's labour force participation masks differences among groups of women. For example, although there is no current information on the number of employed or unemployed Aboriginal women or women of colour, the 1986 census indicates that Aboriginal women have restricted access to the labour force as their participation rate is lower than that of women in general with only four in ten Aboriginal women in the labour force. Disabled women also experienced restricted access. Women of colour, however, have the highest percentage of workers with almost two out of three (or 64.5 percent) in the labour force. This is much higher than the 1986 average of 55 percent for all women (Khosla 1993).

## Unemployment and Underemployment

High rates of mass unemployment characterize the current labour market, but this has not always been the case.[2] In 1966, the official unemployment rate for all workers was just above 3 percent, but over the next twenty years it rose to nearly 10 percent. This represents a more than 280 percent increase in two decades (McBride 1992). The rate of unemployment has continued to increase for women with 689,000 or 11 percent of women officially unemployed by the beginning of 1993 (Khosla 1993).

Unemployment rates differ for women depending on their marital status. Rates are lowest among women who are either part of a common-law or legal marriage and highest among women who generally cannot depend upon a partner's income for support: 16 percent of young women under 24, 14 percent of single women, 13 percent of separated or divorced women, and 13 percent of women who were heading families were officially listed as unemployed in March 1993 (Khosla 1993). As noted earlier, Aboriginal women have even less access to the paid labour force than most other women. In 1985 almost a quarter (22 percent) of Aboriginal women were listed as unemployed (Khosla 1993: Canadian Labour Congress 1993).

While these figures are high, they hide the fact that there are many more unemployed people than the official figures indicate. Official figures do not include "discouraged workers" such as those who have stopped looking for work because they do not believe that there is any, women who are not in the work force because jobs and day care are not available, participants in government sponsored training programs, students who would prefer to work if jobs were available, and former workers who are forced into early retirement. The official figures also do not include women's "underemployment" or the part-time, short-term jobs that many women take because they cannot find full-time work. Official rates, constantly reported in the media, do not represent the "real" rate of unemployment which is estimated to be over 20 percent for both women and men (Khosla 1993).

Part-time work represents the fastest-growing segment of the paid labour force and is a common work form for many women, particularly for those married with children. Approximately one out of every four women in the Canadian labour force works part time and one of every three women in the labour force who is married with children is a part-time worker (Khosla 1993). While part-time work might help some women balance work and family responsibilities in a society that does not supply adequate support for mothers to work full time, it has serious short-term and long-term drawbacks. Part-time work provides no job permanency. This reduces the ability of part-time workers to borrow money for housing, cars, or other consumer products. Part-time employment generally pays low wages and rarely provides unionization or benefits that are equivalent to those of full-time jobs. For example, few part-time workers have access to paid vacations, overtime, health care plans, sick and disability leave, and, most of all, pension benefits. Even when they do have access to pension benefits, their pension contributions and the matching contributions of their employers are based on incomes that are substantially lower than those of full-time employees. As a result, the pensions of retired part-time workers are  substantially lower than those of full-time employees.

## The Gendered Wage Gap

As noted earlier, the shift from a household economy to a wage labour economy in the nineteenth century brought with it an unequal wage structure due partly to the ideology of "the family wage." This inequality formed the basis for the unequal pay structure or "wage gap" that currently exists between women and men. In 1991, women who worked in full-time, permanent jobs earned an average of $26,842, which was 69.6 percent of what men earned (Khosla 1993). This wage gap does not include the approximately 50 percent of women workers who are employed in part-time, part-year jobs. When part-time work is included in wage gap calculations, women's average earnings were only $18,050, or less than 62 percent of men's $29,328 average wage (Khosla 1993).

In 1991, the wage gap for full-time, permanent workers widened as women aged. Young women earned 84 percent of young men's wages; women between 35 and 44 years of age, who make up about 25 percent of the female work force, earned 59 percent compared to men the same age; and women between 55 and 64 earned 54 percent of the wages of men in the same age category (Zukewich Ghalan 1993). While there are no published 1991 figures for the wages of visible minority and Aboriginal women, the 1986 figures indicate that these women earn less than other women and certainly less than all men. In 1985, the average wage for all women was $20,100. The average wage for Aboriginal women was $18,500 which was $7,900 less than for Aboriginal men. For visible minorities, the average wage for women at $18,900 was $9,000 less than that of visible minority men at $27,900 (Khosla 1993). Needless to say, more women than men are part of the working poor. In 1991, more than three out of five of women (61 percent) earned less than $20,000 as compared to two out of five men (40 percent). As far as the percentage of women who are high wage earners, less than one in twenty-five women earns a salary of more than $50,000 per year as compared to one in six men (Statistics Canada 1993a).

The difference between women's and men's average wage does not result from individual employers paying women less for doing the same job as men in the same industry. Gunderson (1993) notes that, when we include employee education, training, and work experience as well as occupation, industry, and geographic location of employment for women and men working in the same jobs in the same establishment, women earn 90 to 95 percent of men's salaries. For example, in academia, female faculty earn 80 percent of what male faculty earn but this difference disappears when teachers in the same field and of equal rank are compared (Lee, Spring 1993). Rather, the wage gap results from the gendered nature of work in general. Men's jobs are distinct from women's jobs. The former are largely full-time, well-paying and secure while women's jobs are part-time, low-paid and transitory.

## Women's Industrial and Occupational Segregation

People work in three major economic sectors: primary, secondary, and tertiary. The primary sector includes agriculture, mining, forestry, and fishing. The few women who work in the primary sector receive low wages. Women employed in agriculture—crop, livestock, and other farming—are the lowest-paid group among all women workers (Statistics Canada 1991c).

The secondary economic sector includes manufacturing and construction. In this sector, raw materials provided by the primary sector are turned into goods. These two sectors, primary and secondary, combine to make up the "goods-pro-ducing sector." Almost 40 percent of men and only 15 percent of women are employed in the goods-producing sector (Khosla 1993). It is in this sector that women are the "last hired and the first fired." As fisheries on both coasts shut down, as factories relocate off shore and construction almost halts, women in large numbers are losing their jobs. In British Columbia, for example, Native women and women of colour (mostly Asian women) are among the first to lose their jobs as fishing canneries close.

Services including communication, health, education, finance, government, travel and tourism, and retail sales make up the tertiary sector. This service sector has been the fastest-growing sector in the Canadian economy over the past three decades and is the sector in which more than four out of five women (85 percent) were employed in 1991 (Khosla 1993).

People work as secretaries, managers, and accountants (occupational titles) in all three industrial sectors.[3] Occupational analysis reveals that most women work in just five occupations—clerical, teaching, nursing, or other health-related occupations, sales, or service. In 1991 more than seven out of ten women (71 percent) were employed in these occupations (Statistics Canada 1991c). About three million women, or half the female work force, are employed in clerical, sales, and service jobs. However, since the early 1980s, free trade, the recession, economic restructuring for the global market, and introduction of computer technology have all contributed to a reduction in full-time jobs in these areas. Clerical positions dropped by 10 percent, sales 3 percent, and service jobs by 4 percent between 1990 and 1992. Part-time work for women generally did not compensate for this reduction in full-time jobs. During the same time period, part-time clerical jobs increased by only 1 percent, sales jobs decreased by 1.5 percent and service jobs increased by just over 5 percent (Khosla 1993).

Over the past two decades, women have been moving into upper-tier occupations with high salaries, opportunities for advancement, benefits, job security, and high degrees of job autonomy. For example, women now comprise almost a quarter of physicians and lawyers, over a third of veterinarians, and up to half of all pharmacists in some areas (Lowe and Krahn 1993). However, women who do make it into upper-tier occupations tend to occupy lower-level positions that yield less money and less power. The experiences of women in academia illustrate these points. In 1960, 11 percent of full-time faculty were women, and by 1989, this figure had risen to 20 percent. But full-time female faculty are not making it into the higher-tier academic positions. In 1989, only 7 percent of full professors were women. In contrast, women made up 50 percent of the lecturers and instructors (Lee; Spring 1993). Despite these advancements, the majority of wage-labouring women occupy lower-tier service jobs: over 80 percent of those who wait tables, clean, or provide clerical, social service work, and health service work are women (Lowe and Krahn 1993).

## Sexual and Personal Harassment

Sexual harassment and institutionalized racism push women out of graduate school (Mandell 1991) and workplaces. Sexual harassment refers to "any sexual advance that threatens a worker's job or well-being. It is usually an expression of power made by someone in authority" (Wishart 1993). These sexual advances are almost always made by a man in a position of power over a woman. Most women in the workforce have men in positions of power over them controlling their job security, salary levels, chances for promotions, and other forms of advancement. Sexual harassment threatens all of these, as well as a woman's sense of personal, psychological, and emotional well-being.

As well as sexual harassment, women workers are subjected to other forms of harassment based on race, ethnicity, religion, and immigrant status, sexual orientation, and disability. This has the same effect as sexual harassment by keeping women marginalized and vulnerable. Although human rights legislation provides protections against these forms of harassment, litigation is time-consuming and expensive, and unless the worker is unionized, can result in job loss.

## REDRESSING THE IMBALANCE

Women have never passively accepted labour force inequalities. From the earliest instances of exploitation in the eighteenth and nineteenth centuries, women have organized, protested, and demanded fair wages and fair employment practices. At the present time in Canada, unions are focusing on issues of equality, access to work, and conditions of work for women and men. Political and labour struggles have brought legislation on employment and pay equity. As in most political solutions, employment equity and pay equity have resulted in contradictory "victories" for women.

## Unions

Although women comprise approximately 45 percent of the labour force, only about 30 percent are unionized (Coates 1993). Women's massive entrance into the labour force over the past three decades has been in the non-unionized service sector—banks, departments stores, fast-food restaurants. Almost one-third of unionized working women were in public sector unions, in education, health care, and social services. As unions moved from predominantly goods-producing to service-producing occupations, women's proportional membership increased while men's decreased.

Recently unions have been seriously eroded by provincial legislation and policies. For example, in Ontario during the summer of 1993, social contract legislation was introduced which rolled back already-negotiated contracts, froze wages for three years, and demanded unpaid leave that cost up to 5 percent of many government workers' salaries. In the private sector, the traditional position of trade unions has been eroded by the introduction of worker participation and employee involvement in management, profit-sharing, and work-sharing programs (Coates 1993).

Despite these setbacks, women have used the trade union movement and have assumed leadership roles as ways to improve their working conditions. This includes Madeleine Parent's involvement with the textile unions in Quebec (Parent 1992), the unionization of banks through SORWUC (Warskett 1992), and the strike by the International Ladies' Garment Workers Union in Montreal in 1983 (Lipsig-Mumme 1992). Women have pushed unions to consider such issues as sexual harassment, day care and pay equity as bargaining items.

## Pay Equity and Employment Equity

In the mid-1980s, five provinces in Canada introduced proactive "equal pay for work of equal value" legislation that requires employers to examine wage inequities between men and women in their organizations and make adjustments to equalize them. The Pay Equity Act in Ontario came into effect January

1988 and was the first proactive legislation in the world to include both the public and the private sectors (Fudge and McDermott 1991). Its goal was to establish a gender-neutral method of job evaluation that compared predominantly female and predominantly male jobs with the same employer (Krahn and Lowe 1993). The criteria used to compare and evaluate are skill level, effort, responsibility, and working conditions. In this way, for example, a secretary's job could be compared with that of a maintenance worker's.

The legislation acknowledges that wage differences are structural in origin and not the fault of individual people, that the job market is neither neutral nor unbiased, and that there are systematic wage inequalities based on gender as well as on race/ethnicity and disability. One of its biggest victories to date has been the awarding of an approximately 15 percent increase in wages to 5,000 women government workers in Manitoba (Lowe and Krahn 1993).

While helpful, pay equity legislation as a solution to the gender-based wage gap is far from perfect, and both its basic assumptions as well as its design and implementation have been substantively criticized (Armstrong and Armstrong 1992). One of the most disturbing criticisms of the legislation is put forward by Pat McDermott (1992). She suggests that pay equity and employment equity legislation, which both have the goal of gender equity in the workplace, may in fact be undermining each other. Employment equity seeks to redress industrial and occupational segregation by focusing only on the number of women, Native, visible minority, and disabled workers in various jobs. It does not address inequalities in pay. Under the current employment equity legislation, it is possible for women to be promoted and not paid the same wage as men who are in their new job level. Or they can be "promoted" through a simple renaming of a job; for example, simply to meet employment equity requirements, a woman "supervisor" may be renamed a "manager" with no change in actual job or salary. Further, some employers may hire people from "designated groups" because people in these groups have historically been "cheap labour" and can thus be hired at lower wages. Employment equity may well spread women and other marginalized people across the occupational structures, but it still leaves them in lower-paying, less secure positions.

## Disabilities

Since women with disabilities tend to get less attention than the other designated groups under employment equity, we will discuss them as a particular example of discrimination in the labour force. In 1991, almost 13 percent of Canadians reported that they were disabled. Of these individuals, about 50 percent were women and 50 percent were men. Of those between ages 15 and 65 and living in households, just over 40 percent were employed. Women with disabilities are less likely to be in the labour force than either men with disabilities or women without disabilities, be they Native, women of colour, or married middle-class women

(Roeher Institute 1992). Hence, they have even more restricted job options than women in general.[3]

While there has been some movement to develop and implement employment equity programs that address the long history of discrimination against people with disabilities, the effect of such programs in increasing the representation of disabled people has been minimal. Many of those with disabilities are unable to gain access to the physical and service supports they need to meet their disability-related needs because of a lack of commitment to, and money for, workplace accommodation. Further, people with disabilities do not have equitable access to training and education programs. These factors serve to greatly restrict their access to the labour force (Roeher Institute 1992).

Employee benefit packages, which are not taxed and therefore represent a type of invisible income supplement, are generally less likely to be a part of traditionally female jobs. For women with disabilities, employee benefit packages create different and distinct problems. Employers may refuse to hire women with disabilities because of concerns that these women will put additional stress on existing employee benefit packages. Further, some of the working women with disabilities find themselves in trouble when health-related problems flare up. Without adequate employee benefits, some of these women are not able to afford required services and drugs. Therefore, they may be forced to continue working until a problem escalates to the point that they are so ill they must leave their job. This not only interferes with their self-respect and autonomy but also affects them economically: some women with disabilities are forced to become dependents of the state rather than active contributors to the labour force and the community.[4]

A recent *Canadian Woman Studies* journal focusing on "Women and Disabilities" demonstrates the commitment and political activism of women with disabilities. Contributors included mothers, teachers, university professors, graduate students, lawyers, political activists, writers, researchers, executive directors, physiotherapists, artists, and poets. These women also have physical or sensory disabilities. What emerges from the words and artwork of these women is the importance of education and training and of a workplace that recognizes their talents and skills and enables them to participate equally in the labour force (Blackford et al 1993).

## WOMEN IN CONTEMPORARY FAMILY SYSTEMS

In this section we explore four arrangements that reflect diversity in contemporary family lives: dual-earner, single-parent, common-law, and lesbian. We also discuss and expand upon the notion of extended family.

### Dual-earner Families

Husband-wife families make up over three-quarters (77 percent) of all Canadian families (La Novera, Summer 1993). In two-thirds of these families the wife supplies part of the family income (Zukewich Ghalan, Spring 1993). Factors such as inflation, the economic recession, high unemployment rates among men, women's education and training, women's desire for economic independence and self-esteem, and the broad social acceptance of working mothers resulted in women entering the labour force at almost three times the rate of men in 1991 (Zuke-wich Ghalan, Spring 1993). During the same period, the family income of dual-earner families increased while that of husband breadwinner families fell. A report by the National Council of Welfare (1993) indicates that without the earnings from wives, the percentage of husband-wife families living below the poverty level would have doubled in 1991 from just over 9 percent to over 19 percent.

This growing trend towards dual-earner families reflects, in part, generational differences. Dual-earning families are much more common among those born after the Second World War than for those born prior to this war. Current dual-earner families are relatively young, with three-quarters of them under age 45; both spouses in these families tend to have more formal education than the population at large and hence a higher stake in the labour force. The younger the couple is, the higher the wife's relative contribution to the family income and the smaller the gap between the husband's and wife's education (Moore 1990).

Affordable day care is one of the central needs of dual-earner families. In 1990, most families with preschool children were dual-earner families. Almost 60 percent of married women with children under three were in the labour force, the majority of them working full time (Theilheimer June 1993). By the late 1980s, more than 1.3 million preschoolers needed day care and an additional 1.5 million school-aged children needed part-time care because both their parents were employed. There were, however, less than 300,000 spaces available in licensed day-care centres in Canada at that time. The shortfall between the need and the available spaces was made up with the placement of over 80 percent of these children in privately organized settings (Burke 1990).

Another problem area for women in dual-earner families centres on the lack of an equitable division of labour in the household. Now that they are contributing to the family income through employment, women expect their husbands to contribute more to the housework and child care. An examination of the time women and men spend on paid employment and unpaid domestic work indicates that, on average, men spend more time at paid work and commuting to work than women, while women's combined hours of paid and unpaid work add up to more than those of men. The average amount of time spent each day by full-time employed women on routine domestic tasks such as cooking, cleaning, house maintenance and repair is three times that by men. Unlike men, women do all the domestic tasks including maintenance and repairs, and do them on a daily basis (Devereaux, Autumn 1993).

These differences are even greater when the time spent on child care is taken into consideration. Women who are employed full time spend up to twice as much time on child care (between five and a half and six hours a day) as compared to three and a half to four hours a day for men. As well, women are more likely to combine caring for a child with performance of other jobs such as cooking and laundry, while men tend only to care for the child without simultaneously doing other household tasks (Devereaux, Autumn 1993).

Three studies on the day-to-day lives of women and men in dual-earner families delve even further into the complexities of domestic labour (Luxton 1990; Hochschild 1989; Hertz 1986). Luxton and Hochschild both found varying degrees of resistance on the part of men to share equally in domestic work and child-care responsibilities even though the women put in a "second shift" of work on top of their paid work. This second shift accounted for as much as an extra month of 24-hour domestic work days every year for women (Hochschild 1989). Despite this time inequity, Luxton found that in a number of cases both women and men held to an ideology of separate spheres and gendered division of labour in the home. Women who wanted more equity in domestic work relations developed strategies to redress the imbalance and these strategies commonly resulted in both resistance on the part of men and tensions and resentments for both women and men. Men went to great lengths to avoid doing—or being seen doing—cleaning, cooking, or laundry. A number of these men would—and did—risk losing their relationships with wives and children rather than wash a dish. Men saw the struggle for domestic labour equality as women's problem, and both men and women grappled with it in the privacy of their own homes with few social models and little collective support (Luxton 1990).

Whereas Luxton studied working-class families and Hochschild studied people from a wide range of socio-economic categories, Hertz looked at dual-career marriages of professional men and women who work in the corporate world. Her findings support the view that the higher the woman's income and position, and the lower the economic differential between the husband and wife, the more bargaining power she has in family negotiations. Regardless of their original attitudes about housework, these men appeared to be hard-pressed to refuse to share meal preparation and child care because they acknowledged that their wives worked long hours in the same upwardly mobile career paths as they did. These men also articulated the relief it was not to be totally responsible as the sole family wage earner, to be able to turn down a transfer and spend more leisure time with their families than if they had felt driven to stay on the fast track (Hertz 1986).

However, one of the points made by Hertz and clearly an issue for feminism is the degree to which one woman's liberation is another woman's oppression. The lowest-paid employment for women in 1990 was for those working in the field of child care (Statistics Canada 1993a). One woman rarely pays another who cleans her house the same hourly wages she receives in her job. With the massive entrance of middle-class and professional women into full-time employment, hiring live-in nannies and housekeepers has once more become a solution to domestic work for some families. As Arat-Koc so clearly outlines, this tends, from official government policies to individual household practices, to be a very exploitive and racist system in Canada. Women from poorer countries are allowed to immigrate temporarily, tied to a particular job and sometimes a specific family, leaving their own children in their countries of origin as they raise another family's children in Canada. These women have had few protections or privileges of citizenship or of labour legislation (Arat-Koc 1990, Silvera 1989).

## Single-Parent Families

One of the most significant changes in families over the past two decades in Canada has been the increase in single-parent families. This form of family has been the centre of considerable attention in the popular media, in academic research, and in government studies and policies (Hudson and Galway 1993). According to Moore 1990, single-parent families have been growing at three times the rate of husband-wife families. As of June 1991 single-parent families made up over 14 percent of all families in Canada. This is almost the same percentage as those in which a man supports an economically dependent wife and children—the male breadwinner, nuclear family that is commonly considered the norm, or, by some, the ideal family form (Moore 1990).

What these statistics do not show is the total number of people who have single-parented at some point in their lives but are remarried or in common-law marriages at the time of Statistics Canada's research. McKie (1993) considers those reflected in the statistics at any one time to be only a fraction of those who have spent some part of their life single-parenting. Using the 1986 Census, Marcil-Gratton suggests that a longitudinal projection indicates that approximately one-third of all mothers will become single parents at some stage of their life cycle (Marcil-Gratton 1993).

Single parenting is not a new phenomenon. There were almost as many single-parent families in 1931 as in 1991 (McKie 1993). Explanations for single parenthood, however, altered. Prior to the late 1960s, death of a parent was the most common reason for single-parent families. Today most single-parenting families result from divorce. The passage of the Federal Divorce Act in 1968, revised in 1986, made divorce more accessible to Canadians than it had been previously (Eichler 1988; Marcil-Gratton 1993).

Another reason for the increase in the number of female-led, single-parent families results from the actions of a new generation of young women who are keeping children born outside of marriage rather than giving them up for adoption. By the early 1980s, 16 percent of all children in Canada were born to women who were not legally married. This represents a four-fold increase on the pre-1960 average of 4 percent (McKie and Thompson 1990). About one-third of these mothers are teenagers and another third are less than 24 years old, but the average age of unmarried mothers is increasing. Some of these women are part of common-law unions—another growing family form. It has been suggested that the large percentage of children born outside of marriage to Native women (60 percent of all births to registered Natives in 1981) might in fact reflect the choice of a woman to live common-law rather than lose her status and that of her children by marrying a non-status man (McKie and Thompson 1990: 129).

Approximately 80 percent of single-parent families are headed by women and about half of these female-led single-parent families are considered to be living below the poverty level (Moore 1990). However, this statistic must be more carefully examined. There is no question that the income level of mothers and children drops significantly when separation occurs and that the income of fathers without custody of children rises. The severe economic deprivation of many single-parent women and their children is a serious social problem. But the fact that a woman and children are poor at one point of their lives does not necessarily mean that they remain poor for the rest of their lives. Some research suggests that the average length of time a woman and children live in subsidized housing or on family benefits is approximately five years (Wright 1990). Other research on single-parent families indicates that some women with low incomes are either in the process of retraining to move into average-paying occupations or just beginning to establish themselves in jobs that hold some promise for future financial increases (Lynn 1994). As well, although the family income is much less, the control over how it is spent results in some women and their children in fact having more disposable income than they had within the marriage (Graham 1987).

Separation and the subsequent female-led single-parent family often mean peace and contentment for both women and children. For many women, the dissolution of a legal or common-law marriage means leaving behind relationships that were economically, socially, and psychologically constricting, controlling, and abusive. Although women parenting alone and working full time experience a high level of stress, the level is not much higher than that of women in dual-earner or in male breadwinner families (Lero and Brockman 1993). Further, some women indicate that in many ways their lives are easier on their own, since, while married, they had done all of the domestic work and child care, worked full-time outside the home, as well as served the needs of a husband (Lynn 1994). As far as the effect of single parenting on children, some studies suggest that children experience psychological trauma because of the loss of contact with a parent, other relatives, and friends. However, the vast majority of studies indicate that, in the long run, it is poverty, not single parenting itself, that damages children's growth and development. If the factor of poverty is controlled for, there are no discernible differences between children from single-parent families and those from two-parent families (Gee 1993).

## Common-law Marriages

Cohabitation, or common-law marriages have, over the past decade, become a particularly attractive alternative to legal marriage for many Canadians.[5] A careful analysis of living arrangements and childbirth indicates that "legal marriage is not the majority choice to begin life as a couple in Canada" (Marcil-Gratton 1993). Between 1981 and 1986, there was a 37 percent increase in the number of common-law partnerships compared with less than a 3 percent growth in married couples. Younger people are more likely to make this choice than older people. About half of all cohabiting couples are under age 30 and about 40 percent of common-law couples eventually marry (Turcotte 1990).

Marcil-Gratton argues that cohabitation has replaced legal marriage as a way of living, having children, and forming families whether as a first-time or subsequent relationship. This trend to having children while living common-law is escalating. In the 1960s over nine out of ten Canadians had parents who were in their first legal marriage and who had not previously cohabited. By 1989 just over half of all children were in this category. The popularity of common-law marriage over legal marriage does have regional variations. It is particularly popular in Quebec where, in 1991, almost a third of births were children born to couples in common-law marriages as compared to 9 percent in the rest of Canada. Although many cohabiting parents do eventually marry, the majority do not and they have a high rate of separation (Marcil-Gratton 1993).

Marcil-Gratton raises several insightful questions with this data. The blurring of boundaries between cohabiting, identifying one's self as common-law, and having an ongoing relationship with one's partner although living in separate households calls into question the categorization of single-parenting. She argues that, in spite of the above statistics, "the proportion of children who are born into families with both their biological parents present has remained as high as ever" (p. 79). What has changed is the flexibility and fluidity of partnering and parenting unions; this has resulted in easier access to changing these relationships and unions. Marcil-Gratton suggests as well that "the portrait of single parents" is being altered as women gain more education, higher-paying jobs, and autonomy over their behaviour. All of these factors enable them to make choices as to how and when they will parent. The other side of this process is the engagement of men as fathers on entirely different bases, not necessarily living full-time with their children or having an exclusive relationship with their children's mother, but having an ongoing economic and social relationship with their children.

## Lesbian Families

"A mother is a mother. Some things are no different, lesbian or otherwise. You still need to feed your kids" (Day 1990: 46). Dian Day, a lesbian mother, in her article based on interviews conducted in Nova Scotia, looks at the similarities and differences between lesbian mothering and heterosexual mothering. In spite of the common concerns and delights of parenting shared by mothers, lesbian mothers have particular issues. Some lesbian mothers are made to feel "politically incorrect" for having children, especially if these children are males. If the children are from a previous marriage, the dangers of a woman losing custody because of her sexual orientation are always present. Some women relinquish rights to their share of property and support in exchange for a custody agreement. It is not easy for a lesbian mother to establish a household and family with another woman and clarify her relationship with the children. The degree to which children should be informed of the nature of the sexual relationship between their mother and her partner is difficult to decide.

Kath Weston (1992) takes this analysis of commonality and difference in lesbian and gay families further by suggesting that in setting up family households and having children, gay and lesbian couples are publicly establishing the commonality of their lives with the heterosexual community despite their sexual differences. At the same time, because their particular family is part of a wider system of kinship and community, they are breaking down the frameworks that define kinship as being related by blood or heterosexual marriage. They are, in effect, bringing the gay and lesbian communities that had originally been seen as replacements for families back into a kinship and family network. Tensions exist in maintaining lesbian or gay identities at the same time as "advancing a claim to kinship" by establishing families of choice and yet not allowing these families to be interpreted as antisocial toward the gay and lesbian community (Weston 1992, p. 128).

## Extended Families and Kinship Systems

While there has been a great deal of angst among the conservative pro-family movement about the death of "the family" as an institution, it is really a particular type of family whose loss is being mourned—the male-breadwinner, nuclear family that is assumed to have limited assistance and support from extended family members (Gairdner 1992). If we begin to think in terms of a postmodern family that is fluid, flexible, and continuously changing, it becomes clear that the parameters of the family are, in fact, expanding. In her study of the postmodern extended family, Stacey (1990) goes beyond the usual assumptions of blood ties and current marriage partners and their families as being the primary basis for inclusion in an extended family. She includes divorced spouses, stepfamily and reconstituted or blended family members as part of an extended family because they stay in contact with each other and frequently provide financial, emotional, as well as physical help and support. The support and services from extended family members include child care, money, housework and maintenance, and transportation. More detailed information about the help and support provided by members of a postmodern extended family is limited because organizations such as Statistics Canada base their enquiries about extended families on the criteria of the traditional extended family. What these figures do show is that parents helped adult children in 39 percent of all cases in which they needed money; daughters contributed over 10 percent of all housework to their parents; and siblings and other relatives constantly engaged in various types of exchanges of resources (Statistics Canada 1992).

Recent studies of families shed light on the ongoing ways that families remain attached. Stacey (1990) notes that there has been an increasing "feminization of kinship" that is centred around women, with men participating only marginally. She attributes this shift to divorce and single-parenting in which women have child custody and become responsible for maintaining complex ties with relatives. As men lose economic authority and access to family members, they are less likely to keep up ongoing contact with relatives. Di Leonardo (1992) analyzes the sending of cards and hosting of family dinners as examples of ways in which women put considerable time, effort, and money into establishing reciprocal relationships of exchange and obligation with one another in a kinship system. As families appear to become fragmented and fractured on some levels, they find ways to reconnect and maintain interdependence on others.

These boundaries of kinship and extended family are pushed even further by Collins (1992) to include members of a wider community. Collins notes the role of "bloodmother, othermother, or community other mother" who takes responsibility for and authority over "their" children in the African-American communities (Collins 1992: 233). These women act on the basis of an "ethics of care" that will uplift and strengthen the entire community, keep vulnerable members protected and celebrate the success of strong members. Native Canadian families and recently arrived immigrant families tend to show the same sorts of community solidarity that is more and more frequently moving into political alignments and empowerment, and thus is connecting family systems to the wider social context of politics and work.

## CONCLUSION

This broad survey demonstrates the diversities and complexities that have always been and still are found in women's lives within families and within the labour force. It can be expected that, in the future, women will spend more time in the labour force but in a shifting labour force that includes both unemployment and underemployment as more people are accommodated and technology and trade change. Women will persist in putting much time and effort into family relationships although these families might not look like families of the past. As women continue to be involved in shaping their own communities and politics, their share of services and opportunities will be more equitable than in the past.

## NOTES

1  A photoessay of the work of photographer Edith Watson published in CWS/cf shows the diversity of women's work in nineteenth and early twentieth century Canada in providing for themselves and their families. These photographs include Newfoundland women drying fish flakes; Maritime women farming; women weaving and making soap in Quebec; Mennonite, Hungarian and Doukobour women in the West gathering wood and harvesting fruit; Cree women gathering crops with their babies on their back; and Haida and Japanese women of the West Coast tending fishing nets (Rooney, CWS/cf 1986).

2  The official unemployment rate, like other labour force statistics, is based on information gathered by Statistics Canada. The rate is determined by dividing the total number of people actively looking for work in the last four weeks by the total number of participants in the labour force (including the unemployed).

3  While a variety of occupations are found in all three economic sectors, there are certain occupations that are found more commonly in one industrial sector than another. For example, teachers, nurses, and retail sales clerks are found more typically in the service sector while farmers and foresters are typically found in the primary sector (Krahn and Lowe 1993).

4  The depth of employment discrimination against those with disabilities is evident in policies and practices such as the Ontario "handicapped permit." Not abolished until 1987, the permits allowed employers to pay a person with a disability less than the minimum wage on the assumption that it reflected the true value of the worker (Sandys 1993.)

5  In 1986 and 1991, Statistics Canada conducted Health and Activity Limitation Studies (HALS). For each of these years, two surveys were conducted. The first was a survey of all persons with disabilities living in households; the second was of adults living in health-related institutions. In this paper, we use only data from the household survey for persons between ages 15-64 years of age. The sources we draw from (Statistics Canada 1993; Roeher Institute 1992) for our snapshot of disabled women in the labour force have compared the responses from the household survey to general census data.

6  Common-law studies are based on information from people who declare themselves to be part of a heterosexual couple.

## BIBLIOGRAPHY

Ambert, A. *Divorce in Canada*. Toronto: Academic Press, 1980.

Amott, Teresa and Matthaei, Julie. *Race, Gender and Work*. Montreal: Black Rose Books, 1991.

Anderson, Karen. *Chain Her by One Foot*. London: Routledge, 1991.

Arat-Koc, S. Importing Housewives. In *Through the Kitchen Window: The Politics of Home and Family*, 2nd ed., edited by Luxton et al., 81-103. Toronto: Garamond Press, 1990.

Armstrong, Pat and Armstrong, Hugh. "Lessons from Pay Equity." In *Feminism in Action: Studies in Political Economy*, edited by M.P. Connelly and P. Armstrong, 295-316. Toronto: Canadian Scholars' Press, 1992.

Baber, K. and Allen K. *Women & Families: Feminist Reconstructions*. New York: The Guildford Press, 1992.

Bach, Michael and Crawford, Cameron. *On Target? Canada's Employment Related Programs for Persons with Disabilities*. Toronto: Roeher Institute, 1992.

Benenson, Harold. The "Family Wage" and Working Women's Consciousness in Britain, 1880-1914. *Politics & Society*, 19-1. 71-108, 1991.

Blackford, Karen et al., eds. *Canadian Woman Studies/les cahiers de la femme: Women and Disability*. 13-4. Toronto: Inanna Publications and Education Inc.

Bourgeault, Ron. Race, Class and Gender: Colonial Domination of Indian Women. In *Race, Class, Gender: Bonds and Barriers*, edited by J. Vorst et al., 87-115. Toronto: Between the Lines, 1989.

Bradbury, Bettina. "Pigs, Cows, and Boarders: Non-Wage Forms of Survival Among Montreal Families, 1861-91." *Labour/Le Travail*, 14, 9-46, 1984.

Brisken, Linda. "Women, Unions and Leadership." In *Work in Canada*, edited by G. Lowe and H. Krahn, 284-291. Scarborough: Nelson Canada, 1992.

Burke, Mary Ann. *Child Care. In Canadian Social Trends*, edited by C. McKie and K. Thompson, 167. Toronto: Thompson Educational Publishing, Inc., 1990.

Calliste, Agnes. Canada's Immigration Policy and Domestics from the Caribbean: The Second Domestic Scheme. In *Race, Class, Gender: Bonds and Barriers*, edited by J. Vorst et al., 133-165. Toronto: Between the Lines, 1989.

Canadian Labour Congress. *Women Workers and the Recession: A Report from the Canadian Labour Congress*. Toronto: Social and Economic Policy Department, 1993.

Castellano, Marlene Brant, et al., eds. *Canadian Woman Studies/les cahiers de la femme: Native Women. 10-2&3*. Toronto: Inanna Publications and Education Inc., 1989.

Chawla, Raj K. The Changing Profile of Dual-earner Families. In Statistics Canada. *Perspectives on Labour and Income*. Cat. 75-001E. Ottawa: supply and Services. p. 22-30, Summer, 1992.

Chinese Canadian National Council, The Women's Book Committee. In *Jin Guo: Voices of Chinese Canadian Women*. Toronto: Women's Press, 1992.

Coates, Mary Lou. Is There a Future for the Canadian Labour Movement? In *Work in Canada*, edited by G. Lowe and H. Krahn, 257-265. Scarborough: Nelson Canada, 1993.

Collins, Patricia Hill. Black Women and Motherhood. In *Rethinking the Family: Some Feminist Questions, 2nd ed.*, edited by B. Thorne and M. Yalom, 215-245. Boston: Northeastern University Press, 1992.

Coontz, Stephanie. *The Way We Never Were*. New York: Basic Books, 1992.

Day, D. "Lesbian/Mother." In *Lesbians in Canada*, edited by S. Stone, 35-47. Toronto: Between the Lines, 1990.

Devereaux, Mary Sue. Time Use of Canadians in 1992. In Statistics Canada. *Canadian Social Trends*. Ottawa: supply and Services. Cat 11-008-E p. 13-17, Autumn, 1993.

di Leonardo, Micaela. The Female World of Cards and Holidays: Women, Families, and the Work of Kinship. In *Rethinking the Family: Some Feminist Questions*, edited by B. Thorne and M. Yalom, 246-261. Boston: Northeastern University Press, 1992.

Duffy, Ann; Mandell, Nancy, & Pupo, Norene. *Few Choices: Women, Work and Family*. Toronto: Garamond Press, 1989.

Duffy, Ann; Kitchen, Brigitte, Mandell, Nancy, Merivale, Jane, Perillo, Carmen, White Fran, Wicks, Doreen. (Eds.). *Canadian Woman Studies/les cahiers de la femme: Women in Poverty*, 12-4. Toronto: Inanna Publications and Education Inc., 1992.

Eichler, Margrit. *Families in Canada Today: 2nd Edition*. Toronto: Gage Educational Publishing Company, 1988.

Eichler, Margrit. "Lone Parent Families: An Instable Category in Search of Stable Policies." In *Single Parent Families*, edited by J. Hudson and B. Galaway, 139-155. Toronto: Thompson Educational Publishing, Inc., 1993.

Elliott, J. and Fleras, A. *Unequal Relations*. Scarborough: Prentice-Hall, 1992.

Fudge, Judy and McDermotte, Patricia. *Just Wages: A Feminist Assesment of Pay Equity*. Toronto: University of Toronto Press, 1991.

Frager, Ruth. "Sewing Solidarity: The Eaton's Strike of 1912." *Canadian Woman Studies/les cahiers de la femme*, 7-3, pp. 96-98, 1986.

Gaffield, Chad. The Social and Economic Origins of Contemporary Families. In *Families: Changing Trends in Canada, 2nd ed.*, edited by M. Baker. Toronto: McGraw-Hill Ryerson Ltd., 1990.

Gairdner, William D. *The War Against the Family*. Toronto: Stoddart Publishing Co. Limited, 1992.

Gee, Ellen. Adult Outcomes Associated with Childhood Family Structure: An Appraisal of Research and an Examination of Canadian Data. In *Single Parent Families*, edited by J. Hudson and B. Galaway, 291-310. Toronto: Thompson Educational Publishing, Inc., 1993.

Graham, Hilary. "Being Poor: Perceptions and Coping Strategies of Lone Mothers. In *Give and Take in Families*, edited by J. Brannen and G. Wilson, 56-74. London: Allen & Unwin, 1987.

The Globe and Mail with Canadian Press. Changes in Family Law Proposed. *Globe and Mail*. p. A1, 1993, Nov. 18.

Gunderson, Morley. Male-Female Wage Differentials and Policy Responses. *Journal of Economic Literature*, 27, 46-72, 1989.

Hertz, R. *More Equal Than Others: Women and Men in Dual-Career Marriages*. Berkeley: University of California Press, 1986.

Hochschild, Arlie. *The Second Shift*. New York: Avon Books, 1989.

Horn, Kahn-Tineta. Interview: Oka and Mohawk Sovereignty. *Studies in Political Economy*, 35, pp. 29-41, 1991.

Hudson, Joe and Galaway, Burt, eds. *Single Parent Families*. Toronto: Thompson Educational Publishing, Inc., 1993.

Iacovetta, Franca. "Trying to Make Ends Meet: An Historical Look at Italian Immigrant Women, the State and Family Survival Strategies in Post-War Toronto." *Canadian Woman Studies/les cahiers de la femme: Mediterranean Women, 8-2*, pp. 6-11, Inanna Publications and Education Inc., 1987.

Khosla, Punam. *Review of the Situation of Women*. Toronto: National Action Committee on the Status of Women, 1993.

Kogawa, Joy. *Obasan*. Markham: Penguin Books, 1981.

Krahn, Harvey and Lowe, Graham. *Work, Industry and Canadian Society*. Scarborough: Nelson Canada, 1993.

Krapielian, Isabel. The Saved: Armenian Refugee Women. *Canadian Woman Studies/les cahiers de la femme: Candian Women's History/L'Histoire Des Femmes Canadiennes:2, 7-4*, pp. 6-9, Inanna Publications and Education Inc., 1986.

Landry, Yves. "Gender Imbalance, Les Filles de Roi, and Choice of Spouse in New France." In *Canadian Family History*, edited by B. Bradbury, 14-32. Mississauga. Copp Clark Pitman Ltd, 1992.

La Novera, Pina. Changes in Family Living. In Statistics Canada. Canadian Social Trends. Cat. 11-008E. Ottawa: Supply and Services Canada. p. 14-14, Summer 1993.

Laxer, James. *False God: How the Globalization Myth has Impoverished Canada*. Toronto: Lester Publishing Limited, 1993.

Lee, Judy. "Women in Academia: A Growing Minority." In *Perspectives on Labour and Income*, Cat.75-001E, Statistics Canada. Ottawa: Supply and Services Canada, Spring 1993.

Lero, Donna and Brockman, Lois. "Single Parent Families in Canada: A Closer Look." In *Single Parent Families*, edited by J. Hudson and B. Galaway, 91-114. Toronto: Thompson Educational Publishing, Inc., 1993.

Li, Peter. *Ethnic Inequality: In a Class Society*. Toronto: Thompson Educational Publishing, Inc., 1988.

Lindstrom-Best, Varpu. *Defiant sisters: A Social History of Finnish Immigrant Women in Canada*. Toronto: Multicultural History Society of Ontario, 1988.

Lipsig-Mumme, Carla. "Organizing Women in the Clothing Trades: Homework and the 1983 Garment Strike in Canada." In *Feminism in Action: Studies in Political Economy*, edited by M.P. Connelly and P. Armstrong, 121-148. Toronto: Canadian Scholars' Press, 1992.

Lowe, Graham and Krahn, Harvey, eds. *Work in Canada: Readings in the Sociology of Work and Industry*. Scarborough: Nelson Canada, 1993.

Luxton, Meg. Two Hands for the Clock. In *Through the Kitchen Window: The Politics of Home and Family*, edited by Luxton et al., 39-55. Toronto: Garamond Press, 1990.

———— *More Than a Labour of Love*. Toronto: The Women's Press, 1980.

Lynn, Marion. "Single Parent Families and Family Transformation." (Upcoming) Unpublished Ph.D. Thesis. Toronto: York University, 1994.

Mandell, Nancy. *Wife Assault: Curriculum Unit for use in Child and Family Studies Programs*. Toronto: Center for Feminist Research, York University, 1992.

Maracle, Lee. Racism, Sexism and Patriarchy. In *Returning the Gaze*, edited by H. Bannerji, 122-130. Toronto: Sister Vision Press, 1993.

Marcil-Gratton, Nicole. "Growing Up with a Single Parent, A Transitional Experience? Some Demographic Measurements." In *Single Parent Families*, edited by J. Hudson and B. Galaway, 73-90. Toronto: Thompson Educational Publishing, Inc., 1993.

McBride, Steven. *Not Working: State, Unemployment and Neo-Conservatism in Canada*. Toronto: University of Toronto Press, 1992.

McDermott, Patricia. Pay Equity in Canada: Assessing the Commitment to Reducing the Wage Gap. In *Just Wages: A Feminist Assessment of Pay Equity*, edited by J. Fudge and P. McDermott, 21-32. Toronto: University of Toronto Press, 1991.

———— "Employment Equity and Pay Equity: And Never the Twain shall Meet?" *Canadian Woman Studies/les cahiers de la femme*, 12-3, 24-27, Inanna Publications and Education Inc., 1992.

McKie, Craig & Thompson, Keith. (Eds.). *Canadian Social Trends*. Toronto: Thompson Educational Press, 1990.

———— "An Overview of Lone Parenthood in Canada." In *Single Parent Families*, edited by J. Hudson and B. Galaway, 53-72. Toronto: Thompson Educational Publishing, Inc., 1993.

Moore, Maureen. "Dual-Earner Families: The New Norm." In *Canadian Social Trends*, edited by C. McKie and K. Thompson, 161-163. Toronto: Thompson Educational Publishing, Inc., 1990.

National Council of Welfare. Poverty Profile Update for 1991. Ottawa: National Council of Welfare, Winter 1993.

The Native Women's Association of Canada. Aboriginal Women and the Constitutional Debates. *Canadian Woman Studies/les cahiers de la femme*, 12-3, 14-17, Inanna Publications and Education Inc., 1992.

Nicholson, L. ed. *Feminism/Postmodernism*. New York: Routledge, 1990.

Ng, Roxana. *Sexism, Racism, and Canadian Nationalism. In Race, Class, Gender: Bonds and Barriers*, edited by J. Vorst et al., 10-25. Toronto: Between the Lines, 1989.

Omatsu, Maryka. *Bittersweet Passage: Redress and the Japanese Canadian Experience.* Toronto: Between the Lines, 1992.

Parent, Madeleine. Fifty Years Feminist Trade Unionist: An Interview. In *Feminism in Action: Studies in Political Economy*, edited by M.P. Connelly and P. Armstrong. Toronto: Canadian Scholars' Press, 1992.

Parr, Joy. *The Gender of Breadwinners.* Toronto: University of Toronto Press, 1990.

Roeher Institute. *On Target?: Canada's employment-related programs for persons with disabilities.* North York, Ont. The G. Allen Roeher Institute, 1992.

Rooney, Frances. "Edith S. Watson: A Photoessay" pp. 48-49. *Canadian Woman Studies/les cahiers de la femme,* 7–3. Toronto: Inanna Publications and Education Inc., 1992.

Sabia, Laura. "You Are Not One of Us": The Roots of My Militant *Feminism. Canadian Woman Studies/les cahiers de la femme, 8-2.,32–36.* Inanna Publications and Education Inc., 1987.

Sandys, Judith. *"It Does My Heart Good": The Perceptions of Employers who have Hired People with Intellectual Disabilities through Supported Employment Programs.* Unpublished Doctoral Dissertation. Toronto: University of Toronto, 1993.

———. *Brave New Families.* San Francisco: Basic Books, 1990.

Statistics Canada. (1993a). *The Daily.* April 13/93. Cat. 11-001E. Ottawa: Supply and Services Canada, 1993a.

——— The Labour Force, March 1993, Cat. 71-001E. Ottawa: Supply and Services Canada, 1993b.

——— *Canadian Social Trends, Winter 1992.* Ottawa: Supply and Services Canada, 1992.

——— *Earnings of Men & Women in 1991.* Cat. 13-217E. Ottawa: Supply and Services Canada, 1991a.

——— *Population Estimates.* Cat.75-91-204E. Ottawa: Supply and Services Canada, 1991b.

——— *Women in the Workforce.* Cat. 11-534E. Ottawa: Supply and Services Canada, 1990c.

——— *Canadian Social Trends.* Cat. 11-008E-E. Ottawa: Supply and Services Canada, 1990.

——— *Women in the Workforce.* Cat. 71-534E. Ottawa: Supply and Services Canada, 1987.

Silvera, Makeda. *Silenced.* (2nd Ed.). Toronto: Sister Vision Press, 1989.

Stone, Sharon, ed. *Lesbians in Canada.* Toronto: Between the Lines, 1990.

Theilheimer, Ish, ed. *Transition: Work and Family: The Balancing Act of the 90's.* Ottawa: Vanier Institute of the Family, June 1993.

———— *Transition: Families of the Future*. Ottawa: Vanier Institute of the Family, Sept. 1993.

Turcotte, Pierre. "Common-Law Unions: Nearly Half a Million in 1986." In *Canadian Social Trends*, edited by C. McKie and K. Thompson, Toronto: Thompson Educational Publishing, Inc., 1990.

Vorst, J. et al., eds. *Race, Class, Gender: Bonds and Barriers*. Toronto: Between the Lines, 1989.

Warskett, Rosemary. Bank Worker Unionization and the Law. In *Feminism in Action: Studies in Political Economy*, edited by M.P. Connelly and P. Armstrong, Toronto: Canadian Scholars' Press, 1992.

Weston, Kath. *Families We Choose: Lesbians, Gays, Kinship*. New York. Columbia University Press, 1991.

———— "The Politics of Gay Families." In *Rethinking the Family: Some Feminist Questions, 2nd ed.*, edited by B. Thorne and M. Yalom 119-139. Boston: Northeastern University Press, 1992.

Welner, N. and Gunderson, M. *Pay Equity: Issues, Options & Experiences*. Toronto: Butterworths, 1990.

Wishart, Cynthia. "Workplace Harassment." In *Work in Canada*, edited by G. Lowe and H. Krahn, 185-89. Scarborough: Nelson Canada, 1993.

Wright, Carol Ann. "Women and Poverty." (Workshop Presentation). Gender, Race and Class Conference. Toronto: York University, 1990.

Zukewich Ghalan, Nancy, Women in the Workplace. In Statistics Canada. *Canadian Social Trends*. Ottawa: Supply and Services Canada. Cat. 11-008E. p. 2-5, Spring 1993.

# THE EDUCATIONAL SYSTEM

*Cecilia Reynolds*

## INTRODUCTION

There are a number of paradoxes surrounding the role of schools in Canada, as elsewhere. On the one hand, schools are places where members of society are prepared for participation in the paid labour force, and this requires some form of sorting and sifting of individuals according to agreed-upon criteria. On the other hand, schools are also places where ideals about democratic participation by diverse members of the society seem possible and can be fostered. Some commentators have argued that schools merely mirror both the best and worst aspects of the societies in which they exist while others maintain that schools are powerful sites of cultural production and places where certain behaviours and ideas are legitimated.

Feminist analyses of schooling have raised questions about how traditional beliefs about males and females have been used in the past and continue to be used as inappropriate and inequitable ways of sorting and sifting males and females into separate areas in society. Thus, a major feminist critique rests on historical analyses that reveal how women and others such as Native peoples, immigrants, and Blacks have been largely excluded from certain types of schooling by traditional structures that have favoured middle-class and upper-class White males. This continues to occur because the distribution of power within educational bureaucracies is based on traditions that have a long history and are supported by existing structures that have remained relatively resistant to attempts at change.

Feminists have also pointed to the replication in schools of sexist practices commonly found in the larger society. Despite evidence that far more variations exist within one sex than can be found between the sexes on measures of abilities and performances, the experiences of males and females differ greatly in our classrooms as do the outcomes of schooling in terms of occupations and monetary rewards. Thus, not only the structures but the formal and informal everyday practices of our schools must be examined and changed if ideals about equity that have long filled our rhetoric about schooling in this country are to become reality. Feminists continue to argue that, despite current problems, schools are important places where democratic ideals can be realized and new and more equitable cultural patterns developed in order to foster behaviours and ideas that would improve the position of girls and women in our future society.

This chapter explores both of these major critiques which encompass elementary, secondary, and postsecondary schools and looks at the roles of women not only as students but also as teachers. It is argued that traditional structures and patterns of classroom interaction continue, at a variety of levels, to combine to form a "chilly climate" for females that mitigates against gender equity within our schools. Also discussed are ongoing attempts at reforms that promise to break long-held silences and foster more equitable structures and patterns within the educational system.

## TRADITIONAL STRUCTURES: A LEGACY OF EXCLUSION AND SEPARATION

In the early history of British North America, formal schooling did not play a large part in most people's lives. Access to schools was easier for some groups than for others and not everyone held schooling experiences in high esteem. Thus, early school traditions and structures were predicated on the needs of only a small and privileged group within the newly developing society.

Our knowledge of native cultures reveals oral traditions and skills training but little formal instruction outside of what may have occurred within Jesuit missions or the Ursuline or Notre Dame convent schools set up in New France in the seventeenth and eighteenth centuries.[1] Since immigrants to New France came largely from urban areas, they were likely to have had some schooling.

Convent and parish schools were largely sex-segregated and run by nuns or priests but some lay teachers were employed and some "petites écoles" in rural areas had both male and female students, although an ordinance issued by the Bishop of Quebec in 1727 specified that teachers should not teach those of the opposite sex.[2] Such early traditions supported the separation of males and females within schools. Such separations were largely predicated on fears about sexuality but also encompassed beliefs about the need for different types of education for females, who were to spend most of their lives in the private sphere, and for males, who were to spend their lives in the public sphere.

Schooling opportunities were not as plentiful for the New England Loyalists who came to Nova Scotia, New Brunswick, or Prince Edward Island after the transfer of Acadia to the British Crown in 1713, or those who immigrated from the British Isles in the 1830s and 1840s after the Napoleonic Wars. For Black children who travelled the underground railroad in the first half of the nineteenth century or for the children of immigrants who pioneered the Canadian West, attendance at a school needed to fit in around the tasks required at home. But, a wide variety of schools existed during this period and, while some catered to the well-to-do, others had a clientele of pupils fairly well mixed by gender, class, race, and ethnic background.[3] Also, while many teachers came from religious orders such as that of the Grey Nuns established in the Red River colony in 1846, others, such as Angelique and Marguerite Nolin, who set up a school for Métis children in Red River in 1829, were part of a growing number of lay women who looked to teaching as a form of paid labour through which they could either support themselves or supplement the income of their household. [4]

By the middle of the nineteenth century in most of Canada, publicly funded "common schools" developed; these were supported by the taxes of property owners and the taxes of business and industry. Most of these common schools included only the elementary grades and were co-educational even though some educators, such as Egerton Ryerson in Ontario, felt that there was a "moral danger" in girls attending school along with boys. In many school buildings of this era there were separate entrances for boys and girls with the separate designations etched in the stone walls above the doorways.[5]

The British North America Act of 1867 declared that schooling issues would come under the control of each province. School boards developed in both rural and urban areas. Elected school trustees had decision-making powers with regard to the hiring of teachers and the building of schools. In many areas, parallel "Catholic" and "Public" boards operated and many previously existing privately funded schools continued, most of them run by clergy of a variety of religious denominations. Thus, while the rhetoric of Canadian educators was that of equality, the realities of school life and the outcomes of schooling varied enormously for rural and urban students, for those from poor and wealthy families, for those from Native Canadian or immigrant backgrounds, and for males and females within each of these categories.

Records of school attendance reveal that female students were more likely than males to attend classes regularly and to complete their formal schooling with graduation from high school.[6] Despite this reality, women were not allowed entrance to the universities. When Emily Howard Stowe wanted to enter medical school in Canada in the 1860s, no school would admit her and she had to go to the United States for her education. It was not until 1883 that two separate women's colleges for medical education were established in affiliation with Queen's University and the University of Toronto. In 1890, Clara Brett Martin was refused admission by the Law Society of Upper Canada and it was not until 1897 that she was allowed, by provincial decree, to become the first woman in the British Empire to practice law. Not until 1941 were women in Quebec able to become lawyers.[7]

And what about women who wanted to become teachers? By the beginning of the twentieth century the growth of "common schools" and the development of secondary schooling,[8] along with many provincial policies requiring compulsory school attendance between the ages of 6 and 16, created a demand for qualified and inexpensive teachers. Despite evidence that trustees and educational experts were initially doubtful about women's abilities to teach, by 1901 three-quarters of all those engaged in the educational profession were women and, indeed, apart from domestic service, teaching was the largest category of paid employment for women in Canada at that time.[9]

However, despite the hiring of female teachers in large numbers, they were usually placed under the control of male teachers, principals, inspectors, or trustees and were seldom allowed to teach in the senior grades. In Victoria, British Columbia, in 1903 the board stated that "in the interests of tactful discipline and the cultivation of strength and character in boys" more male teachers should be hired.[10] Often, as in Toronto in 1870, there were differences in salaries paid to men and women teachers despite comparable teaching credentials (the average female salary was $220-$400 per year while the average male salary was $600-$700 per year).[11]

Historical records also reveal different patterns of participation in teaching and administrative roles in schools for males and females. In Canada, men have tended to teach older students and to predominate numerically as professors in universities. Men have also been far more likely than women to become school principals or hold the most powerful administrative roles such as that of the director of the school board. Women, on the other hand, have tended to teach young children and have only recently been appointed as school principals or professors in universities in percentages equivalent to those of men.[12] Formal policies barring women teachers in the 1800s and requiring women to resign from teaching upon marriage in the 1900s have been overcome and yet, despite ostensibly equal access, most women and men still continue to follow different career patterns within the teaching occupation in this country.[13]

Both as students and as teachers, females have needed to argue for acceptance within the educational system at all levels. Formal barriers excluding women students have diminished in Canada and, in 1989, 53 percent of all bachelor's degrees in this country were earned by women, up from 42 percent in 1975. Women in 1989 also earned 45 percent of all master's degrees and 30 percent of all doctoral degrees, a substantial growth from having earned only 28 percent of master's and 16 percent of doctoral degrees in 1975. However, break-downs by field of study reveal that women's participation varies in every field and at all levels from that of men. Women continue to earn fewer degrees than men in mathematics and the physical sciences and in engineering and the applied sciences and they earn more degrees than men in health and educa-tion.[14] Thus, while women have had formal access to most forms of schooling for over 100 years in Canada, their participation in such schooling has been dif-ferent than that of their male peers. This raises many questions about how formal structures and informal patterns which still exist channel students by gender into different positions within the educational system.

In the 1960s, many feminists began to raise questions about equal access for men and women teachers and students within Canada's educational system. Throughout the 1970s and 1980s there was much documentation of the numer-ical disparities by gender within our schools. Such documentation revealed the patterns just described but did little to explain them or suggest steps toward fos-tering equality. Indeed, a debate arose about whether equality, defined as same-ness, was what women really needed or wanted from schooling. Perhaps, some feminists suggested, we do not want women and men to be the same, especially if that means that females as students or teacher/administrators have to fit into a male model. Although breaking down formal and informal barriers for women in terms of access was a part of the solution to the "problem" and something that continued to need attention, many feminists began to discuss the need to study such issues as female experiences in classrooms, the transference of female schooling experiences into activity in the paid labour force, and the whole issue of power within schools and its distribution and its maintenance mechanisms. It is to these three areas that we will now turn.

## Experiences in schools

To understand the part that gender plays in a person's experiences of schooling, we need to grapple with theories about how gender roles develop. We need also to consider how gender is connected to other factors such as race, class, age, and "abelism". School experiences are only one part of a complex system of social-ization in our society, but as "official" state-run or state-sanctioned institutions they carry out a legitimization function that is important.

Much controversy exists about the beginnings of status differences between men and women and about differences across cultures regarding understandings of gender and its importance.

Biological theories emphasize differences in chromosomes, hormones, and genitals that allow us to distinguish between two sexes, male and female. Social and cultural theories emphasize learned behaviours and focus on gender as mas-culine or feminine.

Thus, we have sex roles based on biology, and gender roles based on social expectations of appropriate behaviours. What some feminists have argued is that this has resulted in a complex and often hidden sex/gender system that dictates certain gender relations based on power. Within such a system, gender stereotypes or oversimplified descriptions of a group of people have developed, and stratification or a differential ranking or valuing of the two groups has formed. In almost every society it is men who decide on the rules, control the economy, and define dominant cultural rituals and ideologies. This control by men of the laws and institutions in such a way that men have superior status to that of women has been defined as patriarchy.[15]

Feminists in the 1960s and 1970s became concerned that schools and their formal curriculum were part of a system of early socialization that helped to sustain gender stereotypes, inform male and female students of their traditional rankings in the society, and thereby act as institutions that perpetuated patriarchy. Early efforts focused on school readers and other textbooks in an effort to counter stereotypical images of girls and women as passive social actors with limited potential beyond motherhood and other nurturing roles. Attempts were made to raise the consciousness of teachers, parents, and students to the shortcomings of a continuation of such traditional patterns in our schools. Unfortunately, much of this early work focused on a "deficit model" which argued that the schools were the place to intervene and compensate for the deficit in parental knowledge and abilities, in societal shortcomings such as those found in the media and indeed in girls themselves who were accused of being afraid of success, having a phobia about mathematics and not being assertive enough for their own good.[16] As with earlier issues of access to education, it was erroneously believed that, if only people knew about the uncovered injustices in our educational system, they would be moved to act in such a way as to alleviate them.

More recent studies stress how the "hidden curriculum" that is passed on by the structures of classroom life and the expressed beliefs of students and teachers alike needs consideration as well as the formal plan of study and the choice of textbooks. Also, theories of social construction such as those outlined by Phillip Shaver and Clyde Hendrick in *Sex and Gender* (1987) posit a biosocial interactionist perspective that argues that both sexuality and gender are constructed within societies for specific purposes. To alter sexism in the schoolhouse, then, means attending to all forms of communication—both verbal and non-verbal—and it means recognizing the social locations of male and female teachers and students.[17]

Studies of classroom interaction patterns in Canada, the United States, Britain, and elsewhere have uncovered sexism from grade school to graduate school. The influential work of Myra and David Sadker[18] in the United States has documented how both male and female teachers across different grade levels give more attention (both positive and negative) to male students, and educators are generally unaware of the impact of their own bias in classroom interaction patterns. Studies also indicate that males in most classrooms make greater use of verbal and nonverbal communication. Largely because of this dominance of "air time," most teachers try to select topics of interest to the males in the group in order to maintain control of the situation, tend to give more praise and reprimands to the males, and assess males as having greater ability overall.[19]

Michelle Stanworth in Britain used the phrase "faceless bunch" to describe the way many teachers dealt with what they perceived as the passivity of female students in their classrooms.[20] Much work in Canada has focused on the "chilly climate" for women in Canadian colleges and universities and on possible interpretations of the relative female silences in classrooms at all levels.[21]

Carol Gilligan's *In A Different Voice* (1982) suggested that we needed to encourage girls and women to break their silences and indeed we needed as researchers and theorists to listen attentively to what was said, recognizing that perhaps existing measures and scales were normed on male and not female experiences. She urged us to consider the importance of differences and not automatically assume that difference meant deficit.

The Canadian Teachers' Federation study, *A Cappella* (1990), and the Canadian Advisory Council on the Status of Women study, *What Will Tomorrow Bring* (1985), looked at the experiences of adolescent females across the country and documented their concerns. The Council of Ontario Universities study, *Women in Graduate Studies in Ontario* (1989), and the Canadian Federation of University Women study, *Women in Universities* (1992), have looked at the experiences of Canadian women in our universities. These studies reveal the reality that, while not all students recognize the gendered nature of classroom life, their comments indicate that they are affected by it in terms of their self-image, aspirations, concerns, and expectations.

One of their concerns is violence against women in its many forms, including sexual harassment in schools.

In her longitudinal study in an elementary school in the United States, Raphaela Best in *We've All Got Scars* (1989) documented the various complex processes that work on a daily basis in classrooms to instruct boys and girls about their sexuality and their gender roles. In *Thumbs Down. A Classroom Response to Violence Against Women* (1990), the Canadian Teachers' Federation states clearly that we can no longer deny the sexuality of students or the realities of abuse and violence in their lives.

Indeed, some resources for teachers in Canadian classrooms are developing largely along the theme that it is not enough to recognize sexism in our schools: we must work collectively to break historical silences in all disciplines about women's experiences and we must do so in a deliberately antisexist way using an overtly "feminist pedagogy"[22] in our interactions with all students. Here, however, we run into a controversy similar to that already discussed around women's access to schooling opportunities. Some feminist reformers believe that what is needed is a more equal redistribution to males and females of the pieces of the existing educational pie; others believe that a new pie needs to be baked.

Gaby Weiner and Madeline Arnot in *Gender and the Politics of Schooling* (1987) suggest that an equal opportunities/girl friendly approach would advocate ways of enticing females into science and technology courses so they could reap the rewards of higher-paying careers in these areas, while the antisexist/girl centred approach would advocate ways of changing traditional ways of teaching science and technology so these disciplines would focus on the concerns of females and use techniques amenable to female students so science and technology itself would be transformed by the increased participation of women. While the anti-sexist approach places questions of power and patriarchy at its core, these are not overtly confronted by those using an equal opportunities approach.

Canadian materials for teachers encompass both approaches and while many are available for science, math and computers, fewer exist for subjects such as history, the arts, or physical education, although individual teachers often work to construct their own resources. Of major importance in this endeavour is the growth of Women's Studies in our colleges and universities.

In 1970, the Royal Commission on the Status of Women stated that Women's Studies courses indicated the necessity for change and helped show the ways this could be accomplished and suggested that such courses could improve the conditions for women in future educational systems. In 1982 The Jean Commission in Quebec concluded that "Women's Studies were essential for the improvement of women's opportunities for learning."[23]

Women's Studies programs not only provide the infrastructure in Canada for continuing study of women's experiences and the provision of material in the various disciplines for feminist teachers to use for their students, but they also assist such teachers in understanding how they themselves are situated as social actors in their attempts to bring about school reform. In *Women Teaching for Change* (1988), Kathleen Weiler studied how difficult it is for feminist teachers to work toward antisexist approaches in their classrooms. Jesse Goodman and Tom Kelly in an article in *Interchange* in 1988 talked about how profeminist male teachers encountered opposition not only from other male teachers but also from students, parents, and female teachers when they tried to work toward antisexist teaching strategies. Also, Patti Lather in *Getting Smart* (1991) has described "student resistance to liberatory curriculum" even within Women's Studies courses.

At the centre of much of this reported resistance is the issue of language and communication, which is central to the educational enterprise. As Dale Spender in *Man Made Language* (1980) points out, until fairly recently conventions that posited the superiority of males and the inferiority of females, such as the use of the "generic he," served to limit our abilities to think in nongendered ways. In the *Oppositional Imagination* (1989), Joan Cocks delineates how even our nonverbal communications have traditionally been predicated on the gender of the persons involved and how our very imaginations have been limited by the gendered vocabularies available to us. Indeed, Deborah Tannen in *You Just Don't Understand* (1990) used data on men and women in same-sex and mixed-sex conversations to describe two "genderlects" and explained that in most public settings, such as classrooms, it is the male conversational style that prevails. Thus, in traditional classroom discourse, females must speak an unfamiliar genderlect: they must, as Adrienne Rich has put it, "tell it slant," an activity that robs them of energy and often serves to silence them. Rich urges us to:

> Listen to a woman groping for language to express what is on her mind, sensing that the terms of academic discourse are not her language, trying to cut down her thought to the dimensions of a discourse not intended for her.[24]

This perspective on language and communication raises feminist questions not only about how students should be treated in classrooms but also about what they should be taught. Jane Roland Martin in *Reclaiming a Conversation: The Ideal of the Educated Person* (1985) has argued that, because the school has traditionally been viewed as preparation for public life, it has been based on the ideal of "the cultivated, educated gentleman," even for females. We have discarded Jean-Jacques Rousseau's ideas of overtly separate educational goals for males in the public sphere and for females in the private sphere. While Martin does not advocate that we return to a "domestic science" approach to the education of female students, she does point out that at present the three Cs (caring, concern, and connection) seem, through informal differentiation of the curriculum by gender, to more frequently be stressed for girls than for boys. This, she argues, is particularly problematic in an era when old paradigms of enlightenment rationality, autonomous individuality, and unlimited consumerism are being called into question by postmodernist theorists in a wide variety of disciplines from physics to art history.

What is important for some feminist educational reformers then is an examination of "epistemology" or knowledge itself. No longer can we unquestioningly accept established canons or lists of great contributions to civilization when these exclude women's accomplishments and experiences. We need to question what is worth knowing and how we have come to know. Mary Belenky and a number of other researchers did just that in a book entitled *Women's Ways of Knowing* (1986). In that work they argued that not only females but many males as well would be better served by a teaching method that posed problems and let learners search for connections between knowledges rather than by lecture techniques that compartmentalized knowledges and asked students to be interested spectators and consumers.

Indeed, Michael Cole and Peg Griffin in *Contextual Factors in Education* (1987) and Sheila Tobias in *They're Not Dumb, They're Just Different* (1990) argue that current teaching techniques used in the teaching of math, science, and technology, especially at the college and university level, are aimed at gatekeeping in such a way that only a few students (who resemble those in power positions within these disciplines in thought patterns, learning styles, and often by such characteristics as gender and race) will be allowed the chance to study and eventually work in these areas. While those who have invested in maintaining the current status quo of any discipline may benefit by this procedure, the development of truly "new" innovations in the discipline is severely hampered.

What feminists suggest is that the experiences of all students, teachers, and school administrators be considered by those involved in the educational system in Canada. Some feminist reformers are focused on improving the participation and success of females; others have focused on countering sexism, racism, homophobia, "abelism," and other forms of harmful discriminatory structures and practices; still others are working toward a transformation in not only pedagogical or teaching techniques that have favoured certain groups of males, but also in the actual knowledge bases used and in the underlying theories about humans and ways they learn and assumptions about their roles in the world. Books such as Ruth King's *Talking Gender* (1991) describe how we can alter traditional communication patterns, Diane Richardson and Victoria Robinson's *Thinking Feminist* (1993) tells us how women's studies concepts are crucial to change, and Patti Lather's *Getting Smart* (1991) encourages us to use research and teaching techniques both to "know and be known" in the world.

Such reforms to be successful, need to consider the interrelationship between education itself and the larger economic and political structures of our time. Thus, we need to consider the connections between the educational system and forms of paid and unpaid work.

## LINKAGES BETWEEN SCHOOL AND WORK

In March of 1993, a Gallup survey using a national sample of 1,041 adults revealed that only 41 percent believed that there was equality in this country between men and women. This was down from 45 percent in 1989 and 47 percent in 1986. Slightly more than three in five of the women surveyed (63 percent) said they had fewer opportunities than men and 49 percent of men surveyed agreed with them. There were regional variations in the results in that 64 percent of those in the Atlantic provinces believed men had more opportunities than women, 62 percent in Ontario, 55 percent in the Prairies and only 42 percent in Quebec.[25]

Census data tell us that the average woman in Canada has a family with young children, has only a high school education, and is a member of the paid labour force. The census also shows that 75 percent of married women between the ages of 25-44 are in the paid labour force, that 28 percent of all marriages end in divorce, and that women hold unequal status in the paid work force. In

1988, more than half of all women who worked for pay did so in clerical, sales, or service positions and earned on average about $13,000 a year. Women classed as the head of their household earned an average income of $26,000 compared to $46,000 for men and 34 percent of female-headed households earned under $15,000 compared to only 7 percent of male-headed households at this poverty level. Even the 30 percent of women in Canada in 1988 who worked as managers or professionals earned only 60 percent of the salaries of men in those same occupational categories.[26]

Barbara Lyn, director of the Hastings County Separate School Board in Ontario, declared in 1993: "Young women in the professions need to be identified as potential leaders and they need to be told this many, many times."[27] Yet studies of women's experiences in many male-dominated areas of the paid labour force continue to reveal barriers and harassment. Indeed, some observers state that we are in a period of "backlash" that makes life very difficult for women. A dramatic example of this was the murder of 14 young women engineering students at the École Polytechnique in Montreal in 1989. As Monique Frize of the University of New Brunswick has written in the introduction to a study of women in engineering, "this catalytic event gave our investigation great impetus and jolted engineers and non-engineers alike into deep contemplation and open discussion about the very issue we were to deal with — namely, the status of women in the profession."[28]

Not everyone in Canada, however, shares the same concerns about women in the paid work force. In September of 1990, Gordon Freeman, a chemist at the University of Alberta, wrote an article that was published in *The Canadian Journal of Physics*. In that article he maintained that in recent years a "state of mind" had been inculcated in the minds of Canadian youth whose mothers worked for pay. He blamed this state of mind for "drug use, insider trading, infidelity, embezzlement, teenage sex, and corrupt political practices." He went on to say that women were by nature equipped to be nurturers and that they worked for pay because they distrusted "males' capacity to make a commitment to marriage."[29]

Dr. Selma Zimmerman of York University led an organized protest against the article that resulted in an official apology but not a retraction of the article itself. She complained that it was "an opinion piece passing as science" and "part of a backlash against gains women have made in recent years."[30] Feminists are concerned about what passes for science in our classrooms. About female expectations of outcomes from the educational system, about what females receive in terms of paid labour, and how best to deal with the current backlash against women.

Since the Second World War, a number of analyses of the relationship between school and work have been offered. While it is not possible here to detail all of this work, four major theories will be discussed.[31] The first is the functional approach of Talcott Parsons in the 1950s and 1960s. In brief, Parsons postulated that schools were institutions that served two major functions for the economy: they socialized students and developed their skills and capacities to be productive, and they allocated students to occupational roles needed in the society. To do so efficiently, schools should make rational use of economic resources. This framework was used by John Porter in Canada in his influential analysis during the 1960s.[32]

Closely related to Parsons' work was that of Howard Becker, who argued that, if a single person could advance in the society through merit and hard work, then the society itself could improve its economic position through educational improvement. In *Human Capital Theory* (1964) Becker argued that investment in education would be positively related to economic growth and that educated workers would be more productive workers.

A contrasting view was put forward by Bowles and Gintis in *Schooling in Capitalist America* (1976). They argued that institutions such as schools reflect the dominance of some groups over others and serve the needs of the dominant groups rather than the collective good. The meritocracy that was a basis for differentiation between students in Parson's theory was viewed by Bowles and Gintis as a camouflage for a system that was stacked from the beginning against working-class students. Among the Canadians influenced by this approach was George Martell, who wrote *The Politics of the Canadian Public School* (1974).

The work of Paul Willis in *Learning to Labour* (1977) added an important new dimension to the theory of Bowles and Gintis. Willis argued that "social reproduction" of a class-biased system was not inevitable. Indeed, he detailed in his study of British working-class "lads" how the individual negotiated in an ongoing way the contested and contradictory processes of schooling and paid work. In Willis' view, the participants in schooling were active agents who produced a culture, a set of decisions, and some concrete behaviours out of their interpretations of the social conditions in which they found themselves. They understood part of what they were contesting, they resisted some of it, and they complied with other aspects in a way that made sense to them.

For Parsons, women's schooling was primarily related to their unpaid domestic work and women were often left out of studies using a functional framework or they were allocated to the category "housewife." For Becker, women's lower rate of return on their educational investment remained a mystery he could not explain. For Bowles and Gintis, class equity was their major concern and, while they noted women's discontent, they themselves did not explore issues of sexism or indeed of racism or other forms outside of class-based discrimination within the educational system. For Willis, males were more interesting than females for the purpose of his theory. His work has come under severe criticism by feminists, such as Angela McRobbie[33] who found that while Willis uncovered misogyny being clearly expressed by the working-class lads, he did not explore this and treated it and other gender-related aspects of his findings as only tangential. His framework, however, has been effectively used by Jane Gaskell in her Canadian study of working-class students in British Columbia in *Gender Matters From School To Work* ( 1992).

Along with different theories about the relationship between school and work, Jack Nelson, Stuart Palonsky, and Kenneth Carlson point out in *Critical Issues in Education* (1990) that our political beliefs affect our views about what schools are supposed to do and whose interests they should serve. On the political "right" are those who believe that government's role is to ensure that parents can be free to choose the kind of education they want for their children and that each of us can best help the less fortunate by contributing to the national welfare rather than by giving handouts or special privileges to certain students.

Those on the political "left" demand that the government guarantee that every child have equally good schooling despite parental circumstances. They argue that to date we have had a system that has not equalized the condition of poor people or women but has instead only allowed them to remain dependent upon the well-to-do, most of whom are White males. They state that whenever improved conditions become available to disadvantaged children, those in the advantaged group find some way to provide some form of additional or improved schooling for their children that negates the gains made.

To varying degrees, feminists, like others in our society, can be found across this spectrum of theories and political locations. What they agree upon, however, is that most female students are less advantaged than most male students when it comes to cashing in on their educational investment. Some feminists believe that this is because female students make some unfortunate choices during their schooling, such as dropping math classes. These choices limit the possibilities for females in the world of paid work. Other feminists argue that there are few role models for females to follow in nontraditional occupations and that this contributes to aspirations by females to work in fields where women have always worked and to avoid trying to enter the less comfortable and somewhat risky terrain of such fields as engineering.

Ways in which schools might alleviate the difficulties experienced by females in the paid labour force include the following: counselling girls and women into taking courses that "keep their options open"; encouraging them to gain first-hand knowledge from female mentors in nontraditional roles for women; educating both male and female students about the realities of and need for increased employment equity policies and practices not only in schools but in the paid labour force as well; equipping students, both male and female, with the desire and skills needed to continue to work toward greater equity for a variety of groups in our economy; and transforming the schools themselves so that those who work within them can offer a model to all students of how paid labour need not be designated by gender and how existing traditions and power structures can be altered to increase equity. It is in regard to this last strategy that we now turn to the final section of this chapter, a discussion of the distribution of power within educational hierarchies.

## THE DISTRIBUTION OF POWER IN EDUCATIONAL HIERARCHIES

The educational system in Canada in the twentieth century could be said to be a bureaucracy. As one of its definitions of this term, Webster's offers that a bureaucracy is "a system of administration marked by officialism, red tape and proliferation."[34] When we trace the historical development of elementary and secondary schooling across the country, we see that over time and particularly following World War Two, the administrative side of schools increased dramatically. For example, in the Toronto Board of Education in 1940, 20.5 percent of the teachers were in such administrative roles as principal or vice-principal. By 1980, that percentage had risen to 47.6 percent and now included such roles as consultant, department head and assistant department head.[35] Clearly, the structures and processes of power had become more complicated than those which were used to operate one-room rural schools. Hierarchies of many varieties had developed. Evidence of such hierarchies was seen in differential salaries paid to those at different levels in administration. Organizational charts of large urban school boards revealed a complex pecking order in terms of decision making.

In terms of postsecondary schooling, again we can trace historically a proliferation of universities and colleges with increasingly complex administrative structures and processes and both official and unofficial hierarchies by discipline, institution, and student groups.

Provincial ministries of education and of colleges and universities also had large staffs of decision makers and policies and procedures for a wide variety of school-related activities that ranged from allocating funds to preparing curriculum guidelines for teachers in various subject areas. In all of this, there was often controversy about an unofficial hierarchy that differentially favoured some schools over others, some subject areas, and some groups of students. Fluctuation in all of this was due to the movement of political figures in and out of office following elections and changes in popular theories about schooling. Despite such fluctuation, a relatively stable group of bureaucrats tended to hold the reins of power over what would happen and when.

Put very simply, much of the distribution of power within these myriad educational hierarchies traditionally favoured secondary and postsecondary students over elementary and particularly primary or nursery school students, large systems over small systems, urban venues over rural venues, "normal" students over those with "special needs," full-time students over part-time students, mental skills over manual skills, and science and technology over all other subject areas.

It has been argued as well that the distribution of power also has traditionally favoured White males of the middle and upper classes. Certainly, if we track the gender, race, and class backgrounds of major decision makers in most Canadian educational systems over the twentieth century, there is considerable evidence for this claim, at least in terms of direct participation in the upper levels of the administrative hierarchies. Another telling factor has been the distribution over time of funds to various student groups, disciplines, and schools.

Because this power distribution pattern has had a long duration, it seems usual to us and it is hard to imagine anything different. There are those who argue, however, that more women, persons of colour, those with disabilities, and those with working-class backgrounds should be participants at the higher levels of the existing hierarchies. It is frequently argued that this would change the distribution of power. What critics of this approach point out is that the structures and processes themselves are so deeply flawed that, even if these groups were to come to these roles, there might be little they could do to change the overall organizational mammoths. Like immigrants to a new land, such newcomers to power may be more interested in fitting in than in working to change a system from which they are now in a position to gain at a personal level.

Some feminists, among others, have suggested that what we really need are alternative nonbureaucratic approaches to the problems of organization in education and elsewhere in our society. Kathy Ferguson in *The Feminist Case Against Bureaucracy* (1984) is only one among many who offer a systematic analysis of the problems of bureaucratization not only for women but for all those in minority positions within the larger society. She also points to examples of alternative structures and cites feminist egalitarian approaches to getting things done as an important site of clarification and resistance to traditional patterns of power distribution.

But there is little to suggest that such a transformation would occur easily. Those interested in maintaining the status quo are unlikely to see merits in change in this direction. Even those currently being exploited by existing systems may not agree with suggested alternatives unless they are assured that these will not just offer a different form of exploitation. There are problems too in helping individuals come to grips with their beliefs and actions at a level beyond lip service and "politically correct" rhetoric.

Policy within current educational systems about employment equity seems to offer a good example of the possibilities for new forms within educational hierarchies. It also offers us examples of the difficulties that must be overcome before any deep-seated and lasting changes can occur.

In 1984, in *Equality in Employment: A Royal Commission Report*, Judge Rosalie Abella stated:

Employment equity is action to achieve equality in the workplace so that no person shall be denied employment opportunities or benefits unrelated to ability and to correct the conditions of disadvantage in employment experiences by women, aboriginal peoples, persons with disabilities and persons, who, because of their race, creed, colour, or religion, are in a minority.[36]

A study conducted in 1990 by the Canadian Educational Association revealed that progress across Canada in provincial ministries of education, school boards and teachers' associations varied greatly according to employment equity policies and procedures and in related matters dealing with such issues as sexual harassment and inclusive language. Overall, the distribution by gender for teachers and administrators continues to show an overrepresentation of men in the highest ranks. Despite some provincial declarations such as Memorandum 111 in Ontario which declared that by the year 2000 women should constitute 50 percent of all administrative positions in the educational system, most policies do not set targets or goals nor do they apply rewards or sanctions to those who comply or fail to comply with the policy. Outcries about "reverse discrimination" have been heard in many sectors, and some regions actually show a decline in the participation of women administrators as a result of recent retirements or amalgamation of school districts.

Within colleges and universities, the Canadian Association of University Teachers, through its Status of Women Committee, has, over many years, made a sustained effort toward employment equity and educational equity. Mirrored in many provincial associations, such committees have kept open for debate the need for a redistribution of power and new possibilities regarding old structures. Much of that debate recently has focused on "the inclusive university" as an alternative to traditional version of "academe." Discussing this theme, Joyce Forbes declares:

> The masculinist power structure of the university has no right to set its own limitations on others. By seeing as tangential all that is not traditional, by naming as whole that which is partial, the university has consolidated into an absolute what is partial vision and partial judgement.... To affirm another's self-respect is to ferret out the words that acclaim diversity. This is to transform education: make it relevant.[37]

Following these ideas, others such as the Canadian Federation of University Women have identified aspects of a "woman-friendly" university that are similar to those discussed by many others in colleges and in elementary and secondary schools when they address what needs attending to with regard to employment equity. This includes such aspects as support services for staff and faculty and for full-time and part-time students that include child care and elder care provision; a safe and harassment-free environment; recognition of work experience; salary equity; incentives for increased participation by women in light of their household and family commitments, including access to scholarships and all academic programs; equity in hiring and promotion procedures and outcomes; attention to the inclusion of female experience in all course content; gender-inclusive language as the norm throughout the institution; and finally, structural recognition of Women's Studies as an accredited area of scholarship.

## CONCLUSIONS

The historical origins of educational systems in Canada reveal that females were somewhat grudgingly admitted to schools primarily designed to meet the needs and learning styles of males. Only relatively recently have the material conditions and lives of students and teachers in classrooms been deemed worthy of study or comment. Examinations of those experiences have indicated that, despite their greater compliance overall with the demands of school life, females have been less valued by teachers, given less attention in classrooms, and have had their experiences and accomplishments largely left out of curriculum materials or treated in a stereotypical fashion.

One explanation for this has been that, in the larger society, particularly in the paid labour force, women have been only grudgingly allowed entrance and their efforts have returned lower rewards than those given to their male counterparts. The schools serve only to mirror societal realities. Girls and women rightly belong in the private sphere of the family and, when they enter the public sphere of the school or the paid labour force, they do so only as short-term visitors who should not expect the same treatment or rewards available to the males for whom that public sphere has been reserved.

As we have seen, the distribution of power in educational systems has been predicated on this view of separate spheres for males and females. Employment equity and educational equity policies and procedures often are hotly debated largely because they offer a direct challenge to such views and indeed suggest that, with the necessary adjustments to structures and procedures, both women and men could live and work in both public and private spheres.

Feminists, as already stated, have diverse views about the importance of the educational system in bringing about improvements in our society for girls and women. They often disagree about what strategies should be employed and what changes are necessary. Those who accept the basic traditions of schooling in this country are working largely to ensure that women and other minorities have equal chances to use schooling to help them gain economic viability. Those who are critical of traditional Canadian schooling practices and structures are working to alter them so that the status quo will be changed and possibilities for new forms of organization can develop over time.

In some ways, feminists concerned with the educational system alternate between fatalism and romanticism. They constantly search for clarity of vision regarding existing realities whether those are realities of the current economic or political climates within which they must work for change, or the realities of classroom life which inform them about the success or failures of their attempts. Perhaps the clearest way to think about how feminists are working within the educational system is to imagine, as Virginia Woolf did in *A Room of One's Own* (1928), that Shakespeare had a sister who, like all great poets, has never died but will come back to life when the opportunity permits. Her possible return motivates many feminists to work for educational reform. As Virginia Woolf explains:

> As for her coming without that preparation, without that effort on our part, without that determination that when she is born again she shall find it possible to live and write her poetry, that we cannot expect, for that would be impossible. But I maintain that she would come if we worked for her, and that so to work, even in poverty and obscurity, is worth while.[38]

## NOTES

1  Alison Prentice et al. *Canadian Women. A History*, 25-57.

2  Ibid., 59.

3  Ibid., 65-67.

4  Ibid., 80.

5  Jane Gaskell et al. *Claiming an Education*, 8.

6  Gaskell et al., Also see Ian Davey "Trends in Female School Attendance in Mid-Nineteenth Century Ontario" in Heap and Prentice *Gender and Education*.

7  Gaskell at al., 10.

8  For a discussion of the growth of secondary schooling in Ontario see Robert Gidney and Wynn Millar *Inventing Secondary Schooling*.

9  Alison Prentice et al. *Canadian Women*, 129. Also, for a discussion of patterns for Canada, Ontario and Toronto for teachers by gender, see Cecilia Reynolds "Ontario Schoolteachers 1911-1971: A Portrait of Demographic Change." Unpublished masters' thesis, University of Toronto.

10  Donald Wilson et al. *Canadian Education. A History*, 317.

11  Elizabeth Graham. "Schoolmarms and Early Teaching in Ontario" in Acton et al. *Women at Work*.

12  Ruth Rees. *Women and Men in Education*.

13  For further discussion see Cecilia Reynolds "Too limiting a Liberation: Discourse and Actuality in the Case of Married Women Teachers" in Frieda Forman et al. *Feminism and Education*.

14  Industry, Science and Technology Canada. *Women in Science and Engineering*, Vol.1, 3.

15  Many of the ideas in this paragraph come from a discussion by Marie Richmond Abbott, *Masculine and Feminine. Gender Roles Over the Life Course*, Second Edition, 3-64.

16  Gaskell et al., 11-21.

17   Philip Shaver and Clyde Hendrick. *Sex and Gender.*

18   Among many publications by these researchers is an influential article titled "Sexism in the Classroom: From Grade School to Graduate School" which was published in 1986 in the March issue of the teachers' journal, *Phi Delta Kappan.*

19   Diane Richardson and Victoria Robinson, eds. *Thinking Feminist.*

20   Ibid., 339

21   For further discussion see "The Campus Climate Revisited: Chilly for Women Faculty, Administrators, and Graduate Students," (1986, October), a publication of the Project on the Status and Education of Women Association of American Colleges. Also, the University of Western Ontario has produced a video, "The Chilly Climate for Women at Canadian Colleges and Universities." Also, see Linda Briskin Gender in the Classroom" in *CORE: Newsletter of the Centre for Support of Teaching* (York), Vol.1 No. 1.

22   Two excellent discussions of feminist pedagogy are contained in Patti Lather *Getting Smart. Feminist Research and Pedagogy with/in the Postmodern*; and Anne-Louise Brookes *Feminist Pedagogy. An Autobiographical Approach.*

23   Somer Brodribb. "Women's Studies in Canada: A Discussion." A Special publication of *Resources for Feminist Research*, 1.

24   Adrienne Rich *On lies, secrets and silence: Selected prose, 1966-1978*, 243-244.

25   "Women get raw deal, pollsters told" in *The Toronto Star*, 8 March 1993, A5.

26   Statistics Canada *Labour Force*

27   "Foster professional leaders," women told in *The Toronto Star*, 8 March 1993, A9.

28   "Engineers treated fairly, council rules" in *The Toronto Star*, 8 March 1993, A11

29   "Canadian Chemist Takes on Working Women" in *Science*, 28 February 1992, Vol. 255, 1065.

30   Ibid., 1065.

31   This section draws from a similar discussion in Gaskell *Gender Matters from School to Work*, 16-30.

32   See John Porter *The Vertical Mosaic*, University of Toronto Press, 1965.

33   Angela McRobbie. "Working class girls and the culture of femininity."

34   *Webster's New Collegiate Dictionary*, 1981, 146.

35   Cecilia Reynolds. "Hegemony and Hierarchy: Becoming a Teacher in Toronto, 1930-1980," 95-119.

36   In Rees. *Women and Men in Education*, 3.

37   Joyce Forbes. "The Inclusive University." *CAUT Status of Women Supplement*, 1993, 3.

38   Virginia Woolf. *A Room of One's Own*, 123.

# BIBLIOGRAPHY

Belenky, M, Clinchy, B., Goldberger, N., and Tarule, J. *Women's Ways of Knowing: The development of self, voice and mind* New York: Basic Books, 1986.

Briskin, L. Gender in the classroom *CORE: Newsletter of the Centre for the Support of Teaching (York)*, V.1 #1, 1990.

Brodribb, S. "Women's studies in Canada: a discussion." A special publication of *Resources for Feminist Research /Documentation sur la Recherche Feministe*, 1987.

Brookes, A. *Feminist Pedagogy. An autobiographical approach.* Halifax: Fernwood Publishing, 1992.

Canadian Federation of University Women. *Women in Universities. Survey of the status of female faculty and students at Canadian universities.* Toronto, 1992.

Canadian Teachers' Federation. *Thumbs Down. A classroom response to violence against women.* Ottawa, 1990.

Council of Ontario Universities. *Women in Graduate Studies in Ontario.* Toronto, 1989.

Cocks, J. *The Oppositional Imagination. Feminism, critique and political theory.* New York: Routledge, 1989.

Crease, R. "Canadian chemist takes on working women." *Science* Vol. 255:1065-1066, 1992, February.

"Engineers treated fairly, council rules," *The Toronto Star*, 8 March 1993, A11.

Ferguson, K. *The Feminist Case Against Bureaucracy.* Philadelphia: Temple University Press, 1984.

"Foster professional leaders, women told," *The Toronto Star*, 8 March 1993, A9.

Gaskell, J. *Gender Matters from School to Work.* Toronto: OISE Press, 1992.

Gaskell, J., McLaren, A. and Novogrodsky, M. *Claiming an Education. Feminism and Canadian schools.* Toronto: Our Schools/Our Selves Education Foundation, 1989.

Gidney, R. and Millar, W. *Inventing Secondary Education.* Montreal: McGill-Queen's University Press, 1990.

Goodman, J. and Kelly, T. "Out of the mainstream: Issues confronting the male profeminist elementary school teacher." *Interchange* V.19 #2:1-14, 1988.

Graham, E. "Schoolmarms and early teaching in Ontario." In *Women at Work 1850-1930.* edited by L. Kealy Canadian Women's Educational Press, 1974.

Holland, D. and Eisenhart, M. *Educated in Romance.* Chicago: University of Chicago Press, 1990.

Industry, Science and Technology Canada. *Women in Science and Engineering. Volume 1: Universities.* University and College Affairs Branch, Science Sector, Ottawa, 1991.

Kimball, M. "A new perspective on women's math achievement." *Psychological Bulletin* 105, 198-214, 1989.

Martin, J. R. *Reclaiming a Conversation: The Ideal of the Educated Woman.* New Haven: Yale University Press, 1985.

McRobbie, A. "Working class girls and the culture of femininity." In *Women Take Issue.* Centre for Contemporary Cultural Studies, Women's Studies Group, Birmingham: University of Birmingham, 1978.

Nelson, J., Palonsky, S. and Carlson, K. *Critical Issues in Education.* Toronto: McGraw-Hill Publishing Company, 1990.

Prentice, A., Bourne, P., Brandt, G., Light, B., Mitchinson, W., Black, N. *Canadian Women. A History.* Toronto: Harcourt Brace Jovanovich, 1988.

Rees, R. *Women and Men in Education. A national survey of gender distribution in school systems.* A report of the Canadian Educational Association, 1990.

Reynolds, C. "Hegemony and hierarchy: becoming a teacher in Toronto, 1930-1980." *Historical Studies in Education/ Revue D'histoire de l'education* Vol.2 No. 1,95-118, 1990.

Reynolds, C. "Too limiting a liberation: discourse and actuality in the case of married women teachers in Canada" in *Feminism and Education*, edited by F. Forman, M. O'Brien, J. Haddad, D. Hallman and P. Masters Toronto: OISE Press, 1990.

Reynolds, C. "Ontario schoolteachers 1911-1971: a portrait of demographic change." Unpublished Master's thesis, University of Toronto, 1983.

Rich, A. *On lies, secrets, and silence: Selected prose, 1966-1978.* New York: Norton, 1979.

Richardson, D. and Robinson, V. *Thinking Feminist. Key concepts in women's studies.* New York: The Guilford Press, 1993.

Richmond-Abbott, M. *Masculine & Feminine. Gender roles over the life course.* Toronto: McGraw Hill, Inc., 1992.

Rosenthal, R. and Rubin, D. "Further meta-analytic procedures for assessing cognitive gender differences." *Journal of Educational Psychology.* 74, 708-712, 1982.

Sadker, M. and Sadker, D. "Sexism in the classroom: from grade school to graduate school." *Phi Delta Kappan*, 1986.

Shaver, P. and Hendrick, C. *Sex & Gender.* Newbury Park: Sage, 1987.

Spender, D. *Man Made Language.* London: Routledge and Kegan Paul, 1980.

Tannen, D. *You Just Don't Understand. Women and men in conversation.* New York : Ballantine Books, 1990.

Tobias, S. *They're Not Dumb, They're Different. Stalking the second tier.* Tucson: Research Corp., 1990.

Weiler, K. *Women Teaching For Change. Gender, class & power* Massachusetts: Bergin & Garvey Pub., Inc., 1988.

Weiner, G. and Arnot, M. "Teachers and gender politics" in *Gender and the Politics of Schooling* edited by M. Arnot and G. Weiner (eds) London: Hutchinson, 1987.

Wilson, D. ed. *Canadian Education. A History*. Scarborough: Prentice Hall, 1970.

"Women get raw deal, pollsters told" *The Toronto Star*, 8 March 1993, A5.

Woolf, V. *A Room of One's Own*. Triad Grafton Books, 1977, 1929.

# WOMEN AND HEALTH: CHALLENGES AND CHANGES

*Pat Armstrong*

## INTRODUCTION

Health is about much more than body parts, their function and treatment. And women's health is about much more than particular reproductive organs and secondary sex characteristics. Health is about whole people located in specific places, times, and relations. It is defined by and shaped in social, psychological, and economic environments and relationships. Bodies and minds, then, cannot be understood apart from their history and culture. This means that health is a social issue and a social construct rather than simply a medical and technical problem to be addressed by experts.

Because health is constructed and defined within social, economic, and physical environments, there are therefore significant differences among women related to class, race, culture, age, location, historical period, and personal history. But because health is constructed within social relationships in which women in general are less powerful and because women have some physical attributes in common, having a female body means that women share at least some health concerns. Women's health is constructed in ways that are often different from those of men and therefore the health issues women face are often different from those of men.

This chapter begins by looking at disputes about what constitutes a female body and a female mind. It next explores the ways medicine has defined and treated women both as a group and as members of particular classes, races, ages, and cultures. It then looks at the ways the structures and relations of the home and the paid work force shape the limits on and possibilities for women's health. It assumes that the political economy and relations between the sexes have a profound impact on how women's health is defined and constituted, although it also recognizes that bodies make a difference. But at the same time, it argues that women are active participants in shaping both how their bodies and minds are treated and how they develop over time. A political economy approach means understanding that the very structure of bodies reflects power relationships and struggles over both access to resources and to the right to define health. And it means understanding that, while women often lose in these struggles, they remain continually active in shaping their own health (Armstrong and Armstrong 1983; Smith 1975).

## FEMALE BODIES

Women's bodies are a contested terrain. While most people would agree that there are physiological differences between women and men, there is little agreement about what these differences are and even less about their consequences for women's health (see Armstrong and Armstrong 1993:ch.4). There is also little agreement about who knows best what these differences are and how they should be understood (Haraway 1989). Some would argue that there are so many differences among women and within groups of men that the very categories of male and female are abstractions without substance in individual experience (Adams and Cowie 1990). They would therefore argue that it makes no sense to talk about "women's" health.

Some differences are seldom disputed. It is clear that menstruation, gestation, and lactation are strictly female processes even though some women never experience any of these. As Jessie Bernard, the author of multiple texts about women, put it, "Men hardly ever get pregnant" (quoted in Bacchi 1990:x). Only men, however, produce sperm. While differences in reproductive organs may seem obvious, they do not always provide a means of distinguishing one sex from another. In many athletic competitions, the presence of the x chromosome is the only criterion used to determine who the men are.

Aside from these differences, there are great debates about the extent and nature of any other characteristics that may separate the sexes. Women cannot always easily be distinguished from men in, for example, terms of hormonal production, breast size, facial hair, muscle mass and upper arm strength. Usually there are differences in degree rather than in kind and there are disagreements about the extent of each degree. Height, a characteristic often assumed to separate the women from the men, varies at least as much between men from different countries as it does between women and men in the same country, yet height is often assumed to be sex-specific (Birke 1986; Fausto-Sterling 1985; Rhode 1990).

Even those who agree that there are some clear differences between women and men still disagree about the consequences of such differences. The debates about consequences are often framed in terms of alternatives. Are menstruation, menopause, pregnancy, childbirth, and breast-feeding natural events that need cause little disruption in women's lives or are they debilitating processes that limit women's capacity to participate in various aspects of daily life and require constant medical intervention?

As Bacchi (1990) points out in *Same Difference*, feminists, in their struggles to gain entry into male areas of work or to gain support for maternity leave and resources for childbirth, have often been forced to choose between these alternatives. By downplaying the differences between males and females, many individual women have been able to enter some male fields but at the cost of conforming to male ways of participating. Denying that these specifically female processes make a difference often means giving up having babies, suffering in silence, or struggling to hide hot flushes or premenstrual cramps. By stressing differences, many women have been able to acquire protection and recognition of their discomfort but at the risk of losing out to men in terms of jobs, pay, promotion, and recognition. Emphasizing female processes often means restrictions on access to a range of activities, excessive medical treatment, and relegation to secondary status. In following these two strategies, feminists are often accused of wanting it both ways—of arguing that women are both the same as men *and* different from them, of seeking both the same treatment *and* special treatment. Women are asked to choose one side, to determine once and for all what the "real" differences are and the "real" consequences of these differences.

But Bacchi (1990:xi) makes it clear that "the question of difference has no meaningful answer." As is the case with all physiological components of people's lives, the limitations attributed to women's bodies are simultaneously social and biological. The physiological cannot be separated from the social because the consequences of physiological processes have meaning only in a social context and because the very biology of being a woman is influenced by the social. That Native women in Canada, for instance, have more than twice as many miscarriages as other women primarily reflects living conditions and access to both food and medical services rather than different bodies (Bobet 1989:12). Similarly, the symptoms associated with menopause vary with diet, exercise, and social location; this suggests that this biological process is, to a large extent, socially constructed.

Because bodies exist only in a social environment, "it makes more sense to talk of genders, not simply gender, because being a woman and being a man change from one generation to the next and are different for different racial, ethnic and religious groups as well as for members of different social classes" (Lorber and Farrell 1991:1). This is not to deny that biology is important in health or that being a woman makes a difference but rather to argue that biology and its consequences are not fixed or separable from the social context. Menstruating, pregnancy, childbirth, breast-feeding, and menopause are never "simply" biological processes that can be scientifically examined and medically managed in isolation from other social relations.

## MEDICAL PRACTICES

In spite of the impressive evidence demonstrating the inextricable relationship between the social and the biological, much of the medical profession persists in treating biological processes as independent variables and women as a set of parts to be fixed by practitioners who alone know what is best for women. As Sherwin (1992:7) persuasively argues in *No Longer Patient*, "the institution of medicine has been designed in ways that reinforce sexism, and the effects of medical practice are often bad for women." There is a considerable body of evidence to support her claim.

There are certainly those who argue that biology limited women's possibilities in the past and that medical science has liberated or can liberate women from the restrictions of menstruation, childbearing and menopause (Firestone 1970; Shorter 1985). But many feminists maintain that the role of medical practitioners cannot be understood simply in terms of the objective application of scientifically established procedures to biologically-determined processes or in terms of general good. In the words of Haraway (1989:6), "Scientific practice is negotiation, strategic moves, inscription, translation," not "just the facts." And women have seldom been in a position to determine what is studied, how it is studied, and what is done with the findings. Moreover, the integral relationship of the biological and the social means that there are few clear facts to determine about biology and that most claims for biological truths are matters of debate or of best guesses.

For example, in Victorian Canada one group of doctors argued that bicycle riding was unhealthy for women whereas another group advocated bicycle riding as a cure for women's ills (Mitchinson 1991). One study in today's Canada found that doctors vary widely in terms of whether they systematically prescribe estrogen therapy for menopausal women "but each physician believed absolutely in the correctness of his or her own particular approach to the menopausal patient" (Kaufert and Gilbert 1987:181). In spite of these discrepancies, "Knowledge in most obstetric and gynecologic textbooks is presented as accomplished 'truth', which disguises its disputed character" (Findlay 1993:116) and often serves to deny women's own knowledge claims.

As Mitchinson (1991:5) says of doctors in Victorian Canada, the "medical profession accepted the limited public role given to women and provided a biological rationale for it." And they claimed scientific evidence for their practices, evidence that was intended to place their methods beyond critique. Science was not used exclusively, or even primarily, to liberate women from the assumed dictates of their bodies, and doctors were seldom on the side of women. Today, "Doctors interpret theory into practice through the bias of their own class, ethnicity, and gender and through that of their patients" (Mitchinson 1991:8). Medicine remains a means of controlling women as well as a means of achieving health: sometimes control takes precedence and health is jeopardized.

This is still the situation even though a rapidly growing number of medical doctors are women and even though these women practice medicine somewhat differently from men. The proportion of physicians and surgeons who are women grew from 21 percent in 1986 to 27 percent in 1991, and women account for more than 40 percent of those enrolled in medical school[1] (Blishen 1991:Table 5.1). Although women are more likely to be in general practice, to work in group practices, and to see fewer patients during their time in practice than men, there are few major attitudinal differences between male and female medical practitioners (Williams et al. 1990). The differences in the way women practice medicine may reflect their household responsibilities while their similarity in terms of attitude may reflect the fact that they are still taught and evaluated mainly by medical men (Armstrong and Armstrong 1992:125-126).

## Drug Prescriptions

Drug prescription practices provide just one example of how physicians often treat women and men differently and of how health care is used as a means of control. Even when they report the same symptoms to the physician, women are much more likely than men to receive prescriptions for tranquilizers (Cooperstock and Lennard 1987; Harding 1986). For example, a Saskatchewan study found that, among those aged 20 to 29, eight times more women than men received antidepressants (Harding 1986:61). Elderly women in particular receive a large number of prescriptions for tranquilizers and other drugs. "Even though the over-prescribing to women is often justified by bio-medical arguments (e.g. problems from reproduction, longevity, etc.), and pain killers are commonly used for such bio-medical problems, no major sex differences existed for these drugs. The major sex differences clearly involved the psychoactives" (Harding 1986:64). In other words, these differences in prescription patterns cannot be primarily explained by women's bodies as defined in medicine, given that women are mainly receiving mood-modifying drugs. Nor can they be explained by women shopping around for several doctors to give them drugs because most prescriptions were received from a single physician. Rather, much of the explanation can be found in physicians' "notions of female passivity and helplessness" and ideas about appropriate female behaviour (McDonnell

1986:6). Whatever the physicians' reasons, the effect is to encourage women to accept their conditions and ignore the social and economic factors that are central in explaining why many women seek medical help.

Breast implants provide an even more obvious example. Interviewed by Regush (1993:74), a man selling implants explained that women are valued for their appearance much more than men are and therefore it makes sense for women to change their image in order to please a man. Although there was "very little serious safety research on breast implants and even less understanding of their short- and long-term physical effects," some doctors gave women the impression that such research had been done and that it had demonstrated the safety of the implants. A group of American doctors lobbying for the implants "even diagnosed small breasts as a 'disease'" (Regush 1993:94). It took a long time for the research indicating the harmful effects of these implants to reach the public and even longer for government action to limit their use. Moreover, while breast cancer affects one in nine Canadian women, breast cancer research receives one-twenty-fifth the money the National Cancer Institute allocates to research (Williams 1994).

## Birth Control

Women have never meekly accepted the practices of the medical profession or relied exclusively on professionals to define women's health. Collectively and individually, women have struggled to control their own health and care. The history of women's health is a history of women's active participation in shaping the conditions of health and care for themselves and their families (see Armstrong, Choiniere, and Day 1993; Kleiber and Light 1978; McDonnell and Valverde 1985; Montreal Health Press, 1990).

Pregnancy and birth are examples of this. Issues of definition and control begin with conception. In *A History of Contraception*, McLaren (1992:3) explains that there has "always been a concern to influence or shape fertility, to reduce or increase conceptions and births" and fertility control is best understood as "a contested outcome"(1991:4). Women have been central protagonists in this contest because reproductive decisions have much more obvious consequences for women than for men. Throughout history, women have developed means to encourage or discourage contraception, often flouting the law in doing so. The laws they flouted were largely male-designed. Feminist theorist O'Brien (1981:49) argues that because men have a more tenuous connection to reproduction, there have been "centuries of strenuous masculine activity to negate the uncertainty of fatherhood, activity of which the institution of marriage is only the most obvious example."

Physicians claiming specialized knowledge of what they define as primarily a biological issue have been particularly prominent in this continuing contest.

Physicians struggled to become the main gatekeepers to birth control and abortion and were successful in doing so until recently. It is still doctors who determine access to the birth control pill and their prescription patterns may have as much to do with their own race, class, and age as they do with an assessment of physical response and scientific evidence. Although doctors no longer legally control access to abortion, primarily as a result of women's individual and collective efforts to change the legislation, in practice women can gain access to abortions only if doctors agree to perform them. Here, too, whether physicians agree to perform an abortion may be related more to the class, age, and sex of the patient than to an assessment of physiological consequences.

## Infertility

It is physicians who define what constitutes infertility and determine which women will have access to which new reproductive technologies. The medical profession now defines "primary" infertility as the "inability to conceive within six months to one year of regular intercourse without contraception" (Rehner 11989:15). After this very brief period of unprotected sex—a period in which a whole variety of factors ranging from exhaustion and tension to old chemicals from the birth control pill and from other medical treatments can interfere with fertility—physicians may initiate complex medical treatments that can significantly alter women's lives. Sexual intercourse may be scheduled by the physician, often with the assistance of chemicals or sperm produced through masturbation may be inserted into the vagina by the doctor. Eggs may be surgically removed from one of the ovaries, fertilized in a glass dish with sperm from the male, and replaced in the uterus or the fertilized egg may be inserted into another woman under contract to carry the child, a woman usually called a surrogate mother. If conception takes place, and this is a big "if" given that in vitro fertilization has a one in ten "success" rate, throughout pregnancy the woman will be continually monitored, treated, and instructed by the doctor. "The treatments may go on for months. They will be time-consuming and expensive and may involve considerable risk to health and emotional stability" (Beck-Gersheim 1989:35). They will all be under the doctor's control. Here, too, women have been resisting medical control. The Royal Commission on New Reproductive Technologies is just one consequence of their efforts, and it may do little to limit doctors' power.

More than one feminist researcher has suggested that doctors use this control to restrict access to those women who meet physicians' criteria for good mothers, criteria that emphasize race, age, heterosexual relationships, and middle-class lifestyles. Moreover, much of this technology uses procedures that may well be dangerous to women's health, procedures that have not been exposed to the kind of scientific research on which physicians base their claims. For example, as

Sherwin (1992:125) points out, the "bioethics literature has not considered the chemical similarities between clomid, an artifical hormone that is commonly used to increase women's rate of ovulation and DES, a drug that has belatedly been implicated as carcinogenic for the offspring of women who were prescribed it decades before." Yet the way these technologies have been developed and used allows physicians not only to apply experimental treatments to women but also to tell women how to behave and how to understand their bodies from before conception until well after birth (Bercovitch 1986; Brodribb 1986; Coffey 1986; Lippman 1986; Overall 1986 and 1987 and Rehner 1989). The more these technologies are used, the more they become acceptable and necessary, just as many "forms of surgery on women's reproductive systems have already been marketed as routine and virtually essential: hysterectomy, caesarean section and episiotomy are well-known examples" (Beck-Gernsheim 1989:28).

## Pregnancy and Childbirth

Although many women conceive without a physician's help or advice, few go through pregnancy without regular consultation with a physician. An increasing number have their pregnancy surveilled through tests such as amniocentesis and ultrasound. In many parts of the world, midwives assist women throughout pregnancy and childbirth. Although electronic surveillance and other forms of intervention are less frequent, survival rates for mother and child are often as high as or higher than those in Canada.

Midwives were common in the early days of this country. However, from the earliest period of European settlement, physicians sought to gain a monopoly over attendance at pregnancy and birth. They claimed midwives were dangerous but they also recognized that midwives were a significant threat to physicians' incomes (Biggs 1990:26-27). Physicians were especially concerned about the wealthy women who gave birth in urban areas: they expended little energy in limiting midwives who practiced in remote areas and in native communities.

By 1865, physicians in Ontario had successfully lobbied the state to grant them the exclusive right to attend childbirth, and, by the end of the century, other provinces had followed suit (Biggs 1990). Their success reflected their political strength more than the effectiveness of their treatment. In 1919, a Saskatchewan medical officer reported that "maternal mortality was much higher in the 50 percent of confinements attended by medical men." Moreover, "a very large number of women were confined without either nurse or doctor in attendance, and in these cases maternal mortality was much lower." When the officer presented this data to a group of physicians, he "was strongly taken to task by some of the members for even compiling the figures" (in Cayley 1985:15). Scientific evidence and women's health did not seem to be their only concerns.

Although doctors increasingly attended births, "until 1938, most births in Ontario took place at home and after that date most took place in hospital" (Oppenheimer 1990:51). The transfer to hospitals coincided with a reduction in both maternal and infant mortality rates, but this improvement was at least as much a result of better living conditions as it was of medical treatment (Oppenheimer 1990:51).

Managed births involved increasingly complicated interventions from medical practitioners. One intervention led to another: pain relief procedures had to be counteracted by other drugs that induced more pain that led to further pain relief that limited women's capacity to push. This could mean the baby must be delivered by forceps (Hunsburger 1992:82). Treatments to induce labour, shaves, enemas, the strapping of women to tables in delivery rooms where admittance was restricted to medical personnel, anaesthetics, and episiotomies occurred frequently more for the convenience of the medical practitioners than for the health of the patient. Some of these practices had no beneficial purpose for the patient and some were harmful (Oakley 1980). All could be seen as a means of increasing control over the women giving birth.

One woman interviewed for Hunsburger's (1992:57) study of pregnancy and childbirth reported that, when a nurse informed a doctor who had ordered an episiotomy that the woman did not want an episiotomy, he responded with "Who's delivering that baby?" Earlier, when the same doctor countered the same woman's request not to be forced to lie flat on her back with the same question, she had responded "I am!"

Indeed, individually and collectively, women have increasingly objected to the transformation of pregnancy and childbirth into medical events controlled by doctors. They have been successful in many of their efforts. In a growing number of hospitals, women can choose the kinds of births they want and the kinds of people with whom they want to share the experience. More and more alternatives to hospital delivery rooms are available, and birthing centres have become increasingly common. In Ontario, a group of women has been successful in breaking the physicians' monopoly over attendance at pregnancy and birth. As of 1993, midwives will be licensed to "catch" babies at home, in birthing centres or in hospitals. The practice of midwifery will be based on the assumption that pregnancy is a state of health and birth a normal process; that women should have a choice about both their caregiver and place of birth and that care should be woman-centred, non-authoritarian, continuous, and personalized, a far cry from medically managed births that have been common in the postwar period (Task Force on the Implementation of Midwifery in Ontario 1987). Moreover, midwives will be paid by the state, and this will make it more possible for women of all classes to have access to such care. Special programs for Aboriginal midwives have been developed to ensure that Native women will also be served. Registration procedures are being designed in ways that will encourage women trained in other countries to acquire a license to practice here. This could mean that women from non-English and French backgrounds will be able to find a midwife who speaks their language and who understands their traditional birth practices.

All this is not to suggest that women have received no benefit from developments in medicine. Certainly some research and medical practice have helped women survive pregnancy and childbirth, breast cancer, and ovarian cancer. They have helped some women control their fertility and live active lives in spite of illness and disability. They may have helped women live longer than men. It is not suggested that medical doctors always or only use their power to control women; however, medicine is not practiced the same way when the patients are women as it is when the patients are men, and that it is more likely to be used to control women than to control men. Medical treatment can be harmful to women's health, especially when control is at stake. Physicians have frequently used women's specific reproductive capacities as a way to control women rather than as a means of providing women with control over their own lives.

## HEALTH AND HOMES

Physicians' offices and hospitals treat illness, or at least what is defined as illness, but the conditions for health are primarily created outside the health care system. Households are particularly important in these terms, to a large extent because they form the basic economic units in our society. They can also be the major source of the social support that is central to well-being.

Economic circumstances are critical in creating the conditions for health. Food, shelter, clothing, recreation, and social support are major determinants of health and all but social support cost money. A large number of women living in households below the poverty line lack access to many of those things that make it easier, or even possible, to be healthy. Even those families that live above the poverty line may not be able to afford the conditions necessary for health. In at least one study (Heller 1986:31), a majority of women said they need more money for health treatment and supplies not covered by insurance and for healthy food or other health-related items.

### Lone-parent Women

Most of the poor are women. Women account for 59 percent of all those over 18 years of age who live in poverty (National Council of Welfare 1993:Table 24) and the disparity is even greater among those parenting alone. In 1991, 15 percent of the households with children under age 18 were headed by lone-parent females, 62 percent of whom lived below the poverty line. This was a significant increase over the 58 percent who were poor in 1980 (National Council of

Welfare 1993:8). Aboriginal women and women from groups classified as a visible minority are more likely than other women to be lone parents and thus more likely to be poor (Lindsay 1992:14). Lone-parent families headed by women spend less than other families on food, clothing, shelter, household furnishings and operations, recreation, transportation, reading, education, and life insurance. They are also less likely than other families to have a washing machine or a dishwasher, a clothes dryer or a microwave oven, an air conditioner or a home computer, a smoke detector or a fire extinguisher. In other words, many cannot afford those things that make people healthy and that can reduce stress. Moreover, women heading such families have fewer social contacts and feel more socially isolated than do women in other households (Lindsay 1992:42-43). That lone-parent families with a female head spend more money per person and a significantly higher proportion of income on health and personal care, while spending less on all other items, suggests that women in such households face more health problems than do those in other households (Lindsay 1992:Table 4.2). As Beardshaw explained in a report to a Winnipeg conference on women, "When women's economic position and low status within society is combined with poverty, the effect on women's health in particular can be absolutely devastating" (quoted in Harding 1986:81).

It is not only lone-parent women who live below the poverty line. Women are also more likely than men to be poor both when they are young and single and when they are old and alone. Women's higher poverty rates reflect the fact that women are paid less than men when they work in the labour force, are less likely than men to have full-time full-year paid jobs, and are less likely than men to have jobs that include a good pension for old age, although women on average do live longer than men. Part of the explanation for women's more limited access to paid jobs and good pensions can be found in their primary responsibility for households and children (Armstrong and Armstrong 1993).

This domestic work of women not only limits their possibilities for paid employment but also adds significantly to their stress. It explains why women "appear to be more consistently time stressed than men" (Frederick 1993:7) and helps explain why women visit doctors more often than men.

## Mothering

Motherwork can be particularly harmful to women's health. Statistics Canada found that "mothers on maternity leave reported feeling exceptionally stressed for time. Having to meet the demands of a new baby left 72% stressed for time" (Frederick 1993:7). The way child-care work is done contributes to the stress. "In addition to having little power to define and control the work of childrearing, isolation from other adults and a lack of feedback on 'job performance' can make motherwork especially stressful" (Lowe 1989:41). Lack of sleep and heavy workloads often lead to chronic fatigue (Duval 1985:9). In her study of early mothering, Rossiter (1988:89) reports that a woman named Maria experienced bouts of depression after the birth of her first child. This depression was largely attributable to her isolation, and both contributed to other signs of poor health. Crying as she talked, Maria said, "I might go out today, but I have no energy. It's always one thing or the other, but I don't know. I'm just so fed up right now" (Rossiter 1988:90). Child care can mean ten-hour work days, "the strain of unrelenting tasks," and exposure to every childhood disease (Duffy, Mandell, and Pupo 1989:57).

Children can bring great joy, but this is more likely when women have help in their child-care work and when they can afford to leave their child-care work for at least a brief period of time. Few women receive regular help from their husbands or from state-supported child care. Many cannot afford alternative care; although women often do support each other in carrying out their child-care work. Some women have gotten together to organize day-care centres and other services to provide support.

## Women as Caregivers

Women are not only primarily responsible for children; they are also the main caregivers for the disabled and the elderly. In her cross-Canada study, Heller (1986:48) found that, although many women feel positive about caring for others, more than two in five looking after elderly relatives said they needed more help in order to carry out their health-care work. This study was undertaken before the most recent move to send patients home early from hospitals and to release many from institutions. The growing number of people at home requiring care likely means that a majority of women need more help in order to avoid putting their own health at risk (Armstrong 1993).

Disabled dependents frequently require "extraordinary, constant care" that can place a severe strain on the caregiver. This is particularly the case if the caregiver has not been trained for the job—a likely situation for many women—and if the caregiver works alone—the most common condition for women at home. With the deinstitutionalization that is very much a part of the new stress on health promotion, more and more women are caring for people who need skilled attention. It takes practice to learn how to assist a person into bed, education to learn how to change bandages and dressings, skill to insert a feeding tube. Without training, women may be putting both themselves and those they are caring for at risk.

Women do much more in the household than care for the elderly, the disabled, and the young. It is mainly women who do the regular household chores and these can be both stressful and dangerous. "More than one-half of full-time working wives in dual earner families with children at home are solely responsible for all daily household chores" and the other women do the majority of the domestic work as well (Marshall 1993:11). Housework is often experienced as monotonous and boring, invisible and repetitive, fragmented and strenuous (Duffy, Mandell, and Pupo 1989; Luxton 1980). Such work can increase stress levels, reduce resistance to disease, and result in more specific health problems.

## Home Health Hazards

Women also face more visible health hazards in the home. As Rosenberg (1990) points out, many of the cleaning products used in the household are dangerous. They can produce hazardous fumes, cause rashes or other allergic reactions, and can kill if injested. Many of the insecticides and gardening products used in the household can cause cancer and birth defects and damage the brain or the liver. Much of the equipment used in the household is unsafe: household accidents are common. New electrical equipment, such as the microwave and the computer, can be dangerous (Brodeur 1989). The hazards are increased when women do industrial sewing or other paid work at home because these processes frequently produce frequently dangerous dust and chemicals.

The combination of all this domestic work can literally make women sick. In Heller's study, women reported that they had no time to look after their own health, to stay in bed, or to visit the doctor. This is particularly so for the majority of women who have another job in the labour force. A woman interviewed for a study of work and family (Macbride-King 1990) said, "I find that with the responsibilities of job, housework, child care, quality family time, other family responsibilities, etc., that it is usually my private needs—personal relaxation time—that are sacrificed. Social life is severely cut back and private time with my husband also suffers. These lacks can lead to mental exhaustion. Sometimes I feel stretched very thinly."

The women in Heller's study also report that they need more moral and social support. "Many want more emotional support from family and friends; others want more recognition, praise or thanks" (1986:31). Conversely, Gannage (1986) in her study of garment workers, found that social support provided by the families of immigrant women made a critical difference to their survival and their health.

## Abusive Relationships

Many women, however, lack such support. Indeed, other household members may constitute a danger to women's health. The physical abuse of women and the sexual abuse of children in the home is far too common (Macload 1987). "Our supposed haven, the home, unfortunately offers us little protection, since most assaults on women and children are by known assailants. If a husband, friend, or relative does not get us there, a stranger might" (Wolfe and Guberman1985:9). Studies of wife abuse indicate that from one in ten to one in four women were abused within the last year and as many as one in three has been abused at some time (Dekeseredy and Hinch 1991: Table 2.1). A Statistics Canada survey indicates that half of all women have experienced some form of physical or sexual abuse at least once in their adult lives (*The Toronto Star*, 1993). Those with disabilities are particularly at risk. Assault causes more than physical injury. It frequently leads to depression, confusion, sleep disturbances, erratic mood swings, eating disorders, and anxiety.

As unemployment and poverty levels rise, tensions in households increase as do women's chances of being attacked. At least one study has indicated that unemployed men are twice as likely as other men to abuse their wives (Lupri 1990). At the same time, because women's economic alternatives are increasingly limited, more women may have little choice about staying in abusive relationships (Morell 1993).

For many women, households are not havens in a heartless world. Rather, they constitute risky workplaces. Poverty can mean women lack adequate food, shelter, and clothing. Living above the poverty line does not guarantee that women have enough money to buy what they need for their health. The isolation of the home increases the danger of the workplace and reduces the opportunities for support. The heavy workload, especially when combined with a second job in the labour force, means women face high levels of stress and exhaustion. Women's low wages in the labour force and limited job opportunities often mean that many women do not have the opportunity to improve their conditions for health in the home.

## HAZARDS IN THE WORKPLACE

Women who have labour force jobs frequently enjoy better health than women who work exclusively at home. The poorer health of women without paid work may partly reflect the nature of the work in the home. Paid work can offer women some economic independence, some contact with others, and some sense of accomplishment. Many of the women at home who are in poor health have been made sick by their labour force jobs. Paid work too can be harmful to women.

The health hazards women face in the labour force tend to be much less visible than those faced by men. There are two reasons for this invisibility. First, the hazards women face are less likely to result in immediate death or obvious injury that is clearly a result of the work. Men in construction, for example, are far too frequently killed or disabled by accidents on the job, but few waitresses or clerical workers face such risks. Computer operators frequently develop headaches from watching a screen all day and waitresses often develop pains in their legs from standing all day in the high heels required by the employer. Such health hazards are not only less visibly linked to the work but are often dismissed simply as women's ills or as "all in their minds." For example, Mergler (1992:38) found that "in this microelectronics plant as in others, affective difficulties and disorders were attributed to women's individual or collective psychological problems."

Second, "research into occupational health has tended to exclude women and research into women's health has tended to exclude occupational variables" (Messing 1991:7). Moreover, much of the material that does discuss women is based on studies of men that ignore the specifics of women's work and women's health (Messing 1991:7). Women have often been hesitant to demand such research because they are afraid that it will be used to limit where and when they can work. Research on pregnant women, for example, has been used as a justification for excluding all women from some work even though any conditions that are dangerous for a fetus are dangerous for everyone and even though some research indicates that males too may transmit, through their sperm, problems created by their working conditions (Stellman 1977).

## Clerical Work

In spite of these limitations, feminist efforts mean there is a growing body of research indicating that women face a wide variety of health hazards in their paid work (see Health and Welfare Canada, 1992). Clerical work provides just one example of the kinds of hazards women face in their paid jobs. Almost one in three women in the labour force does clerical work. Although this "white collar" work often seems relatively harmless, it constitutes a range of risks for women. Very few of the women doing clerical work are secretaries who do a variety of chores in a bright office next to the boss. Most are bank tellers, telephone operators, computer operators, and mail sorters, or they are in similar jobs that are generally dull, repetitive, boring, and closely supervised (Armstrong and Armstrong 1983).

Much of the work is done at high speed under close supervision. Telephone operators and airline booking agents have only seconds to answer calls. They are required to answer questions with prescribed scripts and to deal with each call in a prescribed time. Their speed is monitored by machine, and their calls frequently listened to by supervisors (Armstrong and Armstrong 1983). A study of postal workers found that women who sort mail at a rapid pace, under close supervision, report more depression, poorer mental health, and more physical symptoms than other women and men (Lowe and Northcott 1986). Although we often associate stress with high-level managers, the research indicates that high-speed work, especially when combined with low levels of control or close supervision, induces high levels of stress. Women office workers who have nonsupportive supervisors are more likely to have heart desease. Women who have few rest periods, do repetitive work, have little opportunity to talk to other women, and face constant demands are more likely to have premature babies (Messing 1991:42). Women's responses to the stress and high-paced work have often been dismissed as hysteria, but research indicates that their symptoms are very much related to the conditions of work (Messing 1991:45).

Much clerical work requires women to stand or sit in the same position all day. This immobility can cause pains in the legs and varicose veins; it impedes blood circulation and causes swelling; it can contribute to miscarriage and still-births. The problems can be made worse by dress requirements that mean women have to wear shoes that provide little support or clothes that are tight or uncomfortable (Messing 1991:49-50; Stellman and Henifin 1983).

Today, most clercial workers spend a great deal of their time at video display terminals. Even though research indicates that radiation may not be a major problem for those who sit in front of a screen for long hours, there is clear evidence that there are other major risks associated with the work. Computers mean that women are no longer required to stop frequently in order to adjust margins, make corrections, put in new paper, or look up spellings. Instead, they just keep typing. Although other countries have been concerned for a long time with the problems caused by repeating the same motion over and over again, repetitive strain injury is just now being recognized in Canada (Armstrong 1984). Computers require women to type constantly at high speed in ways that can leave their muscles permanently damaged. Screens can also cause eye fatigue and reduce the capacity to distinguish colours (Messing 1991:60). The stress associated with the work may be the reason higher miscarriage rates have been reported for women working long hours in front of a computer. Like other high-speed work, computer work often leads to depression, anxiety, and an inability to concentrate. Stress also reduces immunity to a whole range of diseases.

Although clerical work is often thought of as clean work—hence the white collar—clerical workers are frequently exposed to a range of chemicals from cleaners, glues, carpets, solvents, inks, photocopy machines, and paper. Many clerical workers are regularly required to lift heavy bundles of papers and dirty, cumbersome files. Offices often have noise levels equivalent to or higher than those in factories, levels that can damage hearing permanently and increase stress. Lighting and equipment can be harmful: much of it is not designed for the worker's health (DeKeseredy and Hinch 1991: Table 5.2; Stellman and Henifin 1983).

In addition to pressure from the work and risk from the physical environment, clerical workers are often exposed to constant pressure from customers. Clerical workers are the front line, and if things go wrong, clerical workers are often blamed by the customers even though they may have had little choice about the deterioration in services or the long lines at the bank. Clerical workers, like other women workers, are also exposed on the job to sexual harassment from customers, from other workers, and from employers. "Sexual harasssment is often made worse in situations where supervisors or employers know of its existence but refuse to take action to stop it" (DeKeseredy and Hinch 1991:103).

Finally, clerical workers are under the constant threat of job loss. The new electronic technologies are replacing workers with machines. The many bank closures reflect this. Fear of unemployment adds considerably to stress levels and increases the pressure to work harder at the job.

While other jobs women do in the labour force involve risks particular to the job, the example of clerical work indicates the range of hazards women face in their paid work. The risks are often different from those of men, in part because most women and men do different work in different workplaces. Risks are also often different for women of colour because these women are disproportionately slotted into the worst jobs. Many of the hazards women face receive little attention, relief, or compensation, in part because women are not seen as "real" workers. Moreover, most of the women who do paid work have two jobs—one at home and one in the labour force. Two jobs necessarily means more stress and less time for leisure.

## CONCLUSION

This article has only touched on the many health hazards women face in their two jobs and on the kinds of treatment women receive from the health-care system. In this short space it was not possible to cover such issues as the pressure on women to be thin (Szekely 1988), the violence women face on the streets, the particular problems faced by women of colour and women with disabilities (Dhruvarajan 1990; Stewart Percival and Epperly 1992) or the health-care work women do in the labour force.

It is designed to introduce many of the major health issues for women and to invite readers to further explore questions about women's health. It is also intended as a warning that women's possibilities for health are deteriorating along with the economy and that the struggle for women's health is far from over.

## NOTES

1  Calculated from Statistics Canada, *91 Census Occupation* (Cat. no. 93-327) Ottawa: Minister of Industry, Science and Technology, 1993, Table l.

## BIBLIOGRAPHY

Adams, Parveen and Cowie, Elizabeth *The Woman in Question*. Cambridge: MIT Press, 1990.

Armstrong, Pat *Labour Pains. Women's Work in Crisis*. Toronto: Women's Press, 1984.

_____ "Closer to Home: More Work for Women." Paper distributed by the Hospital Employee's Union: British Columbia, 1993.

Armstrong, Pat and Armstrong, Hugh *A Working Majority. What Women Must Do For Pay.* Ottawa: Supply and Services Canada for the Canadian Advisory Council on the Status of Women, 1983.

_____ "Sex and the Professions in Canada." *Journal of Canadian Studies.* 27(1, Spring):118-135, 1992.

_____ *The Double Ghetto: Canadian Women and Their Segregated Work.* 3d ed. Toronto: McClelland and Stewart, 1993.

Armstrong, Pat, Choiniere, Jacqueline and Day, Elaine *Vital Signs. Nursing in Transition.* Toronto: Garamond, 1993.

Bacchi, Carol Lee. *Same Difference.* Sydney: Allen and Unwin, 1990.

Beck-Gernsheim, Elisabeth. "From the Pill to Test-Tube Babies: New Options, New Pressures in Reproductive Behaviour," In *Healing Technology,* edited by Kathryn Strother Ratcliff (ed.) Ann Arbor: The University of Michigan Press, 1989.

Bercovitch, Joan. "Civil Law Regulation of Reproductive Technologies." *Canadian Journal of Women and the Law.* 1(2):385-406, 1986.

Biggs, C. Lesley "The Case of the Missing Midwives: A History of Midwifery in Ontario from 1795-1900." In *Delivering Motherhood,* edited by Katherine Arnup, Andree Levesque and Ruth Roach Pierson, 20/35. London: Routledge, 1990.

Birke, Lynda. *Women, Feminism and Biology.* Brighton: Harvester, 1986.

Blishen, Bernard, *Doctors in Canada: The Changing World of Medical Practice.* Toronto: University of Toronto Press, 1991.

Bobet, Ellen. "Indian Mortality." *Canadian Social Trends.* 15 (Winter):11-14, 1989.

Brodeur, Paul. *Currents of Death: Power Lines, Computer Terminals and the Attempt to Cover Up the Threat to Your Health.* New York: Simon and Shuster, 1989.

Brodribb, Somer. "Off the Pedestal and onto the Block? Motherhood, Reproductive Technologies and the Canadian State." *Canadian Journal of Women and the Law.* 1(2), 1986.

Cayley, David. *Doctoring the Family.* Montreal: CBC, 1985.

Coffey, Mary Anne. "Of Father Born. A Lesbian Feminist Catalogue of the Ontario Law Reform Commission Recommendations on Artificial Insemination." *Canadian Journal of Women and the Law.* 1(2), 1986.

Cooperstock, Ruth and Lennard, Henry. "Role Strains and Tranquilizer Use." In *Health and Canadian Society, 2d ed.,* edited by Coburn, D'Arcy, Torrance and New (eds.) Markham: Fitzhenry and Whiteside, 1987.

Dekeseredy, Walter and Hinch, Ronald. *Woman Abuse*. Toronto: Thompson, 1991.

Dhruvarajan, Voraja. *Women and Well-Being*. Montreal: McGill-Queen's University Press for CRIAW, 1990.

Fausto-Sterling, Anne. *Myths of Gender. Biological Theories About Women and Men*. New York: Bruce Books, 1985.

Findlay, Deborah. "The Good, the Normal and the Healthy: The Social Construction of Medical Knowledge About Women." *The Canadian Journal of Sociology*. 18(2, Spring):115-136, 1993.

Firestone, Shulamith. *The Dialectic of Sex*. New York: Bantam, 1970.

Frederick, Judith. "Tempus Fugit...Are You Time Crunched?" *Canadian Social Trends*. 31 (Winter): 6-10, 1993.

Haraway, Donna. *Primate Visions. Gender, Race and Nature in the World of Modern Science*. New York: Routledge, 1989.

Harding, Jim. "Mood-modifiers and Elderly Women in Canada: The Medicalization of Poverty." In *Adverse Effects*, edited by Kathleen McDonnell, 51-86, Toronto: Women's Press, 1986.

Health and Welfare Canada. Proceedings of the Research Round Table on Gender and Workplace Health. Ottawa: Office of the Senior Advisor, Status of Women, Health and Weflare Canada, 1992.

Heller, Anita Fochs. *Health and Home: Women as Health Guardians*. Ottawa: Canadian Advisory on the Status of Women, 1986.

Hunsberger, Winfred Wallace. *One Woman to Another. Canadian Women Talk About* Pregnancy and Childbirth. Saskatoon: Fifth House Publishers, 1992.

Jannage, Charlene. *Double Day: Double Bind*. Toronto: Women's Press, 1986.

Kaufert, Patricia and Gilbert, Penny. "Medicalization and the Menopause." In *Health and Canadian Society. 2d ed.*, edited by Coburn, D'Arcy, Torrance and New, Markham: Fitzhenry and Whiteside, 1987.

Kleiber, Nancy and Light, Linda. *Caring for Ourselves: An Alternative Structure for Health Care*. Vancouver: BC Public Health, 1978.

Lindsay, Colin. *Lone-Parent Families in Canada*. (Cat. no. 89-522E) Ottawa: Minister of Industry, Science and Technology, 1992.

Lippman, Abby. "Access to Prenatal Screening Services: Who Decides?" *Canadian Journal of Women and the Law*. 1(2):434-445, 1986.

Lorber, Judith and Farrell, Susan. *The Social Construction of Gender*. London: Sage, 1991.

Lowe, Graham. *Women, Paid/Unpaid Work and Stress. New Directions for Research*. Ottawa: Canadian Advisory Council on the Status of Women, 1989.

Lowe, Graham and Northcott, Herbert. *Under Pressure: A Study of Job Stress.* Toronto: Garamond, 1986.

Lupri, Eugen. "Male Violence in the Home." In *Canadian Social Trends*, edited by Craig McKie and Keith Thompson, Toronto: Thompson, 1990.

Marshall, Katherine. "Dual Earners. Who's Responsible for Housework?" *Canadian Social Trends.* 31(Winter):11-15, 1993.

MacBride-King, Judith. *Work and Family: Employment Challenge of the '90s.* Ottawa: Conference Board of Canada, 1990.

Macleod, Linda. *Battered But Not Beaten...Preventing Wife Battering in Canada.* Ottawa: Canadian Advisory Council on the Status of Women, 1987.

McDonnell, Kathleen. "Introduction. Finding a Common Ground," pp.1-8 in McDonnell, ed., 1986.

McDonnell, Kathleen and Valverde, Mariana. *The Health Sharing Book.* Toronto: Women's Press, 1985.

McLaren, Angus. *A History of Contraception.* Oxford: Blackwell, 1992.

Mergler, Donna. "Women in the Microelectronics Industry," pp. 37-39 in Health and Welfare Canada, 1992.

Messing, Karen. *Occupational Safety and Health Concerns of Canadian Women.* Ottawa: Women's Bureau, Labour Canada, 1991.

Mitchinson, Wendy. *The Nature of Their Bodies. Women and Their Doctors in Victorian Canada.* Toronto: University of Toronto Press, 1991.

Montreal Health Press. *Menopause: A Well Woman Book.* Montreal: Montreal Health Press, 1990.

Morrell, Catherine. Returning to Abusive Situations: Impact of Selected Factors Concerning Social Assistance on Women's Decision. Ottawa: CRIAW, 1993.

National Council of Welfare. *Poverty Profile. Update for 1991.* Mimeo: Ottawa, 1993.

Nicholson, Linda, ed. *Feminism/Postmodernism.* New York: Routledge, 1990.

Oakley, Ann. *Women Confined.* Oxford: Martin Robertson, 1980.

O'Brien, Mary. *The Politics of Reproduction.* London: Routledge and Kegan Paul, 1981.

Oppenheimer, Jo. "Childhood in Ontario: The Transition From Home to Hospital in the Early Twentieth Century," pp. 51-74 in Arnup et al., 1990.

Overall, Christine. "Reproductive Ethics: Feminist and Non-Feminist Approaches." *Canadian Journal of Women and the Law.* 1(2):271-278, 1986.

———— "Sexuality, Parenting and Reproductive Choices." *Resources for Feminist Research.* 16(3, September):42-45, 1987.

Regush, Nicholas. *Safety Last*. Toronto: Key Porter Books, 1993.

Rehner, Jan. *Infertility. Old Myths. New Meanings*. Toronto: Second Story Press, 1989.

Rhode, Deborah, ed., *Theoretical Perspectives on Sexual Difference*. New Haven: Yale University Press, 1990.

Rosenberg, Harriet. "The Home is the Workplace: Hazards, Stress and Pollutants in the Household," In *Through the Kitchen Window*, edited by Meg Luxton, Harriet Rosenberg and Sedef Arat-Koc, pp.57-80. Toronto: Garamond, 1990.

Rossiter, Amy. *From Private to Public. A Feminist Exploration of Mothering*. Toronto: Women's Press, 1988.

Sherwin, Susan. *No Longer Patient. Feminist Ethics and Health Care*. Philadelphia: Temple University Press, 1992.

Shorter, Edward. *Bedside Manners*. New York: Simon and Shuster, 1985.

Statistics Canada. *91 Census. Occupation*. (Cat no. 93-327). Ottawa: Minister of Industry, Science and Technology, 1992.

Stellman, Jeanne. *Women's Work: Women's Health*. New York: Pantheon, 1977.

Stellman, Jeanne and Henifin, Mary Sue. *Office Work Can Be Dangerous to Your Health*. New York: Pantheon, 1983.

Stewart, Houston; Percival, Beth and Epperly, Elizabeth. *The More We Get Together*. Charlottetown: Gynergy Books, 1992.

Szekely, Eva. *Never Too Thin*. Toronto: Women's Press, 1988.

Task Force on the Implementation of Midwifery. *Report of the Task Force on the Implementation of Midwifery in Ontario*. Ontario: Ministry of Health, 1987.

"Violence To Women." *The Toronto Star*, 6 Dec. 1993.

Williams, Paul; Domnick-Pierre, Karen; Vayda, Eugene; Stevenson, Michael and Burke, Mike. The Feminization of Canadian Medicine: Implications for Health Care Delivery. North York: York University Institute for Social Research, 1990.

Williams, Penelope. "Shadow of Doubt. Breast Cancer: Special Report." *Homemakers Magazine*. March:14-32, 1994.

Wolfe, Margie and Guberman, Connie. "Introduction." In *No Safe Place*, edited by Connie Guberman and Margie Wolfe, 9-18. Toronto: Women's Press, 1985.

# A CHRONOLOGY
# OF WOMEN IN CANADA

*William Whitla*

c 25,000-
16,000 BCE
Peoples began to settle in North America during the last Ice Age. Archaeological evidence of habitation found at Bluefish Caves in the Northern Yukon includes chipped stone artifacts embedded in deposits with the bones of extinct fossil animals (mammoths and bison, fish and birds), which exhibit marks of stone tools. Carbon dating indicates a period between 18,000 and 12,000 years ago, and hence suggests some form of habitation or intrusion of hunting parties in the late Pleistocene period.

before 1000
Beothuk Indian and Dorset Inuit peoples were neighbours in sub-arctic Labrador and northern Newfoundland from 3,000 – 2,500 BCE and continued there until about 1,500 CE. In both cultures women shared in the decision making and were responsible for the cutting and drying of meat, and the preparation of hides for boats, shelter, and clothing. These peoples were identified as "Skraelings" in the *Graenlendinga Saga* and in the revision and partial expansion of that saga, *Eiriks Saga*, both of which refer to events around the year 1,000.

c 1004-7
Gudrid Thorbjørnsdatter (b. 980) was the first recorded European woman to colonize North America. Her life is recorded in both the *Graenlendinga Saga* and *Eiriks Saga*. She had married

Thorstein, the son of Eric the Red, and accompanied him on an unsuccessful trip to Vinland (very probably northern Newfoundland). After his death she married Thorfinn Karlsefni and accompanied him on a colonizing expedition to Vinland, probably to the site at L'Anse aux Meadows, where they settled for three years, and where she bore her son, Snorri. She later returned to Iceland, made a pilgrimage to Rome, returned to Iceland, and became a nun and anchoress. Another woman, Freydis, a daughter of Eric the Red, also made two expeditions to Vinland; in one she was involved in treachery, murder, and robbery (*Graenlendinga Saga*, 8) and in another she fought single-handed against the Skraelings when pregnant (*Eiriks Saga*, 11). Excavations at L'Anse have uncovered a spindle and other weaving tools dating from the Viking invasions.

*1500s* Iroquois society in North America was matrilineal: establishing kin depended on the maternal line. It was also matrilocal: a male, uniting with a female, moved in with the woman's kin. Iroquois women grew crops and held influential positions in the community. Such roles continue in the Iroquois confederacy to the present day.

*c 1600* The Constitution of the Iroquois Confederation of Nations guaranteed to women the sole right and power to regulate peace and war, and to select the tribal leaders. Those rights continue to this day.

*1617* Marie Rollet (d. 1649), the spouse and assistant of the apothecary and farmer, Louis Hébert, at Quebec, was the first married European woman to come to settle in New France permanently.

*1634* The Compagnie des Cent-Associés, was set up by Cardinal Richelieu to establish the French Empire in North America and began, with the help of agents of the entrepreneurs and the religious communities of France, to recruit young women from France to marry men in the colony of New France. Over the next years, 250 women were recruited.

*1639* Marie Guyard, who took the name Marie de l'Incarnation (1599–1672), founded the convent of the Ursulines at Quebec, the first in Canada, and supervised its construction. She became Superior of the order. Her 13,000 letters are important historical documents. Her work for the Native peoples was also highly influential, and included a dictionary of French and Algonquian. She was beatified in 1877 and canonized in 1990.

*1641*  Jeanne Mance (1606–73) arrived in Canada from France; she moved to Montreal to set up in 1643 its first medical dispensary, the Hôtel-Dieu, and so was the founder of nursing in Canada.

*1658*  Marguerite Bourgeoys (1620–1700), who had emigrated to Canada with Paul de Chomedey, Sieur de Maisonneuve, began educational work in Quebec. She was the first school teacher in Montreal of local children and First Nation girls. In 1669 she founded the secular (uncloistered) order of the *Congrégation de Notre Dame*. She was canonized in 1982.

*1663*  The first of some 800 "filles du roi," young girls of marriageable age, often beggars and orphans from Paris, were shipped to New France under French royal authority with a trousseau and dowry. A number of the "filles du roi" were taught by Marguerite Bourgeoys.

*1680*  Death of Kateri Tekakwitha (b. 1656), the "Lily of the Mohawks." Converted to Christianity by the Jesuits, she lived a life of simplicity, chastity, and heroism in the face of rejection by her people. She died at the mission at Chaughnawaga. She was the earliest First Nation person in North America to be a candidate for sainthood. She was beatified in 1980.

*c 1705*  Agathe de Saint-Père, Madame de Legardeur de Repentigny of Montreal (1657–1747), established the textile industry in Montreal by ransoming nine English weavers who had been captured when a supply ship went down. She had looms made and engaged apprentices, turning her home into a workshop with over twenty looms.

*1717*  Death of Thanadelthur, a Chippewa who had guided White explorers through Cree and Chippewyan territories in the northern prairies. She had negotiated peace between the Cree and Chippewyan peoples in Canada and had worked on relations between her peoples and the Hudson's Bay Company at York Factory. Hers is one of the few early documented lives of First Nation women.

*1734*  A Montreal slave, Marie-Joseph Angélique, about to be sold to another owner, attempted to escape and set a fire in the house. It could not be contained and eventually damaged half of Montreal. She was caught, tortured, and hanged. This first recorded resistance by a woman to slavery brought attention to the conditions of slaves in Canada.

| | |
|---|---|
| *1736* | Birth of Koñwatsi'Tsiaiéñni, Mary or Molly Brant (1736–96), Mohawk leader and sister of the hereditary chief of the Mohawks, Joseph Brant. In 1752 she was married, according to Mohawk rites, to Sir William Johnson and negotiated peaceful diplomatic relations between the Six Nations and the English loyalists during the period of the English-American wars. She died at Cataraqui, near Kingston, in 1796. |
| *1769* | Frances Brooke (1724–89), English writer, published the first novel written in Canada, *The History of Emily Montague*, an epistolary account of her experiences in the Quebec garrison when she was posted there with her husband (1760-68). |
| *1783* | More than 5,000 Blacks, having been promised land grants by the British, left the U.S. as United Empire Loyalists to live in the Maritimes, Quebec, and Ontario. They received either very small grants, poor land, or none at all. |
| | Rose Fortune (1744–1864), a Black woman, became the first woman police officer in North America and the British Empire, in Annapolis Royal, Nova Scotia. |
| *1793* | The importing of slaves was prohibited by the first parliament of Upper Canada in the same law that freed slaves 25 years old or more. Although the law did not completely abolish slavery, Upper Canada was the first British territory to legislate against it. |
| *1803* | Mary Fubbester, known as "the Orkney Lass," disguised as a man began work as a clerk in a Hudson's Bay trading post in Rupert's Land. In 1807 she was discovered and fired when she gave birth. |
| *1813* | Laura Ingersoll Secord (1775–1868), Canadian heroine of the War of 1812, learned from American troops billeted at her house at Queenston of the planned surprise attack on the British at Beaver Dams in the Niagara Peninsula. She drove her cow 19 miles through swamps and the American lines to warn Lieutenant James Fitzgibbon to take preparatory action. She had been born in Massachusetts but had gone to Canada with her parents at the time of the American Revolution. Her action was finally recognized in 1860 with the gift of £100. |
| *1823* | Madame Gilbertin, Canada's first woman prospector, discovered gold in the Chaudière River in Quebec. |
| *1824* | Julia Beckwith Hart (1796–1867), novelist, published the first novel in Canada by a person born in Canada, *St. Ursula's Convent; or, The Nun of Canada, Containing Scenes of Real Life*. It was written when she was 17. |

| | |
|---|---|
| *1825* | Presbyterian Women in Prince Town (Malpeque, P.E.I.) established The Prince Town Female Society for Propagating the Gospel and Other Religious Purposes. |
| *1829* | With the death of Shawnandithit (b. 1801), the Beothuk Indians of Newfoundland became extinct. She was the last speaker of Beothuk as a mother tongue. Her people, together with the Inuit of Labrador, had been about the year 1000 the first to have contact with the European colonizers. In the year before her death from tuberculosis she provided valuable information concerning the language and customs of her people. |
| *1834* | Slavery ended in all British territories on July 31. |
| *1835* | Catharine Parr Traill (1802–99) published *The Backwoods of Canada; being Letters from the Wife of an Emigrant Officer; Illustrative of the Domestic Economy of British America*. It included advice to settlers in Canada about the harsh realities of living, and recommendations for supplementing the diet with native plants. She also published *The Female Emigrant's Guide, and Hints on Canadian Housekeeping* (1854), and guides to the wild flowers of Canada (1868, 1885). |
| *1838* | Anna Brownell Jameson (1794–1860), Irish writer, art historian, and feminist, published *Winter Studies and Summer Rambles in Canada*, an account of her stay in Canada in 1836. |
| *1840* | Mrs. Wilson Abbott, a Black woman, established in Toronto the Queen Victoria Benevolent Society, the first organization to offer aid to Black women, indigents, and fugitive slaves. |
| *1844* | The first professional medical care was brought to the Red River Colony in Manitoba by four Sisters of Charity from Montréal. |
| *1850s* | Ruth Addams invented the cook stove and was the first Canadian woman to receive a patent. |
| *1851* | Mary Ann Shadd (1823–93) founded the Anti-Slavery Society in Toronto. In 1853 she was the first Black woman to establish and edit (until 1858) a newspaper in North America. Her *Provincial Freeman* was published in Windsor, Toronto, and later Chatham for Backs who had fled from the U.S. to Canada under the Fugitive Slave Law of 1850. She established schools in Windsor and was the first Black woman lecturer. After the Civil War she studied law at Howard University, Alabama. The first female law student there, she was denied her degree until 1883. She was also active in the National Women's Suffrage Association in the U.S. |

| | |
|---|---|
| *1852* | Susanna Moodie (1803–85), the sister of Catharine Parr Traill, published *Roughing it in the Bush* (1852; serially 1838–52), a study of pioneer conditions for women in Canada. She had already published works linking her with the anti-slavery campaign in the U.S. |
| *1854* | Abigail Becker (1830–1905), "the Heroine of Lake Erie," rescued the captain and six crew of the schooner *Conductor*, shipwrecked off Long Point. She waded into the water, encouraged them to swim separately to her, and hauled each exhausted sailor ashore. |
| *1855* | First concert of Dame Emma Albani (Marie Louise Emma Lajeunesse, 1847–1930), soprano, at age of eight. Her debut was in Verdi's *Un Ballo in Maschera* (1869), followed by a triumph in Bellini's *La Somnambula*, repeated in London, Paris, and New York. She was attached to Covent Garden in London but also sang at the Metropolitan Opera in New York. She toured Canada about a dozen times between 1883 and 1906. |
| *1857* | Miranda Barry (1794–1865) was appointed inspector-general of hospitals. She had from early youth disguised herself as a man, assuming the name of James Barry, and had graduated from Edinburgh University in medicine in 1812. She served in South Africa and in the Crimean War where she met Florence Nightingale. On coming to Canada she worked in the military hospitals to improve sanitary conditions and the quality of food and medical practice. Her gender was revealed only on her death. |
| *1860* | The Ontario Temperance Act prohibited women from selling liquor or working in public houses. |
| *1864* | The first anthology of Canadian poetry, *Selections from Canadian Poets*, edited by Edward Hartley Dewart, included selections from such women poets as Augusta Baldwyn, Margaret Gill Currie, Jennie E. Haight, Mary and Sarah Herbert, Clotilda Jennings, Helen Mar Johnson, Eleanora Leprohan, Susanna Moodie, and Pamela Vining Yule. |
| *1870* | Women in St. John, New Brunswick, organized the first Canadian Young Women's Christian Association (YWCA) that provided shelter, support, education, and recreation, and eventually set up boarding homes, soup kitchens, and shelters. |
| *1872* | The Ontario legislature passed the Married Women's Property Act that conferred on married women the right to their own earnings independent of the control of their husbands. |

1874    Letitia Youmans (1827–96) established a branch of the international Women's Christian Temperance Union in Picton, Ontario. It advocated the prohibition of alcohol as a means of ameliorating social ills. Realizing that their goals could not be achieved without political power, the WCTU was also instrumental in sponsoring some of the leaders in the suffrage and women's rights movements. Youmans became the first president of the Ontario WCTU in 1877 and the first national president in 1883.

1875    Grace Annie Lockhart was awarded a B. Sc. degree in science and English literature by Mount Allison University, New Brunswick, the first bachelor's degree awarded to a woman in the British Empire.

Henrietta Louise Muir Edwards (1849–1931) founded the Working Girls' Association in Montreal and edited the first women's magazine, *Women's Work in Canada*. An advocate of divorce on equal grounds for women and men, for prison reform, and for the equal rights of women in the law, she was later involved as one of the plaintiffs in the *Persons* case (1929).

Jennie Trout (1841–1921) was the first Canadian woman licensed to practice medicine in Canada. She was not allowed to enroll in any Canadian medical school and so studied at the Women's Medical College of Pennsylvania, graduating in 1875, the same year that she passed the registration examinations of the Ontario College of Physicians and Surgeons. She was one of the founders of the Women's Medical College in Kingston, Ontario.

1876    Emily Howard Stowe (1831–1903), physician and feminist, established the Toronto Women's Literary Club, the first suffrage group in Canada. (See 1880, 1889, and 1893.)

1877    Mary Crossen was the first woman permitted to take classes with men in the study of English literature at Victoria College, then located in Cobourg, Ontario.

1880    Emily Howard Stowe, having graduated from the New York Medical College for Women in 1867, returned to Canada and began to practice medicine in Ontario, though illegally, since she was not granted a licence until 1880 (See 1876, 1889, and 1893.) Her daughter, Ann Augusta Stowe-Gullen (who had enrolled at the Toronto School of Medicine in 1879), was the first woman graduate in medicine in Canada (1883).

| | |
|---|---|
| *1881* | Felicite Angers (1845–1924), the first French-Canadian woman novelist, using the pseudonym Laure Conan, published *Angeline de Montbrun,* serialized 1881–82. In 1886 she addressed a patriotic appeal to French-Canadian women in *Si les Canadiens le voulaient.* |
| *1882* | The Toronto Labour Council supported the principle of equal pay for equal work. |
| | A branch of the Girls' Friendly Society, an Anglican organization, was establshed in Canada to provide support and shelter for single immigrant girls. |
| | Elizabeth Shadd Shreve, a Black preacher, established the Women's Home Missionary Society in Ontario. |
| *1883* | The Canadian Women's Suffrage Association was founded in Toronto from the Toronto Women's Literary Club (founded 1876) by Emily Howard Stowe and Augusta Stowe-Gullen. |
| | The Ontario Medical College for Women was established. |
| | Ada Marean taught the first kindergarten class in the public school system in Canada in the Louisa Street Public School in Toronto. |
| *1884* | Nellie Greenwood of Victoria College was the first woman to receive the B. Sc. from the University of Toronto. |
| | Isabella Valency Crawford (1850–87), novelist and poet, privately published her only volume of poetry, *Old Spookses' Pass, Malcolm's Katie, and Other Poems,* selling only a few copies. After the death of her father in 1875 she supported her family with her writing of serialized fiction. She became better known as a poet after J. W. Garvin published her *Collected Poems* (1905), but her place as a major narrative poet was not recognized until the 1970s. |
| *1885* | Hanna Grier Coome (1837–1921), mother-foundress of the Anglican Sisters of St. John the Divine, Toronto (1884), went with a group of nuns and nurses to care for the sick and wounded and to set up hospitals in Moose Jaw in the second Northwest Rebellion. |
| *1886* | Sara Jeanette Duncan (1861–1922), journalist, was the first woman employed full-time by the Toronto *Globe.* |
| *1887* | Founded by Anna Leonowens (1834–1915), the Nova Scotia College of Art was opened. She had supported her two children by working as a court governess in the court of Siam (her autobiography was the |

source for *The King and I*, 1951, by Richard Rodgers and Oscar Hammerstein) and eventually emigrated to Canada in 1876, where she organized women in Halifax, founded the College, and helped to establish the first local Council of Women. She also served on the National Council of Women as an advocate for women's suffrage and lectured at McGill University on Sanskrit.

*1888*        Women replaced men as switchboard operators for the Bell Telephone Company; their efforts to improve hours and wages and to establish a union with the International Electrical Workers in 1907 resulted in a strike and a Royal Commission. Before it could report, Bell had either forced those who joined the union to resign from it or had fired them.

Death of Anna Haining Swan (b. 1846), the "Nova Scotia Giantess." In 1862 she had joined P. T. Barnum's American Museum in New York, advertised as 246 cm (8'1") but in reality 228 cm (7'6") tall. In a tour of Europe she met and married a Kentucky giant, Martin van Buren Bates, and was presented to Queen Victoria.

*1889*        Emily Howard Stowe founded the Dominion Women's Enfranchisement Association. (See 1893.)

*1890*        Kathleen Blake Coleman (1864–1915), the first syndicated columnist in Canada, began a column for women called "Woman's Kingdom" in the Toronto *Mail and Empire*, which she continued to 1911 under the pseudonym of "Kit." (See 1898.)

*1892*        Pauline Johnson, Tekahionwake (1861–1913), daughter of the hereditary Mohawk chief and a White mother, began a series of international tours across Canada, the U.S., and England, in which she spoke and read her poetry that celebrated her heritage. Her collected poetry, *Flint and Feather*, was published in 1912. She was the first woman in Canada to have a commemorative stamp issued in her honour.

*1893*        Lady Aberdeen (Ishbel Maria Marjoribanks Gordon, 1857–1939), the Scottish wife of the governor general of Canada, established, with the help of others including Henrietta Edwards, the National Council of Women of Canada.

Lady Aberdeen was elected president of the International Council of Women at its Congress at the Chicago World's Fair.

The National Council of Jewish Women was established.

Emily Howard Stowe founded the Dominion Woman Suffrage Association in Canada. (See 1876, 1880, and 1889.)

1894    Maude Elizabeth Seymour Abbott (1869–1940), pathologist and educator, known as "The Beneficent Tornado," graduated as a medical doctor from Bishop's University, having been barred from medicine at McGill because she was a woman. McGill awarded her an honorary M.D. in 1910. She was appointed to the faculty of McGill in 1912 and achieved an international reputation for her work on heart disease and the use of medical museums in teaching. She was never promoted beyond the rank of assistant professor.

Margaret Marshall Saunders (1861–1947) published *Beautiful Joe*, the story of an abused dog, for an American Humane Society competition. After winning first prize, the story was translated into over 14 languages and was the first Canadian novel to sell more than a million copies.

1895    Emilie Carrier LeBlanc, under the pseudonym of "Marichette," began a series of letters concerning Acadian women to *L'Evangeline*, the leading French Maritime newspaper, on the subjects of education for women, temperance, and suffrage.

1896    May Irwin (1862–1938), motion picture actress, played in *The Kiss*, the first film to show a couple kissing. It caused a sensation.

1897    Adelaide Hoodless (1857–1910), educational and social reformer, established the first Women's Institute, a movement that eventually was worldwide. With Lady Aberdeen, in the same year she helped found the Victorian Order of Nurses in Canada, and also assisted in the founding of the National Council of Women and the YWCA. She advocated the teaching of domestic science in schools and the preparation of women for motherhood.

Clara Brett Martin (d. 1923) was the first woman in the British Empire to earn a law degree and to practice law. She was admitted to the Law Society of Upper Canada after a protracted battle that eventually resulted in two amendments to provincial legislation to permit women to be admitted.

1898    Kathleen "Kit" Blake Coleman was the first Canadian woman to serve as a war correspondent. In Cuba she covered the Spanish–American war for the Toronto *Globe and Empire*.

Margret Benedictsson (1866–1956), Manitoba suffragist, and her husband, Sigfus, published the first woman suffrage paper in

Canada, *Freyja* [Woman] that appeared from 1898–1910. Directed primarily to the Icelandic community in Canada, it reported widely on the suffrage movement in Canada, Iceland, and the world. Margret Benedictsson formed the first Icelandic Suffrage Association in North America (1908) and linked it, and its local chapters, to the Canada Suffrage Association.

Margaret Anglin (1876–1956), actress, had her first success in New York in *Cyrano de Bergerac*. She was born in the Parliament Buildings, Ottawa, where her father was speaker of the House of Commons. She became one of the most distinguished dramatic actresses of her age.

1900    The Imperial Order of the Daughters of the Empire (IODE) was founded by Margaret Polson Murray of Montreal. Its interests were promoting education, immigration, child welfare, social health, and community services, as well as British imperialism.

1901    Ella Cora Hind (1861–1942), journalist and women's rights activist, joined the staff of the *Winnipeg Free Press* as agricultural editor as the first woman journalist in the Canadian west. She was president of the Canadian Women's Press Club in 1904.

The Canadian Census recorded that there were 30,900 female teachers in Canada. Only 47 of 857 professors were women.

Mary Matilda Winslow became the first Black woman to enter the University of New Brunswick. She graduated with honours and won the Montgomery–Campbell Prize. She became a teacher in Nova Scotia.

1902    A Royal Commission on Chinese and Japanese immigration concluded that Asians were "unfit for full citizenship, …obnoxious to a free community, and dangerous to the state." On this basis the entry or "Head Tax" of 1884 was raised from $100 to the huge sum of $500, effectively eliminating Chinese and Japanese immigration and virtually excluding the bringing of wives and families. At the same time provincial legislation in British Columbia excluded Chinese and Japanese from most professions, from the civil service, and from teaching.

The Socialist Party of Canada was the first political party to admit women as full members.

1903    Emma Baker was the first woman to earn a Ph. D. in philosophy when she graduated from the University of Toronto.

*1904*    The Canadian Women's Press Club was founded by thirteen women journalists returning from covering the St. Louis World's Fair. The founders included Kathleen Blake, Kate Simpson (who was the first female author who published west of Ontario with *Prairie Pot-Pourri* of 1895, under her pseudonym, Mary Markwell), Emily Murphy, Cora Hind, and Nellie McClung.

Pauline Donalda (1882–1970), soprano, made her operatic debut in Massenet's *Manon* at Nice. She subsequently sang at Covent Garden with Enrico Caruso, and throughout the world, eventually teaching singing in Montreal, where she was born.

*1905*    Mina Hubbard, explorer, was the first person to explore and map the Naskaupi-George river route through Labrador to Ungava Bay.

*1907*    Nellie McClung (1873–1951), feminist, campaigner for women's rights and the vote, politician, and author, joined the Canadian Women's Christian Temperance Union (WCTU). She was the personification of the "first-wave feminism" (referring to the suffragette struggles of the nineteenth and early twentieth centuries) in Canada, campaigning for prohibition and the vote across the country. Born in Chatsworth, Ontario, she moved with her family to Manitoba in 1880. At the age of 16 she taught school near Manitou, Manitoba. In 1915 she published *In Times Like These*. She held a seat in the Alberta legislature from 1921–26. (See 1967.)

British Columbia disenfranchised all South Asian immigrants, excluding them from all professions, the civil service, teaching, political office, and labour on public works.

Marie Gerin-Lajoie, Caroline Beique, and Josephine Marchand-Dandurand established the Federation Nationale Saint-Jean-Baptiste, a francophone and Catholic organization for women concerned with education, social service, and the relations of women's lives to the economy in wages, working conditions, trade unions, and other associations.

Kathleen Parlow (1890–1963), violinist, made her professional debut in Berlin and subsequently toured the world. In 1941 she returned to Canada to teach at the Toronto Conservatory where she established the Parlow String Quartet that became well known internationally and that toured across Canada until 1958.

*1908*    Lucy Maud Montgomery (1874–1942), a novelist from Prince Edward Island, published *Anne of Green Gables* depicting turn-of-the-century Canadian life in a novel for children that was an immediate bestseller and is now translated into more than 30 languages.

The federal government passed an immigration requirement for South Asian immigrants, requiring that they must immigrate with a continuous ticket from their country of origin, an arrangement impossible from South Asia (India, Pakistan, Ceylon [Sri Lanka]). Hence wives and families were excluded from joining their husbands and fathers in Canada.

*1909*　　　Elizabeth Arden (Florence Nightingale Graham, 1884–1966), cosmetics manufacturer, moved to the U.S. to work in a beauty salon. She then borrowed money to set up her own salon and began to manufacture cosmetics to use in it, eventually building the sale of her products into a multi-million dollar empire.

*1911*　　　Women comprised 21.6 percent of the Canadian workers: 40 percent in manufacturing; 22 percent in clothing industries; 15 percent as domestic servants; 9 percent as saleswomen; 9 percent in secretarial work; 5 percent as nurses; 3 percent as teachers. Immigrants comprised 24 percent of the labour force.

*1912*　　　Carrie Matilda Derick (1862–1941), botanist, was the first Canadian woman appointed full professor — of morphological botany at McGill University. In the same year she was active in helping found the Montreal Suffrage Association. She introduced the teaching of genetics and was an ardent social activist on behalf of compulsory schooling, care for abnormal children, women's rights, and birth control.

*1913*　　　Average wage for a female factory worker in Canada was $5 per week, or $261 per year. A living wage was $390 per year, according to Carrie Derick, writing in the *Labour Gazette*.

Death in poverty of Harriet Tubman (b. 1821? into slavery), heroine of the underground railroad at the outbreak of the American Civil War. She made more than 19 trips from her home in St. Catharines, Ontario, into Maryland to lead slaves to safety in Canada. On 2 June 1863, she led the only military campaign in American military history planned and led by a woman, an action that freed more than 750 slaves at Combahee River in South Carolina.

Frances Loring (1887–1968) and Florence Wyle (1881–1968), sculptors, moved from Chicago to Toronto, setting up the studio they shared for 50 years. Both were founding members of the Sculptors' Society of Canada.

<table>
<tr><td>1914</td><td>

Almanda Walker-Marchand founded the Federation des femmes canadiennes-françaises (FFCF), the first organization in Canada for francophone women outside Quebec, and remained president until 1946. Sections were established in Ontario and Western Canada.

</td></tr>
</table>

*1914*

Almanda Walker-Marchand founded the Federation des femmes canadiennes-françaises (FFCF), the first organization in Canada for francophone women outside Quebec, and remained president until 1946. Sections were established in Ontario and Western Canada.

The delegation advocating women's suffrage having been refused in Manitoba, Nellie McClung and the Political Equality League staged a "Women's Parliament" in a Winnipeg theatre to full houses in order to raise money for the suffrage campaign.

Marie Dressler (1869–1934), film actress of the silent and early talkie period, made her film debut as a comedian in *Tillie's Punctured Romance*. She was best known for her role in *Tugboat Annie* (1932).

*1915*

The first International Congress of Women with delegates from 150 countries met at The Hague to promote world peace. Under the leadership of Austrian pacifist, Bertha Von Süttner (b. 1843), it established the Women's International League for Peace and Freedom. Branches established throughout the world included Canada, where Agnes MacPhail served as honourary president. In the 1930s the Congress protested against cadet training in high schools, reviewed school textbooks to lobby against militarism in them, and in 1931 campaigned for universal disarmament.

*1916*

Women 21 and over got the vote in provincial elections in Alberta, Manitoba, and Saskatchewan.

Mary Irene Parlby (1868–1965), feminist and politician, was elected president of the Women's Auxiliary of the United Farmers of Alberta and eventually transformed it into a body of united action that pressed for legislation concerning women's rights. In 1921 she was elected to the provincial legislature for the UFA, holding her position for 14 years and becoming cabinet minister without portfolio. In 1929 she was one of the plaintiffs in the *Persons* case and in 1930 was appointed Canadian delegate to the League of Nations.

*1917*

Women 21 and over got the vote in provincial elections in British Columbia and Ontario.

Under the Canadian Military Voters Act nurses were given the right to vote in federal elections in Canada.

Helen Gregory MacGill (1864–1947), journalist, feminist, and reformer, was appointed the first female judge in British Columbia as the result of pressures brought by women's groups, including the University Women's Club of Vancouver. She had been the first woman graduate of Trinity College, Toronto, with a degree in music.

1918    Women 21 and over got the right to vote in Canada in federal elections, and in provincial elections in Nova Scotia.

Mary Ellen Smith (1863–1933) was the first woman elected to the Legislative Assembly in British Columbia and was the first woman in the British Empire to serve as a cabinet minister.

1919    Women 21 and over were given the right to vote in provincial elections in New Brunswick.

In the Winnipeg General Strike, women were the first to walk off the job with 500 telephone operators leaving their positions in the early dawn of May 15. Led by Helen Armstrong, the president of the Women's Labour League, members prepared 1,500 meals a day for striking women.

1920    E. Marjorie Hill received her B. Sc. degree from the University of Toronto and was the first female architect in Canada.

1921    Agnes Campbell MacPhail (1890–1953), a candidate of the United Farmers of Ontario, was the first woman elected as a member of parliament in Canada. She supported women's rights and was instrumental in initiating prison reform, including the establishment in Canada of the Elizabeth Fry Society.

Women employed in the Canadian federal civil service were obliged to resign when they married.

Alice A. Chown (1866–1949), feminist, socialist, and pacifist, published *The Stairway*, an autobiographical novel based on her extensive diaries. She was actively involved in the Canadian suffrage movement, the Canadian Suffrage Association, and her own organization—the Equal Franchise League that had been established in 1912 to promote the vote as well as other far-reaching reforms in women's equality. Inspired by Emma Goldman, she was also an active trade union organizer, against, for example, the monolithic T. Eaton Company. Late in her life she was a strong worker for the League of Nations Society.

British Columbia passed the first maternity leave legislation.

*1922*   Women 21 and over got the right to vote in provincial elections in Prince Edward Island and so throughout all Canada, except in Quebec.

Rebecca Buhay (1896–1953), political activist, was an organizer for unions among the garment workers in Montreal and joined the Workers' Party of Canada, serving on its national executive.

*1923*   Aimee Semple McPherson (1890–1944), evangelist, opened a 5,000-seat Angelus Temple of the Four Square Gospel in Los Angeles. After revivalist tours throughout the world, she divorced her second and third husbands and suffered a series of moral and financial scandals.

The "Head Tax" of $500 on Chinese immigrants was removed, only to be replaced by other legislation that virtually eliminated Chinese immigration and made it impossible for male Chinese workers to bring in their wives and families. Hence July 1, 1923, is known as "Humiliation Day" in the Chinese community.

*1924*   Establishment of the Federation of Medical Women of Canada.

Ada Mackenzie (1891–1973) founded in Thornhill, Ontario the first golf club restricted to women when men's clubs refused women adequate playing time. She won the Canadian Ladies Open Amateur title five times, and in 1933 was named Canadian athlete of the year.

*1925*   Women 25 and over were given the right to vote in Newfoundland.

*1926*   Savella Stechishin, teacher and promoter of Ukrainian language and culture, was the founding president of the Ukrainian Women's Association, organized in Saskatoon.

*1928*   Anna Dexter was the first Canadian woman radio broadcaster.

Fanny "Bobbie" Rosenfeld (1903–1969), athlete, entered the Amsterdam Olympics among the first women to be admitted to the Olympics, and won the silver medal in the 100m race. Ethel Catherwood was the first Canadian woman to win a gold medal — for the high jump.

*1929*   Nellie McClung, Emily Murphy. Louise McKinney (1868–1931), Irene Parlby, and Henrietta Muir Edwards petitioned in 1927 for an interpretation of "person" in the British North America Act with specific reference to the appointment of a woman to the Senate (Section 24). Emily Murphy (1886–1933), who had become in Alberta the first woman magistrate in the British Empire, was challenged in her first case by the defence lawyer on the grounds that as a woman she was not legally a person, though her position was upheld by the Supreme Court of Alberta in 1916. After an adverse ruling by the Supreme Court of Canada in 1928 that women were not "fit and qualified persons" eligible to serve in the Senate as specified in the Act, they appealed to the Judicial Committee of the [British] Privy Council who ruled in 1929 that women were persons and so eligible for appointment to the Senate. This decision is known as the *Persons* case.

1930    Cairine Reay Wilson (1885–1962), philanthropist and politician, was the first woman appointed to the Canadian Senate, and in 1949 became the first woman delegate to the United Nations.

The Saskatchewan Farm Women's Movement and the United Grain Growers' Convention pressed for birth control information and the availability of contraceptive devices.

1931    Annie Buller (1895–1973), political activist, was arrested for organizing the coal miners in Estevan, Saskatchewan, and was jailed for a year. She had joined the Workers' Party of Canada in 1922 and was business manager of the *Western Clarion* when she was again arrested in 1939 and spent until 1942 in jail.

1932    The first family planning clinic in Canada was established by Dr. Elizabeth Bagshaw in Hamilton, Ontario.

1934    Helen Alice Kinnear (b. 1894) was the first woman to argue a case before the Supreme Court of Canada. She was also appointed King's Counsel in 1934, the first woman lawyer so appointed in the British Empire.

Oliva Dionne gave birth to the Dionne quintuplets in Corbeil, Ontario, only to have the provincial authorities remove them from their parents' farm, care, and value systems, and place them in a specially constructed building under the supervision first of the doctor who delivered them, and then, in 1936, under the control of Dr. William Blatz, who conformed them to his system of discipline and scientific child study as a controlled experiment. Protests in 1938 by Catholics and Francophones returned them to their parents, but the rift between them was by then too great to be healed.

Elizabeth Sterling Haynes, actress and teacher of drama, established the first school for drama at Banff that evolved into the Banff School of Fine Arts.

| | |
|---|---|
| *1936* | Lydia Emily Gruchy (1895–1992) was the first woman ordained as a minister in the United Church of Canada. She graduated from St. Andrew's College, Saskatoon, in 1923. Her ordination had been opposed by the General Council of the United Church for 13 years. |
| *1937* | Trans-Canada Air Lines set regulations for the minimum height (5 ft. 3 in.) and maximum weight (125 lbs.) for women flight attendants. |
| *1940* | White women over 21 got the vote in provincial elections in Quebec; Japanese-Canadian and Chinese-Canadian women got the franchise several years later and First Nation peoples in Quebec in 1969. |
| | Death in Toronto of Emma Goldman (1869–1940), anarchist, free speech activist, feminist. She founded a journal, *Mother Earth*, and spoke in favour of birth control (1916). |
| *1941* | Quebec allowed women to practice law. |
| | Portia White (1910–68), Black contralto, made her debut in Toronto. Born in Truro, Nova Scotia, she began a singing career at the age of six in the local Baptist church. After her Toronto appearance she won international acclaim, touring Latin America and giving recitals in New York, often being compared with Marian Anderson. |
| *1942* | The Canadian government, reacting to the Japanese bombing of Pearl Harbour (1941), ordered the removal of all Japanese-Canadians within 160 km of the Pacific coast. After being held in cattle sheds in the grounds of the Pacific National Exhibition in Vancouver, they were sent to internment centres in the interior of British Columbia until the end of the war, on the grounds that they had to be controlled so as not to pose a threat to Canada's security, though no Japanese-Canadian was ever charged with disloyalty. Over 20,000 persons were relocated; families were split up so that the men were sent to one camp, women and children to another; and their homes, farms, boats, businesses, and personal effects were sold. At the end of World War One they were given the choice between deportation or relocation in central Canada. In 1949 they were given the right to vote. |
| | The Canadian Women's Army Corps (CWAC, established 1941) was incorporated into the Canadian armed forces. |

*1944*
Elizabeth Lawrie Smellie (1884–1968) was the first woman appointed to the rank of colonel in the Canadian army. Educated at Toronto and Johns Hopkins University, she undertook graduate work in public health nursing at Simmons College, Boston, and served in the Canadian Army Medical Corps in World War One, being mentioned in dispatches and decorated. She became assistant matron-in-chief of the Canadian Army Nursing Service (1918–20) and chief superintendent of the Victorian Order of Nurses for Canada (1924–47). In 1940 she was appointed matron-in-chief of the Royal Canadian Medical Corps and in 1941 supervized the organization of the Canadian Women's Army Corps.

Over one million women in Canada were engaged in paid work; 36,000 were in the armed forces.

*1945*
Death of the painter, Emily Carr (b. 1871), the recorder of West Coast Haida and other traditional First Nation life. Her first solo show was held in Vancouver in 1938. In 1941 her autobiography, *Klee Wyck*, won the Governor-General's Award for nonfiction.

*1946*
Carrie Best (b. 1903), Black poet, journalist, and civil rights activist, began to publish a church bulletin that eventually became a national newspaper, *The Clarion* that continued until 1956 as the first black newspaper published in eastern Canada. It resumed publication under her editorship in 1992.

Viola Desmond, a Black woman, sat in a "Whites Only" section of a theatre in Nova Scotia and thereby caused a reaction that resulted in her being arrested, imprisoned overnight, and fined. The event, widely reported in the national and international press, began the mobilization for civil rights in Nova Scotia.

Madeline Parent (b. 1918), trade unionist and organizer, tried to organize textile workers in Quebec from 1940 on, but her efforts culminated in the textile strike in Montreal and Valleyfield involving 6,000 workers and clashes with police who used tear gas and threatened with machine guns. After three months the strike ended when the employers allowed the formation of a union.

*1947*
Married women were dismissed from jobs in the Canadian civil service and the Canadian Broadcasting Corporation on the basis that their wartime employment was only temporary.

Francophone Canadian novelist Gabrielle Roy (1909–1981) was the first woman to be admitted to membership in the Royal Society of Canada. Her novel *Bonheur d'occasion* (in English translated as

*The Tin Flute*) won the Prix Femina in Paris and the Literary Guild of America Award in the U.S.

Discriminatory legislation against Chinese immigrants was repealed. Chinese and East Indian-Canadians got the vote. South Asians were allowed to immigrate on an annual quota system: India, 150; Pakistan, 100; Ceylon, 50.

Dorothy Livesay (b. 1909), poet, won the Governor-General's Award for poetry a second time, first for *Day and Night* (1944) and second for *Poems for People*. That same year she wrote a long poem, *Call My People Home* as a commentary for a radio broadcast on the plight of Japanese Canadian families in British Columbia during and following World War Two.

1948    Mona Campbell (d. 1989) was the first woman to graduate from the Ontario Veterinary College with a degree in Veterinary Science. She was excluded from practice because no practicing veterinarian would hire her. After working in the U.S., she returned to set up her own practice at Manotick near Ottawa.

Barbara Ann Scott (b. 1928) won the Olympic, World, and European figure skating championships.

1949    Hilda Marion Neatby (1904–75), historian and educator, was the only woman appointed to the Massey Royal Commission on Arts, Letters, and Sciences. In 1953 she published a critique of Canadian education, *So Little for the Mind*.

Japanese-Canadians received the franchise.

Gwenneth Lloyd (b. 1901) and Betty Farrally (1915–89), dancers and choreographers, founded the Royal Winnipeg Ballet, the first professional dance company in Canada.

1950    Edith Margaret Fulton Fowke (b. 1913), folklorist, began to broadcast "Folk Song Time" on the CBC, playing many of the songs she recorded in her collecting tours in Canada. In 1954 she published the first of two volumes of *Folk Songs of Canada* and later *Folklore of Canada* (1974) as well as many other collections.

1951    Death of Nellie McClung, feminist, author, school teacher, and member of Alberta legislature from 1921–26. Her most memorable phrase was "Never retract, never explain, never apologize — get the thing done and let them howl." (See 1907, 1929.)

Charlotte Whitton (1896–1975) was elected Canada's first woman mayor by the people of Ottawa. For nearly thirty years she lived with Margaret Grier, a federal civil servant, in an economic and mutual support partnership.

Kay Livingstone (d. 1974), Black actress and broadcaster who hosted her own program on the CBC, was the founding president of the Canadian Negro Women's Club that later became the Canadian Women's Negro Association. She was also the Chair of the National Black Coalition of Canada, the Canadian Council of Churches, and the president of the Women's Section of the United Nations Association.

Addie Aylestock (b. 1909), of the British Methodist Episcopal Church, was the first ordained Black woman in Canada.

Winnie Roach Leusler was the first Canadian to swim the English Channel.

Celia Franca (b. 1921), dancer and choreographer, founded the National Ballet of Canada.

*1952*    Soprano Lois Marshall (b. 1928) made her New York debut at Town Hall. Arturo Toscanini engaged her for a performance of Beethoven's *Missa Solemnis* with his NBC Orchestra. In 1957 she made her London debut with Sir Thomas Beecham and began a long recording and concert career.

Marilyn Noell, a quadriplegic, was the first person in a wheelchair to enter the School of Social Work at the University of Toronto. She had to be carried up and down stairs from class to class. After graduating she was the first person in a wheelchair to be a medical social worker in a Toronto hospital. She then worked for the Children's Aid Society and was the founding president of the first consumer-based agency for assisting the disabled in Canada, the Centre for Independent Living. Her autobiography, *Another Path to My Garden*, was published in 1992.

*1954*    Marilyn Bell (b.1939), swimmer, was, at sixteen, the first person to swim across Lake Ontario. In 1955 she was the youngest person to swim the English Channel and in 1956 was the first Canadian to swim the Strait of Juan de Fuca, off Victoria, British Columbia.

*1955*    Women from the West Indies were recruited for immigration to Canada. Under a program called "the Domestic Scene," they were granted immigrant status but had to work as domestics for a year before seeking other employment.

Restrictions were removed on the employment of married women in the Canadian federal public service.

Jean Little (b. 1932), children's writer, graduated from Victoria College, University of Toronto. Rejected in Ontario for teacher training because of her limited vision, she went to Utah and trained to teach handicapped children. Returning to teach at the Guelph Crippled Children's Centre, she began writing books for children that often had a handicapped child as a hero. She has been awarded the Canadian Children's Book Award for *Mine for Keeps* and the Vicky Metcalf Award of the Canadian Library Association. Her autobiography, *Little by Little*, was published in 1987.

1956    Violet Archer (b. 1913), composer and teacher, completed her *Piano Concerto No. 1*, a landmark in Canadian music. She had studied with Bela Bartók and Paul Hindemith in New York, and after teaching in the U.S. she returned to Canada to teach at the University of Alberta from 1962 until her retirement in 1978.

Maureen Forrester (b. 1930), contralto, made her New York debut to rave reviews. She has made an international career in opera, oratorio, lieder, on radio, television, and recordings. In 1976 she was made a Companion of the Order of Canada and subsequently was the first woman head of the Canada Council.

1957    Death of Martha Louise Black (b. 1866), botanist and politician, who joined the Klondike Gold Rush (1898), received the OBE for assistance to Yukon soldiers in World War One, was elected fellow of the Royal Geographical Society for her work with Yukon flora, and was elected to the Canadian House of Commons as the second woman member in 1935.

Ellen Fairclough (b. 1905) was the first woman to serve as a federal cabinet minister. She was appointed secretary of state in the Conservative government of John Diefenbaker. Elected to Parliament in 1950, she became the Conservative labour critic and subsequently introduced a bill requiring equal pay for equal work.

Ludmilla Chiriaeff, a Latvian-born dancer trained in ballet at the Bolshoi, established Les Grands Ballets Canadiens in Montreal.

1958    Blanche Margaret Meagher (b. 1911) was the first Canadian woman to be appointed ambassador. She served as ambassador to Israel (1958–61), Austria (1962–69), and Sweden (1969–73).

| | |
|---|---|
| *1959* | Alice Willard Turner, mathematician, was appointed the first woman faculty member at York University. |

Teresa Stratas (b. 1938), soprano, won the Metropolitan Opera auditions in New York. In 1960 she joined the company and became one of the leading singers of the next decades.

Marie-Claire Blais (b. 1939), Quebec writer, published her first book, *La Belle Bête* (1959), translated as *Mad Shadows*, to acclaim and controversy over its rejection of conventional Catholic morality. She was nineteen years old. *Une Saison Dans la Vie d'Emmanuel* (1965) won the Prix France-Canada and the Prix Medicis and has been the subject of well over 2,000 reviews, articles, books, and theses.

*1960s*     Buffy Sainte Marie (b. 1941), Cree singer and songwriter, began singing folk songs that became popular in the anti-war and civil rights movements but that also for the first time focused attention on the situation of the First Nation peoples.

*1960*     The Canadian branch of the Voice of Women was established as a voluntary association of women to oppose violence and war, and to promote disarmament and peace. It has been active in sponsoring conferences, including two international conferences, educational projects, and government lobbying.

Kenojuak Ashevak (b. 1927) published *The Enchanted Owl*, one of the best-known Inuit prints. It was used on a Canadian stamp in 1970. She was the first woman to join the printmaking shop at Cape Dorset. In 1970 she received the Order of Canada.

*1961*     Women comprised 30 percent of the work force in Canada; 15.5 percent of working women were in the professions. Women comprised .25 percent of the engineers; 2.6 percent of the lawyers; 4.5 percent of the dentists; and 7.3 percent of the doctors. The average earning of women was $2,051; of men, $4,178.

Planned Parenthood of Canada was founded. The birth control pill was developed for general use. Advertising or selling contraceptives was illegal. Condoms were labelled and sold "for the prevention of disease only."

*1965*     The Ontario Medical Association accused working women of being bad mothers. Women were defended by Laura Sabia, president of the Canadian Federation of Women.

Marilyn Noell was the first woman appointed to the board of the Canadian Paraplegic Association.

Adrienne Clarkson (b. 1939), television journalist, was appointed host of the CBC program "Take 30," on which, as in other programs as "The Fifth Estate," she addressed topics rarely discussed in the media such as abortion, rape, menopause, and breast cancer.

1966     Jean Sutherland Boggs (b. 1922) was appointed director of the National Gallery of Canada, the first woman in the world to direct a national gallery.

La Federation des femmes du Quebec was founded.

1967     The First Women's Liberation groups were formed in Chicago and in Toronto.

The Canadian Royal Commission on the Status of Women was established with Florence Bayard Bird as chair. The report was issued in 1970. The forming of Women's Liberation groups and the establishment of the Commission inaugurated "second wave feminism" in Canada. (See 1907.)

The average income for men in Canada was $5,331; for women, $2,303 (43 percent of the average for the men).

1968     The Presbyterian Church of Canada ordained its first women clergy.

Anglophone liberation began in Quebec when the McGill Student Society published the illegal *Birth Control Handbook* and became involved in abortion counselling.

Birthright, an anti-abortion activist group, was established to contend with the forthcoming reforms in the Criminal Code on abortion and to provide help for unmarried mothers.

Nancy Greene (b. 1943), athlete, won gold and silver medals in slalom skiing at the Winter Olympics.

1969     The Canadian Amendment to the Criminal Code on abortion was passed. It forbade abortion on eugenic or medico-social grounds, allowing it only after a three-person medical team approved it in an accredited hospital in circumstances where continuation of the pregnancy would endanger the life of the mother. Disputes and court cases abounded for the next 20 years. The same amendment removed as a criminal offence the dissemination of information concerning birth control.

Margaret Benston of Vancouver (d. 1991) published an article, "The Political Economy of Women's Liberation" (*Monthly Review*

21) in which she argued that housework is an important part of labour.

1970s    Judith Snow, a paraplegic, enrolled at York University, began pressing for the implementation of services for the disabled, and helped make York the first wheel-chair accessible university in Canada.

1970    An Abortion Caravan set out from Vancouver and converged with other groups in Ottawa to demand abortion on demand in the legislation.

The Report of the Canadian Royal Commission on the Status of Women was issued. It set out four principles: women are free to seek employment outside the home; the care of children is a shared responsibility for mother, father, and society; society has a responsibility for women because of pregnancy and childbirth, and so special treatment for reasons of maternity is necessary; and women in certain areas need special treatment to overcome adverse effects of discriminatory practices. It also recommended amending the Criminal Code to allow a qualified medical practitioner to perform an abortion on the request of the pregnant woman. *The Toronto Star* described the report of the Royal Commission as "a bomb already primed and ticking." The report provided the women's movement with an agenda for reform. When the government was slow to respond, Laura Sabia led the movement to establish the Ad Hoc Committee which in 1972 became the National Action Committee on the Status of Women (NAC).

There were 2,690,000 women, both employed and unemployed, in the labour force in Canada. This number represented 32 percent of the total labour force.

1971    Women comprised 8 percent of Canada's medical doctors and 99 percent of the nurses.

Women were allowed to serve as jurors in Quebec for the first time.

The Canada Labour Code was amended to prohibit discrimination on the grounds of sex and marital status.

1972    Rosemary Brown (b. 1930) was elected to the British Columbia legislature. She was the first Black woman to win a seat in a provincial legislature in Canada.

The Ontario Native Women's Association was established with headquarters in Thunder Bay, Ontario.

*1973*    The first national lesbian conference was held at the YWCA, Toronto.

The first Canadian lesbian journal, *Long Time Coming*, was established in Montreal.

First National Congress of Black Women was held.

The Supreme Court of Canada denied Irene Murdoch, an Alberta divorcee, any proceeds from the family farm, even though she had worked on it equally with her former husband.

Muriel Ferguson was appointed first woman Speaker of the Canadian Senate.

A Rape Relief Centre opened in Vancouver and a Rape Crisis Centre in Toronto.

Vera Cudjoe, who had immigrated to Canada from Trinidad in 1960, established Black Theatre Canada.

Jeanette Corbiere Lavell an Ojibwa from Manitoulin Island, and Yvonne Bedard, born on the Six Nations reserve near Brantford, had lost their Indian status when they married non-Indians (under section 12.I.b of the Indian Act of 1876). They took their cases to the Supreme Court of Canada with no support from their communities, band councils, or national organizations. The decision against them was greeted as a victory for First Nation rights and as a defeat for First Nation women. (See 1977.)

Karen Kain (b. 1951), dancer, won the silver medal at the Moscow International Ballet Competition. She became principal dancer with the National Ballet of Canada.

*1974*    Canadian Association for the Repeal of the Abortion Law (CARAL) was established. In 1980 it became the Canadian Abortion Rights League.

Pauline Jewett (1922–92), educator and politician, was the first woman appointed president of a major co-educational university in Canada. She was president of Simon Fraser University from 1974–78.

The Native Women's Association of Canada was founded.

Pauline Emily McGibbon (b. 1910) was the first woman appointed lieutenant-governor in Canada. She was lieutenant-governor of Ontario, 1974–80, her first salaried job.

The National Film Board set up Studio D to promote films by and about women.

Liona Boyd (b. 1950), classical guitarist, issued her first album, *The Guitar—Liona Boyd*, selling over 30,000 copies. She came to the attention of an even wider audience when she toured with Gordon Lightfoot in 1976. She won a Juno award in 1978.

1975    The First United Nations World Conference on Women was held in Mexico City.

International Women's Year was proclaimed by the United Nations, the first year of a Decade for Women on the themes of peace, development, and equality.

Grace Hartman was elected president of the Canadian Union of Public Employees, the first woman to lead a national trade union.

1976    The Anglican Church ordained the first six women in Canada as priests.

Canadian women won seven medals at the summer Olympics in Montreal.

Carroll Baker (b. 1949), singer and songwriter from Nova Scotia, sang "I've Never Been This Far Before" at the Juno awards telecast, becoming a star of Canadian country music.

For every 100 marriages in Canada, there were 28 divorces. The average income for a family headed by a woman was $9,001, and by a man, $21,551.

1977    Women Against Violence Against Women (WAVAW) was established in Canada.

Marion Ironquill Meadmore was the first Aboriginal woman to be admitted to the bar of Manitoba and in all of Canada.

The Canadian Humans Rights Act forbade discrimination on the basis of sex and ensured women equal pay for work of equal value.

Madame Jehane Benoît (b. 1904), chef and author, gave the first two microwave cooking demonstrations in Canada. She also published *The Encyclopedia of Canadian Cooking* (1970).

Sandra Lovelace, a Tobique from New Brunswick, had married a non-Indian and lost her legal status under the Indian Act. She took her case to the United Nations Committee on Human Rights and won in a ruling that declared that Canada had contravened the International Covenant in denying her the right to live in her own cultural community.

1978    *Fireweed*, a national magazine for women of colour and for women's community, was first published in Toronto. *Canadian Woman Studies/Les Cahiers de la Femme*, a feminist quarterly, was first published in Toronto edited by Shelagh Wilkinson.

The first "Take Back the Night" action by women to claim the right to safety on the streets was organized in Vancouver.

One woman in 10 in Canada, a total of 500,000 women, was beaten by the man with whom she lived.

1979    The Feminist Party of Canada was established at a conference of 700 women in Toronto.

Death of Mary Pickford (b. 1893), film actress of the silent era, known after her 1907 success as "America's Sweetheart." She made over 200 films and in 1919 formed United Artists with Charlie Chaplin, D.W. Griffiths, and Douglas Fairbanks Sr., whom she also married.

The United Nations designated the year as the Year of the Child, with special emphasis on abused children, an idea proposed by Montreal journalist, Mary Van Stolk.

Death of Dora Mavor Moore (b. 1888), actress. She was the first Canadian to graduate from RADA (Royal Academy of Dramatic Art) in London. She acted in the U.S. and at the Old Vic in London, and, on her return to Canada, she established the New Play Society that produced 47 new plays (1946–56). She was influential in establishing the Stratford Shakespearean Festival in 1952.

Doris Anderson (b. 1925), former editor of *Chatelaine* (1958–77), was appointed head of the Federal Advisory Council on the Status of Women. As editor she had brought to her readership issues that questioned women's traditional roles.

Angella Taylor (b. 1958), Black athlete, won silver and bronze medals in the Pan-American Games and two gold medals in the 1982 Commonwealth Games. She was the fastest Canadian woman sprinter.

Antonine Maillet (b. 1929), the "Voice of Acadia," won the Prix Goncourt for her novel *Pelagie-la-Charrette*, an account of the life of Acadians returning from enforced deportation. Her monologue novel about an old Acadian woman, *La Sagouine* (1974) was reworked for the theatre to wide acclaim.

Yvonne Peters and Pat Danforth, disabled feminists, sat on the board of the Coalition of Provincial Organizations of the Handicapped and pressed for the resolution of issues that concerned women with disabilities.

*1980*   Jeanne-Mathilde Sauve (1922-93) was the first woman speaker of the House of Commons.

Alexa McDonough was elected the leader of the Nova Scotia NDP, the first woman to lead a Canadian political party.

Women comprised 50.3 percent of the work force.

Death of Judy LaMarsh (b. 1924), politician and broadcaster. She was a member of parliament, the second woman cabinet minister, and a tireless worker for women, especially in taking responsibility for the Canada Pension legislation and national medicare. Her last work was a report that was severely critical of violence in the media. She estimated that children between five and 15 would see some 13,000 violent deaths on television, whereas in real life it would be unusual for most people to see a single example.

Lois Wilson (b. 1927) was elected as the first woman moderator of the United Church of Canada.

*1981*   Canada ratifies the United Nations Convention on the Elimination of All Forms of Discrimination Against Women.

A conference on women and the constitution was cancelled by Lloyd Axworthy, then the federal minister in charge of women's issues. Doris Anderson resigned from the presidency of the Federal Advisory Council. Two weeks after the cancellation, 1,300 women from across Canada gathered in Ottawa to talk and plan for action to enshrine women's rights in the constitution. They were successful when it was proclaimed in 1982.

Thérèse Casgrain (1896–1981) died in Montreal after a lifetime of campaigning for the rights of women in Quebec. She established many organizations to promote the franchise before World War Two, was the leader of the provincial CCF, and was the founder of the Quebec branch of the Voice of Women in 1961, and of the Federation des femmes du Quebec in 1966.

Abby Hoffman (b. 1947), athlete, was appointed director of Sport Canada, a government agency responsible for promoting amateur sport. She first played in the Little Toronto Hockey League. When her team made it to the all-star team competition, it was discovered that she was a girl playing on a boy's team. Although she was allowed to finish the year, she was not permitted to join the boys' league. After entering competitive swimming and winning the Ontario championship in backstroke and breaststroke, she then entered track and field, winning a gold medal in the Commonwealth Games of 1966.

*1982* Madame Justice Bertha Wilson (b. 1923) was the first woman appointed to the Supreme Court of Canada.

Karen Baldwin (b. 1963) was the first Canadian to win the Miss Universe beauty contest.

Members of parliament greeted with jeers an all-party committee report that one in ten women is regularly beaten by her husband. As a result, special shelters for battered women were set up.

*1983* One out of four women in Canada is sexually assaulted at least once in her life; one in 17 is raped; 2 percent of those charged with rape are convicted.

The Canadian Coalition Against Media Pornography was established.

REAL Women (Realistic, Equal, Active, for Life) was established in Canada in opposition to feminist political action, abortion, the equality clauses in the Charter of Rights, equal pay clauses, affirmative action for women in employment practices, no-fault divorce, and gay rights.

Hide Shimizu was named a member of the Order of Canada for a lifetime of volunteer work. She was the first person of Japanese heritage to teach in Canada.

Death of Pitseolak Ashoona (b. 1904), at Cape Dorset, Baffin Island, Inuit graphic artist who became well known from the late 1950s for her depictions of the traditional customs and way of life of the Inuit peoples. She was born on Nottingham Island, Northwest Territories, bore 17 children, and was elected a member of the Royal Canadian Academy of Arts in 1974.

*1984* Jeanne-Mathilde Sauve was the first woman appointed governor-general of Canada. She served from 1984–90.

Anne E. Cools (b. 1943) was the first Black woman appointed to the Senate. As a social worker she had worked to educate the public on issues of violence in the family.

The Canadian Constitution was amended to affirm that aboriginal and treaty rights for First Nation peoples were guaranteed equally to both female and male persons.

The Canadian secretary of state announced funding for the establishment of five chairs of Women's Studies at Canadian universities.

Daurene Lewis, a seventh-generation Nova Scotian descended from Rose Fortune (see 1783) was elected the first Black woman mayor in Canada.

*1985*   The Canadian Indian Act was amended. This revision restored status and the right to be considered for band membership to Indian women who had lost their status by marriage to non-Indians.

The Canadian divorce law was amended to reduce the separation period from three years to one, to eliminate the concept of fault, and to emphasize the economic self-sufficiency of divorced spouses.

Margaret Atwood (b. 1939) published *The Handmaid's Tale*, a feminist dystopia.

*1986*   Gail E. Greenough, Canadian equestrian, was the first Canadian and North American to win the World Championship in show jumping.

Sharon Wood became the first Canadian woman to climb Mount Everest.

The Canadian Employment Equity Act was passed. Applicable to Crown corporations and federally regulated businesses, it redressed historic and systematic discrimination against women, the disabled, Aboriginal peoples, and visible minorities.

Shirley Carr was the first woman chosen as president of the Canadian Labour Congress.

Of 56 universities and colleges surveyed in Canada, only eight (Acadia, Carleton, Dalhousie, Laurentian, McMaster, Waterloo, Western, and York) reported that they were encouraging affirmative action hiring programs to recruit women faculty.

*1987*   Dr. Geraldine Kenney-Wallace was appointed chair of the Science Council of Canada.

Death of Margaret Lawrence (1926-87), novelist, who had published *The Stone Angel* (1964) and *The Diviners* (1974), novels in a cycle of fiction concerning women's lives in the fictional Manitoba town of Manawaka.

Sandra Bernier, aged 11, was barred by G. Emmett Cardinal Carter from serving at the altar at a special mass to mark the centennial of Sacre Coeur church in Toronto where she had already been a server. She was told that female servers were against church law and could not be shown in the mass that was to be televised nationally.

Statistics Canada reported that of 1,762 union executive board members in Canada, 19.3 percent were women, up one percentage point from 1978, but down slightly from 1979.

Jean Augustine (b. 1937), Black activist, was designated the first recipient of the Kay Livingstone Award, sponsored by the Congress of Black Women.

The average income of Canadian two-parent families with children was $48,600; of single-parent families headed by women, $18,900.

DisAbled Women's Network (DAWN) was established at the founding national meeting in Winnipeg.

*1988*   The Supreme Court of Canada struck down the federal law on abortion as illegal, invoking the Charter of Rights.

Thirty-nine women were elected to Parliament in Canada, and six women were appointed to the Cabinet.

The International Lesbian and Gay People of Colour Conference was held in Toronto.

k. d. lang, Alberta country music singer, was chosen "Woman of the Year" by *Chatelaine*.

*1989*   Further abortion legislation and decisions in Canada did not settle the question of its criminality; meanwhile Dr. Henry Morgantaler continued to defy the law by opening an abortion clinic in the Maritimes and continuing to operate his clinic in Toronto.

Audrey McLaughlin (b. 1936) became the leader of the New Democratic Party of Canada, the first woman in Canada heading a federal party.

The Progressive Conservative government eliminated $2 million from the Women's Programme of the Secretary of State, decreasing funding for many groups by 15 percent. As well, $3 million was cut from the Native Citizens Programme and $2 million from multiculturalism.

Fourteen young women engineering students at the ecole Polytechnique in Montreal were massacred by Marc Lepine who shouted, "You're all a bunch of feminists." The massacre focused public attention on violence against women and is commemorated annually on 6 December.

1990    Marie-Marguerite D'Youville (1701–1771) was the first Canadian-born person to be canonized; she was founder of the Grey Nuns of Montreal and a pioneer of charity and social work in Canada. In the same year Marie de l'Incarnation was canonized. (See 1672.)

Canadian federal and provincial ministers responsible for the Status of Women issued a Declaration Against Violence Against Women.

Death of Florence O'Neill-Hutchison (85), educator, who was a literacy advocate from the time she began to teach in the one-room schools of Newfoundland at the age of 18. Her autobiography, *Beside Me in the Wilderness*, is still used as a textbook.

1991    The Supreme Court of Canada ruled that, in rape trials, barring evidence of the complainant's sexual history could violate the accused's right to a fair trial.

Death of Angela Sidney (89), last fluent speaker of the Tagish language once widely spoken in the S. Yukon, but a language that disappeared with the Klondike gold rush at the turn of the century.

Death of Margery Hinds (90), author of an Inuit dictionary and other books on the north.

Zanana Akande (b. 1937) was the first Black woman elected in the Ontario legislature and also was the first Black woman cabinet minister.

1992    Dr. Roberta Lynn Bondar (b. 1945), neurologist, was the first Canadian astronaut in space.

Barbara Frum (1937–92) died of leukaemia. Regarded by many media analysts as Canada's top journalist, in 1967 she was appointed host of CBC's radio news context program, "As It Happens" and after fifteen years moved to TV as the host of "The Journal."

Death of Helen Sawyer Hogg Priestley (b. 1905), astronomer and expert on globular star clusters, who had a star named after her, Minor Planet No. 2917, as Sawyer Hogg.

In the National Referendum on the Constitution, the president of the National Action Committee on the Status of Women, Judy Rebick (b. 1945), campaigned on the "no" side, on the grounds that the constitution did not sufficiently recognize the position of women in Canadian society. Under Judy Rebick, the NAC introduced a policy that tried to integrate anti-racial positions and issues with all other matters on NAC's agenda, including education, training, reproductive technology, employment, and political action.

Death of Rose Park (b. 1900), philanthropist. She had worked as a young woman in the garment industry in Montreal. Later in her life she worked for many charitable institutions and was a generous supporter of the State of Israel, the Hebrew University of Jerusalem, the Canadian National Institute for the Blind, and various hospitals in Winnipeg.

*1993*     Sunera Thobani (b. 1947), a Tanzanian-born single mother, was the first woman of colour to be chosen president of the National Action Committee on the Status of Women. Her bid was unopposed by the more than 200 delegates at the annual meeting as an effort to heal a long-standing rift over the role of "minority" women in the feminist movement. As part of the attack on her candidature, questions were posed in the House of Commons by Ontario MP John MacDougall who wrongly labelled her an illegal immigrant. Over a quarter of the NAC's executive was composed of women from visible minorities.

At the tenth biennial Conference of the National Association of Women and the Law in Vancouver, women of colour argued that they were often "invisible" to the White women who formed the executive and membership of the organization. To address this issue two workshops were organized for the first time on "Women of Colour Strategies" that presented resolutions on funding a permanent advisory committee on women of colour to take an advocacy role. The resolutions were accepted.

Alanis Obomsawin (b. 1932), and Abenaki singer and film-makers, won the Toronto-City Award for the Best Canadian feature film (first time for a documentary), for *Kahehsatake: 270 Years of Resistance* (1992). At the NFB in 1967 she began writing, directing, narrating, and producing films on First Nation traditions, history, and culture. They have won over 24 national and international awards. In 1983 she was appointed to the Order of Canada.

*1994*  Virginia Matthews was consecrated the first woman bishop of the Anglican Church of Canada in Toronto.

Myriam Bedard of Quebec won two gold medals in the biathlon at the Winter Olympics in Lillehammer, Norway.

# BIBLIOGRAPHY

Acton, Janice; Goldsmith, Penny; and Shepard, Bonnie, eds. *Women at Work Ontario: 1850-1930*. Toronto: Women's Press, 1974.

Armour, Moira and Staton, Pat. *Canadian Women in History: A Chronology*. Toronto: Green Dragon Press, 1990. This detailed compilation contains lavish information from Statistics Canada, comparative data on incomes, day-care spaces, percentages of women in all professions, dates of women's accomplishments, especially for the period from 1970 to 1990, and much more.

*Black Studies: A Resource Guide for Teaching*. Toronto: Ministry of Education, 1983.

Briskin, Linda and Yanz, Lynda, eds. *Union Sisters: Women in the Labour Force*. 2d ed. Toronto: Women's Press, 1985.

Burt, Sandra; Code, Lorriane; and Dorney, Lindsay, eds. *Changing Patterns: Women in Canada*. 2d. ed. Toronto: McClelland and Stewart, 1993.

*The Canadian Encyclopedia*. Edmonton: Hurtig, 1985. 3 vols.; 2d ed. 4 vols. 1988.

*Canadian Feminist Periodicals*. Ottawa: Catalyst Research, 1988.

Carty, Linda, ed. *And Still We Rise: Feminist Political Mobilizing in Contemporary Canada*. Toronto: Women's Press, 1993.

Cleverdon, Catherine. *The Woman Suffrage Movement in Canada*. 2d ed. Toronto: Univ. of Toronto Press, 1974.

Clio Collective. *Quebec Women: A History*. Toronto: Women's Press, 1987.

Cochrane, Jean. *Women in Canadian Politics*. Toronto: Fitzhenry and Whiteside, 1977.

Cochrane, Jean; Hoffman, Abby; and Kincaid, Pat. *Women in Canadian Sports*. Toronto: Fitzhenry and Whiteside, 1977.

Cohen, Marcia. *The Sisterhood*. New York: Simon and Schuster, 1988.

D'Oyley, Enid and Braithwaite, Rella. *Women of Our Times*. Toronto: Canadian Negro Women's Association, 1973.

Dranoff, Linda Silver. *Women in Canadian Law*. Toronto: Fitzhenry and Whiteside, 1977.

French, Marilyn. *Beyond Power*. London: Cape, 1986.

Fulford, Margaret. *The Canadian Women's Movement, 1960-1990: A Guide to Archival Resources*. Toronto: ECW Press, 1992. For the Canadian Women's Movement Archives.

*Good Housekeeping*, (February 1990) (Special Anniversary Issue).

*The Good Housekeeping Woman's Almanac*. New York: Newspaper Enterprise Association, 1977.

Government of Canada. Canadian Women's Bureau.

*Women at Work in Canada: A Fact Book on the Female Labour Force of Canada, 1964.* Ottawa: Department of Labour, 1965.

Government of Canada, Status of Women Canada, Communications Directorate:
"Towards Equality for Women — A Canadian Chronology." Produced for International Women's Day, 1992.
*Perspectives.* 2:2 (1989).

Government of Canada. Canadian Advisory Council on the Status of Women Publications:
"As Things Stand." 1983.
"Fact Sheet No. 1: Women and Work."
White, Julie. "Women and Unions." April, 1980.

Gurney, Helen. *Girls' Sports: A Century of Progress in Ontario High Schools.* Toronto: Ontario Federation of School Athletic Associations, 1979.

Hacker, Carlotta. *The Book of Canadians: An Illustrated Guide to Who Did What.* Edmonton: Hurtig, 1983.

Hill, Lawrence. *Trials and Triumphs: The Story of African Canadians.* Toronto: Umbrella Press, 1993.

Iacovetta, Franca and Valverde, Mariana eds. *Gender Conflicts: New Essays in Women's History.* Toronto: Univ. of Toronto Press, 1992.

Johnston, Jean. *Wilderness Women: Canada's Forgotten History.* Toronto: Peter Martin, 1973.

Kelly, Joan. *Women, History, and Theory.* Chicago: Univ. of Chicago Press, 1984.

Lerner, Gerda. *Teaching Women's History.* New York: American Historical Association, 1981.

L'Esperance, Jeanne. *The Widening Sphere: Women in Canada, 1870-1940.* Ottawa: Public Archives Canada, 1982.

Levine, Suzanne and Lyons, Harriet, eds. *The Decade of Women: A MS. History.* New York: Paragon, 1980.

Light, Beth and Strong-Boag, Veronica. *True Daughters of the North: Canadian Women's History: An Annotated Bibliography.* Toronto: OISE Press, 1980.

Light, Beth and Pierson, Ruth Roach. *No Easy Road: Women in Canada, 1920s to 1960s.* Toronto: New Hogtown Press, 1990. Documents in Canadian Women's History. Vol. 3.

Lloyd, Trevor. *Suffragettes International.* London: Library of the 20th Century, 1971.

Matheson, Gwen, ed. *Women in the Canadian Mosaic.* Toronto: Peter Martin, 1976.

Miles, Rosalind. *A Women's History of the World.* London: Michael Joseph, 1988.

*The New Internationalist.* 201 (Nov. 1989).

Offen, Karen; Pierson, Ruth Roach; and Rendell, Jane, eds. *Writing Women's History: International Perspectives.* Bloomington: Indiana Univ. Press, 1991.

Papachristiou, Judith. *Women Together: A History in Documents of the Women's Movement in the United States*. New York: Knopf, 1976.

Pederson, Diana L. *Changing Women, Changing History: A Bibliography of the History of Women in Canada*. Toronto: Green Dragon Press, 1992.

Pierson, Ruth Roach. *They're Still Women After All: The Second World War and Canadian Womanhood*. Toronto: McClelland and Stewart, 1986.

Pierson, Ruth Roach. *Canadian Women's Issues*. Vol. 1. Strong Voices. Toronto: James Lorimer, 1993.

Prentice, Alison; Bourne; Paula; Brandt; Gaile Cuthbert; Light; Beth; Mitchison; Wendy; and Black, Naomi, eds. *Canadian Women: A History*. Toronto: Harcourt Brace Jovanovich, 1988.

Prentice, Alison and Light, Beth. *Pioneer and Gentlewomen of British North America: 1713-1867*. Toronto: New Hogtown Press. 1980. Documents in Canadian Women's History. Vol. 1.

Prentice, Alison and Theobald, Marjorie R., eds. *Women Who Taught: Perspectives on the Theory of Women and Teaching*. Toronto: Univ. of Toronto Press, 1991.

Rasmussen, Linda, comp. *A Harvest Yet to Reap: A History of Prairie Women*. Toronto: Women's Press, 1976.

Raven, Susan and Weir, Alison, eds. *Women of Achievement*. New York: Harmony Books, 1981 (published in England as Women in History. London: Weidenfeld and Nicolson).

Sadlier, Rosemary. *Leading the Way: Black Women in Canada*. Toronto: Umbrella Press, 1994.

Sarachild, Kathie, ed. *Feminist Revolution*. New York: Redstockings, 1975.

Strong-Boag, Veronica. *The New Day Recalled: Lives of Girls and Women in English Canada, 1919-1939*. Mississauga: Copp Clark Pitman, 1993.

Strong-Boag, Veronica and Fellman, Anita Clair, eds. *Rethinking Canada: the Promise of Women's History*. 2d ed. Toronto: Copp Clark Pitman, 1991.

Story, Norah. *The Oxford Companion to Canadian History and Literature*. Toronto: Oxford Univ. Press, 1967.

Treichler, Paula A. "Teaching Feminist Theory." In *Theory in the Classroom*, edited by Cary Nelson. 57-128. Chicago: Univ. of Illinois Press, 1986.

Trofimenkoff, Susan Mann and Prentice, Alison, eds. *The Neglected Majority: Essays in Canadian Women's History*. Toronto: McClelland and Stewart, 1977-85. 2 vols.

Tuttle, Lisa. *Encyclopedia of Feminism*. London: Longman, 1986.

*Union Farmer*. (September 1975).

Van Kirk, Sylvia. "Thanadelthur." *The Beaver* (Spring 1974): 40-45.

Vineberg, Ethel. *The History of the National Council of Jewish Women*. Montreal: National Council of Jewish Women, 1967.

Wallace, W. Stewart, ed. *The Macmillan Dictionary of Canadian Biography*. Rev. by W. A. McKay. Toronto: Macmillan, 1978. 4th ed.

Winks, Robin W. *The Blacks in Canada: A History*. Montreal: McGill-Queens Univ. Press, 1971.

*Women Artists' Book of Days*. New York: Hugh Lauter Levin, 1988.

*Women of Canada*. Toronto: Federation of Women Teachers' Associations of Ontario, 1982. (Three packages of course materials for teachers at the Primary, Junior, and Intermediate levels in Ontario.)

# Notes on Contributors

**PAT ARMSTRONG:** Pat Armstrong is Director of Canadian Studies, Carleton University. She is author, or co-author of a wide range of publications, including *The Double Ghetto: Canadian Women and Their Segregated Wor;, Vital Signs: Nursing in Transition; A Working Majority: What Women Must Do For Pay; Theorizing Women's Work* and *Take Care: Warning Signals for the Canadian Health System.*

**BARBARA CASSIDY:** Barbara Cassidy is a Navajo woman who is working on her M.A. in the Graduate Programme in Women's Studies at York University. Her main areas of interest are the impact of Bill C. 31, an Act to Amend the Indian Act on native women and their families and the disproportionately high suicide rates among First Nations women and children.

**ANN DUFFY:** Ann Duffy is an Associate Professor of Sociology at Brock University where she also teaches in the Women's Studies and Labour Studies Programs. Long interested in the impact of violence on women's lives, she was on the Board of Directors of the Hamilton Rape Crisis Centre for several years. Her recent work continues to focus on implications of feminism for contemporary social analysis.

**PATRICIA ELLIOT:** Patricia Elliot is Co-ordinator of Women's Studies at Wilfrid Laurier University where she also teaches in the Department of Sociology and Anthropology. She is author of *From Mastery to Analysis: Theories of Gender in Psychoanalytic Feminism* (Cornell University Press, 1991) and has an ongoing interest in feminist psychoanalytic, poststructuralist and pedagogical theories.

**NIKKI GERRARD:** Nikki Gerrard is a community psychologist practicing at the Saskatoon Mental Health Clinic. Her research interests, practice, and publishing focus on psychology of women, anti-racism and anti-sexism in mental health systems, and rural mental health. Her Ph.D. is in Community Psychology from the Ontario Institute for Studies in Education, University of Toronto.

**NAYYAR S. JAVED:** Nayyar S. Javed was born and raised in Pakistan, and has taught psychology at the University of Peshawar, Pakistan. Currently she works as a psychologist at the Saskatoon Mental Health Clinic. Her area of research includes women in engineering and she has published papers on the politics of difference, refugee women, and psychology of racialized women. She received an M.Ed. in Educational Psychology at the University of Saskatchewan, and an M.Ed. in Adult Education from the University of Colorado.

**ROBINA LORD:** Robina Lord is an African-Canadian woman who is a Graduate of York University's bilingual undergraduate Women's Studies programme at Glendon College. She is working towards a Graduate Degree in Black-Canadian history with emphasis on race, gender and class analysis.

**MARION LYNN:** Marion Lynn is a Visiting Professor in Women's Studies at Trent University. She has published in the areas of family, work, and violence against women. Her current research is on single-parent families and on students at Community Colleges. Her new family book on "Diversity in Families in Canada" will be published by Nelson Canada in 1995.

**NANCY MANDELL:** Nancy Mandell is an Associate Professor of Sociology at York University's Centre for Feminist Research. Her recent publications include studies on gender tracking in high schools, married women's juggling of wage and domestic labour, adolescent's interpretations of work, family, and school life, poverty in Canada, and violence against women.

**KATHLEEN MARTINDALE:** Kathleen Martindale is an Associate Professor of English, and Co-ordinator of the Women's Studies Programme in the Faculty of Arts at York University. She publishes in feminist and lesbian ethics and lesbian literary theory.

**SUSAN A. McDANIEL:** Susan A. McDaniel, Professor of Sociology, University of Alberta, is author of five books and more than 150 research articles and book chapters on family and women's issues. She serves on the Canada Committee for the International Year of the Family, is appointed to the National Statistics Council advisory to the Chief Statistician of Canada and is Editor of *The Canadian Journal of Sociology*. She is a Fellow of the Royal Society of Canada and is listed in *Canadian Who's Who*.

**SHARON McIRVIN ABU-LABAN:** Sharon McIrvin Abu-Laban is Professor of Sociology at the University of Alberta, specializing in Comparative Family, Gender, Social Gerontology and International Development. Her scholarly work has appeared in a wide range of professional journals and anthologies and she is co-editor of *Muslim Families in North America* and *The Arab World: Dynamics of Development*.

**NORMAN MORRA:** Norman N. Morra is a Doctoral Candidate and Research Assistant in the Department of Sociology at York University. His most recent work, "The Interpersonal Sources of Violence in Hockey: The Influence of the Media, Parents, Coaches, and Game Officials," will appear in *Children and Youth in Sport*. His areas of interest include gender, violence, and culture.

**MARY JANE MOSSMAN:** Mary Jane Mossman is a Professor of Law at Osgoode Hall School. She has taught law in Canada, Australia and the U.S. and has developed courses about womens' claims to legal equality. She also writes and teaches in the areas of family law, property law, and access to justice.

**CECILIA REYNOLDS:** Cecilia Reynolds is an Associate Professor in the Faculty of Education at Brock University. She recently served a term as the Director of the Women's Studies Program. Her publications and research include historical and sociological interests in gender equity in schools, women in educational administration and leadership, teachers' worklives, and relationships between mothers, daughters and grandmothers from cross-cultural perspectives.

**MICHAEL SMITH:** Michael D. Smith was a professor in the Department of Sociology and director of the LaMarsh Centre for Research on Violence and Conflict Resolution at York University in Toronto. He published recent articles on violence against women in the Journal of Interpersonal Violence, Gender and Society, Violence and Victims, and Canadian Journal of Sociology. He is the author of *Violence and Sport* (Butterworths, 1983).

**MILANA TODOROFF:** Milana Todoroff, Ph.D. is a researcher at Ryerson Polytechnic University on a project investigating educational barriers to professional careers for students with disabilities. Her personal/research interests include entrepreneurialism for women, disability issues and women's issues.

**WILLIAM WHITLA:** William Whitla is Professor of English and Humanities at York University. He teaches in the fields of literary theory, Victorian literature and culture. He has published widely on Victorian poetry, including Robert and Elizabeth Browning, Christina Rossetti, and the Pre-Raphaelites. His new book is a critical annotated edition of *Essays and Reviews 1860,* co-authored with Victor Shea that will be published by University Press of Virginia in 1995.